SECONDARY PARALLELISM

Society of Biblical Literature

Academia Biblica

Adele Berlin,
Old Testament Editor

Mark Allan Powell,
New Testament Editor

Number 15

SECONDARY PARALLELISM
A Study of Translation Technique
in LXX Proverbs

SECONDARY PARALLELISM
A Study of Translation Technique
in LXX Proverbs

Gerhard Tauberschmidt

Society of Biblical Literature
Atlanta

SECONDARY PARALLELISM

Copyright © 2004 by the Society of Biblical Literature

All rights reserved. No part of this work may be reproduced or transmitted in any form or by any means, electronic or mechanical, including photocopying and recording, or by means of any information storage or retrieval system, except as may be expressly permitted by the 1976 Copyright Act or in writing from the publisher. Requests for permission should be addressed in writing to the Rights and Permissions Office, Society of Biblical Literature, 825 Houston Mill Road, Atlanta, GA 30329, USA.

Library of Congress Cataloging-in-Publication Data

Tauberschmidt, Gerhard.
  Secondary parallelism : a study of translation technique in LXX Proverbs / by Gerhard Tauberschmidt.
    p. cm. —(Academia Biblica ; no. 15)
  Includes bibliographical references and index.
  ISBN 1-58983-076-8 (pbk. : alk. paper)
  1. Bible. O.T. Proverbs. Greek—Versions—Septuagint. 2. Bible. O.T. Proverbs—Translating. 3. Hebrew language—Translating into Greek. 4. Hebrew language—Parallelism. 5. Bible. O.T. Proverbs—Criticism, Textual. I. Title. II. Academia Biblica (Series) (Society of Biblical Literature) ; no. 15
BS744.T37 2004b
223'.70486--dc22
                              2004003616

08 07 06 05 04   5 4 3 2 1

Printed in the United States of America
on acid-free paper

I dedicate this book to my wife
Hiltrud
and our children
Manuel and Marietta

Table of Contents

Preface	xi
Acknowledgements	xiii
Abbreviations	xv

INTRODUCTION 1

1. HEBREW PARALLELISM RENDERED IN A MORE EXACTLY PARALLEL FASHION 19

1.1	INTRODUCTION	19
1.2	SEMANTIC AND GRAMMATICAL RELATIONSHIPS RENDERED MORE NEARLY PARALLEL	30
1.2.1	SEMANTIC RELATIONSHIPS	31
1.2.1.1	Lexical Aspect	33
1.2.1.2	Emphatic Phrases or Various Figures of Speech	39
1.2.1.3	Near-Synonymous Parallelisms Transformed into Antithetical Forms	43
1.2.1.4	Near-Antithetical Parallelisms Rendered with a Clearer Contrast	50
1.2.1.5	Additional Aspects	61
1.2.1.5.1	Parallelisms of logical relations	62
1.2.1.5.2	Parallelisms of addition relations	67
1.2.1.5.3	Parallelisms of comparisons	69
1.2.1.5.4	Emblematic parallelisms	71
1.2.1.5.5	Less closely parallel or single-sentence constructions	74
1.2.1.5.6	Near-synonymous parallelisms with three parts	75
1.2.1.5.7	Triplets	79
1.2.1.5.8	Phrases	80
1.2.1.6	Conclusion, Application and Further Discussion	81
1.2.2	GRAMMATICAL RELATIONSHIPS	85
1.2.2.1	Second Person, Paired with Impersonal Construction	85
1.2.2.2	Preposition plus Adjective, Paired with Noun	86
1.2.2.3	Personal Object, Paired with Impersonal Object	86
1.2.2.4	Second Person Imperfect (and Third Person Object), Paired with Third Person Imperfect (and Second Person Object)	87
1.2.2.5	Imperative, Paired with Imperfect	88
1.2.2.6	Construct Form, Paired with Participle	89
1.2.2.7	Direct Quotation, Paired with Direct Quotation	90
1.2.2.8	Direct Quotation, Paired with Indirect Quotation	90
1.2.2.9	Exclamation with מַה־, Paired with Statement	91

1.2.2.10	Elliptical Constructions	91
1.2.2.10.1	Complement, omitted in colon B	92
1.2.2.10.2	Verb (or adverb), omitted in one half	92
1.2.2.10.2.1	Verb (or adverb), omitted in colon B	93
1.2.2.10.2.2	Verb, omitted in colon A	98
1.2.2.11	Verbal Clause, Paired with Nominal Clause	100
1.2.2.12	Conclusion	100
1.2.3	POSSIBLE NON-TRANSLATIONAL DEVIATIONS	101
1.3	CONCLUSION	105
2.	HEBREW PARALLELISM RENDERED AS A LESS NEARLY PARALLEL FORM	109
2.1	COHESION AND PARALLEL FORMS	109
2.1.1	LINGUISTIC SIGNALS OF COHESION IN GENERAL	109
2.1.1.1	Connectives, Markers or Particles	110
2.1.1.2	Agreement in Tense/Aspect or Person and Number	113
2.1.1.3	Participant Reference	116
2.1.1.4	Deixis or Deictic Links	120
2.1.1.5	Conclusion	122
2.1.2	LINGUISTIC SIGNALS OF COHESION OR INCREASED COHESIVENESS INFLUENCE PARALLEL FORMS	122
2.1.2.1	Parallelism and Agreement in Tense/Aspect or Person and Number	122
2.1.2.2	Parallelism and Participants	123
2.1.2.3	Parallelism and Deictic Links as well as Other Discourse Considerations	125
2.1.3	COHESIVE TIES AND THEMATIC GROUPINGS	128
2.1.3.1	Cohesive Ties and Thematic Groupings in General	128
2.1.3.2	Cohesive Ties and Thematic Groupings as Affecting Parallel Forms	130
2.2	LINGUISTICS, TRANSLATION, INTERPRETATION AND PARALLEL FORMS	133
2.2.1	VARIOUS LINGUISTIC AND TRANSLATIONAL CONSIDERATIONS INFLUENCE PARALLEL FORMS	133
2.2.2	PROBLEMS RELATED TO THE HEBREW CONSONANTAL TEXT(S) (UNDERSTANDING OR TAKING THE HEBREW DIFFERENTLY, OR INNER-TEXTUAL CORRUPTION) INFLUENCE PARALLEL FORMS	146
2.2.3	INTERPRETATION AND THEOLOGY INFLUENCES PARALLEL FORMS	155
2.3	CONCLUSION	161

3.	PARALLELISM AND TEXTUAL CRITICISM	165
3.1	THE VALUE OF THE LXX	165
3.2	EVALUATION OF TEXTUAL WITNESSES	169
3.3	TRANSLATIONAL CASES OF PARALLEL FORMS	172
3.3.1	SEMANTIC (AND GRAMMATICAL) RELATIONSHIPS	173
3.3.1.1	Lexical Aspect	173
3.3.1.2	Emphatic Phrases or Various Figures of Speech	184
3.3.1.3	Near-Synonymous Parallelisms Transformed into Antithetical Forms	187
3.3.1.4	Near-Antithetical Parallelisms Rendered with a Clearer Contrast	193
3.3.1.5	Additional Aspects	211
3.3.1.5.1	Parallelisms of logical relations	211
3.3.1.5.2	Parallelism of addition relations	213
3.3.1.5.3	Parallelisms of comparisons	213
3.3.1.5.4	Less closely parallel or single-sentence constructions	217
3.3.1.5.5	Near-synonymous parallelisms with three parts	218
3.3.1.5.6	Triplets	218
3.3.1.5.7	Conclusion	220
3.3.2	GRAMMATICAL RELATIONSHIPS	220
3.3.2.1	Noun Phrase Subject, Paralleled with Prepositional Noun Phrase	220
3.3.2.2	Elliptical Constructions	221
3.3.2.2.1	Verb (adverb), omitted in B	221
3.3.2.3	Structural Differences	222
3.4	CONCLUSION	223
GENERAL CONCLUSIONS		227
Appendix		231
Bibliography		235
Index		247

PREFACE

This is a dissertation (with minor revisions) presented for the degree of Ph.D. at the University of Aberdeen, Scotland, Department of Divinity with Religious Studies, in 2001.

In this study I show that the translator of LXX Proverbs frequently rendered Hebrew parallelism in a form that is more closely parallel than the MT, that is, the colons of couplets correspond more closely to each other semantically and/or grammatically. The argument is based on the hypothesis that the Hebrew source of LXX Proverbs is similar to the MT in the cases discussed. It is true that there are recognizable differences between the MT and the source or *Vorlage* of the LXX that cannot be explained on the basis of applied translation techniques etc., but this area goes beyond the scope of this study. The translator's fondness for producing closely corresponding lines needs to be considered when using LXX Proverbs as a source of variant readings. The thesis will assist in evaluating the Greek translation of Proverbs, thus avoiding the misuse of LXX Proverbs for the sake of "better" parallelisms.

The fact that Hebrew parallelism is not as regular as has been thought in the past but is dynamic, as has been demonstrated by recent scholars, supports my findings.

There are, however, cases of parallelisms in LXX Proverbs which appear to be less closely parallel than the MT. But these exceptional instances can be accounted for by one of several reasons: the translator's strong desire to produce a cohesive translation beyond the couplet (on the paragraph level), his linguistic and translational alterations, his theological tendencies, and his understanding or taking the Hebrew consonantal text differently or even misunderstanding his *Vorlage*. These considerations at times overrule the tendency towards producing more closely corresponding forms.

I have demonstrated in this study that when the translator produced forms that are more closely parallel this was due to the application of his translation technique. If this is taken into account, it will be seen that in a considerable number of cases where the translator has been thought to follow a different *Vorlage*, the differences from the MT are in fact of a translational nature, giving rise to freer rather than literal word-for-word renderings of the MT.

Thus, the translator's tendency to produce forms that are more closely parallel than those in his Hebrew *Vorlage* has relevance for differentiating translational and text-critical cases.

Acknowledgements

I would like to express my sincere thanks to all who contributed to the development of this thesis in one way or another. First of all I wish to express my appreciation to my supervisor Prof. Francis Watson and thank him for his excellent guidance and insightful suggestions in the development of the dissertation.

I am grateful to Prof. William Johnstone who read my work and made useful suggestions.

I would also like to thank Emeritus Profs. I. Howard Marshall, David W. Gooding, and Bruce Waltke, who read parts of my thesis material, for their encouraging comments.

I thank my SIL colleagues who gave me feedback on (parts of) my work. In particular I would like to mention Tony Pope and thank him for his helpful comments and his suggestions for improving the English. I alone, however, am responsible for the remaining errors.

Finally, I wish to thank my wife Hiltrud for supporting me in writing this dissertation.

ABBREVIATIONS

ABD	*Anchor Bible Dictionary on CD-ROM*
Aq.	Aquila
Ar.	Arabic
ATA	Alttestamentliche Abhandlungen
BDB	Brown, F., S. R. Driver, and C. A. Briggs. *A Hebrew and English Lexicon of the Old Testament*
BHK	*Biblia Hebraica*, ed. R. Kittel, 1937
BHS	*Biblia Hebraica Stuttgartensia*
Bib	*Biblica*
BIOSCS	*Bulletin of the International Organization for Septuagint and Cognate Studies*
BT	*The Bible Translator*
CBQ	*Catholic Biblical Quarterly*
CEV	Contemporary English Version
Copt.	Coptic
De Proverbio	*An Electronic Journal of International Proverb Studies*
DSS	Dead Sea Scrolls
EBC	*The Expositor's Bible Commentary on CD-ROM*
Epic. Men.	Epicurus, Letter to Menoikeus
Eth.	Ethiopic
G or OG	Old Greek translation
GN1	Die Gute Nachricht in heutigem Deutsch, 1982
GN2	Gute Nachricht Bibel, 1997
GRBS	*Greek, Roman and Byzantine Studies*
HfA	Hoffnung für Alle, 1996
HOTTP	Hebrew Old Testament Text Project
HUBP	Hebrew University Bible Project
HUCA	*Hebrew Union College Annual*
HUSLA	*Hebrew University Studies in Literature and the Arts*
IB	*Interpreter's Bible*. Edited by G. A. Buttrick et al. 12 vols. New York, 1951–1957
IOSCS	International Organization for Septuagint and Cognate Studies
JB	*Jerusalem Bible*
JBL	*Journal of Biblical Literature*
JETS	*Journal of the Evangelical Theological Society*
JNSL	*Journal of Northwest Semitic Languages*
JSJ	*Journal for the Study of Judaism*
JSP	*Journal for the Study of the Pseudepigrapha*
JOTT	*Journal of Translation and Textlinguistics*
JQRS	*Jewish Quarterly Review Supplement*
JSOT	*Journal for the Study of the Old Testament*

JTS	*Journal of Theological Studies*
KJV	King James Version
LXX	Septuagint
MT	Masoretic Text
NAB	New American Bible
NASB	New American Standard Bible
NCV	New Century Version
NEB	New English Bible
NIDOTTE	*New International Dictionary of Old Testament Theology & Exegesis*. Edited by W. A. VanGemeren. 5 vols. Grand Rapids, 1997
NJB	New Jerusalem Bible
NJPS	*Tanakh: The Holy Scriptures: The New JPS Translation according to the Traditional Hebrew Text*
NLT	New Living Translation
NOL	*Notes on Linguistics*
NOT	*Notes on Translation*
NRSV	New Revised Standard Version
OTS	Old Testament Studies
OtSt	*Oudtestamentische Studiën*
PAAJR	*Proceedings of the American Academy for Jewish Research*
Q	Qumran
REB	Revised English Bible
RSV	Revised Standard Version
Sa.	Sahidic (official dialect of Egypt)
SBLSCS	Society of Biblical Literature Septuagint and Cognate Studies
SCS	Septuagint and Cognate Studies
SH	Syro-Hexaplar
SIL	Summer Institute of Linguistics
SJOT	*Scandinavian Journal of the Old Testament*
SP	Samaritan Pentateuch
Symm.	Symmachus
Syr.	Syriac
Tg.	Targum
TC	*Textual Criticism: A Journal of Biblical Textual Criticism*
Th.	Theodotion
THAT	*Theologisches Handwörterbuch zum Alten Testament*. Edited by E. Jenni, with assistance from C. Westermann
TRu	*Theologische Rundschau*
TS	Tur-Sinai, Naftali Herz (German translation which follows the MT closely)
TWNT	*Theologisches Wörterbuch zum Neuen Testament*. Edited by G. Kittel and G. Friedrich

UBS	United Bible Societies
Vulg.	Vulgate
VL	Vetus Latina
VT	*Vetus Testamentum*
VTSup	Vetus Testamentum Supplements
ZAW	*Zeitschrift für die alttestamentliche Wissenschaft*

INTRODUCTION

A number of scholars have argued that the Septuagint[1] ought to be studied primarily as a religious document in its own right, rather than as a corrective to some Hebrew text of which we have a copy.[2] On the other hand, for many scholars the significance of the LXX still lies primarily in its contribution to the textual criticism of the Hebrew Bible.[3] In fact, the LXX may provide useful insights both as a religious document as well as for textual criticism. With regard to textual criticism, most commentaries and Bible translations consulted use the Septuagint to varying degrees as a textual witness.

In any case, it is important to first of all view the LXX as translation(s) and investigate the translation techniques that were applied by the various translators. In this study I deal particularly with the rendering of Hebrew parallelism in LXX Proverbs and demonstrate that the translator of Proverbs had a tendency to produce forms that are more closely parallel than those in his source, assuming that the *Vorlage* of LXX Proverbs was similar to the MT in the cases discussed. The consideration of his translation practice is important especially when using LXX Proverbs as textual witness in order to be able to separate translational cases from text-critical cases.

Historically the translation of the Septuagint was a Jewish work, and was at first held by Greek-speaking Jews in high regard,[4] but on the whole within

---

[1] The name Septuagint (from Latin *septuaginta* = 70) is commonly applied to the Greek version of the OT. In Jewish tradition only the Pentateuch was translated by "the Seventy," but from the second century B.C.E. on, Christian writers began to ascribe the translation of the whole Bible in Greek to the original company of interpreters. So the name "Septuagint" was given to the whole Bible in Greek. E. Bickerman, "The LXX as a Translation," *PAAJR* 28 (1959): 5–6.

[2] M. K. H. Peters, "Septuagint," n.p., *ABD on CD-ROM*. Version 2.1, 1997. According to J. Cook the LXX was the first exegetical commentary on the Hebrew Bible and it "should not be seen as relevant only, or even primarily, for textual criticism." Johann Cook, *The Septuagint of Proverbs–Jewish and/or Hellenistic Proverbs? Concerning the Hellenistic Colouring of LXX Proverbs* (Brill, 1997), 2. Against: M. V. Fox differs from J. Cook's view that the Septuagint should principally be seen as an exegetical commentary. In his opinion the "LXX-Prov is primarily a *translation*, one aiming at a faithful representation of the Hebrew, and it is best understood in terms of that goal." Michael V. Fox, *Proverbs 1–9: A New Translation with Introduction and Commentary* (New York: Doubleday, 2000), 361.

[3] Harry M. Orlinsky, "The Septuagint as Holy Writ and the Philosophy of the Translators," *HUCA* 46 (1975): 89–114. Orlinsky often argues in favor of the LXX reading. He thinks the translation was produced from one whole manuscript (tradition), not like the MT from many; also he regards the translation as fairly literal and does not allow for a lot of translational changes.

[4] Although the Preface to the Greek Ben Sira is critical of the LXX, and the apology for it in Aristeas may imply that some were critical.

Judaism the LXX was never held in such high esteem as in Christianity, because the Jews possessed an inspired Hebrew Bible, while to most of the Christians the LXX was the only sacred source of the OT.[5] Nevertheless, by both groups the Septuagint was regarded as product of divine inspiration,[6] first in Judaism[7] and then in Christianity.[8] Over time, the translation became viewed as an inspired document,[9] and by the time of Jerome and Augustine the LXX had become, in Augustine's thinking (which reflects the more popular position of the Church at the time), a *supplanter* of (or substitute for) the original by right of divine inspiration.[10]

With the Hexapla, a six-columned presentation of various Greek versions of the OT,[11] Origen's aim was to establish a relationship between the LXX (fifth column) and Hebrew (first column) texts of the OT. His motivation was not purely text-critical, but he also wished to establish for the Church a sound basis

---

[5] Emanuel Tov, "The Septuagint," in *Mikra: Text, Translation, Reading and Interpretation of the Hebrew Bible in Ancient Judaism and Early Christianity* (ed. M. J. Mulder and H. Sysling, eed.; Assen/Maastricht: Van Gorcum. Philadelphia: Fortress, 1988), 163. According to A. Rahlfs the Jews became alienated from the LXX a short time after its adoption by the Christian Church. Alfred Rahlfs, *Septuaginta* (Stuttgart: Deutsche Bibelgesellschaft, 1935/79), LVII. For further information on this topic see Karen H. Jobes and Moisés Silva, *Invitation to the Septuagint* (Grand Rapids: Baker; United Kingdom: Paternoster, 2000), 82–85.

[6] The main reason that the idea of inspiration of the LXX came about according to B. W. R. Pearson is "primarily to provide those who depended on the LXX as their primary source for truth and practice with an unassailable argument against those who would suggest that it possibly did not completely convey the ideational thrust of the original." Brook W. R. Pearson, "Remainderless Translations? Implications of the Tradition Concerning the Translation of the LXX for Modern Translation Theory," in *Translating the Bible* (ed. S. E. Porter and R. S. Hess; Sheffield Academic Press, 1999), 74.

[7] According to Pearson, against Orlinsky ["The Septuagint as Sacred Writ," *HUCA* 46 (1975): 94–96], the concept of divine inspiration concerning the LXX is a relatively late development: "Neither Ben Sira, Aristobulus nor the Letter of Aristeas refers to the translation process as a divinely inspired one." Pearson, "Remainderless Translations?", 71–72. By Philo's time, the idea of a divinely inspired translation had developed. He describes the process of translating the LXX as "giving an oracular interpretation of divinely inspired laws" (*On the Life of Moses* 2.6.34). *Ibid.*, 72–74.

[8] The early Christian writers after Justin Martyr all take for granted the inspiration of the LXX (e.g. Irenaeus, c. A.D. 175; Clement of Alexandria, A.D. 150–212; Tertullian, b. c. A.D. 160; and Chrysostom, A.D. 344–407) except Eusebius. *Ibid.*, 75.

[9] *Ibid.*, 80.

[10] *Ibid.*, 79.

[11] These columns contained the following texts: 1. Hebrew text. 2. Transliteration of the Hebrew text into Greek letters. 3. Aquila's translation. 4. Symmachus's translation. 5. Translation of the Seventy (=Septuagint). 6. Theodotion's translation. Jobes and Silva, *Invitation*, 48.

in its dialogue with Judaism. So the Hexapla showed those passages which were accepted either only by Jews or only by Christians.[12]

The problem with Origen's Hexapla is that he inserted Greek texts from Aquila, Symmachus, and Theodotion into the fifth column of the Septuagint and marked it to correspond to his Hebrew text.[13] But unfortunately those markings were not always preserved. Consequently later on when the fifth column was copied separately the manuscripts of the "Septuagint" had a mixed text. Therefore the great task of Septuagint textual criticism is to reconstruct the pre-Hexaplaric text.[14]

In addition to the recension of the Septuagint in the Hexapla, Jerome mentioned two further LXX recensions circulating in the fourth century in different parts of the Christian world. In the "Preface to Chronicles" he wrote:

> Alexandria and Egypt in their Septuagint acclaim Hesychius as their authority, the region from Constantinople to Antioch approves the copies of Lucian the martyr, the intermediate Palestinian provinces read the MSS which were promulgated by Eusebius and Pamphilius on the basis of Origen's labors, and the whole world is divided among these three varieties of texts.

These three recensions are often called, the "Trifaria Varietas" after Jerome's Latin phrase.[15]

---

[12] Origen's approach is set out in his reply to a letter from Julius Africanus (ca. 240 B.C.). He writes, "I make it my endeavour not to be ignorant of their [LXX's] various readings, lest in my controversies with the Jews I should quote to them what is not found in their copies, and that I may make some use of what is found there, even although it should not be in our Scriptures." D. C. Parker, "The Hexapla of Origen," n.p., *ABD on CD-ROM*. Version 2.1, 1997. See also Jobes and Silva, *Invitation*, 51.

[13] If one of these other translations contained a reading that in his opinion corresponded well to the Hebrew reading, he inserted that reading into the Greek of the fifth column, placing it between an asterisk and a metobelus. *Ibid.*, 53.

[14] *Ibid.*

[15] S. K. Soderlund, "Septuagint," in *The International Standard Bible Encyclopedia* (ed. G. W. Bromiley; vol. 4; Grand Rapids: Eerdmans, 1988), 405. Scholars have been unsuccessful in identifying a Hesychian recension among the manuscripts, although most biblical books have an Egyptian text form which may be the basis for Jerome's comment. Jobes and Silva, *Invitation*, 47.

The LXX remained the Bible of the Church also through its Latin translation, the Vetus Latina, which was later replaced by Jerome's Vulgate.[16] While the Vulgate, although not the only translation in the Church, was widely used in the Western world,[17] the Septuagint was widely used in the Eastern Church. Today, the LXX is still considered a sacred book by the Greek Orthodox Church.[18] In regard to deuterocanonical writings the following stance is taken:

"On the basis of Athanasius's arguments, the Orthodox Churches have retained the deuterocanonical writings, and have reaffirmed this position in the 17th century. These writings can accordingly be freely used in church practice, but may not be made the basis of dogmatic decisions."[19]

Today it is generally accepted that there are three main recensions of the LXX, as suggested by Jerome. Therefore, the first task of LXX textual criticism is as far as possible to identify and eliminate these Origenian or Hexaplaric, Lucianic, and Hesychian elements and to restore the "original" text or proto-LXX. After the death of Lagarde (the initiator of this project), his student Rahlfs took over the project and was able to produce the first critical editions: Ruth (1922), Genesis (1926), Psalms (1931). His popular edition, based on three major uncials (Vaticanus, Sinaiticus, and Alexandrinus),[20] was published in 1935, just before his death. The Göttingen "Septuaginta-Unternehmen" is now the only active institute involved in the preparation of LXX texts.[21] Most books of the LXX are now published, but for some books editors are still to be found. So far a critical LXX edition of Proverbs has not been published yet. The Cambridge project is now defunct. It uses the text of Codex Vaticanus (B) as base text and where the text is lacking, mainly the text of Codex Alexandrinus

---

[16] Martin Luther wrote in his Table-Talk of God's Word: "St Jerome, after he had revised and corrected the Septuagint, translated the Bible from Hebrew into Latin; His version is still used in our church. Truly, for one man, this was work enough and to spare. . . . Interpreters and translators should not work alone; for good *et propria verba* do not always occur to one mind." William Hazlitt, *The Table-Talk of Martin Luther* (Philadelphia: Lutheran Publication Society, 1997).

[17] "At the time of Reformation, the unique authority of the Latin Vulgate was challenged by Protestants. The books of the Protestant Old Testament were translated afresh from the Hebrew canon, which does not include the additional Greek books." Jobes and Silva, *Invitation*, 51.

[18] Tov, "The Septuagint," 163.

[19] E. Oikonomos, "Die Bedeutung der deuterokanonischen Schriften in der orthodoxen Kirche," in *Die Apokryphenfrage im ökumenischen Horizont* (ed. S. Meurer; Stuttgart: Deutsche Bibelgesellschaft, 1989), 39.

[20] But many other sources were used extensively.

[21] Peters, "Septuagint," n.p. Soderlund, "Septuagint," 405.

(A) is used. No attempt is made to provide a reconstructed or "true" Septuagint text.[22]

Since the Reformation and Enlightenment, arguments were advanced to examine the MT carefully for copyists' errors. When the Septuagint was seen to correct these, it became a source (and along with it other ancient versions such as the Syriac and the Vulgate, and later the DSS) for the establishment of the text for translation.[23]

Today most of the (English and German) translations (except e.g. KJV, similarly TS) use the LXX to varying degrees as a textual witness for the parts of the MT which are unclear or corrupt. That means, only when the MT is in clear error would an alternative textual reading be acceptable.[24]

It is, however, not agreed by all scholars that the MT preserves the oldest and best text tradition. There are scholars who regard the Hebrew text underlying the LXX as good and valuable as the MT, and in some cases, such as Samuel, the LXX is regarded as more valuable.[25] A. G. Auld has argued that the Hebrew source text behind the LXX of Joshua consistently bears witness to an

---

[22] Ellis R. Brotzman, *Old Testament Textual Criticism: A Practical Introduction* (Grand Rapids: Baker, 1994), 78. J. W. Wevers states: "What is now abundantly clear is that we can never return to those days of Swete when the text of Codex B was reprinted, errors and all, and manuscripts were collated to it. No NT scholar would dream of accepting such a text, and there is no good reason for Septuagint scholars to do so either." J. W. Wevers, "The Göttingen Septuagint," *BIOSCS* 8 (1975): 23. Wevers stresses the importance of a critical text and gives as an example Gen 15:15 (MT: תקבר) where a very early copyist erred by adding a ρ after τ writing τραφεὶς "being nourished" instead of the original ταφεὶς "being buried" (Rahlfs edition). This error occurs in both codex A and codex B. J. W. Wevers, "An Apologia for LXX Studies," *BIOSCS* 18 (1985): 27.

[23] R. S. Hess, "Reflections on Translating Joshua," in *Handbook of Classical Rhetoric in the Hellenistic Period 330 B.C.–A.D. 400* (ed. S. E. Porter; Leiden, New York, Köln: Brill, 1997), 126.

[24] A new era began with the publication of the RSV in 1952. The revisers opened the door to a limited number of textual adoptions, particularly where the LXX or another version lent support. Carl E. Armerding, *The Old Testament and Criticism* (Grand Rapids: Eerdmans, 1983), 116. After this breakthrough other translations followed, such as the JB of 1966 and the NEB of 1970. The NASB and the NIV, two more recent translations by evangelical scholarship, however, "resisted the trend toward a more eclectic text" as Armerding puts it. *Ibid.*, 118–119.

[25] E. Tov, *Textual Criticism of the Hebrew Bible* (Minneapolis: Fortress; Assen/Maastricht: Van Gorcum, 1992) and, E. Tov, *The Text-Critical Use of the Septuagint in Biblical Research* (Jerusalem: Simor, 1997). According to Tov although readings found in the MT are, on the whole (or statistically), preferable to those found in other texts, the MT is not more reliable than LXX or certain Qumran texts in all biblical books. Tov, *Textual Criticism*, 299–300.

older text.[26] M. Müller[27] holds the LXX in high esteem. In his view the LXX cannot just be ignored, considering that it is also a witness to the transmission of traditions. The question Müller asks is whether the LXX should be regarded as merely a translation, i.e. as a more or less reliable text witness of an "original" Bible, or as a witness to the process of transmitting tradition.[28] Since it does not seem that the Hebrew Bible was already a fixed entity in the third and second centuries B.C.E., on the basis of which the Greek translation can be evaluated, the Greek translation may according to Müller very well be seen as evidence of a process reflecting changing traditions which only gradually came to a standstill once a particular Hebrew text became normative.[29]

Also, the differences in some books, such as Daniel, Esther, Jeremiah, Job and Proverbs, are so great that it must be assumed according to Müller that the Hebrew text underlying the Greek translation must have been different from the MT. This gives evidence for the fluid nature of the Hebrew text throughout the third and second centuries B.C.E., reflecting a dynamic shift of traditions in the existing "books." Müller writes: "It is a question of two processes running partly parallel, and it is no longer possible automatically to give priority to the current Hebrew text."[30] Müller says that we must insist that the LXX is part of the canon, a witness of the handing on of traditions.[31] Yet there are other scholars such as R. T. Beckwith[32] and D. W. Gooding[33] who would insist on the opposite view.

According to E. Tov there are differences that were presumably created at an earlier stage, that of the literary growth of the books. The differentiation between these two types of readings, however, is very difficult, and sometimes almost impossible.[34]

---

[26] A. Graeme Auld, *Joshua, Moses and the Land: Tetrateuch-Pentateuch-Hexateuch in a Generation of Study since 1938* (Edinburgh: T & T Clark, 1980). Cf. Hess, "Reflections," 127.

[27] Mogens Müller, *The First Bible of the Church: A Plea for the Septuagint* (Sheffield Academic Press, 1996).

[28] *Ibid.*, 99.

[29] *Ibid.*, 102.

[30] *Ibid.*, 102–104.

[31] *Ibid.*, 122. For a similar approach for the NT see D. C. Parker, *The Living Text of the Gospels* (Cambridge University Press, 1996). Parker thinks that the Gospels cannot be properly understood as texts without taking into consideration their physical existence as manuscripts. He argues that the search for an original text of the Gospels overlooks the way in which the early church passed down its traditions.

[32] See in R. T. Beckwith, *The Old Testament Canon of the New Testament Church* (London: SPCK, 1985).

[33] Personal correspondence.

[34] Tov, *Textual Criticism*, 314.

Tov's view is supported by B. Albrektson who writes:

> Where do we draw the borderline between on the one hand additions which may still be regarded as belonging to the stage of growth of the text and on the other hand additions which are to be regarded as glosses or marginal notes by a scribe and which should therefore be deleted? In other words, this is the question of the boundary between literary criticism and textual criticism.[35]

According to Tov, for all the differences that were created at the literary level, no preference for one text or another is to be expressed.[36]

> As a rule, this branch of textual criticism aims neither at the compositions written by the biblical authors, nor at the previous oral stages, if such existed, but only at the stage of the composition which is attested in the textual evidence. Textual analysis does not aim at oral or literary stages beyond this evidence. The assumption of earlier stages is based merely on logical deductions and cannot be proven.[37]

Both groups, HOTTP and HUBP, agree that period one, the period of the so-called Ur-text, falls outside the province of textual criticism *in sensu stricto*.[38] According to D. W. Gooding, "decisions based on a study of translation-technique are less subjective than those based on literary criticism."[39] Thus it seems best to approach the textual situation using the findings gained by studying the translation-techniques of the LXX.

The problem with Müller's position is that he sees the Septuagint as a new edition of Judaism's holy books, which neither seeks to bring the readers to the

---

[35] Bertil Albrektson, "Textual Criticism and the Textual Basis of a Translation of the Old Testament," *BT* 26/3 (1975). In contrast with textual criticism or "lower criticism," so-called "higher criticism" e.g. literary criticism, deals with issues such as composition, origin, date, structure, authorship, authenticity and uniformity, although in practice the two cannot always be separated neatly. Tov, *Textual Criticism*, 17. Or to put it another way: "literary criticism deals with the first area, the stage of the development of the biblical books, whereas textual criticism operates within the second stage, that of the books' copying and transmission." *Ibid.*, 315.

[36] Tov, *Textual Criticism*, 313–349, here 348. Also, in *Text-Critical Use*, 261, Tov writes: "In our view, textual evaluation should not be applied to data that were not created during the textual transmission," that is data that were created "at an earlier stage, namely, that of the literary growth of the books."

[37] Tov, *Text-Critical Use*, 2–3.

[38] J. A. Sanders, "Hermeneutics of Text Criticism," *Textus* 18 (1995): 7.

[39] Dominique Barthélemy, David W. Gooding, Johan Lust, and Emanuel Tov, *The Story of David and Goliath* (Göttingen: Vandenhoeck & Ruprecht, 1986), 115.

source text, as would be the case in an unduly literal translation as for example in Aquila's translation, nor intends to bring the source text to the reader as in a paraphrastic translation, but aims to express how Hellenistic Jews understood the Scripture.[40] This view, however, cannot be maintained on the basis of the kind of translational alterations made by the LXX translators.[41] Also, the Septuagint cannot be judged as a single translation, since different translation techniques were employed by the different translators. Therefore it is necessary to judge each book individually and discuss translation principles/techniques as they are applied in a particular book.

As regards the value of the LXX for textual criticism, there are different opinions among Old Testament text critics. The traditional view has been to give greater value to the readings of the Masoretic Text and less value to the LXX, but it has been argued that the MT is only one of several witnesses and should not be considered more valuable than any other. In my opinion we cannot give automatically priority to the MT in every case, although on the whole the MT readings may be preferable to those found in other texts. For further discussion on this issue, see 3.2.

In any case, textual decisions should not be made on the basis of scholarly fashion. Each individual textual case needs to be judged on its own merit. But before we can use the LXX as a textual witness we need to look closely at the translation techniques (the same would apply to any other translation such as the Syriac and the Vulgate) and my work is a case study on that issue.

The reason I chose to investigate the rendering of Hebrew parallelism in LXX Proverbs is because in the process of writing my earlier work on "Principles of Bible Translation and the Septuagint"[42] I discovered over and over again that the translator of Proverbs seemed to have adapted dynamic Hebrew couplets translationally to make the lines correspond more closely. Since there exists no Hebrew *Vorlage* that LXX Proverbs could be compared to, the MT will be used instead, on the assumption that it corresponds closely to the Hebrew source of LXX Proverbs, at least concerning the examples used in the thesis as they are generally based on passages where the deviations between MT and LXX[43] can be explained in terms of translational etc. adjustments.

As for the Hebrew text of Proverbs E. Tov thinks that two parallel editions existed which originated during the period when the book was first set down in writing.[44] Similarly R. J. Clifford holds that a different Hebrew recension of

---

[40] Müller, *First Bible*, 110.

[41] Cf. Gerhard Tauberschmidt, "Principles of Bible Translation and the Septuagint," M.Phil. diss., University of Aberdeen, 1997.

[42] *Ibid.*

[43] For the issue of rearrangements, additions and omissions in LXX Proverbs see the comment in 1.1 *Introduction*.

[44] Tov, *Textual Criticism*, 337.

Proverbs was the basis for LXX Proverbs.[45] In his opinion "LXX has an important role in Proverbs text criticism."[46] Clifford criticizes HOTTP because, according to his view, it "seldom recommends emendations on the basis of LXX."[47] Also R. N. Whybray regards the LXX of Proverbs as an important witness in restoring the Hebrew Text, since the others (Targum, Syriac and Vulgate) follow the Hebrew in the main,[48] while the LXX represents a different tradition.[49] But in regard to the differences in the order in which the different parts of the book are arranged Whybray says that "it is not clear whether either LXX or the Hebrew has preserved the 'original' order, or whether the book had not yet received a definite order when the LXX translation was made."[50] A. P. Ross speaks of the possibility that LXX additions may have come from a different Hebrew source,[51] but he still prefers the MT: "The Hebrew text is arguably in fair condition. Where the LXX differs in a number of places, the MT is usually far more satisfying."[52] Some of the recent commentaries (e.g. Meinhold, Scherer) attempt to explain the MT with very little support from the LXX for superior readings. For a survey of the preferences of different commentaries and Bible versions with regard to textual decisions in Proverbs, see "Appendix."

In general it can be said that the Septuagint of Proverbs has been used frequently as a tool for reconstructing the Hebrew text in order to produce

---

[45] Richard J. Clifford, *Proverbs: A Commentary* (Louisville: Westminster John Knox, 1999), 28.

[46] Richard J. Clifford, "Observations on the Texts and Versions of Proverbs," in *Wisdom, You Are My Sister* (ed. M. L. Barre; CBMS 29; Washington, DC: Catholic Biblical Association, 1997), 56.

[47] *Ibid.*

[48] So Tov, *Textual Criticism*, 337.

[49] R. N. Whybray, *The Book of Proverbs: A Survey of Modern Study* (Leiden, New York, Köln: Brill, 1995), 161.

[50] *Ibid.*

[51] "Throughout the book the LXX adds proverbs (which may be from a different Hebrew *Vorlage* [underlying text]) but deletes others." A. P. Ross, "Proverbs," n.p., *EBC on CD-ROM* (Grand Rapids: Zondervan, 1991).

[52] Ross, "Proverbs," under "5. Canon and Text," n.p. Similarly B. Waltke in regard to Prov 14:32 assumes that the MT is superior although he thinks that the LXX rendering goes straight back to a Hebrew source text that is different from the MT. Bruce Waltke, "Proverbs: Theology of," in *NIDOTTE* (ed. W. A. VanGemeren; vol. 4; Grand Rapids: Zondervan, 1997), 1091–1092.

"better" parallelism[53] without taking into consideration the translator's technique in regard to producing "better" parallelisms.

In my present work I will show that the translator of Proverbs did not produce a literal translation but made many translational changes particularly concerning the production of forms that are more parallel grammatically and/or semantically.

Therefore, it may be problematic to quickly turn to LXX Proverbs as support for superior readings concerning "better" parallelisms without having looked closely at the translator's technique. The insights into his translation practice provide important guidance in deciding whether an apparent divergence between the LXX and the MT is due to a different *Vorlage* or rather to the translator's effort.[54]

E. Tov expresses the importance of considering translational factors in the following statement:

> When analyzing the LXX translation for text-critical purposes, one should first attempt to view deviations as the result of . . . inner-translational factors . . . Only after all possible translational explanations have been dismissed should one address the assumption that the translation represents a Hebrew reading different from MT.[55]

Furthermore, Tov states,

> the more one knows about the nature of the translation, and the more thoroughly inner-translational deviations are analyzed, the less one is inclined to ascribe translational deviations to Hebrew variants. Many injudicious retroversions of variants could have been avoided by a better analysis of the translators' practices.[56]

Thus insights into the translator's techniques are a prerequisite for determining cases where the LXX is different from the MT for translational reasons and separating them from cases where it is different from the MT

---

[53] Adele Berlin supports this view in *The Dynamics of Biblical Parallelism*, (Bloomington: Indiana University Press, 1985), 130, where she writes, ". . . the practice of emending the text in order to create 'better' parallelism has no basis . . . We must adopt a broader view of parallelism, taking into account the wide range of linguistic possibilities for its construction."

[54] Cf. Wevers, "Apologia," 38.

[55] Tov, *Text-Critical Use*, 40.

[56] *Ibid.*, 44. Tov treats inner-translational deviations under a section called "Exegesis" which is divided into a. "Additions," b. "Omissions," and c. "Substitutions." However, the labels given to a. and b. could be misleading since in these categories he deals with purely linguistic and translational elements which should not be called additions and omissions in relation to the translators' practices. See *ibid.*, 45–50.

because of differences in the *Vorlage* of the LXX. Differences between the two may also be due to inner-textual corruption[57] (cf. 2.2.2).

It is not always easy to distinguish between translational and text-critical cases. A literal translation, of course, can be relatively easily retroverted, whereas a translation in the manner of LXX Proverbs makes it more difficult to reconstruct the original achieving satisfactory results. The knowledge of the translation techniques of the translator, however, will help us make quite reliable decisions.

The following example may serve to illustrate my approach.

Prov 3:12

MT: כִּי אֶת אֲשֶׁר יֶאֱהַב יְהוָה יוֹכִיחַ וּכְאָב אֶת־בֵּן יִרְצֶה
"for whom the Lord loves, he reproves, even as a father the son in whom he delights"

LXX: ὃν γὰρ ἀγαπᾷ κύριος παιδεύει μαστιγοῖ δὲ (=וַיַּכְאִב)
πάντα υἱὸν ὃν παραδέχεται
"for whom the Lord loves, he disciplines, and scourges every son whom he receives"

In Prov 3:12 the suggestion has been made to emend the MT on the basis of the LXX (the LXX version is also quoted in Hebr 12:5–6) and to read μαστιγοῖ δὲ = וַיַּכְאִב "and he will make suffer" for וּכְאָב "and like a father," e.g. C. H.

---

[57] These are especially differences created by copyists. Such errors in copying have been called *parablepsis* (= "oversight" or "faulty seeing" which occurred when a scribe overlooked part of his text. This happened when the scribe's eye skipped to another identical or similar sequence further on in the text. Because of that the words or phrases in between the two sequences were lost); parablepsis may be caused by *homoioarkton* and *homoioteleuton* (a loss of text occurred when identical or similar sequences of letters in the beginning or at the end of two words or phrases were read as one), and *graphic confusion* (letters that were similar in shape such as ו and י, and ב and כ were sometimes confused by the scribes). Such errors may be found in the MT as well as in the *Vorlage*. On "inner-textual corruption" see Tov, *Textual Criticism*, 233–285. Tov, *Text-Critical Use*, 50–56. P. Kyle McCarter, Jr., *Textual Criticism: Recovering the Text of the Hebrew Bible* (Philadelphia: Fortress, 1986), 26–61. Ernst Würthwein, *Der Text des Alten Testaments* (Suttgart: Deutsche Bibelgesellschaft, 1988), 118–124. Brotzman, *Textual Criticism*, 107–121.

Toy,[58] B. Gemser,[59] NEB, REB, *BHS*, and even R. N. Whybray somehow favors the LXX.[60] And the HOTTP committee is equally divided.[61]

The consonants of the two readings look alike and thus there is the possibility that a scribe dropped the letter י in the MT tradition. It is more likely, however, that the translator of LXX Proverbs altered the Hebrew form in his source text—and we are working on the basis of the hypothesis that the shape of the MT was similar to that of the translator's *Vorlage*—to improve the parallelism, making the second half match the first half, since this seems to be his common practice as we shall see in the thesis. In addition, it may be noted that the translator frequently dropped comparisons and similes and/or rendered them differently, e.g. Prov 1:12b; 7:22; 11:28; 12:4; 18:8b,11b,19; 23:28a,32,34; 26:1. Thus it is unsafe to rely on the LXX reading in this case. Anyhow, the reading of the MT makes good sense: God disciplines (Prov 3:12; cf. Deut 8:5; 2 Sam 7:14) and displays the same attitude as a father (Prov 13:24).[62]

In the present work I am concerned with the rendering of Hebrew parallelism in the LXX of Proverbs, in which the translator took the same liberty as in his rendering of other linguistic features. He frequently modified Hebrew parallelisms to produce more regular and symmetrical or antithetical forms. Similar translational adaptations of parallel constructions can be found in some of the other more freely translated LXX books (see "INTRODUCTION," "Parallelism in the LXX"), although not to the same extent as in LXX Proverbs.

Furthermore, the linguistic structure of Hebrew differs from that of Greek.[63] The same applies to style (style may be specific to the individual and to the

---

[58] Crawford H. Toy, *The Book of Proverbs: A Critical and Exegetical Commentary* (Edinburgh: T & T Clark, 1899), 64–65.

[59] Berend Gemser, *Sprüche Salomos* (Tübingen, 1963), 26.

[60] According to Whybray the LXX would be syntactically an improvement, but he thinks that the MT may be correct without giving any reason. R. N. Whybray, *Proverbs: New Century Bible Commentary* (Grand Rapids: Eerdmans, 1994), 65.

[61] Dominique Barthélemy et al., *Preliminary and Interim Report on the Hebrew Old Testament Text Project* (vol. 3 of *Poetical Books*; New York: United Bible Societies, 1973–1980).

[62] A. Lemeire, "Education," n.p., *ABD on CD-ROM*. Version 2.1, 1997. Similarly C. J. H. Wright, *New International Dictionary of Old Testament Theology & Exegesis* (5 vols.; Grand Rapids: Zondervan, 1997), 1:221. Also in favor of the MT reading are, e.g. Clifford, *Proverbs*, 50. Arndt Meinhold, *Die Sprüche* (2 vols.; Theologischer Verlag Zürich, 1991), 1:77–78. Rolf Schäfer, *Die Poesie der Weisen: Dichotomie als Grundstruktur der Lehr- und Weisheitsgedichte in Proverbien 1-9* (Neukirchener Verlag, 1999), 85. Most of the translations follow the MT, also William McKane, *Proverbs: A New Approach* (London: SCM, 1970) and Roland E. Murphy, *Proverbs* (Nashville: Nelson, 1998).

[63] Cf. J. W. Wevers, "The Use of Versions for Text Criticism: The Septuagint," in *La Septuaginta en la Investigacion Contemporanea* (ed. N. Fernández Marcos; Madrid, 1985), 15–19.

language/culture), and in adaptations of parallel forms we are mainly dealing with differences in style; style is normally described at the language structure or discourse level.[64] Similarly, recent Greek grammars treat parallelisms, e.g., synonymous and antithetical, as stylistic devices at the discourse level.[65] Therefore, it may be quite normal if Hebrew parallelisms differ from Greek forms[66] and this may especially be true if we consider the individual style of a translator.[67]

Thus, the starting point for our study must be an investigation of the nature of Hebrew parallelism, and only then should we look at the Greek renderings.

---

[64] See also Tauberschmidt, "Principles."

[65] See in Willibald Heilmann, Kurt Roeske, and Rolf Walther, τύποι *Griechische Kurzgrammatik* (Frankfurt am Main: Moritz Diesterweg, 1994), 129–130. Winfried Elliger et al., *ΚΑΝΘΑΡΟΣ Griechisches Unterrichtswerk* (Stuttgart: Klett, 1996), 22–23.

[66] For instance, the literal King James translation simply copied the Hebrew poetic form. But CEV and NLT recast the original form into a more natural and appropriate English form. Similarly the GN 1/2 employed common German forms such as the pentameter for Job (as in Schiller's Glocke). The Song of Songs had to be cooled down for German readers. The following meters were used: iambics, trochaic, dactylic, anapaestic. The Song of the Vineyard in Isa 5 was modelled on "Im Märzen der Bauer" (W. Hensel, *Der singende Quell*, Kassel and Basel: Bärenreiter).

[67] The individual character of translators can be observed, for instance, in the Pentateuch. In the book of Leviticus θανάτῳ plus cognate verb translating an infinitive absolute construction occurs frequently. In Exodus also θανάτῳ plus cognate verb occurs several times translating an infinitive absolute construction, but other than in Leviticus different verbs are used for the sake of stylistic variation. Z. Frankel (1801–1875) already observed the individual character of the Pentateuch translators. Z. Frankel, *Über den Einfluß der palästinischen Exegese auf die alexandrinische Hermeneutik* (Leipzig, 1851). See also Wevers, "Apologia," 20. Cf. Tauberschmidt, "Principles," 130–131.

The Nature of Hebrew Parallelism

Parallelism, while it occurs also in other languages,[68] is an outstanding characteristic of Hebrew poetry.[69] According to A. Berlin "Parallelism is the most prominent rhetorical figure in ancient Near Eastern poetry, and is also present, although less prominent, in biblical prose."[70]

Berlin defines parallelism as "the repetition of the same or related semantic content and/or grammatical structure in consecutive lines or verses."[71] "Because there are infinite possibilities for activating linguistic equivalences, there are infinite possibilities for constructing parallelisms."[72]

According to D. L. Petersen and K. H. Richards parallelism occurs in the interaction of semantic and grammatical equivalence and opposition. "[Hebrew] parallelism is not something that is predictable, and no mechanical system or set of categories can confine it. Rather, we must carefully observe the individual words as well as their relationships at the level of the colon, multi-colon, and

---

[68] Parallelism can be found in the literature of other languages as well. According to L. I. Newman parallelism "is discoverable in some degree in almost every literature." L. I. Newman, *Studies in Biblical Parallelism. Part I: Parallelism in Amos* (Semicentennial Publications of the University of California, 1868–1918), 3. In Egyptian poetry parallelism, the key feature of Hebrew poetry, has been found to occur even before 2000 B.C.E. [see also D. K. Berry, *An Introduction to Wisdom and Poetry of the Old Testament* (Nashville: Broadman & Holman, 1994), 221] in "A Dispute over Suicide." James B. Pritchard, ed., *Ancient Near Eastern Texts: Relating to the Old Testament* (Princeton: Princeton University Press, 1969), 405–407. According to Berry, "Egypt employed parallelism long before the development of Hebrew poetry." Berry, *Wisdom and Poetry*, 231. And in Newman's opinion, Egyptian "poetry delighted in synonyms and antitheses; it even transcended Hebrew in its 'rhythmic arrangements, in the balance of lines, the close correspondence of clause to clause and the strict observance of rhythmic laws.' (See A. Erman, *Die aegyptische Literatur* in *Die orientalischen Literaturen*, p. 29). Breasted affirms, indeed, that parallelism is the usual form of Egyptian poetry. *Biblical World*, I, 55." Newman, *Biblical Parallelism*, 22. For examples of synonymous and antithetic parallelism see 23–24. Late Egyptian poetry of the Greek-Roman period is even more structured and symmetrical. On the whole a higher degree of meter, strophe, and parallelism can be found in it than in early Egyptian compositions. *Ibid.*, 27. For synonymous and antithetical parallelisms in Greek see Epicurus, Letter to Menoikeus 131 and Plato Apology 17b, quoted in Heilmann, τύποι, 130.

[69] But it is of course not the only characteristic of Hebrew Poetry; see also Wilfred G. E. Watson, *Classical Hebrew Poetry: A Guide to its Techniques* (Sheffield Academic Press, 1995), 118.

[70] Adele Berlin, "Parallelism," n.p., *ABD on CD-ROM*. Version 2.1, 1997.

[71] *Ibid.*

[72] *Ibid.*

entire poem in order to comprehend the range of parallelisms utilized in the Hebrew Bible."[73]

Certainly, Hebrew parallelism cannot be fitted neatly into a mechanical system. J. L. Kugel has argued that, although R. Lowth is the man generally credited with the discovery of biblical parallelism, by setting up three types of parallelism (synonymous, antithetical and synthetic parallelism) he forced everything to fall into one of three boxes.[74] This has had a disastrous effect on subsequent criticism, because synonymity was often imposed where it did not exist.[75]

A. Berlin, although commending Lowth for his insights,[76] agrees with Kugel that "there is no reason that his [Lowth's] views of parallelism should remain canonized," as in her opinion biblical parallelism is dynamic.[77] She says, "Most of the credit goes to Kugel, who offered the longest, most anti-Lowthian description of parallelism."[78]

---

[73] David L. Petersen and Kent Harold Richards, *Interpreting Hebrew Poetry* (Minneapolis: Fortress, 1992), 35.

[74] Although Bishop Robert Lowth was not the first to discover parallelism, he gave the most extensive treatment in his *De sacra poesi Hebraeorum* (London, 1753) [ET: *Lectures on the Sacred Poetry of the Hebrews* (London, 1835)] and his *Isaiah: A New Translation with a Preliminary Dissertation and Notes Critical, Philological, and Explanatory* (London, 1778), and consequently his definition, as expressed in the introduction to *Isaiah*, became the classic definition of parallelism: "The correspondence of one Verse, or Line, with another I call Parallelism. When a proposition is delivered, and a second is subjoined to it, or drawn under it, equivalent, or contrasted with it, in Sense; or similar to it in the form of Grammatical Construction; these I call Parallel Lines; and the words or phrases answering one to another in the corresponding Lines Parallel Terms."

[75] J. L. Kugel, *The Idea of Biblical Poetry: Parallelism and Its History* (Yale University Press, New Haven and London, 1981), 12, 15. Cf. T. R. Schneider, *The Sharpening of Wisdom: Old Testament Proverbs in Translation* (Pretoria: OTSSA, 1992), 33.

[76] Berlin, *Dynamics*, 64.

[77] *Ibid.*, 4.

[78] *Ibid.*, 64. In Kugel's view the second line always goes beyond the first one. He says that "Biblical parallelism is of one sort, "A, and what's more, B," or a hundred sorts; but it is not three." Kugel, *Idea*, 58. Berlin, however, faults Kugel for equating parallelism with poetry and making no distinction between poetry and prose. She writes that Kugel "tacitly accepts the equation of parallelism with poetry (even as he rejects it – *Idea*, 70) and then, wherever he finds parallelism he is forced to call it poetry – but, since he knows it isn't poetry, he calls it 'elevated style.'" Berlin, *Dynamics*, 4. Berlin goes on to say that "parallelism is not in and of itself a mark of poetry as opposed to prose, or even of elevated style as opposed to ordinary discourse; it is a common feature of all language. And yet, . . . in a certain sense parallelism *is* the essence of poetry." *Ibid.*

In a similar vein, R. Alter spoke of the "consequentiality" of parallel lines. He too viewed parallelism not as something static but as something dynamic, a point he demonstrates.[79]

According to R. G. Bratcher and W. D. Reyburn "An objective look at parallel lines in Hebrew poetry leads one to the conclusion that the possible relations between lines are nearly limitless."[80]

Even F. Delitzsch already remarked on parallelism that, "The relation of the two lines to each other is very manifold."[81]

In summary, parallelism is the heart of Hebrew poetry. Its many different forms cannot easily be categorized and captured in a fixed mechanical system, as there are innumerable possible combinations. Thus the three categories of R. Lowth, which are used to classify the whole spectrum of Hebrew parallelism, are too narrow: they cover only a few frequently occurring cases and impose synonymity where it does not exist. Hebrew parallelism, however, is dynamic rather than static, as a number of recent studies (e.g. Alter, Berlin, Kugel, and Watson) have demonstrated.

This is important to keep in mind when using the LXX (of Proverbs) to achieve "better" parallelism in text criticism. For we cannot automatically assume that the LXX translators rendered their source text word-by-word. In the next section we will look at parallelism in some freely translated LXX books.

PARALLELISM IN THE LXX

Parallelism can also be found in the LXX, not just as a copy of Hebrew parallelism, but it may occur as an independent Greek form.[82]

Especially those books of the LXX that are translated less literally contain freer and more natural parallel forms. This statement is supported by the following examples of Hebrew parallelisms from the MT, which were altered by the translators of the LXX.

---

[79] See Robert Alter, *The Art of Biblical Poetry* (New York: Basic Books, 1985), also R. Alter, "The Dynamics of Parallelism," *HUSLA* 11/1 (1983): 71–101. Berlin, however, faults both Alter and Kugel for being too extreme: "Both Kugel and Alter came to the study of the Bible from literary criticism, and both brought their finely honed skills as readers to parallelistic texts. But literary criticism often eschews precise analysis in favor of more diffuse observations. So, while achieving a reorientation of the view of parallelism, Kugel and Alter achieve it only at a level of extreme generality. They offer only the vaguest definitions of parallelism and do not provide the criteria for deeper analysis of its workings." Berlin, "Parallelism," n.p.

[80] Robert G. Bratcher and William D. Reyburn, *A Translator's Handbook on the Book of Psalms* (New York: United Bible Societies, 1991), 5.

[81] Franz Delitzsch, *Biblical Commentary on the Proverbs of Solomon* (trans. M. G. Easton; Grand Rapids: Eerdmans, 1971), 7.

[82] Friedrich Blass, Albert Debrunner, and Friedrich Rehkopf, eds., *Grammatik des neutestamentlichen Griechisch* (Göttingen: Vandenhoeck & Ruprecht, 1979), 420–421.

1. Isa 52:1

MT: עוּרִי עוּרִי לִבְשִׁי עֻזֵּךְ צִיּוֹן לִבְשִׁי בִּגְדֵי תִפְאַרְתֵּךְ יְרוּשָׁלַםִ עִיר הַקֹּדֶשׁ
"Awake, awake, put on your strength, O Zion; put on your beautiful garments, O Jerusalem, the holy city"

LXX: ἐξεγείρου ἐξεγείρου Σιων ἔνδυσαι τὴν ἰσχύν σου Σιων καὶ ἔνδυσαι τὴν δόξαν σου Ιερουσαλημ πόλις ἡ ἁγία
"Awake, awake, Zion; put on your strength, O Zion; and put on your glory, Jerusalem the holy city"

In Isa 52:1 the translator repeated "Zion." He also dropped the figure "garments," and replaced it by "glory," thus making the second colon more parallel with the first.

2. Gen 37:33

MT: וַיַּכִּירָהּ וַיֹּאמֶר כְּתֹנֶת בְּנִי חַיָּה רָעָה אֲכָלָתְהוּ טָרֹף טֹרַף יוֹסֵף
"He recognized it and said, The robe of my son, a bad living thing (animal) devoured him, it surely tore Joseph to pieces"

LXX: καὶ ἐπέγνω αὐτὸν καὶ εἶπεν χιτὼν τοῦ υἱοῦ μού ἐστιν θηρίον πονηρὸν κατέφαγεν αὐτόν θηρίον ἥρπασεν τὸν Ιωσηφ
"And he recognized it, and said, It is my son's coat, an evil wild beast has devoured him; a wild beast has carried off Joseph"

In Gen 37:33 the LXX repeats θηρίον "wild beast" thus producing an independent parallel structure.

There are cases where the altered form of the Hebrew parallelism is quoted in the NT as in the following examples.

3. Isa 40:3

MT: קוֹל קוֹרֵא בַּמִּדְבָּר פַּנּוּ דֶּרֶךְ יְהוָה יַשְּׁרוּ בָּעֲרָבָה מְסִלָּה לֵאלֹהֵינוּ
"A voice cries out, in the wilderness prepare the way of the Lord, make straight in the desert a highway for our God"

LXX: φωνὴ βοῶντος ἐν τῇ ἐρήμῳ ἑτοιμάσατε τὴν ὁδὸν κυρίου εὐθείας ποιεῖτε τὰς τρίβους τοῦ θεοῦ ἡμῶν
"The voice of one crying in the wilderness, prepare the way for the Lord, make straight the paths of our God"

In Isa 40:3 "in the desert" is left out the second time in the LXX and "highway" is changed to "paths." Also in the MT the words "in the wilderness" modify "prepare," whereas in the LXX they go with "cry." Matt 3:3 follows the LXX fairly closely.[83]

Another example of this would be Prov 3:34 which is quoted in 1 Pet 5:5 according to the altered LXX translation, and similarly Prov 3:12 where the altered form is quoted in Hebr 12:6.[84]

In summary, these examples taken from Genesis and Isaiah show how some of the LXX translators departed from a literal rendering of Hebrew parallelism and used forms that were more natural to them stylistically. Some of these adapted parallelisms were even quoted by NT authors.

The LXX translator who translated Proverbs, however, is the one who took most liberty in rendering Hebrew parallelism (and other features). This will be demonstrated in the following Chapter One.

---

[83] Matthew (apart from adding the orienter: "This is the one of whom the prophet Isaiah spoke when he said") followed the LXX in leaving out "in the desert" the second time. But he makes a further alteration, changing "(the paths of) our God" to "his (paths)" thus leaving out "God." In Greek fewer full noun phrases are used than in Hebrew, and this may have led to the change from "of our God" to "his." But perhaps Matthew made this change not for linguistic reasons but because he wanted to refer clearly to the Lord Jesus.

[84] There are also similar examples of Greek parallelism in the book of Wisdom, e.g. 7:7,8; 8:13,14,17. According to R. E. Murphy "Without the Greek cultural background that blanketed the Mediterranean world a book like the Wisdom of Solomon would never have been written. Although it remains an intensely Jewish book, it is to be read in the light of Hellenistic culture." Roland E. Murphy, "Wisdom in the OT," n.p., *ABD on CD-ROM*. Version 2.1, 1997.

1. HEBREW PARALLELISM RENDERED IN A MORE EXACTLY PARALLEL FASHION

1.1 Introduction

In my earlier work "Principles of Bible Translation and the Septuagint" I have written on aspects of the translation techniques of the LXX translators and have classified the LXX books with regard to their literalness on a scale ranging from free through middle to literal.[1] According to this classification LXX Proverbs falls in the group of free translations.[2] In my present study I concentrate on the book of Proverbs only and show how the translator adapted Hebrew parallelism so as to produce couplets that are more closely parallel as regards their structure and/or semantics. This presupposes that the shape of his Hebrew *Vorlage* was similar to that of the MT. These adaptations led to "better" parallelisms in LXX Proverbs. The fact that Hebrew parallelism is dynamic, as has been demonstrated by recent scholars (Alter, Berlin, Kugel, Watson), lends support to my findings. There are, however, cases of couplets in LXX Proverbs the lines of which may be regarded as less closely parallel than in the MT, but these can be explained on the basis of the translator's love for cohesion (beyond the couplet, i.e., on the paragraph level) and other factors, all of which can overrule the closely corresponding lines of the couplet and lead to less closely parallel forms. LXX Proverbs should therefore only be used for "better" parallelism (or for textual criticism in general) after careful consideration of the translator's technique.[3] The present work will provide guidance to this end, as the translation

---

[1] See also Tov, "The Septuagint," 173. And Sidney Jellicoe, *The Septuagint and Modern Study* (Oxford: Clarendon, 1968), 318.

[2] Tauberschmidt, "Principles." The book of Proverbs is clearly on the free side with regard to translation techniques employed. This is shown by the survey of translating the infinitive absolute plus cognate verb (5x). There is no occurrence of a literal rendering. In addition, there are three cases where appropriate adverbs are used. There are also many cases where the LXX translator was free to alter a Hebrew poetic form so that the second half of the parallelism corresponded with the first half or vice versa, and to paraphrase similes completely. The Hebrew comparative מִן ... טוֹב has been translated freely in all occurrences (19x). Also, בְּנִי where it occurs as vocative is rendered υἱέ without possessive pronoun in all occurrences, and אִמּוֹ (5x) is rendered freely 4x without possessive pronoun. *Ibid.*, 127. See also G. Gerleman, *Studies in the Septuagint, III, Proverbs* (Lunds Universitets Årsskrift, 1956), 12. H. St. J. Thackeray, *A Grammar of the Old Testament in Greek acc. to the Septuagint, I* (Cambridge University Press, 1909), 13.

[3] According to J. W. Wevers "It is imperative that one have some clear understanding of the mind of the translator and how he operated before drawing textual conclusions which presuppose a different parent text." Wevers, "Apologia," 38.

technique of LXX Proverbs has not been researched extensively nor has any analysis been done of the translator's[4] method of rendering Hebrew parallelism with particular regard to his tendency to produce forms that are more parallel semantically and/or grammatically.

The first critical contribution to the study of LXX Proverbs was made by P. A. de Lagarde in 1863.[5] His work aimed primarily at reconstructing the Greek text. The second nineteenth-century contribution was by A. J. Baumgartner in 1890.[6] In his opinion the LXX *Vorlage* hardly differed from the MT and he thought the deviations were a result of the translator's peculiar translation method. However, neither of these works presented any study of the methodology of the translator.[7]

In the twentieth century a major contribution was made by G. Gerleman, in *Studies in the Septuagint, III, Proverbs,* (1956). He criticizes the earlier studies for the lack of "a clear exposition of the translator's nature and aims"[8] and claims that his "study is an attempt to take up the task of fixing the general character of the LXX Prov."[9] Gerleman, in this study, as well as in his earlier study "The Septuagint Proverbs as a Hellenistic Document," (1950), provides the most extensive treatment of the subject. He argues that the translator of LXX Proverbs adapted Hebrew parallelism in conformity with Hellenistic literary

---

[4] The style of translation throughout LXX Proverbs (see whole thesis) suggests that there may have been only one translator involved, and apparently the person who translated Job was a different one according to the findings of John G. Gammie, "The Septuagint of Job: Its Poetic Style and Relationship to the Septuagint of Proverbs," *CBQ* 49/1 (1987): 14–31, against the position of Gerleman, *Studies*, 59–60. J. Cook agrees that throughout LXX Proverbs the *basic approach* is the same, but he thinks that the translation may have been the result of teamwork as "it is probably a tall order to expect one person to have completed such a daunting task [as translating Proverbs]." Cook, *Proverbs*, 322. But this argument is not very convincing. In R. L. Giese's opinion, however, "the style of Greek is quite inconsistent, revealing various hands at work in the process of translation." Ronald L. Giese Jr., "Dualism in the LXX of Prov 2:17: A Case Study in the LXX as Revisionary Translation," *JETS* 36/3 (1993): 289. But Giese does not provide any proof for his claim.

[5] Paul A. de Lagarde, *Anmerkungen zur griechischen Übersetzung der Proverbien* (Leipzig, 1863).

[6] A. J. Baumgartner, *Étude critique sur l'état du texte du Livre des Proverbes d'après les principales traductions anciennes* (Leipzig, 1890).

[7] A further work on the Greek text is G. Mezzacasa, *Il libro dei proverbi di Salomone: Studio critico sulle aggiunte greco-alessandrine* (Roma: Instituto Biblico Pontificio, 1913); also some of the commentaries discuss the Greek text: McKane, *Proverbs*, especially 33–47; Toy, *Proverbs*; and to some extend Otto Plöger, *Sprüche Salomos (Proverbia)* (Neukirchener Verlag, 1984).

[8] Gerleman, *Studies*, 3–5. Cf. also Cook, *Proverbs*, 4.

[9] *Ibid.*, 5. Gerleman goes on to say: "Only if this task can be accomplished will it become possible to form an opinion of the value of this translation in criticising MT."

tradition, transforming synonymous parallelisms into antithetic forms[10] and trying to make the contrast in Hebrew antithetical parallelisms more precise and clear-cut,[11] as well as employing other adaptations.[12] Gerleman's opinion (1950) is that the adaptations in LXX Proverbs affected both style and ideas due to the "friendly attitude to Hellenistic culture." He writes,

> The Greek reshaping of the book of Proverbs relates to the form as well as to the content, to the style as well as to the ideas.[13]

> The friendly attitude to Hellenistic culture which has stamped the Septuagint Proverbs has left its most distinct marks in the style of the translation. But at the same time it is incontestable that Hellenistic ideas, first and foremost of the Stoic type, have found their way into it also.[14]

In his later monograph, Gerleman presented a more comprehensive study of Hellenistic influence in LXX Proverbs at the level of stylistic form and the world of ideas.[15]

In contrast to Gerleman's analysis, S. Segert in his article "Hebrew poetic parallelism as reflected in the Septuagint," (1985), expressed a more cautious view:

> In relatively frequent instances where the Greek translation exhibits parallelistic structures against non-parallelistic verses in the Hebrew Masoretic text, it is difficult to prove whether this parallelism was preserved from the pre-Masoretic text or whether the Greek translator

---

[10] G. Gerleman, "The Septuagint Proverbs as a Hellenistic Document," *OtSt* 8 (1950): 15–17.

[11] Gerleman, *Studies*, 22–24.

[12] Further adaptations are described in relation to e.g. assonance, anaphora, meter, additions, metaphor, spiritualizing, religious-moralizing. *Ibid.*, 11–57. H. St. J. Thackeray in his article, "The Poetry of the Greek Book of Proverbs," *JTS* 13 (1911): 46–66, observes that there are many instances of metrical arrangements in LXX Proverbs that represent hexameter and iambic meters. Gerleman, while agreeing with Thackeray especially concerning hexameter endings, has some reservations and calls for caution particularly regarding the iambics proposed by Thackeray. Gerleman, *Studies*, 15–17. According to A. Taylor, "Metrical studies of proverbs have rarely escaped the temptation to employ the elaborate classical system of metrics, and have consequently failed to discover the essential traits." Archer Taylor, "The Style of Proverbs," *De Proverbio* 5/1 (1999): 1.

[13] Gerleman, "Septuagint Proverbs," 15.

[14] *Ibid.*, 27.

[15] Gerleman, *Studies*.

attempted to regularize or symmetrize the asymmetry of the original.[16]

In 1997 a monograph on LXX Proverbs (chapters 1, 2, 6, 8, 9, and 31) by J. Cook appeared.[17] He agrees with Gerleman's view "that this translator had a predilection for sharp antithesis."[18] But he disagrees that this preference for sharp contrast was only applied for the purpose of literary effect. To Cook's mind the translator of Proverbs also had religious intentions with his antithesis.[19] Against Gerleman[20] he writes in an earlier article:

> It is undoubtedly true that the Greek version of Proverbs has many more examples of antithetical parallelism than has the Hebrew. However, whether this should at the same time prove Greek (Hellenistic) influence is an issue of another order.[21]

Cook disagrees with Gerleman on two crucial points: 1) he maintains that the translator made certain adjustments not solely for the sake of literary effect,

---

[16] S. Segert, "Hebrew Poetic Parallelism as Reflected in the Septuagint," IOSCS 18 (1985): 133–148, (here 142). Against H. St. J. Thackeray's understanding, that the translator imitated the most common Greek verse types of hexameter and iambic lines (Thackeray, "Poetry," 46–66), S. Segert holds that parallel forms in general were translated without substantial change, since "in translation from Hebrew into Greek, considerable correspondence between grammatical categories of these languages makes a close rendering of parallelistic structure possible." Segert, "Hebrew Poetic," 133. One may not agree with Thackeray in every detail, nevertheless, the translator of LXX Proverbs adapted Hebrew parallelism in accordance with his translation technique in the direction of closer corresponding forms, as this thesis demonstrates.

[17] Cook, *Proverbs*. C. Cox in his review of this book was quite critical and did not recommend it. C. Cox, "Review of Cook, The Septuagint of Proverbs," *TC: A Journal of Biblical Textual Criticism* 3 (1998). N. Fernández Marcos, however, in his review drew a more positive picture: "In sum, the book is well developed and argued within the limits imposed." Review of J. Cook, *The Septuagint of Proverbs–Jewish and/or Hellenistic Proverbs? Concerning the Hellenistic Colouring of LXX Proverbs*, *JSJ* XXX 1 (1999): 96.

[18] Cook, *Proverbs*, 7.

[19] *Ibid.*

[20] L. Greenspoon comments on Cook's contribution (in L. Greenspoon and O. Munnich, eds. *VIII Congress of the International Organization for Septuagint and Cognate Studies: Paris 1992*. SBLSCS 41, Atlanta: Scholars Press, 1995) as follows: "In one sense Cook's final position is not far from that of Gerleman, who emphasized that the LXX Proverbs was a Hellenistic document, but noted that the acceptance of Hellenistic culture and ideas was minimal when compared to the Hellenization seen in Philo. Gerleman supposes continuity, Cook, intellectual resistance. The fulcrum may be the dating of the text." Cook's article appeared in writing under the title "Hellenistic Influence in the Book of Proverbs," *BIOSCS* 20 (1987): 30–42.

[21] *Ibid.*, 33.

but also to express explicit religious viewpoints (or a Jewish way of thinking);[22] and 2) he faults Gerleman for putting too much emphasis on Greek philosophical influence on the translator, especially his claims that Stoic perspectives found their way into the Greek text of Proverbs.[23]

It may very well be that G. Gerleman tends to over-emphasize the influence of Hellenistic thought and ideas in LXX Proverbs, especially as far as Stoic philosophy is concerned.[24] Certainly, the LXX translators were not neutral, that is, free from the influence of their own background,[25] but the question remains open as to whether the translator of Proverbs was primarily influenced by Hellenistic (Gerleman) or Jewish (Cook) ideas.[26] There are also a number of shorter studies that may be mentioned which concentrate on various influences on LXX Proverbs: G. Bertram (1936) thinks that LXX Proverbs exhibits a definite Hellenistic Jewish *Tendenz*;[27] J. Weingreen (1973) holds that the LXX version of Proverbs "may be described as a Targum" or a "Rabbinic-type

---

[22] Cook, *Proverbs*, 7.

[23] *Ibid.*, 12.

[24] See in Gerleman, "Septuagint Proverbs," 15–27. According to Martin Hengel, in *Judentum und Hellenismus* (Tübingen, 1973), there is very little influence of philosophical ideas in the LXX in general with only some exceptions, 189–190, which can be found especially in Job and Proverbs, 209–210 and 292–295. But it is not Hengel's primary aim to detect such philosophical influence, as he states in his introduction, 6: "Es geht nicht primär darum, je und je angebliche 'griechische Einflüsse' nachzuweisen, zumal oft zwischen Analogien und wirklichen Beeinflussungen nicht unterschieden werden kann, vielmehr soll versucht werden, das innere Gefälle des jüdisch-palästinischen Denkens in der Spannung zwischen Rezeption und Abwehr des hellenistischen Zeitgeistes darzustellen."

[25] See Tauberschmidt, "Principles," 110.

[26] In J. Cook's opinion, "Hellenistic influence was restricted to the domain of the literary," Cook, *Proverbs*, 9, and he excludes any Hellenistic influence at the level of "world of ideas." *Ibid.*, 320. This view is, however, too narrow. Note, for instance, that the LXX translators in order to avoid misunderstandings did not translate the figure צוּר "rock" literally where it refers to God (even in LXX books that are regarded as literal translations), because in the Hellenistic religions stone or rock is a symbol or the embodiment of a god.

[27] Georg Bertram, "Die religiöse Umdeutung altorientalischer Lebensweisheit in der griechischen Übersetzung des AT," *ZAW* NF 13 (1936): 153–167.

commentary";[28] M. B. Dick (1990) emphasizes the moralizing tendency of the translator,[29] and R. L. Giese Jr. finds evidence for a stronger component of compassion to the lowly[30] and thinks that the translator focused on economy and social issues rather than moral and religious ones regarding the topics of wealth and power.[31] In connection with Dick's (1990) and Cook's 1987 article R. J. Clifford remarks that "recently attention has shifted away from textual matters to ideology."[32]

It is beyond the scope of this study to answer the question of the primary influence on LXX Proverbs in any detail. Certainly, no translation is free from biases, and we may not be certain as to whether an adaptation was motivated by the translator's philosophical/religious background or interests (or those of his target audience), or whether it was due to linguistic and translational factors, or both. But it is important to employ an adequate methodology for determining how the translator seems to have operated. In J. Cook's opinion in order to be able also to observe religious motives in the translation, one needs to have "a broader definition of translation technique, for a strictly linguistic approach will not automatically bring such perspectives to the fore."[33] I agree with Cook in that all possible influences need to be kept in consideration when evaluating a translation. But to my understanding, any approach to defining a translator's technique should filter out the elements which are not linguistically and translationally motivated and which go beyond the intention of the original

---

[28] J. Weingreen, "Rabbinic-Type Commentary in the LXX Version of Proverbs," in *Proceedings of the Sixth World Congress of Jewish Studies* (ed. A. Shinan; Jerusalem: World Union of Jewish Studies, 1973), 407–415. Weingreen's view that the LXX version of Proverbs "may be described as a Targum" or a "Rabbinic-type commentary" is quite one-sided. He even seems to deny that the "LXX version of Proverbs represents the work of the translators" and holds that "the glosses and editorial notes, representing the official interpretation of the passages concerned, had been incorporated into the Alexandrian Hebrew text before them and that they were already established in this text before the process of translating the Hebrew into Greek had been inaugurated." *Ibid.*, 413.

[29] Michael Brennan Dick, "The Ethics of the Old Greek Book of Proverbs," in *The Studia Philonica Annual: Studies in Hellenistic Judaism* (ed. D. T. Runia; vol. II; Atlanta 1990), 20–50.

[30] Ronald L. Giese Jr., "Compassion for the Lowly in Septuagint Proverbs," *JSP* 11 (1993): 109–117.

[31] Ronald, L. Giese Jr., "Qualifying Wealth in LXX Proverbs," *JBL* 111/3 (1992): 409–425.

[32] Clifford, "Observations", 52.

[33] Cook, *Proverbs*, 30. Cook seems to refer to the so-called "Helsinki-school." *Ibid.* See also J. Cook, "Aspects of the Translation Technique followed by the Translator of LXX Proverbs," *JNSL* 22/1 (1996): 143–144.

author, as these may be regarded as deficiencies in a translation.[34] Thus, in defining the translation technique of a particular LXX translator we may investigate both the way he tended to render linguistic features,[35] as well as the way he tended to interpret his source text(s): whether he emphasized the spiritual, religious, natural, or philosophical realm. It is, however, not always clear if the alterations were motivated merely by the translator's translation technique and style[36] or by his ideas, or both. But it may be better to investigate the style of the translation and the linguistic and translational aspects first and as a second step look at the religious or philosophical motives of the translator as the former field seems to be more clear-cut than the latter considering the many diverse and opposing views,[37] although it is not always possible to separate the two categories.[38]

---

[34] Cf. Tauberschmidt, "Principles," under 2.3 Deficiencies of the LXX. In a good translation the factual information, ideas, the authorial intention, and the effect contained in the original text should be retained in the translation.

[35] This may include any part of speech or linguistic construction starting from the word level up to the discourse level.

[36] The different views on "style" can be divided into three categories: 1) When the reference to reality is central, style can be seen as a possible form for a specific content. 2) From the perspective of writer or speaker, style can be seen as the choice of specific forms. 3) From the perspective of the reader or listener, language can be seen as a deviation from a given expectation. J. Renkema, *Discourse Studies: An Introductory Textbook* (Amsterdam/Philadelphia: John Benjamins, 1993), 97. In our approach the option 2) may apply. According to P. Newmark "the individual uses of language of the text-writer and the translator do not coincide. Everybody has lexical if not grammatical idiosyncrasies, and attaches "private" meanings to a few words. The translator normally writes in a style that comes naturally to him, . . ." Peter Newmark, *Approaches to Translation* (Oxford, New York, Toronto, Sydney, Paris, Frankfurt: Pergamon, 1981), 8.

[37] It is true that ideally the translator should turn his attention both to the ideas and the words and arrangement before he can operate his techniques and undertakes his "compromises." But it may be considered that in poetry the form may be more important than the meaning, whereas in non-literary work the facts are more important than the style. Cf. Newmark, *Approaches to Translation*, 21–23.

[38] According to F. Watson, although "translation is always also a political act," there are certain criteria of (relative) "objectivity" for textual interpretation, one of which implies a relative freedom from local interests (and the translator is included here). This means that a rendering may be primarily motivated by the concern to render the Hebrew words as accurately as possible. Francis Watson, *Text and Truth: Redefining Biblical Theology* (Grand Rapids: Eerdmans, 1997), 107–126, here 113–114.

Although Gerleman's study (1956) may be regarded as the most extensive on the nature of parallelism in LXX Proverbs so far,[39] it lacks any description of the translator's individual style and especially his dominant characteristic of cohesion. In addition, he limits the translator's more precise and clear-cut parallelisms to antithetical forms, thus apparently excluding synonymous parallelism. The problem with Gerleman's analysis may be that he compares the Greek style of Proverbs exclusively with Hellenistic Greek (this may also concern the world of ideas) and gives too little attention to the individual style[40] and technique of the translator.

E. Tov makes the criticism that scholars have tended to ascribe the deviations of LXX Proverbs from the MT to the "translator's whims" rather than to its Hebrew *Vorlage*.[41] Tov's criticism is justified in so far as the method and style of translation of LXX Proverbs has not been studied sufficiently, and this has often led to *ad hoc* decisions on text-critical questions. Among his examples there are, however, some cases that he treats as text-critical[42] although they can be explained as being due to the translator's style and translation practice.[43]

As I have already stated, LXX Proverbs is a rather free translation. If the OG of Proverbs had been a literal translation, we could assume that the parallelisms that vary from the MT reflect a different Hebrew source text. In the case of LXX Proverbs, however, this is simply impossible considering the freedom the translator used in his translation, although like all LXX translators he did not apply his principles consistently. And in the rendering of Hebrew parallelism the translator of LXX Proverbs took the same liberty as in his

---

[39] J. Cook's book, *The Septuagint of Proverbs–Jewish and/or Hellenistic Proverbs?*, is of course more detailed on all levels and more current, but it covers only a number of chapters and is thus not comprehensive, and in addition, its emphasis is more on ideology. In some of his articles, however, he does deal with various aspects of translation technique and these are discussed in the thesis.

[40] My own experience as a translation advisor/consultant has taught me that individual style can differ greatly. We may take Mark's Gospel as an example from the NT to illustrate some of his stylistic devices: Mark's use of εὐθύς "immediately" (41 times), see Paul Ellingworth, "How soon is 'immediately' in Mark?," *BT* 29/4 (1978): 414–419; similarly Mark's frequent use of the historic present (151 times) is of a stylistic nature although he may have used it for a particular purpose, see Stanley E. Porter, *Idioms of the Greek New Testament* (Sheffield Academic Press, 1992), 30–31; Mark uses eight different words that mean "amazed" in English, some of which occur over twenty times in the Gospel of Mark; finally we may mention his frequent use of *kai* "and, also, etc." although it may be due to Semitic influence.

[41] Emanuel Tov, "Recensional Differences between the Masoretic Text and the Septuagint of Proverbs," in *Of Scribes and Scrolls, Studies on the Hebrew Bible, Intertestamental Judaism, and Christian Origins Presented to John Strugnell* (ed. H. W. Attridge et al.; Lanham, Maryland, 1990), 43–44.

[42] *Ibid.*

[43] E.g. Prov 3:2,16,22; 11:10–11; 18:21.

rendering of other linguistic features. So it is not surprising that he frequently modified Hebrew parallelisms to produce more regular and symmetrical or antithetical forms.

The comparative study of the characteristics of parallelism in LXX Proverbs and the MT is based on the assumption that the Hebrew *Vorlage* or source text of the LXX did not differ extensively from the MT.[44] The examples used in the thesis are generally based on passages where there is little reason to doubt the truth of this assumption, as they can be explained on the basis of the translator's technique. I do not ignore the fact that there are rearrangements of the text,[45] but most of these bigger variations are irrelevant to the issue of the thesis, since they do not affect the problem of textual variants at a more detailed level within passages that are in both the MT and the LXX. There are, however, clauses that were apparently added or omitted by the translator. Only in cases where sufficient evidence can be provided that the translator's technique led to such "additions"[46] and "omissions" are they treated in the study.

The Bible editions used for the analysis are the *BHS*[47] and Rahlfs, as the critical LXX edition of Proverbs has not been published yet.

---

[44] See also Jellicoe, *Septuagint*, 317. W. McKane, *Proverbs*, 34. Cook, *Proverbs*, 334. Also N. Fernández Marcos who states: "In particular I basically agree with Cook's statement that the translator of Proverbs deliberately adapted his parent text and that he is not following a different Hebrew Vorlage." Marcos, Review J. Cook, *Proverbs*, 96.

[45] "The most obvious differences between it [the Septuagint] and the Hebrew text lie in the order in which the different parts of the book are arranged." Whybray, *The Book of Proverbs*, 161. C. T. Fritsch thinks, "The order found in the Greek text is probably older than that of the Hebrew." Charles T. Fritsch, "The Treatment of the Hexaplaric Signs in the Syro-Hexaplar of Proverbs," *JBL* 72 (1953): 169. E. Tov thinks that there were two parallel editions of the Hebrew text of Proverbs. The different order of chapters 24–31 and some (but not all) of the additional verses are an indication in favor of this assumption. Tov, *Textual Criticism*, 337. See also Tov, "Recensional Differences," 43–56.

[46] One kind of addition has been called "double translation" in LXX studies. Z. Talshir uses "'double translation' to describe a given situation in which one unit in the Vorlage has for its equivalent two alternate units in the translation." Zipora Talshir, "Double Translations in the Septuagint," in *LXX VI Congress of the International Organization for Septuagint and Cognate Studies, Jerusalem 1986* (ed. C. E. Cox; SCS 23; Atlanta 1987), 21–63, (here 27). But Talshir does not discuss LXX Proverbs except for the mention of one case in Prov 6:3. *Ibid.*, 36. S. Talmon, however, takes "double translations" as "the work of copyists who combined alternative renderings of a single Hebrew word or a single Hebrew expression found in different MSS of the version in question." Shemaryahu Talmon, "Double Readings in the Massoretic Text," *Textus* 1 (1984): 144–184, (here 151). Talmon does, however, not discuss LXX Proverbs. For a discussion of "double translation" see also Cook, *Proverbs*, 12–16. In this thesis, the terminology "double translation" has been avoided.

[47] Note that the BHQ (Biblia Hebraica Quinta) has not been completed yet.

As regards genre *Proverbs* (*māšāl*) designates a wide range of literary types. According to R. J. Clifford, "The book of Proverbs consists of several collections of instructions, speeches, poems, and two-line sayings."[48] Concerning the origins of the Hebrew *māšāl*[49] there are many uncertainties. It is normally assumed that "the collection of Hebrew Proverbs (MT) is the end result of a long and extensive development."[50] In W. McKane's view (drawing from J. Schmidt[51]) "the single-limbed verse is the primitive form (*Urform*) of the popular proverb," and "the two-limbed verse is the basic stylistic element (*Stilform*) of the literary *māšāl*. . . . When two limbs are similarly constructed, *parallelismus membrorum* is produced."[52] In McKane's view, "*parallelismus membrorum* is not native to Old Testament wisdom literature, but derives from the influence of poetry and a form of elevated speech on that literature."[53] According to A. Meinhold the two-line saying, the so-called *parallelismus membrorum*, was known in the whole ancient orient.[54] He writes:

> In der altorientalischen Umwelt Israels sind die Weisheitstraditionen Mesopotamiens vorrangig von Spruchweisheit bestimmt gewesen. Die alttestamentlichen Sprüche weisen ein poetisches Merkmal auf, das sich auch sonst in der altorientalischen Literatur findet, den Parallelismus membrorum. Damit ist die Gestaltung einer

---

[48] Clifford, *Proverbs*, 1.

[49] "In the Hebrew Bible *māšāl* designates a wide range of literary types—taunt, allegory, lament, simile, and so on—but its etymology implies likeness and, in the view of some interpreters, authoritative word (from *mšl*, 'to rule'). The fundamental feature of the sayings within the book therefore seems to be 'comparison.' Brief proverbial sayings set one image over against another, making an explicit or implicit comparison. Not every isolated saying compares two things, however, and some sayings extend considerably beyond a single distich, in the process multiplying the number of likenesses under consideration." J. L. Crenshaw, "Proverbs, Book of," n.p., *ABD on CD-ROM*. Version 2.1, 1997.

[50] Cook, *Proverbs*, 32. According to R. J. Clifford, "the author-editors of Proverbs not only collected instructions and sayings but also rearranged and reshaped them." Clifford, *Proverbs*, 2.

[51] J. Schmidt, "Studien zur Stilistik der alttestamentlichen Spruchliteratur," ATA 13/1 (1936): 1-2.

[52] McKane, *Proverbs*, 1.

[53] *Ibid*, 2. "Because the literature grew out of popular wisdom and was not originally poetry, something of the prosaic still attaches to its form and content." *Ibid*. Cf. Cook, *Proverbs*, 33. R. J. Clifford thinks that "Israel's authors created a subgenre, the bicolon proverb, which attained definite shape well before the late eighth century, when King Hezekiah's clerks added their collection to an already existing one." Clifford, *Proverbs*, 19.

[54] "Die Kunstform der Sentenz zeigt sich darin, daß der im ganzen Alten Orient bekannte Parallelismus membrorum verwendet wird." Plöger, *Sprüche*, XVIII.

> Langzeile mittels zweier Hälften gemeint, die eng aufeinander bezogen sind und in dieser Bezogenheit ihre Aussage machen. Das führt in den meisten Fällen zu einer Doppelung der Vorstellungen und Gedanken und eröffnet beinahe unerschöpfliche Möglichkeiten des Variierens und Nuancierens.[55]

In any case, whether proverbs were actually borrowed from outside Israel[56] or whether Israel simply based its poetry on the content and usage of its milieu,[57] the parallel lines of the *parallelismus membrorum* were dynamic, as I have shown above. The translator of Proverbs, however, adapted dynamic Hebrew parallelisms into forms that were more exactly parallel semantically and/or grammatically. The question is whether these differences are mainly due to the translator's style or to Hellenistic Greek style in general.

The following authors have noted stylistic differences between Hebrew and Greek. According to J. L. Kugel "those who first attributed meter to the Bible were Hellenized Jews, and later, Greek-speaking Christians, . . . [their] desire [was] to parallel the excellencies of Greek poetry with their own sacred texts . . ."[58] J. L. Crenshaw states that "The Greek text [of Proverbs] has about 130 stichs more than the Hebrew, many of them highly Hellenized."[59] S. Jellicoe writes about the translator of Proverbs that he "adapts his original to its new environment. . . . Greek rather than Hebrew standards determine the style. Yet it remains essentially the Hebrew Book of Proverbs though its dress is Greek."[60] Even S. Segert, who does not allow for the presence of considerable translational changes in the parallelisms of the LXX (cf. INTRODUCTION), admits that "Parallelistic structures were not unknown in the original Greek poetry of the Hellenistic period."[61]

---

[55] Meinhold, *Sprüche*, 1:17.

[56] According to R. J. Clifford, "It is generally agreed that "The Words of the Wise" (Prov 22:17–24:22), drew upon the Egyptian *Instruction of Amenemope*." Clifford, *Proverbs*, 17.

[57] According to D. K. Berry, "We cannot say that Israel's poetry 'came from' Egypt, or Ugarit, or Babylon, but Israel 'based its poetry' on the content and usage of its milieu. From another perspective, Israel based its poetry on the expressions of its ancestors, but these ancestors were not yet Hebrews." Berry, *Wisdom and Poetry*, 238.

[58] Kugel, *Idea*, 301.

[59] Crenshaw, "Proverbs," n.p.

[60] Jellicoe, *Septuagint*, 317–318.

[61] Although he believes that "such intention [in the LXX] may be rather ascribed to the tendency to imitate a characteristic formal feature of the Hebrew original as compensation for considerable changes in content and conceptual level." Segert, "Hebrew Poetic," 141.

Although differences between general Greek style and general Hebrew style may have led the translator to adapt his Hebrew *Vorlage* stylistically, I will give more consideration to the translator's individual style and how he applied certain translation techniques, as this area can be measured more objectively. While the differences between Hebrew and Greek style lend support to my findings, my main arguments are based on 1) the translator's individual style in the translation of LXX Proverbs, 2) recurring patterns in couplets and his application of cohesion, 3) the free character of his translation.

Methodologically the following approach has been taken: in each case there is first a short discussion of the form in the MT to establish the Hebrew text according to possible interpretations as presented in commentaries. This is followed by a comparison of that text with the OG translation and its deviations in order to elucidate the structural characteristics of the parallel.

The alteration of dynamic Hebrew parallelisms in the direction of forms that are more parallel grammatically and/or semantically does not imply that there is always a total correspondence of all constituents or phrases (verb phrase and noun phrase) grammatically and semantically. But there is agreement in at least one significant aspect grammatically or semantically (synonyms[62] or antonyms[63]). The following section gives evidence for this position.

1.2 Semantic and Grammatical Relationships Rendered More Nearly Parallel

Hebrew parallelism may be best described using a linguistic model that takes into consideration not only its semantic relationships but also its grammatical

---

[62] Note: Among synonyms (words that are very similar in meaning) that occur in languages, very few are exact synonyms. More often such synonyms are close or near synonyms. Mildred L. Larson, *Meaning-based Translation: A Guide to Cross-Language Equivalence* (University Press of America, Lanham, New York, London, 1984): 73. "For two items to be synonymous, it does not mean that they should be identical in meaning, i.e. interchangeable in all CONTEXTS, and with identical CONNOTATIONS—this unlikely possibility is sometimes referred to as 'total synonymy.'" David Crystal, *A Dictionary of Linguistics and Phonetics* (Blackwell, 1991) 340.

[63] "In its most general sense, [antonymy] refers collectively to all types of semantic oppositeness, with various subdivisions then being made (e.g. between **graded antonyms**, such as *big ~ small*, where there are degrees of difference, and **ungraded antonyms**, such as *single ~ married*, where there is an either/or contrast)." Crystal, *Dictionary*, 20.

aspects and relationships,[64] like the model of A. Berlin (1985),[65] for which R. Jakobson laid the foundations.[66] The model used in this thesis also has a linguistic emphasis, although it may not correspond to Berlin's approach in every detail.

The translator of LXX Proverbs took great pains to translate dynamic Hebrew parallelisms often less dynamically with closer corresponding lines semantically and/or grammatically, as the following sections demonstrate.

1.2.1 SEMANTIC RELATIONSHIPS

The semantic relationships between parallel lines or the semantic aspect of parallelism may be described as "the sense of one line and its relationship to the sense of the parallel line," or it may be called the "flesh and blood" of the parallelism, as opposed to the grammatical aspect that provides the skeleton.[67]

R. Lowth categorized the semantic relationship as synonymous, antithetic, and synthetic. J. L. Kugel described this relationship as "A, what's more, B."

---

[64] "Despite some borderline, transitional formations, there is in language a definite, clear-cut discrimination between these two classes of expressed concepts—material and relational—or, in more technical terms, between the lexical and grammatical aspects of language." Roman Jakobson, "Poetry of Grammar and Grammar of Poetry," in *Verbal Art, Verbal Sign, Verbal Time* (ed. Krystyna Pomorska and Stephen Rudy; University of Minnesota Press, 1985), 37.

[65] Berlin, *Dynamics*. This is the broadest and most recent study on this topic. See also a detailed summary of it in *ABD* under "Parallelism." The phonological aspect, however, is not treated in my analysis, as it has no bearing on the thesis. L. Zogbo and E. R. Wendland are right in saying that "parallel structures are built not only on similarity of meaning and grammatical form, but on sound patterns as well. Parallel lines have similar or regular stress patterns, which add to the overall feeling of rhythm and balance." Lynell Zogbo and Ernst R. Wendland, *Hebrew Poetry in the Bible: A Guide for Understanding and for Translating* (United Bible Societies, 2000), 36. However, according to A. Niccacci, "Phonologic parallelism is normally established according to individual taste, without controlled criteria." Alviero Niccacci, "Analysing Biblical Hebrew Poetry," *JSOT* 74 (1997): 90. In any case, it is difficult to adapt phonologic parallelism in translation.

[66] Jakobson had a great impact on the study of parallelism. In his well known pronouncement he stated: "Pervasive parallelism inevitably activates all the levels of language—the distinctive features, inherent and prosodic, the morphological and syntactic categories and forms, the lexical units and their semantic classes in both their convergences and divergences acquire an autonomous poetic value." Roman Jakobson, "Grammatical Parallelism and Its Russian Facet," *Language* 42 (1966): 423.

[67] Berlin, *Dynamics*, 64.

Moreover, A. Berlin spoke of semantic equivalence[68] between parallel lines which may be perceived as either paradigmatic[69] or syntagmatic.[70] She uses the two categories for word pairs (lexical equivalents)[71] as well as parallel lines. In her opinion differentiating paradigmatic and syntagmatic relations helps to describe more precisely the exact relationship of the lines, since a couplet may consist of both a paradigmatic as well as a syntagmatic relation, e.g. Isa 40:9.[72]

In this work the various semantic relationships of parallelisms have been differentiated and treated separately in the following sections. Each parallelism is analysed in as much detail as necessary, although Berlin's terminology of paradigmatic and syntagmatic relations has not been used.

---

[68] "Semantic equivalence is a much broader term than Lowth's synonymous parallelism, and would include much that he might have considered 'synthetic parallelism.' 'Contrast' is also broader than 'antithetic parallelism' and includes not only semantic opposites but also other types of contrast (which Lowth might have thought of as synonymous), such as 'Water he asked; Milk she gave' (Jud 5:25)." *Ibid.*, 95.

[69] "A basic term in LINGUISTICS for the set of substitutional relationships a linguistic UNIT has with other units in a specific CONTEXT." Crystal, *Dictionary*, 249. A paradigmatic lexical relation is a pattern of association between lexical units that share one or more core semantic components, belong to the same lexical category, fill the same syntactic position in a syntactic construction, and have the same semantic function. Some common paradigmatic lexical relations in English are synonymous lexical relations such as "happy," "joyful," "glad," or lexical relations of opposites such as "student–teacher," "patient–doctor." "Paradigmatic lexical relation," under "Linguistic Bookshelf" in *LinguaLinks Library CD-ROM*. Version 4.0 LT, SIL International, 1999.

[70] "A fundamental term in LINGUISTICS, originally introduced by the Swiss linguist Ferdinand de SAUSSURE to refer to the SEQUENTIAL characteristics of speech, seen as a STRING of CONSTITUENTS (sometimes, but not always) in LINEAR order." Crystal, *Dictionary*, 341. A syntagmatic lexical relation is a pattern of association between pairs of lexical units (A1–B1, A2–B2, A3–B3 . . .) where the two members of each pair (A1 and B1) have compatible semantic components, are in a fixed syntactic and semantic relationship to each other, and are typically associated with each other. The corresponding members of each pair (A1, A2, A3 . . .) belong to the same lexical category, fill the same syntactic position in a syntactic construction, and have the same semantic function. Some examples of syntagmatic lexical relations in English are actor, undergoer, location, instrument, benefactor. "Paradigmatic lexical relation," *LinguaLinks*, n.p.

[71] According to Berlin's view there is no reason to limit such word pairs to fixed or frequently recurring pairs. She takes lexical equivalents in a very broad sense: "The process whereby terms are paired in parallelism is similar to the process which generates associations in psycholinguistic word association games. That is, parallel word pairs are the product of normal linguistic association. Every word has a potential mate, and it does not require any special training or talent to produce one." Berlin, "Parallelism," n.p.

[72] "We usually think of semantic parallelism only as paradigmatic—that is, one thought can substitute for the other. But we should not exclude the possibility of a syntagmatic semantic relationship where the two lines contain a semantic continuation, a progression of thought." Berlin, *Dynamics*, 90.

1.2.1.1 Lexical Aspect

In the category of lexical aspect (similarly 1.2.1.2 "Emphatic phrases or various figures of speech") the pairing of words or phrases in parallel lines may be considered.[73] The translator tends to use word pairs and phrase pairs that are more closely parallel synonymously (and antithetically cf. 1.2.1.4) than in the Hebrew.

The following cases demonstrate the translator's technique in adapting his source text with regard to synonymous word and phrase pairs to produce more closely corresponding colons.

1. Prov 1:23b,c[74]

MT: הִנֵּה[75] אַבִּיעָה לָכֶם רוּחִי אוֹדִיעָה דְבָרַי אֶתְכֶם
"behold, I will pour out to you my spirit (or: thoughts), I will make known my words to you"

LXX: ἰδοὺ προήσομαι ὑμῖν ἐμῆς πνοῆς ῥῆσιν διδάξω δὲ ὑμᾶς τὸν ἐμὸν λόγον
"behold, I will bring forth to you the utterance of my breath, and I will instruct you in my speech"

In Prov 1:23 ("behold, I will pour out to you my spirit (or: thoughts), I will make known my words to you") רוּחִי "my spirit" or "my breath" can also mean "my thoughts."[76] Although "thoughts" are related to "words" these are not exactly parallel, since a thought normally precedes the actual words spoken. In the LXX ("behold, I will bring forth to you the utterance of my breath, and I will instruct you in my speech"), however, the translator added ῥῆσιν (first colon) in close resemblance to λόγον, דבר (second colon), but he kept ἐμῆς πνοῆς (the literal equivalent of רוּחִי), which in the whole LXX occurs only here together with

---

[73] Cf. *ibid.*, 65.

[74] The whole verse may be regarded as a triplet (*IB*, 4:790; Toy, *Proverbs*, 23), or as a conditional sentence (NEB, NIV, Ross, "Proverbs," n.p.). The second and third clauses, however, are near-synonymous.

[75] הַבִּיעָה "is a common figurative word, expressive of the free pouring forth of thoughts and words." Delitzsch, *Proverbs*, 1:71.

[76] See also RSV, NRSV. "Frequently [רוּחַ] denotes the seat of cognition and volition, those activities involved in thinking, aptitude, and decision-making." M. V. Van Pelt/W. C. Kaiser, Jr./D. I. Block, *NIDOTTE*, 3:1075. Or else spirit may be understood as "the active power of the words," Delitzsch, *Proverbs*, 1:71; or as endowment of wisdom, a charismatic gift, McKane, *Proverbs*, 274.

ῥῆσις as this combination appears to be quite uncommon in Greek;[77] for a similar translational adaptation see Prov 1:24, 1.2.1.2. This case clearly shows how the translator sought to make the two colons correspond to each other in a synonymous parallel manner.[78] This conclusion is supported by the following cases.

2. Prov 3:9

MT: כַּבֵּד אֶת־יְהֹוָה מֵהוֹנֶךָ וּמֵרֵאשִׁית כָּל־תְּבוּאָתֶךָ
"Honor the Lord with your wealth, and with the first fruits of all your produce"

LXX: τίμα τὸν κύριον ἀπὸ σῶν δικαίων πόνων καὶ ἀπάρχου αὐτῷ ἀπὸ σῶν καρπῶν δικαιοσύνης
"Honor the Lord with your just labors, and give him the first of your fruits of righteousness"

Prov 3:9, a near-synonymous parallelism, is the only cultic demand in the book of Proverbs[79] ("Honor the Lord with your wealth, and with the first fruits of all your produce"). The translator, however, reinterpreted the cultic demand ethically[80] rendering "the first fruits of all your produce" by "the first of your fruits of righteousness." In fact, καρπῶν δικαιοσύνης "fruit of righteousness" (second colon) seems to be one of the translator's favorite phrases, as it occurs also in 11:30 and 13:2. In the latter case the translator also interpreted the

---

[77] I agree with S. P. Brock when he writes, "The un-Greek character of the translation simply lies in the way the individual lexical items are sometimes strung together." Sebastian P. Brock, "The Phenomenon of the Septuagint," OTS 17 (1972): 32. "As far as vocabulary alone is concerned it is quite clear that LXX Greek is very much part of the spoken language of early Ptolemaic Egypt." *Ibid.* For LXX Proverbs on the whole, however, the free character of the translation is obvious. Brock too speaks of "the freedom that the Greek translator of *Proverbs* had used." Sebastian P. Brock, "Aspects of Translation Techniques in Antiquity," *GRBS* 20 (1979): 76.

[78] J. Cook too regards this case as reflecting the creative approach of the translator, and he even states that "ῥῆσιν has been added in order to harmonise stichs b and c." Cook, *Proverbs*, 87. On page 98 Cook gives stylistic reasons of alliteration for the addition of ῥῆσιν, and furthermore on page 106 he claims, in his so-called final analysis, that the addition of ῥῆσιν is religiously motivated. In my view this is, however, reading too much into the text.

[79] McKane, *Proverbs*, 293–294.

[80] Similarly A. Meinhold: "Die Septuaginta . . . überträgt das konkrete kultische Verständnis des Verses auf die religiös-ethische Seite." Meinhold, *Sprüche*, 1:76. According to J. Weingreen "the moral judgement interpolated into the Greek translation would seem to represent a type of interpretation which may be designated as Midrashic or, if you will, as Rabbinic." Weingreen, "Rabbinic-Type Commentary," 410.

Hebrew text ethically[81] as he rendered "A man shall eat good (things) from/by the fruit of his mouth (words)" by "A good man shall eat of the fruits of righteousness." In none of these three occurrences is the translator translating the MT literally. Considering the translator's propensity for increased symmetry it is not at all surprising that he did not translate מֵהוֹנֶךָ "with your wealth" literally either, but adjusted it to ἀπὸ σῶν δικαίων πόνων "with your just labors" (first colon) to make it agree better with the second colon. Thus this case demonstrates clearly that the translator even when he reinterprets his text seeks to maintain parallel lines. For a further translational adjustment see 1.2.2.10.2.1.

3. Prov 3:25

MT: אַל־תִּירָא מִפַּחַד פִּתְאֹם וּמִשֹּׁאַת רְשָׁעִים כִּי תָבֹא
"Do not be afraid of sudden terror, neither of the devastation/ruin of the wicked when it comes (=of the moment when wicked men are destroyed)"

LXX: καὶ οὐ φοβηθήσῃ πτόησιν ἐπελθοῦσαν οὐδὲ ὁρμὰς ἀσεβῶν ἐπερχομένας
"And do not be afraid of alarm coming upon you, neither of approaching attacks of ungodly men"

In Prov 3:25 "sudden" terror and "coming" destruction (lit.: destruction . . . when it comes) are paralleled ("Do not be afraid of sudden terror, neither of the devastation/ruin of the wicked when it comes"). Presumably the translator chose the verb ἐπέρχομαι "come upon" to render פִּתְאֹם "sudden" (first colon) in parallel fashion to ἐπερχομένας "approaching" (MT: כִּי תָבֹא "when it comes") in the second half ("And do not be afraid of alarm coming upon you, neither of approaching attacks of ungodly men"). In order to express the suddenness of the action, he used the aorist tense/aspect ἐπελθοῦσαν, whereas for the second verb he used the present tense ἐπερχομένας expressing imperfective aspect in agreement with the Hebrew imperfect verb. So he seems to have tried to convey the differences in aspect. Still, the LXX rendering can be regarded as more nearly parallel lexically.

4. Prov 12:14

MT: מִפְּרִי פִי־אִישׁ יִשְׂבַּע־טוֹב וּגְמוּל יְדֵי־אָדָם יָשׁוּב לוֹ
"From the fruit of his mouth a man will be satisfied with good, and the recompense (or: work) of a man's hands will return to him"

---

[81] Cf. also Prov 22:11 under 3.3.1.5.4.

LXX: ἀπὸ καρπῶν στόματος ψυχὴ ἀνδρὸς πλησθήσεται ἀγαθῶν ἀνταπόδομα δὲ χειλέων αὐτοῦ δοθήσεται αὐτῷ
"From the fruits of his mouth the soul of a man will be filled with good, and the recompense of his lips will be given to him"

Prov 12:14 teaches "that proper speech and diligent work result in good things"[82] ("From the fruit of his mouth a man will be satisfied with good, and the recompense of a man's hands will return to him"). C. H. Toy describes the parallelism in the Hebrew as "progressive parallelism: in first cl. wise, kindly, righteous speech brings reward; in second cl. all actions bring requital."[83] The LXX rendering, however, is not progressive as χειλέων "lips" (second colon) seems to be a translational alteration to make a parallel with στόματος "mouth", MT: פִּי, (first colon) in place of the MT יְדֵי "hands." Thus the translator produced a form that is more parallel lexically while excluding the aspect of work or action ("From the fruits of his mouth the soul of a man will be filled with good, and the recompense of his lips will be given to him").

5. Prov 20:23

MT: תּוֹעֲבַת יְהוָה אֶבֶן וָאָבֶן וּמֹאזְנֵי מִרְמָה לֹא־טוֹב
"Diverse weights are an abomination to the Lord, and a false balance is not good"[84]

LXX: βδέλυγμα κυρίῳ δισσὸν στάθμιον καὶ ζυγὸς δόλιος οὐ καλὸν ἐνώπιον αὐτοῦ
"A double weight is an abomination to the Lord, and a deceitful balance is not good in his sight"

Prov 20:23 is regarded as a near-synonymous parallelism[85] in the second half of which part of the complement is implied but not explicitly stated[86] ("Diverse weights are an abomination to the Lord, and a false balance is not good"). The LXX ("A double weight is an abomination to the Lord, and a deceitful balance is not good in his sight"), while following the MT closely, is more nearly parallel since ἐνώπιον αὐτοῦ "in his sight" (second colon) has been added by the translator to resemble יְהוָה / κυρίῳ "to the Lord" (first colon) and thus produce colons that are more nearly parallel.

---

[82] Ross, "Proverbs," n.p. Also *IB*, 4:853.

[83] Toy, *Proverbs*, 251.

[84] NIV: "The LORD detests differing weights, and dishonest scales do not please him." NLT: "The LORD despises double standards; he is not pleased by dishonest scales."

[85] Toy, *Proverbs*, 393. Meinhold, *Sprüche*, 2:343. and Plöger, *Sprüche*, 238.

[86] Cf. Prov 20:10 and 11:1 where it is clearer that both lines contain a reference to the Lord.

6. Prov 20:30

MT: חַבֻּרוֹת פֶּצַע תַּמְרִיק בְּרָע וּמַכּוֹת חַדְרֵי־בָטֶן
"Blows and wounds (=a severe beating) cleanse away evil, and beatings (make clean) the inward parts of the belly (or: the innermost parts)"

LXX: ὑπώπια καὶ συντρίμματα συναντᾷ κακοῖς πληγαὶ δὲ εἰς ταμίεια κοιλίας
"Bruises and contusions befall evil men, and blows (will come) into the inward parts of (their) belly"

In Prov 20:30 the focus is on corporal punishment[87] ("Blows and wounds cleanse away evil, and beatings (make clean) the inward parts of the belly"). The verb תַּמְרִיק "cleanse" applies to both halves, with regard to cleansing away evil as well as purifying the inner being. In the LXX, however, the lines are more nearly parallel semantically ("Bruises and contusions befall evil men, and blows (will come) into the inward parts of (their) belly"). It is likely that the translator took the impersonal object רָע "evil" (first half) as personal, κακοῖς "evil men,"[88] parallel to the personal object κοιλίας "(their) belly" (בָטֶן) (second half). Consequently he altered תַּמְרִיק "cleanse" to συναντᾷ "it befalls" (in "contusions befall evil men"). In the light of the first change this alteration makes sense and also runs fairly parallel to εἰς "(will come) into" (the inward parts of their belly).

7. Prov 24:11

MT: הַצֵּל לְקֻחִים לַמָּוֶת וּמָטִים לַהֶרֶג אִם־תַּחְשׂוֹךְ
"Deliver them that are taken away to death, and those who go staggering/tottering to the slaughter/execution,[89] oh stop them[90]"

---

[87] Ross, "Proverbs," n.p. Similarly McKane, *Proverbs*, 540.

[88] W. McKane writes, "LXX 'evil men' (κακοῖς) is in all probability an inaccurate rendering of [רָע] and so confirms MT." McKane, *Proverbs*, 540.

[89] According to G. R. Driver "tottering to execution" is too strong compared with "taken away to death." He thus suggests the emendation to "ready for execution," i.e., "at the point of execution." G. R. Driver, "Problems in Proverbs," *ZAW* 50 (1932): 146.

[90] Cf. Delitzsch, *Proverbs*, 2:131. Similarly Meinhold, *Sprüche*, 2:399. "If אִם is interpreted as a particle of adjuration, then אִם־תַּחְשׂוֹךְ is equivalent to: I adjure thee, forbear not (cf. Neh. xiii. 25 with Isa. lviii. 1), viz. that which thou hast to do, venture all on it (LXX., Syr., Jerome)." Delitzsch, *Proverbs*, 2:131.

LXX: ῥῦσαι ἀγομένους εἰς θάνατον καὶ ἐκπρίου κτεινομένους, (μὴ φείσῃ)
"Deliver them that are led away to death, and redeem them that are appointed to be slain; (do not refrain)"

Prov 24:11 may either be about the judicial process[91] or it may be taken as having a general application to rescue those that are in mortal danger.[92] Apparently the translator added ἐκπρίου "redeem" (second colon) in parallel with ῥῦσαι "rescue, deliver"; MT: הַצֵּל (first colon), and interpreted the first part (second colon) of וּמָטִים לַהֶרֶג אִם־תַּחְשׂוֹךְ "and those who are staggering to the slaughter, oh stop them" as an elliptical construction (". . . and redeem them that are appointed to be slain"). This is supported by the fact that he also provided a rendering for the final verb phrase (". . . do not refrain").

8. Prov 31:6

MT: תְּנוּ־שֵׁכָר לְאוֹבֵד וְיַיִן לְמָרֵי נָפֶשׁ
"Give strong drink to one who is perishing (or: dying), and wine to those (lit.: whose soul is) in bitter distress"

LXX: δίδοτε μέθην τοῖς ἐν λύπαις καὶ οἶνον πίνειν τοῖς ἐν ὀδύναις
"Give strong drink to those who are in sorrow, and the wine to drink[93] to those who are in distress/pain/grief"

Prov 31:6, a near-synonymous parallelism, recommends giving strong drink to relieve bodily suffering and mental distress ("Give strong drink to one who is perishing, and wine to those in bitter distress"). Apparently the translator adapted his source text and did not render לְאוֹבֵד "to him who is perishing" literally but translated it by τοῖς ἐν λύπαις "to those who are in sorrow" (first half) parallel to τοῖς ἐν ὀδύναις "to those who are in grief/distress/pain"; MT: לְמָרֵי (second half).[94] Thus the LXX rendering ("Give strong drink to those who are in sorrow, and the wine to drink to those who are in distress") can be regarded as a closer parallel semantically.

To sum up, this section gives evidence of the translator's effort to produce word and phrase pairs that are more closely synonymous. For further examples of "lexical aspect" see Chapter Three under 3.3.1.1 where similar cases are discussed with regard to textual criticism.

---

[91] Plöger, Sprüche, 282.

[92] Ross, "Proverbs," n.p. According to R. J. Clifford, it is not clear as to whether this is about the judicial process or more generally about the necessity of every person to stand up for justice in serious cases. Clifford, Proverbs, 215.

[93] "To drink" is probably taken from the first word in the following verse 7, יִשְׁתֶּה.

[94] This is supported by J. Cook who states, "These two Greek lexemes clearly have related semantic fields." Cook, Proverbs, 301–302.

A common feature in Hebrew parallelism is the use of poetic devices, as described in the following section, in which near-synonymous couplets are treated.

1.2.1.2 *Emphatic Phrases or Various Figures of Speech*

In the verses to be considered in this section the two lines are fairly parallel (near-synonymous), with a step-up of intensity or poetic feeling brought about in the second line by e.g. a figure of speech which matches the less emphatic/dynamic expression in the first line.

The cases in this section may be compared to the so-called "step parallelism"[95] or step-up of poetic feeling or intensity, as R. G. Bratcher and W. D. Reyburn put it.[96] Although the two lines or colons may be semantically parallel, the second line may be dynamic "through the use of a more specific, figurative, or dramatic term or image."[97]

1. Prov 1:24

MT: יַעַן קָרָאתִי וַתְּמָאֵנוּ נָטִיתִי יָדִי וְאֵין מַקְשִׁיב
"Because I called (or: summoned you) and you refused to listen, I have stretched out my hand and no one has heeded"

LXX: ἐπειδὴ ἐκάλουν καὶ οὐχ ὑπηκούσατε καὶ ἐξέτεινον λόγους καὶ οὐ προσείχετε
"Because I called, and you did not listen, and I spoke at length, and you gave no heed"

In Prov 1:24 "I stretched out my hand" (second colon) may be a conventional Semitic gesture that accompanied words for rhetorical effectiveness,[98] or it may be used as a gesture of appeal to beckon people to come[99] ("Because I have called and you refused to listen, I have stretched out my hand and no one has heeded"). In any case, there are several translational adjustments in the LXX, see also 1.2.2.1. The action נָטִיתִי יָדִי "I have stretched out my hand" (second

---

[95] Stephen A. Geller, *Parallelism in early Biblical Poetry* (Scholars Press, 1979), 31. Step-parallelism is also called climactic parallelism and is found "where one member (or part of a member) in one line is repeated in the second, and made the starting-point for a fresh step." T. H. Robinson, *The Poetry of the Old Testament* (1947), 23.

[96] Bratcher and Reyburn, *Psalms*, 6.

[97] *Ibid.*, 9. For a detailed classification of different types of parallelisms see Watson, *Classical*, 114–159.

[98] McKane, *Proverbs*, 274–275. Similarly GN2 which translated: "Ich habe immer wieder geredet, doch ihr habt gar nicht zugehört. Mit erhobener Hand habe ich gerufen, und niemand hat darauf geachtet."

[99] *IB*, 4:790. Similarly Delitzsch, *Proverbs*, 1:71–72.

colon) was dropped and its meaning expressed more directly by
ἐξέτεινον λόγους "I stretched out words (or: spoke at length)." The verb,
however, was maintained and rendered literally. This led to a seemingly
uncommon expression. For a similar translational adaptation see Prov 1:23,
1.2.1.1. This shows clearly the translator's attempt to parallel the lines more
closely even to the detriment of the poetic effect that is expressed in Hebrew if
the first interpretation is taken.

2. Prov 17:26

MT: גַּם עֲנוֹשׁ לַצַּדִּיק לֹא־טוֹב לְהַכּוֹת נְדִיבִים עַל־יֹשֶׁר
"Also[100] to punish the just is not good, nor to strike princes for equity (for being honest)"

LXX: ζημιοῦν ἄνδρα δίκαιον οὐ καλόν οὐδὲ ὅσιον ἐπιβουλεύειν δυνάσταις δικαίοις
"It is not good to punish a righteous man, nor is it holy/pious to plot against righteous princes"

Interpretations of Prov 17:26 ("Also to punish the just is not good, nor to strike princes for equity") vary according to the way in which עַל־יֹשֶׁר is understood. W. McKane takes it to mean "improper" or "contrary to what is right."[101] According to F. Delitzsch "עַל־יֹשֶׁר means here neither against nor beyond what is due, but: on the ground of honorable conduct, making this (of course mistakenly) a lawful title to punishment,"[102] and he translates "on account of his rectitude." This view is followed by NRSV where it is rendered "for their integrity,"[103] and similarly NLT et al.[104] W. G. E. Watson lists Prov 28:19;

---

[100] "Also" may indicate that the proverb was once paired with another which it resembles and goes beyond. D. Kidner, *Proverbs*, 126. Similarly McKane, *Proverbs*, 506. But according to O. Plöger it can be translated as *schon* (even) in the sense of a *Steigerung*. Plöger, *Sprüche*, 199.

[101] *Proverbs*, 506–507. Similarly A. Meinhold who translates, "ist gegen jedes Recht." Meinhold, *Sprüche*, 2:293. And O. Plöger renders, "ist gegen die Ordnung." Plöger, *Sprüche*, 199.

[102] Delitzsch, *Proverbs*, 1:371.

[103] The RSV rendered the second line "to flog noble men is wrong," emending the MT.

[104] For a similar view see Clifford, *Proverbs*, 164,167.

25:15; and 17:26 under the poetic device of oxymoron.[105] Its effect in general is to drive a point home with vigor. It is also related to irony.[106] In any case, the deviation in the LXX may simply be due to the translator's desire to improve the symmetry. He may have repeated the adjective δίκαιος "righteous" in the second line as a substitute for עַל־יֹשֶׁר "for equity," thus producing a more closely parallel form semantically, and also grammatically as described in 1.2.2.10.1.

3. Prov 22:8

MT: זוֹרֵעַ עַוְלָה יִקְצָר־אָוֶן וְשֵׁבֶט עֶבְרָתוֹ יִכְלֶה
"He who sows injustice will reap calamity, and the rod of his anger/arrogance[107] (or: hubris[108]) will fail/end"

LXX: ὁ σπείρων φαῦλα θερίσει κακά πληγὴν δὲ ἔργων αὐτοῦ συντελέσει
"He who sows evil/wickedness shall reap troubles, and the punishment of his deeds he shall complete (fully receive)"

Prov 22:8 may be regarded as synonymous[109] or more precisely near-synonymous,[110] as the second half informs what is entailed in reaping calamity: his reign of terror will end[111] ("He who sows injustice will reap calamity, and the rod of his anger/arrogance will fail/end"). Presumably the translator rendered the figure שֵׁבֶט "rod"[112] as πληγὴν "blow/punishment" the same as he did in Prov 29:15, and in consequence of that change read עברתו "his anger/arrogance/hubris" as עבדתו "his deeds," which only requires taking ד for ר, and

---

[105] Oxymoron may be defined as "the yoking together of two expressions which are semantically incompatible, so that in combination they can have no conceivable literal reference to reality." G. N. Leech, *A Linguistic Guide to English Poetry* (London: Longmans, 1969), 132. Also Watson, *Classical*, 312. Or, "An oxymoron is a collocation of words that have contradictory or sharply incongruous meanings." Edward P. J. Corbett, *Classical Rhetoric for the Modern Student* (New York: Oxford University, 1971), 491. Some examples of oxymorons in English are "conspicuous by his absence," "cruel kindness," "thunderous silence," "make haste slowly."

[106] Watson, *Classical*, 313.

[107] G. B. Struthers, *NIDOTTE*, 3:316.

[108] McKane, *Proverbs*, 570.

[109] Toy, *Proverbs*, 416. *IB*, 4:908.

[110] R. Alter lists this example under less parallel cases of narrative development where the second verset follows the first. Alter, *Art*, 172–173.

[111] Cf. NLT.

[112] "The symbol of the rod here represents his power for doing evil." Ross, "Proverbs," n.p.

he took יִכְלֶה (qal) "will finish/disappear" as יְכַלֶּה (pi'el) "he shall complete" ("and he shall fully receive the punishment of his deeds"). As a result, he produced a parallelism that is somewhat different, but it may be regarded as a slightly closer parallel semantically, as the idea of sowing injustice (MT) or wickedness (LXX) and reaping calamity/troubles (first half) is re-expressed in the second half by "the punishment of his (evil) deeds," whereas in the Hebrew only the idea that his reign of terror or arrogance will end is expressed.

4. Prov 23:21

MT: כִּי־סֹבֵא וְזוֹלֵל יִוָּרֵשׁ וּקְרָעִים תַּלְבִּישׁ נוּמָה
"for the drunkard and the glutton will become poor, and slumber/drowsiness[113] will clothe (them) with rags"

LXX: πᾶς γὰρ μέθυσος καὶ πορνοκόπος πτωχεύσει καὶ ἐνδύσεται διερρηγμένα καὶ ῥακώδη πᾶς ὑπνώδης
"for every drunkard and whoremonger/fornicator will become poor, and every sluggard will clothe himself with tatters and ragged garments"

Prov 23:21 is a couplet whose lines are somewhat parallel, but not identical. The first line states that drunkenness and gluttony lead to poverty, while the second line more specifically describes one aspect of poverty, the lack of adequate clothing, as well as expressing in poetic language the effect of too much partying as leading to drowsiness and laziness. In the LXX, however, the translator expressed the poetic language (metaphor), וּקְרָעִים תַּלְבִּישׁ נוּמָה "drowsiness will clothe (them) with rags," more straightforwardly by ἐνδύσεται διερρηγμένα καὶ ῥακώδη "(he) will clothe himself with tatters and ragged garments" (second half) and in parallel with πτωχεύσει "(he) will become poor" = יִוָּרֵשׁ (first half). In addition the translator added πᾶς ὑπνώδης "every sluggard" (second colon) in parallel with πᾶς . . . μέθυσος "every drunkard"—MT: סֹבֵא "the drunkard" (first colon). Thus in the LXX rendering the colons are clearly more closely parallel.

To sum up, the translator rendered the parallelisms of various poetic devices to produce more closely parallel forms semantically—but often also grammatically cf. 1.2.2—regardless of the poetic effect of the Hebrew figure. This predilection of the translator is important to keep in mind when using the LXX of Proverbs as a source of variant readings, cf. 3.3.1.2.

The translator not only adjusted near-synonymous or near-antithetical Hebrew parallelisms to produce more closely synonymous or antithetical renderings, but he even transformed parallelisms into antithetical forms.

---

[113] "**Drowsiness** comes from overeating and overdrinking." *IB*, 4:914. A. Meinhold translates נוּמָה (which occurs only here as a noun) as "(Rausch-)Schläfrigkeit." Meinhold, *Sprüche*, 2:389.

1.2.1.3 Near-Synonymous Parallelisms Transformed into Antithetical Forms

This section gives evidence of the translator's freedom to transform near-synonymous parallelisms into antithetical forms.[114]

1. Prov 15:(22b),23

MT: (15:22b: וּבְרֹב יוֹעֲצִים תָּקוּם)
"but with many counselors they (=plans) are established"

Q: וברב יועצים תקום

LXX: ἐν δὲ καρδίαις βουλευομένων μένει βουλή
"but counsel abides in the hearts of counselors")

MT: שִׂמְחָה לָאִישׁ בְּמַעֲנֵה־פִיו וְדָבָר בְּעִתּוֹ מַה־טּוֹב
"A man has joy by the answer of his mouth (in an apt answer), and a word spoken in due season, how good it is!"

Q: מֶחה [לאיש במענה] פיו ודבר בע[תו מה] טוב [115]

LXX: οὐ μὴ ὑπακούσῃ ὁ κακὸς αὐτῇ οὐδὲ μὴ εἴπῃ καίριόν τι καὶ καλὸν τῷ κοινῷ
"A bad man will by no means attend to it (=counsel); neither will he say anything seasonable, or good for the common (weal)"

In Prov 15:23 the parallelism may be regarded as somewhat synonymous semantically.[116] The translator, however, seems to have altered it into an antithesis to v. 22b by inserting "bad (man)"[117] and negating the verbs ("will by no means attend" . . . "neither will he say"). The fact that the item βουλή "counsel" in v. 22b is referred to by αὐτῇ "it" in v. 23a indicates a close

---

[114] This is supported by G. Gerleman who writes, "the synonymous parallelisms of the Hebrew text have, to a large extent, had their places taken by antitheses" and lists many examples. Gerleman, *Studies*, 18–22. Similarly J. Cook who states that "contrast is actually a 'translation technique' of this specific translator." Cook, *Proverbs*, 314. Cf. Johann Cook, "Contrasting as a Translation Technique in the LXX Proverbs," in *The Quest for Context and Meaning: Studies in Biblical Intertextuality in Honor of J. A. Sanders* (ed. C. A. Evans and S. Talmon; Brill, 1997).

[115] Jan de Waard, "4QProv and Textual Criticism," *Textus* 19 (1998): 90. Source: E. Tov, *The Dead Sea Scrolls on Microfiche* (Leiden: Brill, 1993). Q agrees with the MT as far as the evidence is concerned.

[116] Cf. Toy, *Proverbs*, 313.

[117] M. B. Dick lists κακός under moralizing tendency. Dick, "Ethics," 22–23.

relationship between the two lines and supports the translational character of v. 23.[118]

2. Prov 17:4

MT: מֵרַע מַקְשִׁיב עַל־שְׂפַת־אָוֶן שֶׁקֶר מֵזִין עַל־לְשׁוֹן הַוֺּת

"An evildoer gives heed to false lips, and a liar gives ear to a naughty tongue"

LXX: κακὸς ὑπακούει γλώσσης παρανόμων δίκαιος δὲ οὐ προσέχει χείλεσιν ψευδέσιν

"A bad man listens to the tongue of transgressors, but a righteous man attends not to false lips"

Prov 17:4 stresses the point that those who listen to malicious talk are in fact malicious themselves,[119] ("An evildoer gives heed to false lips, and a liar gives ear to a naughty tongue"). The translator seems to have altered the near-synonymous parallelism into an antithetical form changing שֶׁקֶר "liar" by rendering it δίκαιος "righteous (man)" (second colon) in contrast to κακὸς "bad (man)" (first colon) due to his general tendency to produce antitheses.[120] The two terms correspond closely antithetically and even grammatically since they are both adjectives, whereas the parallel terms in the Hebrew have slightly less correspondence since מֵרַע "evildoer" is a verb (*hipʿil* participle from רעע) and is also more generic in meaning[121] than שֶׁקֶר "liar" which is a noun.

In addition to his general predilection, the translator may have been influenced by the context of antithetical forms, as the following cases seem to indicate.

3. Prov 11:7

MT: בְּמוֹת אָדָם רָשָׁע תֹּאבַד תִּקְוָה וְתוֹחֶלֶת אוֹנִים אָבָדָה

"When a wicked man dies, his hope will perish (or: this is the end of hope), and the expectation in his strength (or: wealth)[122] perishes"

---

[118] See under "Agreement in tense/aspect or person and number" 2.1.1.2.

[119] Ross, "Proverbs," n.p.

[120] M. B. Dick lists δίκαιος under moralizing tendency. Dick, "Ethics," 22–24.

[121] Cf. also Dan 11:27 and Isa 9:16.

[122] אוֹנִים can mean "strength" (e.g. Delitzsch, Murphy, NLT, NIV; also R. Wakely who writes, "The word is used of the physical strength of humans . . . possibly Prov 11:7," *NIDOTTE*, 1:316), or "riches/wealth" (e.g. McKane, Clifford, Meinhold, TEV, REB, NCV, GN2). Another possibility is to interpret the Hebrew form as plural of אָוֶן "evil," belonging to another word, e.g. NJPS gives "evil men." (N)RSV follow the LXX τῶν ἀσεβῶν "the godless."

LXX: τελευτήσαντος ἀνδρὸς δικαίου οὐκ ὄλλυται ἐλπίς τὸ δὲ καύχημα τῶν ἀσεβῶν ὄλλυται
"When a just man dies his hope does not perish, but the boast of the ungodly perishes"

For Prov 11:7 ("When a wicked man dies, his hope will perish, and the expectation in his strength perishes") various interpretations and emendations have been suggested.[123] For our analysis, however, it will suffice to note that apparently the translator adapted the colons in line with his predilection for antithetic forms. In addition, he may have been influenced by the prevalence of antithetic forms in the preceding context. Apparently it was this that led to recasting אָדָם רָשָׁע "wicked man," rendering it ἀνδρὸς δικαίου "just man"[124] and correspondingly changing תֹּאבַד "it perishes" to οὐκ ὄλλυται "it does not perish" (first colon). Then in antithetic parallelism he inserted τῶν ἀσεβῶν "the ungodly"[125] (second colon), thus producing an antithetical and also more closely parallel form. The environment of preceding antithetic forms may have influenced the translator's decision.

4. Prov 15:10

MT: מוּסָר רָע לְעֹזֵב אֹרַח שׂוֹנֵא תוֹכַחַת יָמוּת
"There is stern correction for him who forsakes the way, (and) he who hates reproof will die"

LXX: παιδεία ἀκάκου γνωρίζεται ὑπὸ τῶν παριόντων οἱ δὲ μισοῦντες ἐλέγχους τελευτῶσιν αἰσχρῶς
"The instruction of the simple is known by them who undergo it,[126] but they who hate reproofs die disgracefully"

There are different views on Prov 15:10 as to the relationship of the two colons ("There is stern correction for him who forsakes the way, and he who hates reproof will die"). According to A. P. Ross, they are probably synonymous,[127]

---

[123] See discussion in McKane, *Proverbs*, 439–440; Meinhold, *Sprüche*, 1:188–189; and Plöger, *Sprüche*, 136. Watson regards the tense of the verb pairs qtl // yqtl as devices that were employed on purpose to avoid repetition. Watson, *Classical*, 279–280.

[124] M. B. Dick lists δικαίου under moralizing tendency. Dick, "Ethics," 22–24. Dick does not consider other possible influences that may have led to the addition.

[125] Toy regards this insertion as "an interpretation of the Greek scribe, under the influence of the later belief in immortality." Toy, *Proverbs*, 223. However, the insertion may simply be due to the transformation into an antithesis.

[126] Another possible but less likely translation: "them who pass by."

[127] He writes, "the 'stern discipline' [מוּסָר רָע] of the first line is parallel to the death [יָמוּת] in the second." Ross, "Proverbs," n.p.

and similarly C. H. Toy,[128] and also F. Delitzsch,[129] but W. McKane regards the relationship of the two halves as one of progression.[130] The translator, however, seems to have altered this parallelism into an antithetical form ("The instruction of the simple is known by them who undergo it, but they who hate reproofs die disgracefully"). Apparently he understood παιδεία "instruction" as having some positive effect on those who endure it. Only those who hate ἐλέγχους "reproofs" die disgracefully. In addition to the translator's love of antithesis, the present context may have influenced his decision to produce an antithetical parallelism.

5. Prov 21:14

MT: מַתָּן בַּסֵּתֶר יִכְפֶּה־אָף וְשֹׁחַד בַּחֵק חֵמָה עַזָּה
"A gift in secret averts anger, and a concealed bribe in the bosom (or: pocket), strong wrath"

LXX: δόσις λάθριος ἀνατρέπει ὀργάς δώρων δὲ ὁ φειδόμενος θυμὸν ἐγείρει ἰσχυρόν
"A secret gift calms anger, but he who forbears to give gifts stirs up strong wrath"

In Prov 21:14 the two halves are near-synonymous in that in the first line the more neutral word מַתָּן "gift" is used, and in the second line the more specific word שֹׁחַד "bribe"[131] ("A gift in secret averts anger, and a concealed bribe in the pocket, strong wrath"). The translator, however, may be responsible for altering the near-synonymous form into an antithetical parallelism by adding ὁ φειδόμενος "he who forbears"[132] in the second half ("A secret gift calms anger, but he who forbears to give gifts stirs up strong wrath"). And because he changed the synonymous parallelism into an antithesis he had to supply the verb ἐγείρει "stirs up" (second colon), whereas in Hebrew there is an elliptical construction. Again, the translator's predilection and perhaps partly the following antithetical parallelism may have been responsible for these changes.

---

[128] Toy, *Proverbs*, 306–307.

[129] Delitzsch, *Proverbs*, 1:321.

[130] "If a person forsakes the (right) road, he must be prepared to submit to severe discipline in order to get back on course. Should he not be amenable to correction, so that he is incapable of learning from a teacher who would set his feet on the way of life, he will die." McKane, *Proverbs*, 479.

[131] Cf. Ross, "Proverbs," n.p.

[132] Toy regards the LXX reading as less probable than that of the Hebrew although the Greek makes good sense. Toy, *Proverbs*, 404.

The translator's fondness for antithetical parallelism may also be reflected by antithetical additions, as in the following examples.

6. Prov 6:11

MT: וּבָא־כִמְהַלֵּךְ רֵאשֶׁךָ וּמַחְסֹרְךָ כְּאִישׁ מָגֵן
"and poverty will come upon you like one that travels (or: vagrant[133]), and your want like an armed man"

LXX: εἶτ' ἐμπαραγίνεταί σοι ὥσπερ κακὸς ὁδοιπόρος ἡ πενία καὶ ἡ ἔνδεια ὥσπερ ἀγαθὸς δρομεύς
"Then poverty comes upon you like an evil traveler, and want like a good courier"

11a ἐὰν δὲ ἄοκνος ᾖς ἥξει ὥσπερ πηγὴ ὁ ἀμητός σου ἡ δὲ ἔνδεια ὥσπερ κακὸς δρομεὺς ἀπαυτομολήσει
"however, if you are diligent your harvest will arrive like a fountain, and poverty will flee like a bad courier"

In the near-synonymous parallelism of Prov 6:11 two similes illustrate the onslaught of poverty[134] ("and poverty will come upon you like one that travels, and your want like an armed man"). The addition in v. 11a is apparently made by the translator as a contrast to the preceding statement[135] ("however, if you are diligent your harvest will arrive like a fountain, and poverty will flee like a bad courier"). Note the contrast between ἀγαθὸς δρομεύς "good courier" (v. 11, second colon) and κακὸς δρομεύς "bad courier" (v. 11a, second colon).[136]

In addition, in v. 11 ἀγαθὸς δρομεύς "good courier" (second colon) is contrastively parallel to κακὸς ὁδοιπόρος "evil traveler" (first colon)[137] ("Then poverty comes upon you like an evil traveler, and want like a good courier"). The positive and negative nuance as expressed by the adjectives is not present in the MT and may be regarded as an expression of the translator's fondness for producing contrasting pairs. The Hebrew parallelism appears to be slightly less close, as אִישׁ מָגֵן "armed man" and מְהַלֵּךְ "one that travels" or "vagrant" have

---

[133] See McKane, *Proverbs*, 324. Also GN2 has "Landstreicher." And NRSV "vagabond."

[134] Ross, "Proverbs," n.p.

[135] Similarly Toy, *Proverbs*, 125. E. Tov too regards v. 11a as translational: "The use in v '11a' of words occurring in the Greek context makes it likely that the addition has been made in Greek rather than Hebrew, and therefore the Hebrew reconstruction of this plus by Lagarde (23) [*Anmerkungen zur griechischen Übersetzung der Proverbien*], . . . , is unwarranted." Tov, "Recensional Differences," 45–46.

[136] G. Gerleman too regards these additional couplets of lines forming an antithesis as added by the translator. Gerleman, *Studies*, 19, 21.

[137] According to J. Cook, "The translator is rendering his parent text in terms of the dualism of good versus bad." Cook, *Proverbs*, 171.

slightly less correspondence semantically. Thus the LXX alteration may be regarded as translational.

7. Prov 17:21

MT: יָלַד כְּסִיל לְתוּגָה לוֹ וְלֹא־יִשְׂמַח אֲבִי נָבָל
"The one who begets a fool gets trouble, and the father of a fool has no joy"

LXX: καρδία δὲ ἄφρονος ὀδύνη τῷ κεκτημένῳ αὐτήν
"the heart of a fool is grief to its possessor"

οὐκ εὐφραίνεται πατὴρ ἐπὶ υἱῷ ἀπαιδεύτῳ υἱὸς δὲ φρόνιμος εὐφραίνει μητέρα αὐτοῦ
"A father does not rejoice over an uninstructed son, but a wise son gladdens his mother"

In Prov 17:21 כְּסִיל "fool" and נָבָל "fool" are put in synonymous parallelism[138] ("The one who begets a fool gets trouble, and the father of a fool has no joy"). As for the LXX there seems to be some confusion in vv. 19–21. The translator rendered only the first half of v. 19 in its proper sequence, adding the second half to v. 16.[139] Apparently he instead paralleled v. 19 A "He who loves transgression/sin loves strife" (MT/LXX) with v. 20 A "He who has a crooked mind finds no good" (MT/LXX), and v. 20 B "And he who is perverted in his language falls into evil" (MT/LXX) with v. 21 A "The one who begets a fool gets trouble" (MT), though v. 21 A LXX ("the heart of a fool is grief to its possessor") has little correspondence with the MT; according to E. Tov "probably . . . the translator read לב instead of ילד."[140] The translator then added to colon B "A father does not rejoice over an uninstructed son" (LXX) of v. 21 an extra colon C "but a wise son gladdens his mother" which corresponds closely with it antithetically (see comment below). The use of δὲ in the second colon of each couplet supports the view that the translator paralleled differently from the Hebrew, and the punctuation in Rahlfs supports this view. In any case, the translator rendered (probably נָבָל by) υἱῷ ἀπαιδεύτῳ "uninstructed son" (colon B) and contrasted it with the added υἱὸς . . . φρόνιμος "wise son" (colon C), being prompted by his love for antithesis and presumably by the following antithetical parallelism. Also the translator added "mother" in the second half of

---

[138] This combination is only used here. According to C. H. Toy the two terms are practically identical in meaning. However, כְּסִיל (which occurs nearly fifty times in Prov) portrays a slow-witted dullard, whether it be in spiritual, intellectual, or moral matters; and נָבָל (which is found elsewhere in Prov only in 17:7 and 30:22, and less than twenty times in the whole Hebrew Bible) primarily focuses on religious folly, one who is morally and religiously indifferent. Toy, *Proverbs*, 348. Also Ross, "Proverbs," n.p.

[139] Cf. also Murphy, *Proverbs*, 131.

[140] Tov, "Recensional Differences," 47–48.

the couplet perhaps for the sake of stylistic variation, or else he may have been influenced by the context as the combination of "father" and "mother" is used in v. 25.[141]

8. Prov 18:22

MT: מָצָא אִשָּׁה מָצָא טוֹב וַיָּפֶק רָצוֹן מֵיְהוָה
"He who finds a wife finds a good thing, and has won favor from the Lord"

LXX: ὃς εὗρεν γυναῖκα ἀγαθήν εὗρεν χάριτας ἔλαβεν δὲ παρὰ θεοῦ ἱλαρότητα.
22a ὃς ἐκβάλλει γυναῖκα ἀγαθήν ἐκβάλλει τὰ ἀγαθά ὁ δὲ κατέχων μοιχαλίδα ἄφρων καὶ ἀσεβής
"He who has found a good wife has found favors, and has received gladness from God"
22a "He who puts away a good wife puts away a good thing, and he who keeps an adulteress is foolish and ungodly"

Prov 18:22 may be regarded as near-synonymous, the second line explaining the first in the sense that finding a wife is the sign of favor from the Lord[142] ("He who finds a wife finds a good thing, and has won favor from the Lord"). While the LXX corresponds somewhat with v. 22 ("He who has found a good wife has found favors, and has received gladness from God"), in regard to v. 22a we can of course not be totally sure whether the translator's *Vorlage* contained this verse or not ("He who puts away a good wife puts away a good thing, and he who keeps an adulteress is foolish and ungodly"). C. H. Toy thinks that it is "a scribal addition intended to bring the thought of the couplet out more fully."[143] According to SH the second couplet is OG and the first is Hexaplaric.[144] However, considering the translator's love of antithesis and his tendency to produce additional antithetical colons, verse 22a may as well have come from him as an addition to the first couplet.[145]

To sum up, the translator felt free to recast (mostly) near-synonymous parallelisms as antithetical forms in accordance with his general preference, though the context of antithetic parallelisms may have played a role in his decision. Most of the adapted forms are also more nearly parallel contrastively.

---

[141] For this same combination of "father" and "mother" elsewhere in the book (MT and LXX) see also 1:8; 4:3; 6:20; 10:1; 15:20; 19:26; 23:22; 30:11,17.

[142] Cf. Ross, "Proverbs," n.p.

[143] Toy, *Proverbs*, 366.

[144] Fritsch, "Hexaplaric Signs," 176.

[145] G. Gerleman lists this case under the stylistic device of anaphora. Gerleman, *Studies*, 14. E. Tov lists 18:22a under inner-translational pluses. Tov, "Recensional Differences," 48.

He even added antithetical parallelisms to contrast with the preceding forms. M. B. Dick ascribes some of the altered forms (Prov 11:7; 15:23; 17:4; also 10:18 under 3.3.1.3) to the translator's moralizing tendency.[146] This additional tendency cannot be ruled out, as translations, especially those that are rendered more freely, tend to have certain biases, but it is better to first approach the subject matter from a translational, linguistic and stylistic point of view, and then as a second step consider moralizing, religious, etc. tendencies. The former approach seems to give a broader perspective on the issue, because it is more clear-cut, concrete and capable of covering a wider range of cases, as can be seen in this section. The translator's predilection to produce antithetic forms, whether it is due to stylistic factors or a moralizing tendency, is important to consider for distinguishing translational cases from text-critical cases, cf. 3.3.1.3.

Similarly the translator's desire for closer correspondence of the lines is reflected in near-antithetical parallelisms, as the following section demonstrates.

1.2.1.4 Near-Antithetical Parallelisms Rendered with a Clearer Contrast

This section deals with near-antithetical Hebrew parallelisms which the translator altered to produce a clearer contrast semantically but often also structurally, employing various linguistic and translational features.[147]

1. Prov 11:21

MT: יָד לְיָד לֹא־יִנָּקֶה רָּע וְזֶרַע צַדִּיקִים נִמְלָט
"Hand to hand (=Be sure of this[148]), an evil man will not be unpunished, but the seed (descendants) of the righteous will be delivered"

LXX: χειρὶ χεῖρας ἐμβαλὼν ἀδίκως[149] οὐκ ἀτιμώρητος ἔσται ὁ δὲ σπείρων δικαιοσύνην λήμψεται μισθὸν πιστόν
"He that unjustly strikes hands will not be unpunished, but he that sows righteousness will receive a faithful reward"

---

[146] Dick, "Ethics," 22–24.

[147] Many of these parallelisms are also listed in Gerleman, *Studies*, 22–24. He comments that "Very often the antitheses already existing in the Hebrew text have not satisfied the translator, and he has tried to make the contrast more precise and clean cut." *Ibid.*, 22.

[148] יָד לְיָד "Hand to hand" means "Be sure of this" or "that it is settled," "one can depend on it," see M. Anbar, "Proverbs 11:21; 16:5: *yd lyd* 'sur le champ,'" *Bib* 53/4 (1972): 537–538.

[149] Cf. Prov 16:5 where the translator rendered the same Hebrew phrase similarly.

Prov 11:21 is a near-antithetic parallelism with an additional phrase or expression of assertion at the beginning of the verse ("Hand to hand, an evil man will not be unpunished, but the seed of the righteous will be delivered"). The translator, however, reduced the verse to two lines ("He that unjustly strikes hands will not be unpunished, but he that sows righteousness will receive a faithful reward") and incorporated the initial phrase into the first colon of the antithetical form to produce a more nearly parallel structure, there being a close contrastive resemblance semantically as well as grammatically between ἐμβαλὼν ἀδίκως "he that unjustly strikes . . ." (first colon) and σπείρων δικαιοσύνην "he that sows righteousness" (second colon). O. Plöger suggests that the LXX exchanged v. 21b with v. 18[150] and it is in fact possible that the translator deliberately did this to achieve a closer correspondence of the lines in both cases.[151] Also ἔσται "he will be" and λήμψεται "he will receive" agree in tense, voice, mood, person and number, whereas in the MT an imperfective verb is paralleled with a perfective verbal aspect. Thus the LXX is clearly a more closely parallel couplet.

2. Prov 11:24

MT: יֵשׁ מְפַזֵּר וְנוֹסָף עוֹד וְחוֹשֵׂךְ מִיֹּשֶׁר אַךְ־לְמַחְסוֹר
"There is he that scatters (=gives freely)[152] and yet increases (or: and yet is always getting richer), and he that withholds more than is meet (or: justly due), only to his loss (or: but it leads to poverty)"

LXX: εἰσὶν οἳ τὰ ἴδια σπείροντες πλείονα ποιοῦσιν εἰσὶν καὶ οἳ συνάγοντες ἐλαττονοῦνται "There are those who scatter their own and make it more, and there are also those who gather yet have less"

In Prov 11:24 a paradox is presented: one must give in order to gain, and the person who does not do so will become poor[153] ("There is he that scatters and yet increases, and he that withholds more than is meet, only to his loss"). In the LXX the first colon corresponds fairly well to the MT except that the translator rendered מְפַזֵּר "he that scatters" by οἳ . . . σπείροντες "those who scatter." But in the second colon he did not translate חוֹשֵׂךְ "he who withholds" literally[154] but

---

[150] Plöger, Sprüche, 134.

[151] In 11:18 the translator contrasted "the ungodly" with "the seed/descendants of the righteous."

[152] "With human subject, the vb. in a positive vein can refer to the generosity of the wise who distribute goods (NIV gives freely) to others (Prov 11:24)." M. D. Carroll R., NIDOTTE, 3:595.

[153] Similarly Clifford, Proverbs, 125.

[154] The occurrences of חשׂך in Proverbs are translated by the verb φείδομαι (10:19; 13:24; 17:27; 24:11), or the negative ἀφειδῶς (21:26), except for Prov 11:24.

rendered it by employing the exact opposite, οἱ συνάγοντες "those who gather" (second colon). Thus the LXX can be regarded as more nearly parallel lexically ("There are those who scatter their own and make it more, and there are also those who gather yet have less"). Not only that, but also grammatically there is a closer correspondence, see under 1.2.2.10.2.1.

3. Prov 12:10

MT: יוֹדֵעַ צַדִּיק נֶפֶשׁ בְּהֶמְתּוֹ וְרַחֲמֵי רְשָׁעִים אַכְזָרִי
"The righteous knows (or: regards) the life of his animal, but the mercies/compassions of the wicked is cruel"

LXX: δίκαιος οἰκτίρει ψυχὰς κτηνῶν αὐτοῦ τὰ δὲ σπλάγχνα τῶν ἀσεβῶν ἀνελεήμονα
"The righteous has pity for the lives of his cattle, but the bowels of the ungodly are unmerciful"

In Prov 12:10 of the MT יוֹדֵעַ "knows" corresponds somewhat with אַכְזָרִי "cruel" antithetically ("The righteous knows/regards the life of his animal, but the mercies/compassions of the wicked is cruel"). The former is to be understood in the sense of "be concerned for."[155] According to D. Kidner "this proverb illustrates the warm, personal quality of the Heb. verb 'to know' . . ."[156] Apparently the translator sought to translate the meaning of יוֹדֵעַ in a way that was more specifically and antithetically parallel to ἀνελεήμονα "are unmerciful" (second half), rendering it οἰκτίρει "he has pity" (first half). This may have been prompted by the phrase רַחֲמֵי רְשָׁעִים "mercies of the wicked" (τὰ . . . σπλάγχνα τῶν ἀσεβῶν).[157] In any case, the couplet in LXX appears to be a more closely parallel form lexically.

4. Prov 12:25

MT: דְּאָגָה בְלֶב־אִישׁ יַשְׁחֶנָּה וְדָבָר טוֹב יְשַׂמְּחֶנָּה
"Anxiety in a man's heart weighs him (alt.: it) down, but a good word makes him (alt.: it) glad"

---

[155] McKane, *Proverbs*, 452. Similarly Ross who writes, "Compassion for animals is an indication of one's character. The righteous are kind to all God's creation (see Deut 25:4) because they have received his bounty." "Proverbs," n.p.

[156] Kidner, *Proverbs*, 96.

[157] This phrase occurs only here in the MT.

LXX: φοβερὸς λόγος καρδίαν ταράσσει ἀνδρὸς δικαίου ἀγγελία
δὲ ἀγαθὴ εὐφραίνει αὐτόν
"A terrible word troubles the heart of a righteous man, but a good message makes him glad"

Prov 12:25 has an implicit or progressive antithesis[158] ("Anxiety in a man's heart weighs him down, but a good word makes him glad"). W. McKane writes that "When a man is anxious, he is depressed and he needs "a good word" to cheer him up."[159] Thus the state or condition of anxiety is overcome by a good word. In the LXX rendering, however, nothing is said about such a condition ("A terrible word troubles the heart of a righteous man, but a good message makes him glad"). Apparently the translator made the first half of the parallelism correspond to the second half by altering דְּאָגָה בְלֵב "anxiety in the heart" to φοβερὸς λόγος καρδίαν ταράσσει "a terrible word troubles the heart" (first half), which is antithetically parallel to ἀγγελία . . . ἀγαθὴ "a good message"; MT: דָּבָר טוֹב "a good word" (second half). Thus the LXX rendering appears to be clearly more parallel semantically.

5. Prov 13:19

MT: תַּאֲוָה נִהְיָה תֶעֱרַב לְנָפֶשׁ וְתוֹעֲבַת כְּסִילִים סוּר מֵרָע
"A desire realized is sweet to the soul, but to turn away from evil is an abomination to fools"

LXX: ἐπιθυμίαι εὐσεβῶν ἡδύνουσιν ψυχήν ἔργα δὲ ἀσεβῶν μακρὰν ἀπὸ γνώσεως
"The desires of the godly gladden the soul, but the works of the ungodly are far from knowledge"

In Prov 13:19 the two lines are difficult and seem unrelated[160] ("A desire realized is sweet to the soul, but to turn away from evil is an abomination to fools"). C. H. Toy suggests that each line has lost its parallel line.[161] W. McKane treats both halves separately.[162] But there are those who see the two halves as connected, as for instance T. T. Perowne who summarizes his solution to the problem as follows, "In spite of the sweetness of good desires accomplished,

---

[158] Toy, *Proverbs*, 256.

[159] McKane, *Proverbs*, 446.

[160] *IB*, 4:859.

[161] Toy, *Proverbs*, 274.

[162] McKane, *Proverbs*, 459 and 460.

fools will not forsake evil to attain it."¹⁶³ The LXX ("The desires of the godly gladden the soul, but the works of the ungodly are far from knowledge"), however, is clearly a more closely parallel couplet than the Hebrew, as in the first colon εὐσεβῶν "the godly" is added as a contrastive parallel to ἀσεβῶν "the ungodly" (second colon).¹⁶⁴ Similarly ἔργα "works" (second half) may have been added as a parallel to ἐπιθυμίαι "desires"—MT: תַּאֲוָה "desire, longing"—(first half), although they do not correspond completely.

6. Prov 13:25

MT: צַדִּיק אֹכֵל לְשֹׂבַע נַפְשׁוֹ וּבֶטֶן רְשָׁעִים תֶּחְסָר
"The righteous eats (or: has enough to eat) to the satisfying of his soul (=appetite), but the belly of the wicked shall want"

LXX: δίκαιος ἔσθων ἐμπιπλᾷ τὴν ψυχὴν αὐτοῦ ψυχαὶ δὲ ἀσεβῶν ἐνδεεῖς
"A just man eats and satisfies his soul, but the souls of the ungodly are in want"

In Prov 13:25 there is a contrast between the righteous who has enough to eat to satisfy his physical needs, and evil men who never have enough to eat and thus go hungry¹⁶⁵ ("The righteous eats to the satisfying of his soul/appetite, but the belly of the wicked shall want"). Here נֶפֶשׁ means "appetite"¹⁶⁶ (first colon) and is contrasted with בֶּטֶן "belly" (second colon). The translator, however, seems to have adapted בֶּטֶן to ψυχαὶ "souls" (second colon) parallel to the occurrence of τὴν ψυχὴν (נַפְשׁוֹ) "his soul" in the first colon to achieve a closer lexical correspondence of the two halves ("A just man eats and satisfies his soul, but the souls of the ungodly are in want").

7. Prov 15:15

MT: כָּל־יְמֵי עָנִי רָעִים וְטוֹב־לֵב מִשְׁתֶּה תָמִיד
"All the days of the afflicted are evil/hard, but a good heart (=he who is of a cheerful heart) has a continual feast"

---

¹⁶³ T. T. Perowne, *The Proverbs*, 103. Cf. 13:12; 29:27. NLT also expresses a relationship between the two lines, "It is pleasant to see dreams come true, but fools will not turn from evil to attain them." W. E. Mouser treats the lines as logically connected with "so": "Desire realized is sweet to the soul; so it is an abomination to fools to depart from evil." William E. Mouser, *Getting the Most out of Proverbs* (Grand Rapids: Zondervan, 1991), 31.

¹⁶⁴ According to W. McKane the LXX reinterprets pietistically. McKane, *Proverbs*, 459.

¹⁶⁵ Similarly McKane, *Proverbs*, 462.

¹⁶⁶ Cf. McKane, *Proverbs*, 462. Toy, *Proverbs*, 279.

LXX: πάντα τὸν χρόνον οἱ ὀφθαλμοὶ τῶν κακῶν προσδέχονται
κακά οἱ δὲ ἀγαθοὶ ἡσυχάζουσιν διὰ παντός
"All the time the eyes of the wicked are looking for evil things, but the good are always quiet (=live a quiet peaceful life)"

In Prov 15:15 ("All the days of the afflicted are evil/hard, but a good heart has a continual feast") there is some contrast between עָנִי "the afflicted" and טוֹב־לֵב "he who is of a cheerful heart" and to some extent between כָּל־יְמֵי ... רָעִים "all the days ... are evil/hard" and מִשְׁתֶּה תָמִיד "continual feast." The translator, however, translated in a slightly more parallel fashion, rendering טוֹב־לֵב by οἱ ... ἀγαθοί "the good" (second colon), in which he was moralizing,[167] and contrasted it with τῶν κακῶν "the wicked" (first colon) in line with his fondness for antithesis despite changing the Hebrew text considerably. The phrase οἱ ὀφθαλμοὶ τῶν κακῶν "the eyes of the wicked" (עיני רשעים, e.g. Job 11:20) was perhaps prompted by the similar looking עני רעים (first colon), and the remainder of the clause προσδέχονται κακά "they are looking for evil things" contrasts with ἡσυχάζουσιν "they live a peaceful life" (second colon).

8. Prov 15:21

MT: אִוֶּלֶת שִׂמְחָה לַחֲסַר־לֵב וְאִישׁ תְּבוּנָה יְיַשֶּׁר־לָכֶת
"Folly is a joy to one who lacks a heart (=has no sense or judgment), but a person of understanding walks straight ahead"

Q: וֶלֶת שמחה להס[ר לב ואיש] תבונה יישר לכת[168]

LXX: ἀνοήτου τρίβοι ἐνδεεῖς φρενῶν ἀνὴρ δὲ φρόνιμος
κατευθύνων πορεύεται
"The ways of a foolish man are void of sense, but a wise man proceeds on his way aright"

The proverb of 15:21 contrasts the person without sense and judgment (lit.: heart[169]), who enjoys folly,[170] with the one who has understanding and thus

---

[167] Cf. McKane, *Proverbs*, 481.

[168] De Waard, "4QProv," 90. Q agrees with the MT.

[169] "Although no human is capable of functioning without a physical heart, individuals are nevertheless described metaphorically as lacking this organ when they exhibit irrational behavior." ". . . the heart among Hebrew speakers was identified as the integrating center of a human's life, where the volitional, cognitive, and emotional choices were processed. To lack such a central point of integration would mean an inability to discriminate between reasonable and unreasonable courses of action." S. Meier, *NIDOTTE*, 2:225–226.

[170] "The term *folly* here has a moral as well as an intellectual content." Toy, *Proverbs*, 312.

follows a straight course[171] ("Folly is a joy to one who has no sense or judgment, but a person of understanding walks straight ahead"). Apparently the translator wanted to achieve a clearer antithesis, which he did by adding τρίβοι "ways" (first colon) as a parallel to κατευθύνων πορεύεται "(he) proceeds on his way aright", MT: יְיַשֶּׁר־לָכֶת, (second colon). This led to a more parallel form semantically.

9. Prov 15:27

MT: עֹכֵר בֵּיתוֹ בּוֹצֵעַ בָּצַע וְשׂוֹנֵא מַתָּנֹת יִחְיֶה
"He who is greedy for gain troubles his own house, but he who hates gifts will live"

Q: [כר ביתו בו]צע בצע ושנא מ[תנת יחיה][172]

LXX: ἐξόλλυσιν ἑαυτὸν ὁ δωρολήμπτης ὁ δὲ μισῶν δώρων λήμψεις σῴζεται
"A receiver of bribes destroys himself, but he who hates the receiving of bribes is safe"

The theme in Prov 15:27 is ill-gotten wealth and greed[173] ("He who is greedy for gain troubles his own house, but he who hates gifts will live"). The relationship of the two halves may be described as fairly parallel antithetically or even as generic-specific. The first half speaks of ill-gotten wealth in general, and the second half speaks of gifts or bribes in particular. The translator seems to have deliberately rendered בּוֹצֵעַ בָּצַע "he who is greedy for gain" (first colon) as δωρολήμπτης "a receiver of bribes/gifts" to make it correspond to δώρων λήμψεις "the receiving of bribes/gifts", MT: מַתָּנֹת "gifts", (second colon). This translational adjustment does not cause surprise because the same Hebrew idiom "greedy for gain" was also rendered freely in Prov 1:19 by τῶν συντελούντων τὰ ἄνομα "(all) that perform lawless deeds." In the latter case the adaptation was prompted by παρανόμων "transgressors" in the previous verse. Also, in the first half of 15:27 MT the man's "own house" or "family"—בֵּיתוֹ "his house"—is troubled by the one who is greedy, whereas in the LXX only the receiver of bribes is affected as he destroys ἑαυτὸν "himself" ("A receiver of bribes destroys himself, but he who hates the receiving of bribes is safe"). The translator seems to have altered the more generic "house" to a more specific "himself" so as to be antithetically parallel to the third person

---

[171] Similarly Ross, "Proverbs," n.p.

[172] De Waard, "4QProv," 88. As far as the evidence is concerned Q agrees with the MT.

[173] McKane, *Proverbs*, 485. "The 'gain' is to be understood as . . . selfish (Ps 119:36; Prov 15:27; Jer 6:13)." J. Clinton McCann, Jr., *NIDOTTE*, 1:695.

singular in the second half. Thus the LXX rendering is clearly a more closely parallel couplet semantically due to the translator's effort.

10. Prov 17:9

MT: מְכַסֶּה־פֶּשַׁע מְבַקֵּשׁ אַהֲבָה וְשֹׁנֶה בְדָבָר מַפְרִיד אַלּוּף
"He who covers over an offence seeks love, but he who repeats a matter/word separates friends"

LXX: ὃς κρύπτει ἀδικήματα ζητεῖ φιλίαν ὃς δὲ μισεῖ κρύπτειν διίστησιν φίλους καὶ οἰκείους
"He who conceals injuries seeks love, but he who hates to hide them separates friends and kindred"

Prov 17:9 is an antithetical parallelism where "he who covers over an offence" of a friend[174] is contrasted with the one who "repeats" the news about it; the former promotes love and the latter separates friends[175] ("He who covers over an offence seeks love, but he who repeats a matter/word separates friends"). The translator of LXX Proverbs, however, sought to produce a clearer antithesis and repeated κρύπτω "cover" in place of שֹׁנֶה "he who repeats" (second colon) to make a parallel with מְכַסֶּה "he who covers" (first colon). At the same time he inserted μισεῖ "he (that) hates"[176] for the sake of the antithesis, thus creating a closer correspondence of the lexical items ("He who conceals injuries seeks love, but he who hates to hide them separates friends and kindred").

11. Prov 22:3

MT: עָרוּם רָאָה רָעָה וְיִסָּתֵר וּפְתָיִים עָבְרוּ וְנֶעֱנָשׁוּ
"A prudent man sees the evil and hides himself, but the simple pass on and are punished"

LXX: πανοῦργος ἰδὼν πονηρὸν τιμωρούμενον κραταιῶς αὐτὸς παιδεύεται οἱ δὲ ἄφρονες παρελθόντες ἐζημιώθησαν
"A clever man seeing a bad man severely punished is himself instructed, but fools/the.ignorant pass by and are punished"

In Prov 22:3 the contrast is between the עָרוּם "prudent" and the פְּתָיִים "simple"[177] ("A prudent man sees the evil and hides himself, but the simple pass

---

[174] According to W. McKane "v.9a refers to the benevolent overlooking of another's foibles and not response to a personal affront." McKane, *Proverbs*, 508.

[175] Ross, "Proverbs," n.p.

[176] There might be the possibility that the translator was prompted to insert μισεῖ by the similar looking שׂנא.

[177] Ross, "Proverbs," n.p.

on and are punished"). Although the LXX deviates from the MT ("A clever man seeing a bad man severely punished is himself instructed, but the ignorant pass by and are punished"), there is some indication that its source text was similar to the MT. The rendering πανοῦργος "clever man," which is recognizably a translation of עָרוּם,[178] is contrasted with ἄφρονες "fools/the.ignorant" (from פְּתָיִים). Also the first verb in the first half "see" agrees in both readings and similarly the first verb in the second half "pass on/by/through." The translator, however, may have taken רָעָה "evil, danger" as freely representing πονηρὸν "evil man" and added τιμωρούμενον κραταιῶς αὐτὸς παιδεύεται "severely punished [he] is himself instructed" (first colon)[179] to explicate what he thought it meant, making an antithetic parallel to נֶעֱנָשׁוּ / ἐζημιώθησαν "they are punished" (second colon).[180]

12. Prov 28:25

MT: רְחַב־נֶפֶשׁ יְגָרֶה מָדוֹן וּבוֹטֵחַ עַל־יְהוָה יְדֻשָּׁן
"A greedy man (lit.: wide of soul) stirs up strife, but he who puts his trust in the Lord will be made fat (=enriched)"

LXX: ἄπληστος[181] ἀνὴρ κρίνει εἰκῇ ὃς δὲ πέποιθεν ἐπὶ κύριον ἐν ἐπιμελείᾳ ἔσται
"A greedy many judges rashly, but he who trusts in the Lord will act carefully"

In Prov 28:25 the רְחַב־נֶפֶשׁ "greedy man" is contrasted with the בּוֹטֵחַ עַל־יְהוָה "the man who trusts in the Lord."[182] The former by his selfishness stirs up strife, but the latter trusts in God and will thus prosper.[183] It seems that the translator took the liberty to alter יְגָרֶה מָדוֹן "he stirs up strife" (first colon), rendering it more specifically as κρίνει εἰκῇ "he judges rashly"—which the

---

[178] Cf. McKane, *Proverbs*, 564.

[179] According to J. Weingreen רעה "is interpreted by the LXX to mean "punishment" which, in turn, it is implied must have been justly meted out to a wicked person." Weingreen, "Rabbinic-Type Commentary," 410.

[180] McKane thinks that the LXX reinterprets rather than misunderstands the MT. McKane, *Proverbs*, 564. Similarly Toy who holds that the sense of the LXX is good in itself but not that of the Hebrew. Toy, *Proverbs*, 414.

[181] The codices B (Vaticanus) and S (Sinaiticus) have ἄπιστος "an unbelieving (man)" instead which corresponds with πέποιθεν ἐπὶ κύριον "he who trusts in the Lord" antithetically. Thus there is the possibility that this reading may be the translator's original rendering.

[182] McKane, *Proverbs*, 627. Ross, "Proverbs," n.p.

[183] According to W. McKane the former person is greedy for wealth and the latter will enjoy true prosperity, McKane, *Proverbs*, 627, whereas R. J. Clifford limits the proverb to unbridled appetite and satisfaction of appetite. Clifford, *Proverbs*, 247.

translator regarded as the cause of stirring up strife. At the same time he made the second colon correspond antithetically by altering יְדֻשָּׁן "(he) will be made fat" to ἐν ἐπιμελείᾳ ἔσται "he will be/act with. care/carefully" (second colon), instead of in the MT—"stirs up strife" (first half) and "will be made fat" (second half)—where there is less correspondence. Thus the LXX ("A greedy many judges rashly, but he who trusts in the Lord will act carefully") can be regarded as a more closely parallel couplet semantically.

13. Prov 28:27

MT: נוֹתֵן לָרָשׁ אֵין מַחְסוֹר וּמַעְלִים עֵינָיו רַב־מְאֵרוֹת
"He who gives to the poor will not lack, but he who hides his eyes (= turns a blind eye) will get many a curse"

LXX: ὃς δίδωσιν πτωχοῖς οὐκ ἐνδεηθήσεται ὃς δὲ ἀποστρέφει τὸν ὀφθαλμὸν αὐτοῦ ἐν πολλῇ ἀπορίᾳ ἔσται
"He who gives to the poor will not be in want, but he who turns away his eye will be in great want/distress"

Prov 28:27 is near-antithetic in that it teaches that "generosity is rewarded but indifference is cursed"[184] ("He who gives to the poor will not lack, but he who turns a blind eye will get many a curse"). The translator, however, produced a clear contrast to οὐκ ἐνδεηθήσεται "will not be in want" (אֵין מַחְסוֹר) by rendering ἐν πολλῇ ἀπορίᾳ ἔσται "will be in great want/distress," whereas the MT has רַב־מְאֵרוֹת "(will get) many a curse."

14. Prov 28:28

MT: בְּקוּם רְשָׁעִים יִסָּתֵר אָדָם וּבְאָבְדָם יִרְבּוּ צַדִּיקִים
"When the wicked rise, men hide themselves, but when they perish, the righteous increase"

LXX: ἐν τόποις ἀσεβῶν στένουσι δίκαιοι ἐν δὲ τῇ ἐκείνων ἀπωλείᾳ πληθυνθήσονται δίκαιοι
"In the places of the ungodly the righteous mourn, but in their destruction the righteous will be multiplied"

In Prov 28:28 the LXX is not without problems, see 2.2.2. But the more general term אָדָם "men" is rendered freely by δίκαιοι "the righteous" (first colon), making a parallel with δίκαιοι, צַדִּיקִים "the righteous" in the second half.[185]

---

[184] Ross, "Proverbs," n.p.

[185] Fritsch in "Hexaplaric Signs," 170, lists δίκαιος of Prov 28:28 etc. under frequently added moralizing terms. Similarly Dick, "Ethics," 22–24.

15. Prov 29:4

MT: מֶלֶךְ בְּמִשְׁפָּט יַעֲמִיד אָרֶץ וְאִישׁ תְּרוּמוֹת יֶהֶרְסֶנָּה
"A king by justice gives a nation stability (lit.: establishes the land), but he that receives gifts (or: gifts; or: raises taxes) overthrows it"

LXX: βασιλεὺς δίκαιος ἀνίστησιν χώραν ἀνὴρ δὲ παράνομος κατασκάπτει
"A righteous king gives a nation stability (lit.: establishes the country), but a transgressor destroys it"

Prov 29:4 contrasts a king who makes the nation secure with one who ruins it[186] ("A king by justice gives a nation stability, but he that receives gifts overthrows it"). The translator may have rendered the prepositional phrase מֶלֶךְ בְּמִשְׁפָּט "a king by justice" by a noun plus adjective βασιλεὺς δίκαιος "a righteous king" (first colon), and the MT: וְאִישׁ תְּרוּמוֹת "but he that receives gifts"[187] by ἀνὴρ δὲ παράνομος "but a transgressor" (second colon) in order to achieve a closer correspondence antithetically. Thus the LXX can be regarded as a more nearly parallel couplet semantically, and also structurally, as both βασιλεὺς δίκαιος "a righteous king" and ἀνὴρ . . . παράνομος "a transgressor" consist of noun plus adjective.

The following case shows that the translator was even capable of dropping lines in order to achieve a more clear-cut antithesis.

16. Prov 11:10–11

MT: 10 בְּטוּב צַדִּיקִים תַּעֲלֹץ קִרְיָה וּבַאֲבֹד רְשָׁעִים רִנָּה
11 בְּבִרְכַּת יְשָׁרִים תָּרוּם קָרֶת וּבְפִי רְשָׁעִים תֵּהָרֵס
"10 When it goes well with the righteous the city rejoices, and when the wicked perish, there is jubilation.
11 By the blessing of the upright the city is exalted, but it is overthrown by the mouth of the wicked"

LXX: 10 ἐν ἀγαθοῖς δικαίων κατώρθωσεν πόλις 11 στόμασιν δὲ ἀσεβῶν κατεσκάφη
"10 When it goes well with the righteous a city prospers, 11 but by the mouths of ungodly men it is overthrown"

---

[186] Also Ross, "Proverbs," n.p.

[187] Note that וְאִישׁ and ἀνὴρ δὲ correspond closely with each other.

Prov 11:10–11 may be regarded as somewhat antithetical[188] ("10 When it goes well with the righteous the city rejoices, and when the wicked perish, there is jubilation. 11 By the blessing of the upright the city is exalted, but it is overthrown by the mouth of the wicked"), but the antithesis in the LXX rendering is clearer ("10 When it goes well with the righteous a city prospers, 11 but by the mouths of ungodly men it is overthrown"). It seems probable that in order to produce a sharper contrast or a straight antithetical parallelism the translator dropped the second half of v. 10 as well as the first half of v. 11, as the second half of v. 10, which is only partly antithetical, could have disturbed the contrast.

To sum up, the translator often altered antithetical parallelisms for the sake of linguistic, translational, and sometimes theological considerations, and at the same time he sought to produce clear contrasts semantically and/or grammatically, even going as far as dropping lines (11:10–11) in order to achieve this goal. In the latter case E. Tov regards the shorter text (LXX) as an indication of a different *Vorlage*.[189] In the light of the translator's predilection to produce clearer contrasts, however, it is likely that this case may be of translational nature.

The translator's fondness to produce a sharper contrast should be considered before using LXX Proverbs as source of variant readings, cf. 3.3.1.4.

In addition to (near) synonymous and antithetical parallelisms, further types of parallel forms may be considered, as the following section demonstrates.

1.2.1.5 Additional Aspects

Parallelisms may be looked at in terms of how the lines relate to one another, e.g. logically, sequentially, comparatively, and emblematically. In the traditional approach of R. Lowth many of these types of parallelism were treated as examples of what he called "synthetic" parallelisms, as they did not fit into the categories of either "synonymous" or "antithetical" parallelisms. They may, however, be defined more precisely as parallelisms of logical relations, parallelisms of addition relations, parallelisms of comparisons, emblematic parallelisms, single-sentence constructions, near-synonymous parallelisms with three parts, triplets, and phrases. These various categories are illustrated in the following sections.

---

[188] "The common theme of this line [v. 10] is joy; it comes from either the success of the righteous or the ruin of the wicked (so an antithetical idea is present)." Ross, "Proverbs," n.p. In the following verse 11 there is "a similar contrast expressing the social effects of words." *Ibid.*

[189] Tov, "Recensional Differences," 56.

1.2.1.5.1 Parallelisms of logical relations

In parallelisms of logical relations colon A and colon B are linked in a cause-effect relation. Within this general group, further more specific relations may be identified, each of which treats the cause-effect relation from a particular point of view, emphasizing some aspect or other involved in it. These cause-effect relations may express e.g. means-purpose, grounds-conclusion, condition-consequence, reason-result, and exhortation-circumstance. However, a verse may be interpreted in different ways and looked at from different viewpoints, thus there may be more than one possible relation.[190]

There are quite a number of cases where the translator rendered parallelisms of logical relations in a parallel manner. The following cases give evidence for the translator's fondness for producing corresponding lines even in rendering logical relations.

1. Prov 4:10

MT: שְׁמַע בְּנִי וְקַח אֲמָרָי וְיִרְבּוּ לְךָ שְׁנוֹת חַיִּים
"Hear, my son, and accept my words, then the years of your life will be many"

LXX: ἄκουε υἱέ καὶ δέξαι ἐμοὺς λόγους καὶ πληθυνθήσεται ἔτη ζωῆς σου ἵνα σοι γένωνται πολλαὶ ὁδοὶ βίου
"Hear, (my) son, and receive my words, and the years of your life shall be increased, that the ways of your life may be many"

In Prov 4:10 ("Hear, my son, and accept my words, then the years of your life will be many") the logical relation may be described as one of protasis and apodosis[191] or condition-consequence (CEV[192]). The LXX basically agrees with the MT in meaning, but the clause ἵνα σοι γένωνται πολλαὶ ὁδοὶ βίου "that the ways of your life may be many" may have been added by the translator, thus paralleling ὁδοὶ βίου "ways of life" with שְׁנוֹת חַיִּים = ἔτη ζωῆς "years of life" (second half) ("Hear, my son, and receive my words, and the years of your life shall be increased, that the ways of your life may be many"). The reason for this addition may have been to connect the verse more smoothly with the figure דֶּרֶךְ, ὁδούς "ways" at the beginning of the following verse 11 and at the same time produce a parallel form.

---

[190] For a similar view cf. Ernst R. Wendland, *Analyzing the Psalms* (SIL, 1998) under 3.3.3.2 Causal correlation.

[191] Toy, *Proverbs*, 91.

[192] "My child, if you listen and obey my teachings, you will live a long time."

2. Prov 17:23

MT: שֹׁחַד מֵחֵיק רָשָׁע יִקָּח לְהַטּוֹת אָרְחוֹת מִשְׁפָּט
"The wicked accepts a concealed bribe from the bosom to pervert the ways/course of justice"

LXX: λαμβάνοντος δῶρα ἐν κόλπῳ ἀδίκως οὐ κατευοδοῦνται ὁδοί ἀσεβὴς δὲ ἐκκλίνει ὁδοὺς δικαιοσύνης
"The ways of a man who unjustly receives gifts in (his) bosom does not prosper, and an ungodly man perverts the ways of righteousness"

Prov 17:23 consists of a single sentence with a means-purpose relationship;[193] the purpose clause explains and clarifies that the intent of the bribe is to pervert the course of justice[194] ("The wicked accepts a concealed bribe from the bosom to pervert the ways of justice"). Apparently the translator changed the single-sentence logical relation into a parallel form, the subject of the first colon λαμβάνοντος δῶρα ... ἀδίκως "a man who unjustly receives gifts" being paralleled in the second colon and described as ἀσεβὴς "an ungodly man." Also, as a parallel to the figure ὁδοὺς "ways"—MT: אָרְחוֹת—(second half), ὁδοί was added in the first colon although it is used in a negative sense. These adjustments together produced a near-parallel couplet without the means-purpose relationship of the MT ("The ways of a man who unjustly receives gifts in his bosom does not prosper, and an ungodly man perverts the ways of righteousness").

3. Prov 24:10

MT: הִתְרַפִּיתָ בְּיוֹם צָרָה צַר כֹּחֶכָה
"If you falter in the day of adversity, your strength is small (or: the limits of your strength are revealed)"

LXX: ἐμμολυνθήσεται[195] ἐν ἡμέρᾳ κακῇ καὶ ἐν ἡμέρᾳ θλίψεως ἕως ἂν ἐκλίπῃ
"He shall be defiled in the evil day, and in the day of affliction until he be utterly consumed"

---

[193] Similarly Mouser, *Proverbs*, 76.

[194] Cf. Ross, "Proverbs," n.p.

[195] This verb seems to belong to v. 10 as in the Cambridge edition; in the Rahlfs edition, however, it goes with v. 9. Apparently the idea of defilement was carried over from the previous verse. This is a common practice of the translator in order to increase cohesiveness.

The logical relationship in Prov 24:10 may be described as grounds-conclusion[196] ("If you falter in the day of adversity, your strength is small"). The LXX is clearly a more closely parallel form since ἐν ἡμέρᾳ θλίψεως "in the day of affliction" (second colon) seems to be added to parallel ἐν ἡμέρᾳ κακῇ "in the evil day" (first colon), whereas the MT is not a parallel couplet as it consists of a one-sentence logical relation. For a further adjustment see 2.1.1.2.

4. Prov 27:11

MT: חֲכַם בְּנִי וְשַׂמַּח לִבִּי וְאָשִׁיבָה חֹרְפִי דָבָר
"My son, be wise, and make my heart glad, so that I may answer whoever reproaches me"

LXX: σοφὸς γίνου υἱε[197] ἵνα εὐφραίνηταί μου ἡ καρδία καὶ ἀπόστρεψον ἀπὸ σοῦ ἐπονειδίστους λόγους
"My son, become wise that my heart may rejoice, and remove from yourself reproachful words"

Prov 27:11 expresses a condition-consequence relationship[198] ("My son, be wise, and make my heart glad, so that I may answer whoever reproaches me"). The translator while following the Hebrew in the first half apparently altered the second half of the logical relation into a coordinate clause καὶ ἀπόστρεψον ἀπὸ σοῦ ἐπονειδίστους λόγους "and remove from yourself reproachful words." This corresponds semantically to σοφὸς γίνου "become wise" (first half), expressing more specifically what it entails to become wise. Thus the translator produced a more closely parallel form.

Within this group of parallelisms that contain logical relations, there are cases where the translator apparently altered his source text in line with his love of antithetical forms, as the following examples demonstrate.

5. Prov 13:14

MT: תּוֹרַת חָכָם מְקוֹר חַיִּים לָסוּר מִמֹּקְשֵׁי מָוֶת
"The law/teaching of the wise is a fountain of life, to (or: so that one may) avoid the snares of death"

LXX: νόμος σοφοῦ πηγὴ ζωῆς ὁ δὲ ἄνους ὑπὸ παγίδος θανεῖται

---

[196] "The verse uses a paronomasia [or play on words] to stress the connection: 'If you falter in the times of trouble [צָרָה], / how small [צַר] is your strength!'" Ross, "Proverbs," n.p. Similarly Meinhold, *Sprüche*, 2:404.

[197] "In Greek possessive pronouns can often be left out, and it is even regarded as good style to use the possessive less frequently than for instance in Hebrew." Tauberschmidt, "Principles," 24–27.

[198] Cf. Toy, *Proverbs*, 487.

"The law/teaching of the wise is a fountain of life, but the man void of understanding shall die by a snare"

Prov 13:14 is a single sentence, the first clause of which contains a comparison expressing the cause (or means), and the second is the effect (or purpose) ("The law/teaching of the wise is a fountain of life, to avoid the snares of death"). The translator, however, rendered the logical relation by an antithetical form inserting ὁ δὲ ἄνους "but the man void of understanding" (second colon) to make a contrast with σοφοῦ / חָכָם "the wise" (first colon). Also, he altered לָסוּר מִמֹּקְשֵׁי מָוֶת "to avoid the snares of death" to ὑπὸ παγίδος θανεῖται "(he) shall die by a snare," which is antithetically parallel to מְקוֹר חַיִּים "(he is a) fountain of life" (πηγὴ ζωῆς) ("The law/teaching of the wise is a fountain of life, but the man void of understanding shall die by a snare").

6. Prov 23:31

MT: אַל־תֵּרֶא יַיִן כִּי יִתְאַדָּם כִּי־יִתֵּן בַּכּוֹס עֵינוֹ יִתְהַלֵּךְ בְּמֵישָׁרִים
"Do not look at wine, when it is red, when it sparkles in the cup, when it goes down smoothly"

LXX: μὴ μεθύσκεσθε οἴνῳ ἀλλὰ ὁμιλεῖτε ἀνθρώποις δικαίοις καὶ ὁμιλεῖτε ἐν περιπάτοις[199]
"Be not drunk with wine, but converse with just men, and converse with them openly"

Prov 23:31 starts with the main clause in imperative mood and the following three parts give the circumstance or condition concerning the wine ("Do not look at wine, when it is red, when it sparkles in the cup, when it goes down smoothly"). The translator appears to have rendered the meaning of the first line directly by μὴ μεθύσκεσθε οἴνῳ "Be not drunk with wine." The circumstantial clauses he transformed into a line that is antithetical to the first and also shifted the topic from "drunk with wine" to the environment in which one ought to be: "but converse with just men" (rather than having fellowship with drunkards). This shift may have been due to the influence of the preceding verse 30 in which also the environment is spoken of, that is, "the places where banquets are." The last colon is fairly parallel to the preceding one but with the further specification of conversing "openly" (with just men). Thus the LXX rendering is clearly

---

[199] The second part of Prov 23:31 is not represented in the MT and may be regarded as an addition to give further explanation: ἐὰν γὰρ εἰς τὰς φιάλας καὶ τὰ ποτήρια δῷς τοὺς ὀφθαλμούς σου ὕστερον περιπατήσεις γυμνότερος ὑπέρου "For if you should set your eyes on bowls and cups, you shall afterwards go more naked than a pestle." According to W. McKane "to be more naked than a pestle" is a Greek proverb meaning to be in a state of dire poverty. McKane, *Proverbs*, 33. Cf. also Gerleman, *Studies*, 33.

translational in nature, reflecting the translator's fondness for antithesis and parallel renderings.

7. Prov 29:9

MT: אִישׁ־חָכָם נִשְׁפָּט אֶת־אִישׁ אֱוִיל וְרָגַז וְשָׂחַק וְאֵין נָחַת
"If a wise man goes to law with[200] (alt.: argues with) a foolish man, there is ranting and ridicule without relief"

LXX: ἀνὴρ σοφὸς κρίνει ἔθνη ἀνὴρ δὲ φαῦλος ὀργιζόμενος καταγελᾶται καὶ οὐ καταπτήσσει
"A wise man shall judge nations, but a worthless man being angry laughs and does not cower"

The relationship of the two halves in Prov 29:9 seems to be of condition-consequence[201] ("If a wise man goes to law with a foolish man, there is ranting and ridicule without relief"). Apparently the translator changed the logical relation into an antithetical form and moved ἀνὴρ δὲ φαῦλος "but a worthless/foolish man" (אִישׁ אֱוִיל) from the first half (MT) to the second half to produce an antithetic parallel to ἀνὴρ σοφὸς = אִישׁ־חָכָם "a wise man" (first half) ("A wise man shall judge nations, but a worthless man being angry laughs and does not cower").

To sum up, the translator altered quite a number of parallelisms of logical relations and changed them into near-synonymous and antithetical forms.

A contrary view is expressed by J. de Waard, who states concerning Prov 23:24[202] ("The father of the righteous will greatly rejoice; (and) he who begets a wise son will be glad in him"), "The translator spells out the reason in Greek for the result of the Hebrew. He does so because he dislikes the synonymous parallelism of the Masoretic text"[203] (LXX: "A righteous father brings up (his children) well, and his soul rejoices over a wise son"). In this section, however, the translator's predilection for recasting parallelisms that consist of logical

---

[200] According to R. J. Clifford, "The verb 'to enter into judgment' does not necessarily mean 'to go to law with' (despite NRSV and REB) but simply 'to dispute, argue with.'" Clifford, *Proverbs*, 251. Cf. Meinhold, *Sprüche*, 2:484–485.

[201] Similarly Ross who states, "The first line presents the condition and the second the effect." Ross, "Proverbs," n.p.

[202] MT: גּוֹל יָגוּל אֲבִי צַדִּיק יוֹלֵד חָכָם וְיִשְׂמַח־בּוֹ "The father of the righteous will greatly rejoice; (and) he who begets a wise son will be glad in him."
LXX: καλῶς ἐκτρέφει πατὴρ δίκαιος ἐπὶ δὲ υἱῷ σοφῷ εὐφραίνεται ἡ ψυχὴ αὐτοῦ "A righteous father brings up (his children) well, and his soul rejoices over a wise son."

[203] Jan de Waard, "The Septuagint of Proverbs as a Translation Model?," *BT* 50/3 (1999): 310.

relations as synonymous and antithetic parallelisms has been demonstrated, and the thesis as a whole shows clearly the translator's fondness for producing forms that are more closely parallel, including synonymous parallelisms. It is true that the translator dislikes repeating the same words (see stylistic variation in Prov 3:13,24; 8:5; 18:15; 20:24, under 3.3) except for cases where he employs the stylistic device of anaphora.[204] However, de Waard's explanation ("He does so because he dislikes the synonymous parallelism of the Masoretic text") is based on one example only and he disregards the general propensity of the translator; nor does he consider the translation technique beyond the couplet. In fact, there may be contextual (or even exegetical) reasons that led the translator to render his source text in a less synonymously parallel fashion (cf. 2.2). The theme of the whole paragraph (vv. 22–25) according to W. McKane is "Honour your father and mother." V. 23 does not harmonize with that theme,[205] and this may have led the translator to leave it out, and he may have even sought to strengthen the command of v. 22 "(My son = LXX) Listen to your father who begot you" by describing further what kind of father he is: Not only did he beget his son, but he is also "A righteous father [who] brings up his children well" (v. 24a, LXX). Thus the command in v. 25: "Let your father and your mother rejoice over you" (v. 25a, LXX). Whatever reasons may have led to changing v. 24, the reason was certainly not that he disliked the synonymous parallelism in v. 24, or even synonymous parallelisms in general, as de Waard seems to indicate.

The translator's technique with regard to altering logical relations into near-synonymous and antithetical forms should be considered before using similar cases as variant readings, cf. 3.3.1.5.1.

The following examples give further evidence for the translator's fondness for producing corresponding lines.

1.2.1.5.2 Parallelisms of addition relations

In the relations of addition treated below, the second half (*B*) is a temporal sequential continuation of the first half (*A*).

1. Prov 17:5

MT: לֹעֵג לָרָשׁ חֵרֵף עֹשֵׂהוּ שָׂמֵחַ לְאֵיד לֹא יִנָּקֶה
"He who mocks the poor reproaches his Maker, (and) he who is glad at calamities/disaster will not go unpunished"

LXX: ὁ καταγελῶν πτωχοῦ παροξύνει τὸν ποιήσαντα αὐτόν
ὁ δὲ ἐπιχαίρων ἀπολλυμένῳ οὐκ ἀθῳωθήσεται
ὁ δὲ ἐπισπλαγχνιζόμενος ἐλεηθήσεται

---

[204] Cf. Gerleman, *Studies*, 14.

[205] McKane, *Proverbs*, 389.

"He who laughs at the poor provokes him that made him (= his Maker), and he who rejoices at the destruction of another shall not be held guiltless, but he who has compassion shall find mercy"

In Prov 17:5 the second half is a continuation of the first; the first half explains that whoever mocks the poor reproaches his Maker, and the second half affirms that he will be punished[206] ("He who mocks the poor reproaches his Maker, (and) he who is glad at calamities/disaster will not go unpunished"). Apparently the translator rendered לְאֵיד "at calamities" by the more specific ἀπολλυμένῳ "the destruction of another" (second colon) parallel to πτωχοῦ / לָרָשׁ "the poor" (first colon). Also the translator seems to have added ὁ δὲ ἐπισπλαγχνιζόμενος ἐλεηθήσεται "but he who has compassion shall find mercy" as a contrastive parallel to the first two lines of the verse; this clause is not represented in the MT. C. H. Toy regards the addition in the Greek as "probably a gloss."[207] It is, however, more likely that the translator added the clause to produce a contrast, cf. Prov 6:11; 17:21; 18:22, 1.2.1.3.

2. Prov 22:15

MT: אִוֶּלֶת קְשׁוּרָה בְלֶב־נָעַר שֵׁבֶט מוּסָר יַרְחִיקֶנָּה מִמֶּנּוּ
"Folly is bound up in the heart/mind of a boy/youth, the rod of discipline (=a good beating) drives it far from him"

LXX: ἄνοια ἐξῆπται καρδίας νέου ῥάβδος δὲ καὶ παιδεία μακρὰν ἀπ' αὐτοῦ
"Folly is attached to the heart/mind of a child, but the rod and discipline are (then) far from him"

In the MT of Prov 22:15 the second half is a continuation of the first half[208] as שֵׁבֶט מוּסָר "the rod of discipline," that is, a good beating, will remove folly mentioned in the first half[209] ("Folly is bound up in the heart/mind of a youth, the rod of discipline drives it far from him"). In the LXX, however, the second colon was made more nearly parallel to the first, as the translator apparently took ῥάβδος . . . καὶ παιδεία "rod and discipline"[210] as being absent from the child when "folly is attached to the heart" ("Folly is attached to the heart/mind

---

[206] Ross, "Proverbs," n.p.

[207] Toy, *Proverbs*, 337.

[208] R. Alter lists this example under narrativity in Proverbs or narrative development. Alter, *Art*, 172–173. Toy too regards this verse as "continuous." Toy, *Proverbs*, 419.

[209] According to Toy "Corporal chastisement of children was probably universal in antiquity . . ." and "The affirmation of the couplet is general, and is not to be put as conditional." *Ibid*.

[210] Rendering the genitive construction of the MT by two coordinated nouns may merely be a translational adjustment.

of a child, but the rod and discipline are (then) far from him"). Thus, the presence of folly and the absence of the rod and discipline form a parallel.

To sum up, in the two parallelisms of time sequence the translator's fondness for closer correspondence, and even antithesis (17:5), is apparent. This translation technique should be considered when using similar cases for textual criticism, cf. 3.3.1.5.2.

1.2.1.5.3 Parallelisms of comparisons

There are parallel lines that express comparison in the comparative. These comparisons are often expressed by an adjective in the comparative plus "than," e.g. "better . . . than," as the following examples indicate.

1. Prov 17:10

MT: תֵּחַת גְּעָרָה בְמֵבִין מֵהַכּוֹת כְּסִיל מֵאָה
"A rebuke strikes deeper into a discerning person than a hundred blows into a fool"

LXX: συντρίβει ἀπειλὴ καρδίαν φρονίμου ἄφρων δὲ μαστιγωθεὶς οὐκ αἰσθάνεται
"A threat breaks down the heart of a man of sense, but a fool, though scourged, understands not"

In Prov 17:10 the comparison[211] ("A rebuke strikes deeper into a discerning person than a hundred blows into a fool") is rendered as an antithetical parallelism (with a close correspondence of the two colons) and this is probably due to the translator's general predilection for antithesis ("A threat breaks down the heart of a man of sense, but a fool, though scourged, understands not"). Along with this change, the implied information in the MT that a fool does not understand despite chastisement is made explicit in the LXX by inserting οὐκ αἰσθάνεται "he understands not," and the meaning of the exaggerated figure מֵאָה . . . מֵהַכּוֹת "a hundred blows"[212] is rendered more directly by μαστιγωθεὶς "scourged"; these alterations are clear indications of the translational character of this verse.[213]

---

[211] "There are no comparative and superlative forms of adjectives in Hebrew, but there are other ways to express both comparative and superlative degree. The preposition מִן may be used to express the comparative." Tauberschmidt, "Principles," 47.

[212] For more details on the number 100 used as an exaggeration rather than an exact figure see Meinhold, *Sprüche*, 2:288.

[213] Unfortunately due to the translational changes some of the dynamics of the original proverb have been lost.

2. Prov 17:12

MT: פָּגוֹשׁ דֹּב שַׁכּוּל בְּאִישׁ וְאַל־כְּסִיל בְּאִוַּלְתּוֹ
"Better to meet a bear robbed of her cubs than a fool in his folly"[214]

LXX: ἐμπεσεῖται μέριμνα ἀνδρὶ νοήμονι οἱ δὲ ἄφρονες διαλογιοῦνται κακά
"Care/thoughtfulness may befall a man of understanding, but fools will meditate evils"

As in the previous example Prov 17:12 consists of a comparison in the comparative: a dangerous animal in a state of rage is less dangerous than a fool[215] ("Better to meet a bear robbed of her cubs than a fool in his folly"). Again the translator rendered the comparison antithetically, contrasting ἀνδρὶ νοήμονι "a man of understanding" (first colon) with οἱ . . . ἄφρονες "fools" (second colon), and likewise he rendered ἐμπεσεῖται μέριμνα "thoughtfulness may befall" as a contrastive parallel to διαλογιοῦνται κακά "(they) will meditate evil"; and consequently he dropped the image of the bear[216] ("Care/thoughtfulness may befall a man of understanding, but fools will meditate evils").

In the last example comparison is expressed as well although different devices are used.

3. Prov 8:10

MT: קְחוּ־מוּסָרִי וְאַל־כָּסֶף וְדַעַת מֵחָרוּץ נִבְחָר
"Receive my instruction, and not silver (or: before silver), and knowledge rather than choice gold"

LXX: λάβετε παιδείαν καὶ μὴ ἀργύριον καὶ γνῶσιν ὑπὲρ χρυσίον δεδοκιμασμένον ἀνθαιρεῖσθε δὲ αἴσθησιν χρυσίου καθαροῦ
"Receive instruction and not silver, and knowledge rather than tried gold, and take perception rather than clean gold"

In Prov 8:10 the two lines each exhibit a comparison and are fairly parallel in thought ("Receive my instruction, and not silver, and knowledge rather than choice gold"). In the LXX the two colons correspond closely to the MT, only that the translator omitted "my" in the first half. This omission is probably due

---

[214] Lit.: "Let a bear robbed of her whelps meet a man, and not a fool in his folly."

[215] Cf. Clifford, *Proverbs*, 166.

[216] Unfortunately by doing so he lost the dynamics of the original. M. B. Dick lists κακός under moralizing tendency. Dick, "Ethics," 22–23. Dick does not consider other possible influences that may have led to the addition.

to the translator's effort to make a parallel (of "instruction") with "knowledge." There is, however, a third line in the LXX (". . . and take perception rather than clean gold"), and the question is whether it reflects a Hebrew source. P. A. de Lagarde regards the third colon as OG and the second colon as the work of a later reviser.[217] C. T. Fritsch holds a similar view.[218] According to J. Cook, the third colon may be a later addition as it is omitted in a number of important MSS.[219] However, on the basis of the translator's technique of employing stylistic variation in comparisons, the addition may be translational, as there are cases where more natural Greek constructions are used in one half of a near-synonymous parallelism and are paralleled with a more literal ὑπέρ phrase[220] for the sake of variation of style, e.g. Prov 8:19; 16:16; 22:1.[221] Although these examples do all reflect a Hebrew text that is similar to the MT, it is possible that in Prov 8:10 the translator added the third colon to produce a line parallel to the previous one as in cf. Prov 4:10 (1.2.1.5.1); and 1:27 (1.2.1.5.7).

To sum up, the translator clearly rendered the comparisons that have been discussed above in a more parallel way semantically and/or grammatically, and produced some contrastive parallel forms, a procedure which is in line with his predilection for antithesis. This tendency needs to be considered before using translational cases of this kind as superior readings, cf. 3.3.1.5.3.

1.2.1.5.4 Emblematic parallelisms

Emblematic parallelism is a parallelism in which one of the lines takes the form of a simile or metaphor[222] whose purpose is to illustrate the other line.[223] In a way emblematic parallelisms can be compared to synonymous parallelisms since one line corresponds to the other. However, in synonymous parallelisms the first half is repeated in the second half, in emblematic parallelisms the first half illustrates the second half. Thus the distinguishing feature, which puts the emblematic parallelisms in a separate group, is the emblem.[224]

---

[217] Paul A. de Lagarde, *Anmerkungen zur griechischen Übersetzung der Proverbien* (Leipzig, 1863), 27.

[218] Fritsch, "Hexaplaric Signs," 180.

[219] Cook, *Proverbs*, 205.

[220] Cf. F. C. Conybeare and St. George Stock, *Grammar of Septuagint Greek* (Hendrickson, 1905/95), 84.

[221] Tauberschmidt, "Principles," 49.

[222] "A metaphor as well as a simile is a figure of speech which involves a comparison. The only difference between a simile and a metaphor is that in a simile the comparison is explicitly stated, using words such as 'like' or 'as,' whereas in a metaphor the comparison is just implied." Tauberschmidt, "Principles," 70.

[223] Berlin, "Parallelism," n.p.

[224] Mouser, *Proverbs*, 57–58.

The following case exemplifies the typical biblical use of humor, and it is the grotesque hyperbole and surrealism of the metaphor that produces the humor.[225]

1. Prov 11:22

MT: נֶזֶם זָהָב בְּאַף חֲזִיר אִשָּׁה יָפָה וְסָרַת טָעַם
"(As) a ring of gold in a swine's snout, (so is) a beautiful woman without discretion"

LXX: ὥσπερ ἐνώτιον ἐν ῥινὶ ὑός οὕτως γυναικὶ κακόφρονι κάλλος
"As an ornament in a swine's snout, so is beauty to an ill-minded woman"

In Prov 11:22 the beautiful woman without discretion is compared to a swine with a gold ring ("[As] a ring of gold in a swine's snout, [so is] a beautiful woman without discretion"). The translator, however, not only adjusted the metaphor to a simile by inserting ὥσπερ ... οὕτως "as ... so," but made the point of comparison clearer by changing the adjective יָפָה of the noun phrase into a separate noun phrase consisting of the noun κάλλος "beauty" (second colon) in parallel with ἐνώτιον "ornament" (first colon), thus producing a more closely parallel structure[226] ("As an ornament in a swine's snout, so is beauty to an ill-minded woman").

2. Prov 26:20

MT: בְּאֶפֶס עֵצִים תִּכְבֶּה־אֵשׁ וּבְאֵין נִרְגָּן יִשְׁתֹּק מָדוֹן
"For lack of wood the fire goes out, and where there is no whisperer/gossip,[227] quarrel subsides"

---

[225] E. L. Greenstein, "Humor and Wit," n.p., *ABD on CD-ROM*. Version 2.1, 1997.

[226] G. Gerleman explains the deviation in the second colon in terms of assonance, which he defines as "the recurrence of a sound in such a manner as to catch the ear." Gerleman, *Studies*, 12.

[227] According to G. V. Smith, "The ni. part., used substantively, is used 4x in Proverbs describing the evil speech of the foolish person. It refers to murmuring about another person behind their back rather than openly complaining about their behavior. This kind of gossip could cause a deep separation between friends (Prov 16:28; 18:8; 26:20, 22)." *NIDOTTE*, 3:1053.

LXX: ἐν πολλοῖς ξύλοις θάλλει πῦρ ὅπου δὲ οὐκ ἔστιν δίθυμος[228] ἡ συχάζει μάχη
"With much wood fire increases, but where there is not a man at variance, strife ceases"

In Prov 26:20 the first line illustrates the second line: the effect of the absence of a gossip is illustrated by using lack of wood for a fire as an emblem ("For lack of wood the fire goes out, and where there is no whisperer/gossip, quarrel subsides"). The translator, however, recast the negative statement of the comparison as a positive statement and thus produced an antithetical parallelism ("With much wood fire increases, but where there is not a man at variance, strife ceases"). Apart from the translator's general fondness for producing antithetical forms, the alteration here is perhaps also due to the influence of the immediate context. In the following verse, "the fire," which is compared to "a quarrel," is burning and the quarrelling of a quarrelsome man is like piling fuel on the fire. Perhaps the translator wanted to make the comparison with wood and a burning fire in both verses agree with each other.

3. Prov 27:15

MT: דֶּלֶף טוֹרֵד בְּיוֹם סַגְרִיר וְאֵשֶׁת מִדְיָנִים נִשְׁתָּוָה
"A continual dripping on a day of steady rain, and a contentious woman are alike"[229]

LXX: σταγόνες ἐκβάλλουσιν ἄνθρωπον ἐν ἡμέρᾳ χειμερινῇ ἐκ τοῦ οἴκου αὐτοῦ ὡσαύτως καὶ γυνὴ λοίδορος ἐκ τοῦ ἰδίου οἴκου
"Drops drive a man out of his house on a wintry day, so a railing woman also (drives him) out of his own house"

In Prov 27:15 the emblem in the first line is compared to a contentious woman: both are irritating and unbearable ("A continual dripping on a day of steady rain, and a contentious woman are alike"). The translator, however, spelled out what he assumed was the point of comparison by adding ἐκβάλλουσιν ἄνθρωπον . . . ἐκ τοῦ οἴκου αὐτοῦ "drive a man out of his house" (first half) and similarly in the second half he added ἐκ τοῦ ἰδίου οἴκου "out of his own house," thus producing a more explicit and parallel structure ("Drops drive a man out of his house on a wintry day, so a railing woman also (drives him) out of his own house)."

To sum up, in the emblematic parallelisms the translator sought to make the point of comparison clearer and at the same time he produced lines that are more

---

[228] At variance; neologism, according to J. Lust, E. Eynikel, and K. Hauspie, comps., *A Greek–English Lexicon of the Septuagint: Part I, A-I* (Deutsche Bibelgesellschaft, 1992), 115.

[229] There is a similar line in Prov 19:13b.

closely parallel. Although the above cases are normally not regarded as text-critical, they support the translator's fondness for closely corresponding lines.

1.2.1.5.5 Less closely parallel or single-sentence constructions

Most of the Hebrew constructions treated in this section consist of a single sentence and are less closely parallel forms, while some of them may not be regarded as parallelisms at all.

1. Prov 7:17

MT: נַפְתִּי מִשְׁכָּבִי מֹר אֲהָלִים וְקִנָּמוֹן
"I have perfumed my bed with myrrh, aloes, and cinnamon"

LXX: διέρραγκα τὴν κοίτην μου κρόκῳ[230] τὸν δὲ οἶκόν μου κινναμώμῳ
"I have sprinkled my couch with saffron/crocus, and my house with cinnamon"

Prov 7:17 is one sentence with three constituents ("I have perfumed my bed with myrrh, aloes, and cinnamon"). The LXX translation is clearly a more parallel structure due to the translator's love for symmetry. Apparently he added τὸν ... οἶκόν μου "my house" (second colon) as a parallel to τὴν κοίτην μου "my couch" (first colon), and dropped the noun phrase אֲהָלִים "aloes."[231]

2. Prov 21:24

MT: זֵד יָהִיר לֵץ שְׁמוֹ עוֹשֶׂה בְּעֶבְרַת זָדוֹן
"The proud, haughty person, named 'Scoffer,' acts with arrogant pride"

LXX: θρασὺς καὶ αὐθάδης καὶ ἀλαζὼν λοιμὸς καλεῖται ὃς δὲ μνησικακεῖ παράνομος
"A bold and self-willed and insolent man is called a pest, and he who remembers injuries is a transgressor"

---

[230] For מֹר "myrrh" (from Arabia) the translator may have substituted κρόκῳ "saffron/crocus" (a local plant). "SAFFRON *(Crocus sativus)* . . . An Egyptian papyrus dated as early as 2000 B.C.E. mentions this plant. . . . Many Jews in the Middle Ages were spice merchants; they were called 'saffron merchants,' and over the ages the yellow color of the spice has been used to mock Jews (cf. the yellow 'Star of David' that the Nazis required Jews to wear)." "Saffron," I. & W. Jacob, "Flora," n.p., *ABD on CD-ROM*. Version 2.1, 1997.

[231] G. Gerleman lists this example among cases the lines of which are more conformable, balanced and made congruent one with another. Gerleman, *Studies*, 24.

The saying in Prov 21:24 defines the scoffer and describes his typical activity[232] ("The proud, haughty person, named 'Scoffer,' acts with arrogant pride"). The syntactical construction is not perfectly clear,[233] but it consists of a single sentence, whereas the translator produced two clauses that have some correspondence: θρασὺς καὶ αὐθάδης καὶ ἀλαζών "A bold and self-willed and insolent man" (first colon) corresponds somewhat with ὃς ... μνησικακεῖ "he who remembers injuries" (second colon) and λοιμὸς καλεῖται "is called a pest" (first colon) with παράνομος "is a transgressor" (second colon). Thus the LXX can be regarded as more nearly parallel structurally.

To sum up, the translator in rendering the single-sentence constructions produced lines that are more nearly parallel structurally and/or semantically. Therefore caution needs to be taken when using such constructions as variant readings, cf. 3.3.1.5.4.

1.2.1.5.6 Near-synonymous parallelisms with three parts

The parallelisms treated in this section consist of phrases or clauses that are often less complete, e.g., verbless and elliptical constructions.

1. Prov 3:18

MT: עֵץ־חַיִּים הִיא לַמַּחֲזִיקִים בָּהּ וְתֹמְכֶיהָ מְאֻשָּׁר
"She is a tree of life to those who lay hold of her, and those who hold her fast, (each one) is called happy"

LXX: ξύλον ζωῆς ἐστι πᾶσι τοῖς ἀντεχομένοις αὐτῆς καὶ τοῖς ἐπερειδομένοις ἐπ' αὐτὴν ὡς ἐπὶ κύριον ἀσφαλής
"She is a tree of life to all who lay hold upon her, and she is a secure help to all who stay themselves on her, as on the Lord"

Prov 3:18 may be regarded as near-synonymous parallelism consisting of three parts.[234] In the MT "wisdom" is described in the first colon as עֵץ־חַיִּים "tree of life," but in the second colon there is no description of her ("She is a tree of life to those who lay hold of her, and those who hold her fast, (each one) is called happy"). In the LXX rendering, however, both colons describe "wisdom" in a parallel manner. In the first half she is described as ξύλον ζωῆς "tree of life" (as in the Hebrew) and in the second half she is ἀσφαλής "a secure help" ("She is a tree of life to all who lay hold upon her, and she is a secure help to all who stay

---

[232] Clifford, *Proverbs*, 193.

[233] Toy, *Proverbs*, 408.

[234] Watson lists this case under "tricolon." Watson, *Classical*, 183. See also the translation of Meinhold, *Sprüche*, 78.

themselves on her, as on the Lord"[235]). Thus the adaptation of the second colon may be regarded as translational.

2. Prov 6:10

MT: מְעַט שֵׁנוֹת מְעַט תְּנוּמוֹת מְעַט חִבֻּק יָדַיִם לִשְׁכָּב
"A little sleep, a little slumber, a little folding of the hands to rest"

LXX: ὀλίγον μὲν ὑπνοῖς ὀλίγον δὲ κάθησαι μικρὸν δὲ νυστάζεις ὀλίγον δὲ ἐναγκαλίζῃ χερσὶν στήθη
"A little sleep (or: You sleep a little), and you rest a little, and you slumber a small (time), and you fold your arms over your breast a little"

While Prov 6:10 in the MT consists of three near-synonymous parts ("A little sleep, a little slumber, a little folding of the hands to rest"), apparently the translator added a fourth part ("A little sleep, *and you rest a little*, and you slumber a small time, and you fold your arms over your breast a little"). The clause ὀλίγον δὲ κάθησαι "and you rest a little" (second part) seems to be added in parallel with the first part מְעַט שֵׁנוֹת "A little sleep" (ὀλίγον μὲν ὑπνοῖς) presumably to produce a corresponding line[236] and also to make the rendering more suitable by using a verb in the second person[237] (similarly in parts three and four). Also, the final word לִשְׁכָּב "to rest" has been dropped in the translation in favor of a rendering that is more closely parallel to the previous parts. Thus the LXX rendering is clearly a more parallel form structurally.[238]

3. Prov 6:23

MT: כִּי נֵר מִצְוָה וְתוֹרָה אוֹר וְדֶרֶךְ חַיִּים תּוֹכְחוֹת מוּסָר
"For the commandment is a lamp, and the teaching a light, and the reproofs of discipline are the way of life"

---

[235] The simile "as on the Lord" seems to be an addition. For "similes" in Proverbs see Tauberschmidt, "Principles," 72, 144, 145.

[236] H. St. J. Thackeray lists this case under "Hexameter endings," Thackeray, "Poetry," 52, and so does G. Gerleman along with Prov 24:33, Gerleman, *Studies*, 16, which speaks in favor of its translational character.

[237] The choice of the second person is for the sake of cohesion with the preceding and following verse.

[238] A similar proverb occurs in Prov 24:33 but without the addition of a line to make it a more parallel form. This shows that even the translator of Proverbs did not apply his translation principles consistently.

LXX: ὅτι λύχνος ἐντολὴ νόμου καὶ φῶς καὶ ὁδὸς ζωῆς ἔλεγχος καὶ παιδεία
"For the commandment of the law is a lamp and a light, and reproof and discipline are the way of life"

Prov 6:23 may be regarded as a near-synonymous parallelism consisting of three parts ("For the commandment is a lamp, and the teaching a light, and the reproofs of discipline are the way of life"). The two stative clauses in Hebrew כִּי נֵר מִצְוָה וְתוֹרָה אוֹר "for the commandment is a lamp and the teaching a light" are rendered by one stative clause ὅτι λύχνος ἐντολὴ νόμου καὶ φῶς "for the commandment of the law is a lamp and a light," corresponding to the one clause in the second colon ("For the commandment of the law is a lamp and a light, and reproof and discipline are the way of life"). In fact, there is a close structural resemblance between the two genitive constructions ἐντολὴ νόμου and ὁδὸς ζωῆς, as well as between the noun phrases λύχνος . . . καὶ φῶς and ἔλεγχος καὶ παιδεία. In addition to the structural resemblance, there is further proof that the translation of the genitive phrase תּוֹכְחוֹת מוּסָר "reproofs of discipline" by two nouns ἔλεγχος καὶ παιδεία "reproof and discipline" is most likely of translational nature. This Hebrew phrase occurs only here as genitive phrase, but the two terms occur quite frequently in reverse order, מוּסָר occurring in the first half of a verse and תּוֹכַחַת in the second half, as in Prov 3:11; 5:12; 12:1; 13:18; 15:10,32. It is possible that the translator was influenced by these occurrences when he separated the genitive phrase. Besides, this kind of adjustment is quite common in his translation, e.g. in Prov 15:33 he also altered a genitive construction into a coordinating phrase and rendered מוּסַר חָכְמָה "a discipline of wisdom" by παιδεία καὶ σοφία "instruction and wisdom."[239] In any case, the parallel structure of the two colons and the consideration of the translator's technique in this regard explain why the translator produced the rendering ἐντολὴ νόμου. J. Cook suggests that this adaptation may have been motivated "with a view to the larger picture" and "to make the point that this is indeed a reference to a Mosaic law."[240] It is possible that this adaptation was partly motivated by a theological bias, but these changes are certainly in line with the translator's technique. Thus the LXX is a more closely parallel couplet due to the translational adjustments made.

---

[239] For this example cf. de Waard, "Septuagint of Proverbs," 309.

[240] Cook, *Proverbs*, 184, 193; and Johann Cook, "The Law in Septuagint Proverbs," *JNSL* 23/1 (1997): 214–215; and Johann Cook, "The Law of Moses in Septuagint Proverbs," *VT* 49:4 (1999): 454–455.

4. Prov 6:35

MT: לֹא־יִשָּׂא פְּנֵי כָל־כֹּפֶר וְלֹא־יֹאבֶה כִּי תַרְבֶּה־שֹּׁחַד
"He will not regard/accept any ransom; neither will he be appeased, though you give many gifts"

LXX: οὐκ ἀνταλλάξεται οὐδενὸς λύτρου τὴν ἔχθραν οὐδὲ μὴ διαλυθῇ πολλῶν δώρων
"He will not give up his enmity for any ransom, neither will he be reconciled for many gifts"

While the near-synonymous verse Prov 6:35 consists of three clauses syntactically ("He will not regard/accept any ransom; neither will he be appeased, though you give many gifts"), the translator reduced it to two clauses that are more closely parallel grammatically ("He will not give up his enmity for any ransom, neither will he be reconciled for many gifts"). The addition of τὴν ἔχθραν "his enmity" is of a translational nature and is due to carrying over the expression of rage (which includes enmity) from the preceding verse 34. According to J. Cook "The whole verse is actually altered semantically and syntactically in order to express this clear intention," which is, "the negative implications of adultery." "Consequently the second hemistich has only one verb, whereas the MT has two."[241] I agree with Cook that the translator altered the whole verse, but to say that all the alterations in the verse are in order to express his intention is only partly true, as it does not leave any space for the translator's general tendency of producing closely corresponding lines. In fact, Cook's analysis of v. 34 is inaccurate. He says, "The Greek translator interprets קִנְאָה a verb as a noun θυμός."[242] The former can hardly be called a verb and the latter is not the corresponding word; rather, ζήλου (or: μεστὸς . . . ζήλου) corresponds to the noun קִנְאָה, similarly in Prov 27:4. As for the rendering θυμός it reflects normally חֵמָה, e.g. Prov 15:1; 16:14; 21:14; 27:4. Thus the statement "It [τὴν ἔχθραν] has the same intention as is the case with θυμός in the previous verse . . ." does not support Cook's point. In my opinion it would be better to first explain the alterations in v. 35, especially the structural changes, in terms of the translator's general predilection for a more nearly parallel form, and then as a second step look at the possibility that the translator may have wished to emphasize the negative implications of adultery. But in any case, the adaptations are of translational (not text-critical) nature.

To sum up, the near-synonymous parallelisms with three parts rendered by two more closely parallel parts give evidence of the translator's love of close

---

[241] Cook, *Proverbs*, 192.

[242] *Ibid.*, 192.

correspondence. This fact needs to be considered when using such parallelisms as variant readings, cf. 3.3.1.5.5.

1.2.1.5.7 Triplets

A triplet, also called "tricolon," may be defined as "A set of three cola forming a single whole, or strophe."[243]

1. Prov 1:27

MT: בְּבֹא כְשׁוֹאָה פַּחְדְּכֶם וְאֵידְכֶם כְּסוּפָה יֶאֱתֶה בְּבֹא עֲלֵיכֶם צָרָה וְצוּקָה
"When terror comes upon you (lit.: your terror) like a storm[244] (alt.: disaster[245]), and your destruction comes like a whirlwind; when distress and anguish come upon you"

LXX: καὶ ὡς ἂν ἀφίκηται ὑμῖν ἄφνω θόρυβος ἡ δὲ καταστροφὴ ὁμοίως καταιγίδι παρῇ καὶ ὅταν ἔρχηται ὑμῖν θλῖψις καὶ πολιορκία ἢ ὅταν ἔρχηται ὑμῖν ὄλεθρος
"And when confusion suddenly comes upon you, and (your) overthrow shall arrive like a tempest; and when tribulation and distress shall come upon you, or when ruin shall come upon you"

In Prov 1:27 there are three colons in the Hebrew (triplet) ("When terror comes upon you like a storm, and your destruction comes like a whirlwind; when distress and anguish come upon you"), whereas in the Greek the translator apparently added a fourth colon at the end of the verse (". . . or when ruin shall come upon you"). This final colon appears to be in parallel with the end of the preceding verse 26 and is introduced by ἢ as is the case with other additions or modifications, as e.g. in 6:8(a) and 7:23. Thus it is possible that the translator simply repeated the last colon of the previous verse with only minor modifications to produce a parallelism of two corresponding colons.[246]

---

[243] Watson, *Classical*, 13. Watson calls it tricolon. *Ibid*.

[244] Cf. Meinhold, *Sprüche*, 1:57; Plöger, *Sprüche*, 12; Clifford, *Proverbs*, 40. Also most of the translations.

[245] Cf. McKane, *Proverbs*, 212.

[246] M. V. Fox does not agree with A. J. Baumgartner who says that the fourth colon was added to provide a parallel to the third line. According to Fox "the LXX does not make major adjustments for literary reasons," Fox, *Proverbs 1–9*, 371–372, but this view cannot be sustained, as the present work shows.

2. Prov 8:34

MT: אַשְׁרֵי אָדָם שֹׁמֵעַ לִי לִשְׁקֹד עַל־דַּלְתֹתַי יוֹם יוֹם לִשְׁמֹר מְזוּזֹת פְּתָחָי
"Happy/blessed is the man who listens to me, watching daily at my doors, waiting at the posts of my doors"

LXX: μακάριος ἀνήρ ὃς εἰσακούσεταί μου καὶ ἄνθρωπος ὃς τὰς ἐμὰς ὁδοὺς φυλάξει ἀγρυπνῶν ἐπ' ἐμαῖς θύραις καθ' ἡμέραν τηρῶν σταθμοὺς ἐμῶν εἰσόδων
"Happy/blessed is the man who shall listen to me, and the person who shall keep my ways, watching daily at my doors, waiting at the posts of my entrances"

Prov 8:34 in the MT consists of three colons ("Happy/blessed is the man who listens to me, watching daily at my doors, waiting at the posts of my doors"), but the LXX translator added a fourth colon in parallel with the first line and following it ("Happy/blessed is the man who shall listen to me, *and the person who shall keep my ways*, watching daily at my doors, waiting at the posts of my entrances"). In the added colon (second clause) ἄνθρωπος "person" corresponds with אָדָם = ἀνήρ "man" (first colon) and τὰς ἐμὰς ὁδοὺς φυλάξει "(he) shall keep my ways" with εἰσακούσεταί μου "(he) shall listen to me"; MT: שֹׁמֵעַ לִי "(he) listens to me." Thus it is most likely that the translator added the second colon to produce a further parallel form.

To sum up, the translator altered triplets into more nearly parallel lines by adding one line, see also in Prov 6:10 treated under "Near-synonymous parallelisms with three parts," 1.2.1.5.6, and applying various other translation techniques. This should be considered when using similar cases as variant readings, cf. 3.3.1.5.6.

1.2.1.5.8 Phrases

Although adaptations towards forms that are more nearly parallel occur mainly at the level of lines, they may also be observed at the phrase level, as the following cases seem to indicate.

1. Prov 3:2a

MT: כִּי אֹרֶךְ יָמִים וּשְׁנוֹת חַיִּים
"for length of days, and years of life ..."

LXX: μῆκος γὰρ βίου καὶ ἔτη ζωῆς
"for length of life, and years of life ..."

In Prov 3:2a ("for length of days, and years of life . . .") יָמִים "days" has been rendered βίου "life," in parallel semantically with ζωῆς "life"; MT: חַיִּים. For a similar case see Prov 5:9, 3.3.1.1.

In Prov 3:16 the translator rendered אֹרֶךְ יָמִים by the same construction μῆκος γὰρ βίου καὶ ἔτη ζωῆς, probably due to the influence of v. 2.[247]

2. Prov 22:29a

MT: חָזִיתָ אִישׁ מָהִיר בִּמְלַאכְתּוֹ
"Do you see a man who is diligent (or: skilful) in his business? . . ."

LXX: ὁρατικὸν ἄνδρα καὶ ὀξὺν ἐν τοῖς ἔργοις αὐτοῦ
"(It is fit that) an observant man (of mental vision) and one who is diligent in his business . . ."

In Prov 22:29a the translator recast the rhetorical question ("Do you see a man who is diligent in his business? . . .") as a statement and rendered חָזִיתָ אִישׁ freely by ὁρατικὸν ἄνδρα "an observant man" as a near parallel to the following phrase מָהִיר בִּמְלַאכְתּוֹ = ὀξὺν ἐν τοῖς ἔργοις αὐτοῦ "one who is diligent/skilful in his business."

To sum up, the translator's predilection for close correspondence may be even observed on the phrase level.

1.2.1.6 Conclusion, Application and Further Discussion

The translator's fondness for producing renderings that are more nearly parallel forms can be observed in his adjustment of less-synonymous/antonymous lexical items to form pairs that correspond more closely and in his expressing poetic language and figures of speech more straightforwardly to achieve closer corresponding colons. The translator not only adjusted near-synonymous parallelisms but also transformed such parallelisms into antithetical forms with a close contrastive correspondence. He also rendered antithetical parallelisms with a clearer contrast compared to his Hebrew source text.

In addition, the translator's predilection for closely corresponding lines, particularly semantically, is apparent in his renderings of parallelisms of logical relations, parallelisms of addition relations, parallelisms of comparisons,

---

[247] In other cases he rendered יוֹם phrases literally, e.g. 10:27; 24:10; 25:19; or he used the more natural χρόνος "period of time" e.g. 15:15; 28:16. J. Weingreen too rules out the likelihood of a variant textual tradition in 3:2,16, but he regards the dual expressions as added notes from Proverbs or other books of the Hebrew Bible according to Rabbinic fashion. Weingreen, "Rabbinic-Type Commentary," 411. E. Tov, however, regards καὶ ἔτη ζωῆς (3:2,16) as "detail beyond the MT" and lists it under "Differences due to the *Vorlage*." Tov, "Recensional Differences," 49.

emblematic parallelisms, and furthermore in less parallel structures that consist of a single sentence, near-synonymous parallelisms with three parts, triplets, and even some phrases.

G. Gerleman, however, expresses a contrary view with regard to synonymous parallelism:

> In the old Hebrew poetry the synonymous parallelism strongly prevails, the same idea being repeated with new words but without antithesis. While cherished by the Orientals this mode of expression is wholly foreign to the Greeks.[248]

> In Hebrew text the dislike of synonymous parallels, as well as the predilection for sharp antitheses, parisosis etc. remains unintelligible, whereas they are easily understood when connected with the translator's familiarity with Greek literary tradition. It is in accordance with this literary tradition that the translator has, sometimes rather roughly, remoulded his original.[249]

Gerleman sees clearly the translator's predilection for sharp antitheses, that is, lines that have a closer correspondence antithetically, as these are common in the Greek literary tradition (cf. 1.2.1.3; 1.2.1.4). However, he gives little attention to the lines that correspond closer synonymously because they are, although not "wholly foreign to the Greeks," less frequent in Greek.[250] Some such cases he does mention, with the following explanations: "Obviously parallel sentences in their Greek garb are much more conformable mutually than

---

[248] Gerleman, *Studies*, 17.

[249] *Ibid.*, 25–26.

[250] τὸ μήτε ἀλγεῖν κατὰ σῶμα μήτε ταράττεσθαι κατὰ ψυχήν "neither to feel any pain in the body nor any disturbance in the soul." Epic. Men. 131, quoted in W. Heilmann, et al., *τύποι Griechische Kurzgrammatik*, 130. See also Perseus Project, G. Crane, ed., "**3042. Pleonasm** (pleonasmos excess), or redundancy, is the admission of a word or words which are not necessary to the complete logical expression of the thought. Such words, though logically superfluous, enrich the thought by adding greater definiteness and precision, picturesqueness, vigour and emphasis; and by expressing subtle shadings of feeling otherwise impossible. Cp. 'All ye inhabitants of the world, and dwellers on the earth.'" "**i.** Amplification by synonymous doublets (especially common in Demosthenes): . . . I beg and beseech Dem. 18.6; . . . visible and clear 14.4. **j.** Parallelism of positive and negative: . . . I will tell you and I will not conceal my opinion on these matters Dem. 8.73; . . . not unbidden but invited Thuc. 6.87." See also G. O. Rowe, "Style," in *Handbook of Classical Rhetoric*, 133 under (12) Synonymia . . . "This *takes away their boldness*, this *twists back their tongues*, *blocks their mouths*, *chokes*, *makes them silent*." (D. *On the Fraudulent Embassy* 19:208).

they are in the MT."[251] And: "Often LXX Prov has two synonymous or nearly synonymous words instead of the single expression of the Hebrew text. These sets of synonyms, so it would seem, not seldom aim at equalizing parallel lines by enlarging one line as to becoming materially conformable to its parallel."[252]

There is much evidence that the translator adapted his source text in order to produce lines that are more closely parallel, not only in the case of near-antithetical parallelisms, but also in the case of near-synonymous forms. This is because the translator applied the principle of cohesion (see below and cf. 2.1) to both types of parallelism. The application of this same principle of cohesion to higher units of discourse beyond the couplet level, however, at times led to less parallel renderings (cf. 2.1.2).

At this point it may be helpful to consider the linguistic feature of cohesion.[253] According to M. A. K. Halliday and R. Hasan cohesion may be divided into grammatical cohesion and lexical cohesion. Cohesion is expressed partly through grammar (the more general meanings) and partly through vocabulary (the more specific meanings).[254] Grammatical cohesion deals with reference, substitution and ellipsis, and conjunction, whereas lexical cohesion deals with the vocabulary or lexical items, e.g. same word (repetition), synonyms/antonyms, near-synonyms/antonyms, superordinate, and word pairs.[255]

Concerning the effect of the two types of cohesion Halliday and Hasan write:

> The effect of lexical, especially collocational, cohesion on a text is subtle and difficult to estimate. With grammatical cohesion the effect is relatively clear: if one comes across the word *he*, for example, there is no doubt that some essential information is called for, and that the identity of the *he* must be recovered from somewhere.

---

[251] Gerleman, *Studies*, 24–25.

[252] *Ibid.*, 25. B. Gemser mentions various areas in which LXX Proverbs continually and intentionally Hellenizes among which he mentions e.g. "Synonyma, Parallelismen," whereby he refers especially to G. Gerleman's research. *Sprüche Salomos*, 9–10.

[253] "The term [cohesion] is used by some linguists to refer to the property of larger units than the MORPHEME to bind together in CONSTRUCTIONS, e.g. ARTICLE + NOUN. In this use, any group of words which acts as a CONSTITUENT of a larger unit can be said to be internally cohesive. In the HALLIDAYAN approach to grammatical analysis, cohesion is a major concept, referring to those SURFACE-STRUCTURE features of an UTTERANCE or TEXT which link different parts of SENTENCES or larger units of DISCOURSE, e.g. the cross-referencing function of PRONOUNS, ARTICLES and some types of ADVERB (as in ***The*** *man went to town.* ***However,*** *he did not stay long* . . .)." Crystal, *Dictionary*, 60–61.

[254] M. A. K. Halliday and Ruqaiya Hasan, *Cohesion in English* (Longman, 1976), 5.

[255] *Ibid.*, 31–292.

> Reference items, substitutes and conjunctions all explicitly presuppose some element other than themselves.
>
> In lexical cohesion, however, it is not a case of there being particular lexical items which always have a cohesive function. EVERY lexical item MAY enter into a cohesive relation, but by itself it carries no indication whether it is functioning cohesively or not. That can be established only by reference to the text.[256]

The effect of grammatical cohesion is more dominant than that of lexical cohesion. So it is not surprising that grammatical cohesion at times overruled the translator's tendency to produce more closely parallel lines. In other words, the application of grammatical cohesion led to less closely parallel forms due to the translator's concern to connect the units more closely; at the couplet level, however, the translator was concerned to produce closely corresponding lines with a high degree of cohesiveness. To achieve what is called "lexical cohesion" he used more synonymous and antonymous word and phrase pairs in his translation, as "the selection of vocabulary items from a common semantic domain adds greatly to the cohesion of a text."[257] Such vocabulary items according to M. L. Larson may be "**synonyms, antonyms, substitution** of more generic words for specific words, **parallel expressions** and so forth."[258]

While the emphasis in section 1.2.1 has been on the semantic relationships of parallelisms, the translator's propensity for modification is not limited to the semantic aspect but often influences the grammar as well in direction of more symmetrical forms, as in e.g. Prov 1:24,27; 3:9; 6:10,35; 7:17; 8:34; 11:21, 22,24; 17:26; 19:28; 21:24; 27:15; 29:4.

Having dealt with the semantic relationships of Hebrew parallelisms and how these forms were altered in the direction of closer corresponding colons, we shall now look at Hebrew parallelisms from a structural viewpoint and how the translator of Proverbs changed these grammatical structures.[259]

---

[256] *Ibid.*, 288.

[257] Larson, *Meaning-based*, 395.

[258] *Ibid.* According to A. Healey, "The lexical unity of a paragraph is signalled by the repetition of roots, words or phrases, and by the occurrence of synonyms, pairs of generic-specific terms, terms in the same semantic domain, and antonyms. The lexical cohesion of a paragraph is signalled by the patterned order in which such lexically related terms occur. Some of the common patterns are listing (B C D E), direct parallelism (AB AC AD AE), contrastive parallelism (FBG HBI), reciprocal parallelism (FBG GBF), the sandwich effect (J B C D E J), and chiasmus (B C C B)." A. Healey, "The Role of Function Words in the Paragraph Structure of Koine Greek," *NOT* 69 (June 1978): 2.

[259] Note: Some of the examples are dealt with under both sections of the thesis due to the separate treatment of the semantic and grammatical aspects.

1.2.2 GRAMMATICAL RELATIONSHIPS

In grammatical parallelisms, according to A. Berlin, "many parallelisms . . . employ lines of different surface structure which can be related back, using the methodology of transformational grammar, to the same underlying deep structure."[260] It is true that the surface structure may be the same in both lines (e.g. Ps 103:10), but it ". . . is identical in only a small percentage of cases."[261] This is supported by the occurrences of the many grammatical combinations discussed below.

Similarly E. L. Greenstein, who recognizes the importance of differentiating surface structure and deep structure, states:

> Where two lines have different surface structures, I first try to examine their deep structures before determining whether they are parallel.[262]

Various grammatical pairs or combinations that can be found in the MT of Proverbs (or elsewhere in the Hebrew Bible) are treated below.

1.2.2.1 Second Person, Paired with Impersonal Construction

In Prov 1:24 ("Because I have called and you refused to listen, I have stretched out my hand and no one has heeded"), see also 1.2.1.2, the translator made the second half parallel to the first half in that he changed the impersonal Hebrew participle construction וְאֵין מַקְשִׁיב "no one has heeded" to second person οὐ προσείχετε "you gave no heed" so as to correspond to the verb of the first colon ὑπηκούσατε "you did not listen." The translator's concern for exactly parallel structure and symmetry can be seen here ("Because I called, and you did not listen, and I spoke at length, and you gave no heed"). In addition to the agreement in number, both verbs are negated by οὐχ/οὐ. In the MT, however, the verb in the first colon is already negative semantically, מאן "refuse," and is thus not negated.

---

[260] Berlin, "Parallelism," n.p.

[261] Berlin, *Dynamics*, 31.

[262] E. L. Greenstein, "How Does Parallelism Mean? A Sense of Text," *JQRS* (1982): 41–70, here 45, fn. 14.

1.2.2.2 Preposition plus Adjective, Paired with Noun

Prov 13:20

MT: הוֹלֵךְ אֶת־חֲכָמִים וַחֲכָם וְרֹעֶה כְסִילִים יֵרוֹעַ[263]
"He who walks with the wise will be wise, but he who consorts with fools will suffer harm"

LXX: ὁ συμπορευόμενος σοφοῖς σοφὸς ἔσται ὁ δὲ συμπορευόμενος ἄφροσι γνωσθήσεται
"He who walks with the wise will be wise, but he who walks with fools will be known"

Although the LXX of Prov 13:20 is a less nearly parallel couplet in one respect due to reading the Hebrew differently, see 2.2.2, it is more symmetrical structurally because ὁ συμπορευόμενος σοφοῖς "He who walks with the wise" (first colon) corresponds closely to ὁ δὲ συμπορευόμενος ἄφροσι "but he who walks with fools" (second colon). The verbs are identical[264] and the predicate nouns in both cases are in the dative. But the MT, although semantically similar, has a slightly different grammatical structure: הוֹלֵךְ אֶת־חֲכָמִים . . . וְרֹעֶה כְסִילִים "He who walks with the wise . . . but he who consorts with fools." Aside from the fact that the verbs differ slightly, the construction in the first half consists of a preposition plus adjective, whereas in the second half a noun is used.

1.2.2.3 Personal Object, Paired with Impersonal Object

Prov 9:6

MT: עִזְבוּ פְתָאיִם וִחְיוּ וְאִשְׁרוּ בְּדֶרֶךְ בִּינָה
"Forsake the foolish, and live; and go in the way of understanding"

LXX: ἀπολείπετε ἀφροσύνην καὶ ζήσεσθε καὶ ζητήσατε φρόνησιν ἵνα βιώσητε καὶ κατορθώσατε ἐν γνώσει σύνεσιν
"Leave folly and live, and seek insight that you shall live, and go straight (succeed) in understanding by knowledge"

---

[263] With Qere.

[264] G. Gerleman lists this case under anaphora due to the repetition of the same word. Gerleman, *Studies*, 14.

In Prov 9:6 ("Forsake the foolish, and live; and go in the way of understanding") the translator apparently paraphrased[265] the personal object פְּתָאיִם "the foolish," rendering ἀφροσύνην "folly" so as to make a parallel to the impersonal object בִּינָה "understanding" (σύνεσιν) in the second half. Furthermore the translator added: καὶ ζητήσατε φρόνησιν ἵνα[266] βιώσητε "and seek insight that you shall live," thus making a parallel with the first colon, except that the first line ἀπολείπετε ἀφροσύνην "leave folly" is negative and the second line ζητήσατε φρόνησιν "seek insight" is positive. But this added line connects more smoothly with the following line which is also positive ("Leave folly and live, and seek insight that you shall live, and go straight (succeed) in understanding by knowledge"). In addition, the verbs that follow the two parts mentioned are quite parallel too, ζήσεσθε and βιώσητε "you shall live" corresponding closely. Thus the translator's concern to produce corresponding lines and phrases is apparent.[267]

1.2.2.4 *Second Person Imperfect (and Third Person Object), Paired with Third Person Imperfect (and Second Person Object)*

Prov 6:25

MT: אַל־תַּחְמֹד יָפְיָהּ בִּלְבָבֶךָ וְאַל־תִּקָּחֲךָ בְּעַפְעַפֶּיהָ
"Do not desire her beauty in your heart, and do not let her capture you with her eyelashes/eyelids[268]"

LXX: μή σε νικήσῃ κάλλους ἐπιθυμία μηδὲ ἀγρευθῇς σοῖς ὀφθαλμοῖς μηδὲ συναρπασθῇς ἀπὸ τῶν αὐτῆς βλεφάρων
"Let not the desire of beauty overcome you, neither be caught by your eyes, neither be captivated with her eyelids"

In Prov 6:25 the first half warns the man not to desire the woman's beauty and the second half changes to the activity of the "evil woman,"[269] this being reflected in the shift of the verb form from second person to third person ("Do

---

[265] This is supported by McKane, *Proverbs*, 361.

[266] This connector is often not a literal representation of the Hebrew text, e.g. 3:6,19,22,23,26; 4:8,9 et al., and 4:10 where it introduces a translational addition.

[267] J. Cook too regards the deviations in the LXX as probably having come from the translator. Cook, *Proverbs*, 254–259, especially 256.

[268] NIV translates "eyes." But according to Ross, The "'Eyes' are singled out here because the painted eyes and the luring glances are symptoms of seduction (see 2 Kgs 9:30)." Ross, "Proverbs," n.p. See also *IB*, 4:822.

[269] According to W. McKane the "evil woman" vv. 24–25 is married. McKane, *Proverbs*, 329.

not desire her beauty in your heart, and do not let her capture you with her eyelashes/eyelids"). The translator, however, rendered all three verbs in the second person for reasons of cohesion ("Let not the desire of beauty overcome you, neither be caught by your eyes, neither be captivated with her eyelids"). He dropped בִּלְבָבֶךָ "in your heart" and rendered instead σε νικήσῃ "(beauty) overcome you" (first colon). This translational change may have been what led to adding an additional colon with the more specific σοῖς ὀφθαλμοῖς "by your eyes" (second colon) thus producing a closely corresponding form with a generic–specific relationship. The second half of the MT is reflected semantically in the third colon of the LXX, but the grammatical structures of cola two and three correspond more closely. This can be seen clearly in μηδὲ ἀγρευθῇς "neither be caught" and μηδὲ συναρπασθῇς "neither be captivated," whereas the MT has third person imperfect (and second person object). Thus it is likely that the whole verse in the LXX is a product of the translator, the second colon being his addition. J. Cook thinks that the translator perhaps added the third stich.[270] It is true that the third colon bears traces of translational adjustments, but it still seems to reflect the second line of the MT. This view is in line with SH where the third colon is regarded as being closer to the Hebrew, whereas the second colon is judged as OG.[271] However, according to C. T. Fritsch, the third colon is Hexaplaric, whereas according to my analysis, the verse as it stands can be explained perfectly well on the basis of the translator's technique.

1.2.2.5 Imperative, Paired with Imperfect

Prov 4:26

MT: פַּלֵּס מַעְגַּל רַגְלֶךָ וְכָל־דְּרָכֶיךָ יִכֹּנוּ
"Keep straight (or: watch) the path of your feet, and all your ways will be sure/secure/established[272]"

LXX: ὀρθὰς τροχιὰς ποίει σοῖς ποσὶν καὶ τὰς ὁδούς σου κατεύθυνε
"Make straight paths for your feet, and order your ways aright"

Prov 4:26 may be regarded as a near-parallel couplet, the second half focusing on the result ("Keep straight the path of your feet, and all your ways will be secure"). In the MT the first verb פַּלֵּס "make straight" is in the imperative mood and the second יִכֹּנוּ "they will be sure/secure" in the imperfective aspect. The

---

[270] Cook, *Proverbs*, 187.

[271] Fritsch, "Hexaplaric Signs," 173.

[272] Cf. REB, NRSV, McKane, *Proverbs*, 217. An alternative but less popular translation is "and let all your ways be correct" Delitzsch, *Proverbs*, 1:114. Similarly NCV.

LXX, however, appears to be more closely parallel at least grammatically, and probably semantically too, as both verbs ποίει "make" and κατεύθυνε "order" are in the imperative mood, active voice, and present tense/aspect ("Make straight paths for your feet, and order your ways aright"). This case demonstrates quite clearly the translator's tendency to make the parallel lines more symmetrical.

1.2.2.6 Construct Form, Paired with Participle

Prov 12:4

MT: אֵשֶׁת־חַיִל עֲטֶרֶת בַּעְלָהּ וּכְרָקָב בְּעַצְמוֹתָיו מְבִישָׁה
"A virtuous woman is a crown to her husband, but she who brings shame is like rottenness in his bones"

LXX: γυνὴ ἀνδρεία στέφανος τῷ ἀνδρὶ αὐτῆς ὥσπερ δὲ
ἐν ξύλῳ σκώληξ οὕτως ἄνδρα ἀπόλλυσιν γυνὴ κακοποιός
"A virtuous woman is a crown to her husband, but as a worm in wood, so an ill-doing woman destroys her husband"

In Prov 12:4 there are two comparisons, one in each line. The one in the first line contains a metaphor and the one in the antithetically parallel line a simile[273] ("A virtuous woman is a crown to her husband, but she who brings shame is like rottenness in his bones"). Grammatically a genitive or construct relationship אֵשֶׁת־חַיִל "a virtuous woman" (first half) is paired with a participle מְבִישָׁה "she who makes ashamed" (second half). The LXX ("A virtuous woman is a crown to her husband, but as a worm in wood, so an ill-doing woman destroys her husband"), however, appears to be more closely parallel in regard to γυνὴ κακοποιός "ill-doing woman" (second colon), as this noun phrase (noun-adj.) may be an adaptation to make a parallel with אֵשֶׁת־חַיִל = γυνὴ ἀνδρεία (noun-adj.) in place of the participle מְבִישָׁה. As for the simile in the LXX, the translator may be held responsible for making the point of comparison more explicit than in the MT. This is not surprising considering the translator's handling of similes, cf. 1:12b; 3:12; 7:22; 11:28; etc.[274]

---

[273] R. Alter sees intensification in the second line as he writes, "A relatively simple maneuver is to match a rather bland simile [or rather metaphor] in the first verset with a more vehement one representing the complementary opposite case in the second verset." Alter, *Art*, 174.

[274] In addition it may be mentioned that one of the translator's favorite words is ἀπώλεια; here the verb is used, which he added for emphasis, e.g. 1:26; 11:6; 13:1,15; 16:26.

1.2.2.7 Direct Quotation, Paired with Direct Quotation

Prov 20:9

MT: מִי־יֹאמַר זִכִּיתִי לִבִּי טָהַרְתִּי מֵחַטָּאתִי
"Who can say, 'I have purified my heart; I am clean from my sin?'"

LXX: τίς καυχήσεται ἁγνὴν ἔχειν τὴν καρδίαν ἢ τίς παρρησιάσεται καθαρὸς εἶναι ἀπὸ ἁμαρτιῶν
"Who will boast that he has a pure heart? Or who will boldly say that he is clean from sins?"

In Prov 20:9 the affirmation that no one can claim to be pure in heart or without sin is made using a rhetorical question[275] ("Who can say, 'I have purified my heart; I am clean from my sin?'"). In the LXX there are several translational adjustments in the direction of a more natural and parallel rendering. First, the translator took the liberty of expressing the direct speech quotation by indirect speech.[276] This kind of translational adjustment can be observed also in other more freely translated LXX books, such as Genesis (3:17; 26:7, 20) and Deuteronomy (11:13–14). Then, καυχήσεται ". . . will boast" (first colon) is used in place of יֹאמַר ". . . will say," explicating the manner in which that speech is uttered, and in parallel with it παρρησιάσεται ". . . will boldly say" (second colon) is used in place of the elliptical construction in the MT. Also τίς "who" (second line) is repeated in parallel with τίς in the first line ("Who will boast that he has a pure heart? Or who will boldly say that he is clean from sins?"). Thus the LXX is a clearly more closely parallel couplet structurally than the MT.[277]

1.2.2.8 Direct Quotation, Paired with Indirect Quotation

Prov 7:4

MT: אֱמֹר לַחָכְמָה אֲחֹתִי אָתְּ וּמֹדָע לַבִּינָה תִקְרָא
"Say to wisdom, 'You are my sister,' and call insight your intimate friend"

---

[275] See also McKane, *Proverbs*, 548. Meinhold, *Sprüche*, 2:335. Ross, "Proverbs," n.p.

[276] "Speech quotations may be expressed differently in different languages. Direct or indirect speech may be preferred. In Hebrew direct speech is used quite frequently as can be seen in the MT, whereas in Greek it is less frequent. Some LXX translators tried to adapt to the Greek way of expressing quotations, that is, where Hebrew expressed such quotations in direct speech they translated these by using indirect speech." Tauberschmidt, "Principles," 94.

[277] G. Gerleman lists this example among cases the lines of which are more conformable, balanced and made congruent one with another. Gerleman, *Studies*, 25.

LXX: εἶπον τὴν σοφίαν σὴν ἀδελφὴν εἶναι τὴν δὲ φρόνησιν γνώριμον περιποίησαι σεαυτῷ
"Say that wisdom is your sister, and gain prudence as an acquaintance for yourself"

Both the MT ("Say to wisdom, 'You are my sister,' and call insight your intimate friend") as well as the LXX of Prov 7:4 ("Say that wisdom is your sister, and gain prudence as an acquaintance for yourself") may be regarded as parallel semantically. Grammatically, however, the translation is more symmetrical since the direct speech quotation in the first half is rendered by indirect speech paralleling the second half. Again, this is clearly a translational device.[278]

1.2.2.9 Exclamation with מָה־, Paired with Statement

Prov 30:13

MT: דּוֹר מָה־רָמוּ עֵינָיו וְעַפְעַפָּיו יִנָּשֵׂאוּ
"There is a generation,[279] O how lofty are their eyes! and their eyelids are lifted up"

LXX: ἔκγονον κακὸν ὑψηλοὺς ὀφθαλμοὺς ἔχει τοῖς δὲ βλεφάροις αὐτοῦ ἐπαίρεται
"A wicked generation have lofty eyes, and exalt themselves with their eyelids"

Prov 30:13 is a fairly parallel couplet in meaning but not in form. Apparently the translator altered the exclamation with מָה־ "O how (lofty are their eyes!)" into a statement ". . . have lofty eyes" (first colon) and thus produced a more closely parallel form grammatically with the statement in the second colon.

1.2.2.10 Elliptical Constructions

An elliptical construction is a construction where, for reasons of economy, emphasis or style, a part of the structure has been omitted. The element that is lacking is recoverable or inferable from the context.[280]

---

[278] See Tauberschmidt, "Principles," 94–97.

[279] Watson calls this form with דּוֹר in the beginning of vv.11–14 "*Repetition-initial* where a series of two or more consecutive lines begin with the same word or phrase." Watson, *Classical*, 276.

[280] Crystal, *Dictionary*, 107–108. "Elliptical construction," *LinguaLinks*, n.p. Gerhard Tauberschmidt, *A Grammar of Sinaugoro: An Austronesian Language of the Central Province of Papua New Guinea* (Canberra: Pacific Linguistics, 1999), 91.

Concerning elliptical constructions in Hebrew parallelism A. Berlin writes:

> The words which are gapped or left unparalleled are those which the verse wants to deemphasize; the emphasis is on the words that are repeated or paralleled.[281]

Although ellipsis occurs also in Greek,[282] the translator of LXX Proverbs filled many gaps in elliptical constructions, which supports the theory that he had a predilection for producing more closely parallel lines structurally.[283]

1.2.2.10.1 Complement, omitted in colon B

In Prov 17:26, see under 1.2.1.2, the translator added οὐδὲ ὅσιον "nor holy/pious" (second colon) as a parallel to לא־טוב = οὐ καλόν "not good" (first colon) ("It is not good to punish a righteous man, nor is it holy/pious to plot against righteous princes"), whereas the clause structure of the MT is elliptical[284] ("Also to punish the just is not good, nor to strike princes for equity"). There is a similar elliptical construction in Prov 18:5 where the translator also added οὐδὲ ὅσιον in the second colon to make a parallel with לא־טוב = οὐ καλόν. Thus the LXX is clearly a more closely parallel couplet grammatically, and also semantically as described under 1.2.1.2.

1.2.2.10.2 Verb (or adverb), omitted in one half

In parallel constructions verbs are frequently omitted in the second half, and also in the first half although less frequently, and are paired with a verbal sentence. The translator frequently added verbs in elliptical constructions, and thus produced forms that are more closely parallel structurally, whereas in a literal translation such additions would be lacking.[285] The following are examples.

---

[281] Berlin, *Dynamics*, 96.

[282] "Ellipse occurs in the case of substantives and pronouns, subject, object, finite verbs, main clauses, and (less often) subordinate clauses." *Perseus Project*, Gregory Crane, Editor-in-Chief, Tufts University. Online: www.perseus.tufts.edu.

[283] This is of course not to say that the renderings in this section are more cohesive.

[284] A. Meinhold too mentions the option of taking this construction as elliptical: "Wenn man die Stilfigur der [Ellipse] aus dem Halbvers 'ist nicht gut' ergänzt, könnte der zweite auch übersetzt werden: 'Vornehme zu schlagen wegen (ihrer) Geradheit (ist nicht gut).'" Meinhold, *Sprüche*, 2:293, fn.

[285] Cf. Tauberschmidt, "Principles," 65–67.

1.2.2.10.2.1 *Verb (or adverb), omitted in colon B*

1. Prov 1:12

MT: נִבְלָעֵם כִּשְׁאוֹל חַיִּים וּתְמִימִים כְּיוֹרְדֵי בוֹר
"Let us swallow them up alive as the grave, and whole, as those that go down into the pit"

LXX: καταπίωμεν δὲ αὐτὸν ὥσπερ ᾅδης ζῶντα καὶ ἄρωμεν αὐτοῦ τὴν μνήμην ἐκ γῆς
"and let us swallow him alive, as Hades (would), and remove the memorial of him from the earth"

The two halves in Prov 1:12 correspond closely semantically,[286] but structurally the second half is elliptical ("Let us swallow them up alive as the grave, and whole, as those that go down into the pit"). The translator, however, added ἄρωμεν "let us remove . . ." (second colon) to make a parallel with καταπίωμεν "let us swallow . . .", MT: נִבְלָעֵם "let us swallow them", (first colon).

2. Prov 3:9

For example and further adjustments see 1.2.1.1.

In Prov 3:9 ("Honor the Lord with your wealth, and with the first fruits of all your produce") the translator seems to have added the second verb ἀπάρχου "offer" (second colon) as a parallel to τίμα "honor" (first colon) ("Honor the Lord with your just labors, and offer him the first of your fruits of righteousness"), whereas in the MT כַּבֵּד "honor" governs both clauses.

3. Prov 5:17

MT: יִהְיוּ־לְךָ לְבַדֶּךָ וְאֵין לְזָרִים אִתָּךְ.
"Let them be only your own, and not strangers with you"[287]

LXX: ἔστω σοι μόνῳ ὑπάρχοντα καὶ μηδεὶς ἀλλότριος μετασχέτω σοι
"Let them be only your own, and let no stranger partake with you"

---

[286] See also Meinhold, *Sprüche*, 1:54, who calls the stylistic device employed in this synonymous parallelism "Ballast-Variante."

[287] NLT: "You should reserve it [sex] for yourselves. Don't share it with strangers." See also Ross, "Proverbs," n.p.

In Prov 5:17 the second half repeats the first half but expresses the positive statement negatively with an elliptical construction ("Let them be only your own, and not strangers with you"). The translator, however, supplied the verb μετασχέτω "partake" (second half) in the verbless clause and thus produced a structure that is more closely parallel grammatically.

4. Prov 7:18

MT: לְכָה נִרְוֶה דֹדִים עַד־הַבֹּקֶר נִתְעַלְּסָה בָּאֳהָבִים
"Come, let us drink deep of love until morning, let us delight ourselves with love"

LXX: ἐλθὲ καὶ ἀπολαύσωμεν φιλίας ἕως ὄρθρου δεῦρο καὶ ἐγκυλισθῶμεν ἔρωτι
"Come, and let us enjoy love until the morning, come, and let us embrace in love"

Prov 7:18 is a fairly parallel couplet, but the translator produced an increased symmetry by adding δεῦρο "come" [288] (second colon) in parallel with the first verb in the first colon ἐλθὲ "come"; MT: לְכָה. Thus the parallelism in the LXX appears to be closer grammatically in this respect.

5. Prov 8:20

MT: בְּאֹרַח־צְדָקָה אֲהַלֵּךְ בְּתוֹךְ נְתִיבוֹת מִשְׁפָּט
"I walk in the way of righteousness, in the paths of justice"

LXX: ἐν ὁδοῖς δικαιοσύνης περιπατῶ καὶ ἀνὰ μέσον τρίβων δικαιώματος ἀναστρέφομαι
"I walk in the ways of righteousness, and conduct myself in the paths of justice"

Prov 8:20 is a near-synonymous couplet with an elliptical construction in the second half ("I walk in the way of righteousness, in the paths of justice"). It can be presumed that the translator made the verb ἀναστρέφομαι "I conduct myself" (second colon) explicit in correspondence to περιπατῶ "I walk" (first colon), thus making the structure more closely parallel grammatically. In addition, it may be mentioned that ὁδοῖς "ways" (MT: אֹרַח "way," first colon) has been conformed in number to τρίβων "paths" (MT: נְתִיבוֹת "paths," second colon).

---

[288] Note that the translator did not simply repeat the first verb but for the sake of stylistic variation chose another synonymous verb. See also under 2.1.4.5 Variation and style, in Tauberschmidt, "Principles," 88–90.

SECONDARY PARALLELISM

6. Prov 9:7

MT: יֹסֵר לֵץ לֹקֵחַ לוֹ קָלוֹן וּמוֹכִיחַ לְרָשָׁע מוּמוֹ
"He that reproves a scoffer gets to himself shame, and he that rebukes a wicked man (gets) himself a blemish (or: gets insults for himself; or: gets hurt)[289]"

LXX: ὁ παιδεύων κακοὺς λήμψεται ἑαυτῷ ἀτιμίαν ἐλέγχων δὲ τὸν ἀσεβῆ μωμήσεται ἑαυτόν
"He that reproves evil men shall get dishonor to himself, and he that rebukes an ungodly man shall disgrace himself"

In Prov 9:7, a fairly synonymous parallelism, a verbal clause with לֹקֵחַ "gets" is used in the first line, but in the second line the second verb is omitted ("He that reproves a scoffer gets to himself shame, and he that rebukes a wicked man (gets) himself a blemish"). The translator, however, expressed the elliptical construction מוּמוֹ "blot/blemish for himself" by the verb μωμήσεται (ἑαυτόν) "he shall disgrace (himself)" and thus produced a more closely parallel couplet structurally.

7. Prov 11:24

For example see 1.2.1.4.

In Prov 11:24 יֵשׁ "there is" covers both halves ("There is he who scatters and yet increases, and he who withholds more than is meet, only to his loss"), whereas the translator of Proverbs repeated εἰσὶν "there are" in the second colon and thus produced a more nearly parallel structure grammatically ("There are those who scatter their own and make it more, and there are also those who gather yet have less") In addition, the second clause of the first half consists of a verbal construction וְנוֹסָף עוֹד "and yet increases," whereas the second clause of the second half is introduced by אַךְ־ "only" which is followed by a nominal construction (לְמַחְסוֹר "to his loss"). In the LXX, however, both corresponding clauses are verbal clauses ("make it more" . . . "yet have less") with a high degree of correspondence. Thus the LXX is clearly more nearly parallel grammatically, but also semantically, see 1.2.1.4.

---

[289] A. Meinhold translates "Schaden" and comments: "Mit 'Schaden' ist ein Wort übersetzt, das 'Makel/Flecken' bedeutet und oft für Schäden an Opfertieren . . . , körperliche Gebrechen bei Priestern . . . oder sonstige Beschädigungen von Menschen . . . gebraucht wird." Meinhold, *Sprüche*, 1:157.

8. Prov 24:30

MT: עַל־שְׂדֵה אִישׁ־עָצֵל עָבַרְתִּי וְעַל־כֶּרֶם אָדָם חֲסַר־לֵב
"I passed by the field of a lazy person, and by the vineyard of a man lacking in sense"

LXX: ὥσπερ γεώργιον ἀνὴρ ἄφρων καὶ ὥσπερ ἀμπελὼν ἄνθρωπος ἐνδεὴς φρενῶν
"A foolish man is like a field, and a senseless man is like a vineyard"

Prov 24:30 is a near-synonymous[290] couplet omitting the verb in the second half. In the LXX this case is different from the others discussed above in that the translator instead of adding a verb omitted one to achieve a more closely parallel form. This may be due to rendering the account of the lazy person (Prov 24:30–31)—a literary device of a fictional but characteristically true picture of the sluggard[291]—by using two similes. Cases that may be compared to the present example are Prov 21:1; 25:14,26 where the translator rendered the figure of metaphor as simile.[292] Furthermore, the translator produced a closer correspondence by changing אִישׁ־עָצֵל "lazy person" to ἀνὴρ ἄφρων "a foolish man" (first colon) in parallel with אָדָם חֲסַר־לֵב = ἄνθρωπος ἐνδεὴς φρενῶν "stupid/senseless man" (second colon).

In the following two elliptical constructions the verb is paired with a noun phrase.

9. Prov 8:4

MT: אֲלֵיכֶם אִישִׁים אֶקְרָא וְקוֹלִי אֶל־בְּנֵי אָדָם
"To you, O men, I call, and my voice (is) to the sons of men"

LXX: ὑμᾶς ὦ ἄνθρωποι παρακαλῶ καὶ προίεμαι ἐμὴν φωνὴν υἱοῖς ἀνθρώπων
"You, O men, I exhort, and utter my voice to the sons of men"

In Prov 8:4 the second half of the near-parallel couplet consists of a verbless and elliptical sentence ("To you, O men, I call, and my voice (is) to the sons of men"). The translator, however, added the verb in the second colon, προίεμαι "utter," in parallel with the verb in the first colon, παρακαλῶ "exhort"; MT: אֶקְרָא ("You, O men, I exhort, and utter my voice to the sons of men"). Thus the translator produced a form that is more closely parallel grammatically.

---

[290] Cf. Watson, *Classical*, 139.

[291] Ross, "Proverbs," n.p. Plöger, *Sprüche*, 288.

[292] Cf. Tauberschmidt, "Principles," 71.

10. Prov 8:6

MT: שִׁמְעוּ כִּי־נְגִידִים אֲדַבֵּר וּמִפְתַּח שְׂפָתַי מֵישָׁרִים
"Hear, for I will speak of excellent things, and the opening of my lips (shall be) right things"[293]

LXX: εἰσακούσατέ μου σεμνὰ γὰρ ἐρῶ καὶ ἀνοίσω ἀπὸ χειλέων ὀρθά
"Listen to me, for I will speak solemn (truths), and will bring forth from (my) lips right (sayings)"

Prov 8:6 may be regarded as a near-synonymous couplet with a verbless and elliptical construction in the second half: וּמִפְתַּח שְׂפָתַי "and the opening of my lips" ("Hear, for I will speak of excellent things, and the opening of my lips (shall be) right things"). The translator, however, rendered it by the verb ἀνοίσω "I will bring forth" in parallel with ἐρῶ "I will speak" (first colon) and thus produced a more closely parallel structure.

The last case in this section differs in that the second line consists of a list of nouns.

11. Prov 1:3

MT: לָקַחַת מוּסַר הַשְׂכֵּל צֶדֶק וּמִשְׁפָּט וּמֵישָׁרִים
"to receive instruction in wise dealing,[294] righteousness, and justice, and equity"

LXX: δέξασθαί τε στροφὰς λόγων νοῆσαί τε δικαιοσύνην ἀληθῆ καὶ κρίμα κατευθύνειν
"to receive turning of words (literary craft), and to perceive true justice and to be straight in judgment"

Prov 1:3 may be regarded as a somewhat synonymous parallelism but there is a certain development, the terms in the elliptical construction of the second line showing how "wise dealing" manifests itself.[295] W. G. E. Watson lists this parallelism under "ballast variant" which he defines as "simply a *filler*, its function being to fill out a line of poetry that would otherwise be too short."[296] In any case, in addition to the noun phrases the verbs νοῆσαί "to perceive" and κατευθύνειν "to be straight" are used in the LXX to convey the meaning of

---

[293] W. McKane translates, "Listen, for my speech is *straightforward*, and my utterances plain," but this difference does not affect our argument here. For a discussion see McKane, *Proverbs*, 345–346.

[294] NLT: "Through these proverbs, people will receive instruction in discipline, . . ."

[295] *IB*, 4:782.

[296] Watson, *Classical*, 344–345.

the Hebrew nouns, the former verb being identical with that in the second colon of the previous verse 2.

1.2.2.10.2.2 Verb, omitted in colon A

The verb may be omitted in the first half of the Hebrew parallelism as the following verses demonstrate, although this happens less frequently than omitting the verb in the second half.

1. Prov 8:2

For example see 3.3.1.5.5.

Prov 8:2 is a near-synonymous couplet which has three parts ("On the heights, beside the way, at the crossroads she takes her stand"). These have apparently been reduced to two parts in the LXX ("For she is on the highest places, and stands in the midst of the ways"). As in the following example, the translator added the verb (here ἐστίν ". . . is") in the first colon and so produced a more closely parallel structure.

2. Prov 8:3

MT: לְיַד־שְׁעָרִים לְפִי־קָרֶת מְבוֹא פְתָחִים תָּרֹנָּה
"Beside the gates at the entrance to the city, at the entrance of the gates she cries aloud"

LXX: παρὰ γὰρ πύλαις δυναστῶν παρεδρεύει ἐν δὲ εἰσόδοις ὑμνεῖται
"For she sits by the gates of princes, and sings in the entrances"

In Prov 8:3 the two halves correspond closely semantically, but grammatically the verb תָּרֹנָּה "she cries" in the second colon covers the whole verse ("Beside the gates at the entrance to the city, at the entrance of the gates she cries aloud"). Apparently the translator added the verb παρεδρεύει "she sits" (first colon) to make a structural parallel with ὑμνεῖται "she sings" (second colon) ("For she sits by the gates of princes, and sings in the entrances"). As a further adjustment the translator may have dropped לְפִי־קָרֶת "at the entrance to the city" to produce a more nearly parallel structure with πύλαις "gates"[297] (first colon) corresponding to εἰσόδοις "entrances" (second colon).

The following case differs from the above in that the verb is omitted in a transitive clause provided the MT is not corrupt.

3. Prov 13:1

MT: בֵּן חָכָם מוּסַר אָב וְלֵץ לֹא־שָׁמַע גְּעָרָה
"A wise son (hears) his father's instruction, but a scorner hears not rebuke"

LXX: υἱὸς πανοῦργος ὑπήκοος πατρί υἱὸς δὲ ἀνήκοος ἐν ἀπωλείᾳ
"A wise son is obedient to his father, but a disobedient son will be destroyed"

Prov 13:1 is antithetically a near-parallel couplet with an elliptical sentence in the first half if we take the MT as it stands[298] ("A wise son (hears) his father's instruction, but a scorner hears not rebuke"), although it has often been regarded as corrupt.[299] As for the LXX, apparently the translator supplied the adjective ὑπήκοος "obedient" in the first colon, and in parallel with it he rendered less literally ἀνήκοος "disobedient" for לֹא־שָׁמַע "hears not" (second colon). Along with this adaptation, the translator repeated υἱὸς "son" in the second colon in parallel with υἱὸς in the first colon. Thus considering these alterations the LXX is a more symmetrical structure.

One may wonder about the phrase ἐν ἀπωλείᾳ "will be destroyed (lit.: in destruction)" as it has no corresponding term in the first half of the verse. However, ἀπωλεία was one of the translator's favorite words which he also used elsewhere in the second part of an antithetical parallelism without any correspondence to the MT, e.g. Prov 11:6; 13:15; 16:26+26a,[300] to emphasize the fate of the transgressors etc. Therefore the translator may have added the phrase in question at this point to complete the line, expressing the fate of the disobedient or scorner.

---

[297] The reason for the insertion δυναστῶν "of princes" is not certain but perhaps it was added for further specification or interpretation. For a similar case see Prov 1:21 where שְׁעָרִים is also rendered πύλαις δυναστῶν. J. Cook regards δυναστῶν as an interpretation of שַׂר instead of שַׁעַר. Johann Cook, "The Hexaplaric Text, Double Translations and other Textual Phenomena in the Septuagint (Proverbs)," *JNSL* 22/2 (1996): 134.

[298] A. Meinhold translates, "Ein weiser Sohn ist (die Verkörperung der) Zucht *des Vaters*, . . ." Meinhold, *Sprüche*, 1:217, maintaining the MT. Similarly W. McKane who renders, "A wise son *submits to his father's discipline*, . . ." McKane, *Proverbs*, 230. But also several emendations have been suggested, for a discussion see *Ibid.*, 453.

[299] Cf. Whybray, *Proverbs*, 200. RSV assumes that "hear" has dropped out, but its inclusion would make an exceptionally long line. *Ibid.*

[300] Here ἀπωλεία occurs in an antithetical line which is apparently added to v. 26.

1.2.2.11 Verbal Clause, Paired with Nominal Clause

Prov 18:12

MT: לִפְנֵי־שֶׁבֶר יִגְבַּהּ לֵב־אִישׁ וְלִפְנֵי כָבוֹד עֲנָוָה
"Before destruction the heart/mind of man is haughty, and before honor is humility (or: but humility goes before honor)"

LXX: πρὸ συντριβῆς ὑψοῦται καρδία ἀνδρός καὶ πρὸ δόξης ταπεινοῦται
"Before ruin the heart of a man is exalted, and before honor it is humbled"

In Prov 18:12 the two halves are antithetically parallel with the point that pride (יִגְבַּהּ) in the heart/mind is the way to destruction, but humility (עֲנָוָה) is the way to honor[301] ("Before destruction the heart/mind of man is haughty, and before honor is humility"). Grammatically, however, the LXX appears to be a more nearly parallel structure since ὑψοῦται "(heart) is exalted" (first colon) corresponds with ταπεινοῦται "(heart) is humbled" (second colon) in number (singular), tense (present), mood (indicative), and person (third), whereas the MT has a verbless clause in the second half.

1.2.2.12 Conclusion

In section 1.2.2 "Grammatical relationships" it has been demonstrated that there are many parallelisms, especially near-synonymous parallelisms, in which the surface structure of the two halves does not correspond one-to-one; in their deep structure or meaning, however, the lines may correspond closely. In translating such verses, the translator was not satisfied with keeping the semantic correspondence but sought to produce colons that were also more closely parallel grammatically. This may partly be due to stylistic differences between Hebrew and Greek, but the main reason for this increased correspondence may be found in the translator's fondness for producing lines that are more symmetrical. This translation technique needs to be considered when using LXX Proverbs as variant text, as has been discussed under 3.3.2 "Grammatical relationships."

---

[301] Cf. Ross, "Proverbs," n.p.

1.2.3 POSSIBLE NON-TRANSLATIONAL DEVIATIONS

In this category cases are treated that are more difficult to explain on the basis of translation techniques. Although an attempt has been made to give translational reasons for the deviations on the basis of the hypothesis that the translator had a similar source text to that of the MT, it cannot be ruled out that some of the deviations are due to differences in the *Vorlage*.

The following is a parallelism of the category "Emphatic phrases or various figures of speech."

1. Prov 19:28

MT: עֵד בְּלִיַּעַל יָלִיץ מִשְׁפָּט וּפִי רְשָׁעִים יְבַלַּע־אָוֶן

"A malicious witness scorns justice, and the mouth of the wicked devour evil"

LXX: ὁ ἐγγυώμενος παῖδα ἄφρονα καθυβρίζει δικαίωμα στόμα δὲ ἀσεβῶν καταπίεται κρίσεις

"He who becomes surety for a foolish child will despise ordinance/regulation/justice, and the mouth of ungodly men shall drink down judgments/justice"

Prov 19:28 is about corrupt witnesses and their disregard for justice and may be regarded as near-synonymous ("A malicious witness scorns justice, and the mouth of the wicked devour evil"). The verb יְבַלַּע (*pi'el*) "it devours" does not seem to fit the line very well and so some have taken it as יַבִּיעַ (*nip'al*) "it gushes" (see *BHS* cf. 15:28). G. R. Driver retains the MT and explains it on the basis of the Arabic *balaga* "enunciates"; this is followed by W. McKane.[302] O. Plöger prefers to take the MT reading figuratively: "Er [der falsche Zeuge] wird eingereiht in die große Kategorie der Frevler, deren Mund das Unheil wie eine begehrte Nahrung förmlich herunterschlingt."[303] Perhaps the translator avoided rendering יְבַלַּע־אָוֶן "devour evil" literally and instead rendered καταπίεται κρίσεις "drink down judgments" because the latter may have been more appropriate than the figure of devouring evil, cf. Prov 26:6,[304] and particularly fitting in that it produced a synonymous word pair with δικαίωμα "ordinance/regulation/justice"; MT: מִשְׁפָּט.

As for the deviation in the beginning of the first half "He who becomes surety for a foolish child" (LXX) in place of "A malicious witness" (MT) it is more difficult to explain. The deviation may go back to a different Hebrew *Vorlage* or it may even be due to giving further explication or specification. If the latter mentioned is the case, the reason for the insertion of παῖδα "child"

---

[302] McKane, *Proverbs*, 529.

[303] Plöger, *Sprüche Salomos*, 227. Similarly Meinhold, *Sprüche*, 2:327. R. J. Clifford also favors the MT, supporting it on the basis of the repetition of similar sounds. Clifford, *Proverbs*, 179.

[304] Similarly in 26:6 the figure of "drinking down violence" is not translated literally.

(first colon), thus making the statement quite specific, may be the translator's desire to make a connection between the "foolish child" (v. 28) and the "(disobedient) son" in the previous verse 27. This led to a less close correspondence of the subjects than in the MT where עֵד בְּלִיַּעַל "a malicious witness" (first colon) and רְשָׁעִים "the wicked" (second colon) correspond closely.

The following cases have additions that are not found in the MT. The first example belongs to the same category as the previous case.

2. <u>Prov 1:14</u>

MT: גּוֹרָלְךָ תַּפִּיל בְּתוֹכֵנוּ כִּיס אֶחָד יִהְיֶה לְכֻלָּנוּ
"Throw in your lot among us; we will all have one purse"

LXX: τὸν δὲ σὸν κλῆρον βάλε ἐν ἡμῖν κοινὸν δὲ βαλλάντιον κτησώμεθα πάντες καὶ μαρσίππιον ἓν γενηθήτω ἡμῖν
"You throw in your lot with us; we will all get a common money bag, and we shall have one purse"

Prov 1:14 is a fairly parallel couplet semantically, the first line being literal and the second figurative; in the first half the more general term גּוֹרָל "lot" is used and in the second half the synecdoche כִּיס אֶחָד "one purse" is employed for the sake of intensification[305] ("Throw in your lot among us; we will all have one purse"). The translator, however, added the second colon[306] apparently to explicate further the figure "one purse"[307] by substituting "common"[308] for "one" (אֶחָד) (κοινὸν ... βαλλάντιον "a common money bag"), and at the same time producing a line that is parallel to the more literally rendered colon that follows ("and we shall have one purse"). But since he had translated πάντες "all" (לְכֻלָּנוּ) in the second colon, he left it out in the third line. This is an attempt to explain the addition translationally based on the hypothesis that the *Vorlage* and the MT were similar in this case.

---

[305] Alter, *Art*, 20.

[306] According to C. T. Fritsch the second colon is OG and the third Hexaplaric, although the Origenian signs are incorrectly noted in SH. Fritsch, "Hexaplaric Signs," 178.

[307] "A common fund of spoil to be equitably distributed among the members of the gang." Toy, *Proverbs*, 16.

[308] In Prov 15:23 κοινός is added translationally.

The following example, a second case with additions, belongs to the category of "Lexical aspect."

3. Prov 5:23

MT: הוּא יָמוּת בְּאֵין מוּסָר וּבְרֹב אִוַּלְתּוֹ יִשְׁגֶּה
"He dies for lack of instruction, and in the greatness of his folly (or: because of his foolishness) he goes astray"

LXX: οὗτος τελευτᾷ μετὰ ἀπαιδεύτων ἐκ δὲ πλήθους τῆς ἑαυτοῦ βιότητος ἐξερρίφη καὶ ἀπώλετο δι' ἀφροσύνην
"Such a man (or: he) dies with the uninstructed, and he is cast forth from the abundance of his own substance/life, and has perished through folly"

Prov 5:23 may be regarded as near-synonymous ("He dies for lack of instruction, and in the greatness of his folly he goes astray") although יִשְׁגֶּה "he goes astray" does not correspond exactly with יָמוּת "he dies," but the former is probably an intentional allusion to v. 19b and v. 20a (תִּשְׁגֶּה "intoxicated").[309] In the LXX the first colon agrees with the MT except that the translator rendered בְּאֵין מוּסָר "without instruction" more freely by μετὰ ἀπαιδεύτων "with the uninstructed." The second colon is somewhat different, corresponding to the MT only in regard to πλήθους "greatness/abundance" (רֹב), which however is used in a positive sense ("the abundance of his own substance") contrary to the MT ("the greatness of his folly"). It may have been added as a commentary on some of the implications of a fool's death, but it is difficult to explain it adequately from the corresponding Hebrew passage.[310] In the third colon the translator then seeks to cover the remaining and so far untranslated words.[311] It may have been this that led to his adding καὶ ἀπώλετο δι' ἀφροσύνην "and has perished through folly," thus producing a closer parallel to יָמוּת as he substituted ἀπώλετο for יִשְׁגֶּה.[312]

---

[309] Plöger, *Sprüche*, 53.

[310] Cf. Gerleman, *Studies*, 8.

[311] There are similar cases where the translator seems to have added one colon to cover some part(s) of the Hebrew text that were not rendered due to translational changes in the preceding colon(s), e.g. Prov 2:19; 17:17; 5:23; 22:11 and 11:16.

[312] *BHS* suggests following the LXX at this point and reading יִסָּפֶה, but this does not seem to be a plausible variant in the source text considering the translator's technique. O. Plöger also speaks against this suggestion. Plöger, *Sprüche*, 53.

In the following case the LXX omits one clause.

4. Prov 3:3

MT: חֶסֶד וֶאֱמֶת אַל־יַעַזְבֻךָ קָשְׁרֵם עַל־גַּרְגְּרוֹתֶיךָ כָּתְבֵם עַל־לוּחַ לִבֶּךָ
"Do not let loyalty and faithfulness forsake you; bind them around your neck, write them on the tablet of your heart"

LXX: ἐλεημοσύναι καὶ πίστεις μὴ ἐκλιπέτωσάν σε ἄψαι δὲ αὐτὰς ἐπὶ σῷ τραχήλῳ καὶ εὑρήσεις χάριν
"Let not mercy and faithfulness forsake you, but bind them about your neck, so you will find favor"[313]

In fact, Prov 3:3 is a triplet in the MT, the second and third lines being nearly parallel. The third line of the parallelism, כָּתְבֵם עַל־לוּחַ לִבֶּךָ "write them on the tablet of your heart," however, is not represented in the LXX,[314] and therefore it has been suggested that v. 3c has been attracted into this verse from 7:3.[315] The LXX translator may have left it out on purpose to achieve a smoother flow of the argument and to produce a straight antithetical parallelism. In v. 3c, or v. 4a according to the Cambridge edition, then the result follows: וּמְצָא־חֵן, καὶ προνοοῦ καλά "so you will find favor . . ." It is true that in Prov 7:3 a similar parallelism is rendered fully in the LXX, but there the argument does not continue in the following verse. Thus the discourse consideration of increased cohesiveness at the paragraph level may have been responsible for the omission of the second part of the parallel form.

To sum up, in cases of major deviations, more extensive additions and omissions, as in the examples above, we cannot be certain whether the differences are due to differences in the *Vorlage* or to translational adjustments, although translational explanations have been given.

---

[313] The last clause, here in v. 3, occurs in the MT in v. 4.

[314] It is omitted by S & B.

[315] Gemser, *Sprüche Salomos*, 26. Cf. also Clifford, *Proverbs*, 50. Whybray, however, thinks that it is the first line which is the added line. *Proverbs*, 60–61.

1.3 CONCLUSION

It has been demonstrated in Chapter One that Hebrew parallelisms were rendered in a more exactly parallel fashion both semantically (1.2.1 Semantic relationships) as well as grammatically (1.2.2 Grammatical relationships), and there are many instances in LXX Proverbs where the two relationships of more nearly parallel forms co-occur. This gives additional support of the translator's predilection to produce more exactly parallel and symmetrical parallelisms.

Hebrew parallelisms have been analyzed in as much detail as necessary beyond the three categories of synonymous, antithetic, and synthetic parallelisms that R. Lowth established to classify the whole spectrum of Hebrew parallelisms. Clear evidence has been provided of the translator's strong predilection for altering dynamic Hebrew parallelisms in the direction of forms that are more nearly parallel semantically and/or grammatically. The approach taken is based on the hypothesis that LXX Proverbs was translated from some Hebrew text that was similar to the Hebrew text we use today, at least in the cases discussed in the thesis.

In the area of semantics (1.2.1), the translator's tendency to render lexical items more parallel synonymously has been demonstrated in Prov 3:12 (see INTRODUCTION); 1:23; 3:9,25; 12:14; 20:23,30; 24:11; 31:6 as discussed under 1.2.1.1. It has been further shown that he often translated emphatic phrases or figures of speech (1.2.1.2) in a more parallel fashion, such as in Prov 1:24; 17:26; 22:8; 23:21 often dropping the figure to the detriment of the poetic effect of the Hebrew.

Although G. Gerleman sees clearly the translator's predilection for sharp antitheses, he gives almost no attention to the lines that correspond closer synonymously because in his view they are wholly foreign to the Greeks. In his two studies Gerleman does not list parallelisms that are more parallel synonymously in the translation, probably because he always compared the translation with the literary tradition in the Hellenistic world (although near-synonymous parallelisms did exist[316]) and did not consider enough the translator's particular style and his general fondness for lexical cohesion which led to producing more synonymous (also antonymous) word and phrase pairs.

The translator not only adjusted near-synonymous parallelisms in the direction of a closer correspondence, but his predilection for closer correspondence is also reflected in renderings that he recast from a near-synonymous Hebrew parallelism into an antithetical form (1.2.1.3), as demonstrated in Prov 15:23; 17:4; 11:7; 15:10; 21:14; and similarly 6:11; 17:21; 18:22 (also 17:5 under 1.2.1.5.2) where he added colons to produce an antithesis. It seems that in many of these cases it may be the occurrence of antithetic parallelisms in the context that helped his decision apart from his general fondness for antithetical forms.

---

[316] Newman, *Biblical Parallelism*, 3, 22–27.

In addition to these near-synonymous parallelisms, there are the following types of parallelism which he transformed into antithetical forms: parallelisms of logical relations, Prov 13:14; 23:31; 29:9 (1.2.1.5.1); a parallelism of addition relations, Prov 17:5 (1.2.1.5.2); parallelisms of comparisons, Prov 17:10,12 (1.2.1.5.3); and an emblematic parallelism, Prov 26:20 (1.2.1.5.4). All of these underwent similar changes in the course of translation.

Also, there are a considerable number of near-antithetical parallelisms which the translator adjusted mainly translationally, rendering them with a clearer contrast semantically (but also grammatically), as in Prov 11:21,24; 12:10,25; 13:19,25; 15:15,21,27; 17:9; 22:3; 28:25,27,28; 29:4; 11:10–11 under 1.2.1.4.

There are further types of parallelisms that have been treated under "Additional aspects" (1.2.1.5), such as "parallelisms of logical relations" (1.2.1.5.1), e.g. Prov 4:10; 17:23; 24:10; 27:11 which are rendered less logically and more synonymously parallel, (and Prov 13:14; 23:31; 29:9; which are cast into antithetical forms, see above). In addition, there are "parallelisms of addition relations" (1.2.1.5.2), Prov 22:15 (and Prov 17:5 see above), that are rendered without the notion of time sequence but in parallel fashion. Also "parallelisms of comparisons" (1.2.1.5.3), Prov 8:10 (and 17:10,12 see above), that are translated more parallel semantically and/or grammatically. Among "emblematic parallelisms" (1.2.1.5.4), Prov 11:22; 27:15 (and Prov 26:20 see above) may be mentioned, all of which are rendered with closer corresponding lines semantically and/or grammatically apart from making the point of comparison clearer and often more explicit. "Less closely parallel or single-sentence constructions" (1.2.1.5.5), Prov 7:17; 21:24, consisting of a single sentence are rendered in parallel fashion. "Near-synonymous parallelisms with three parts" (1.2.1.5.6), Prov 3:18; 6:10,23,35, are all translated in a more parallel way by two corresponding lines. "Triplets" (1.2.1.5.7), Prov 1:27; 8:34, are changed by adding one line to make them more parallel forms. In addition, the tendency to make items correspond can even be observed in "Phrases" (1.2.1.5.8), Prov 3:2; 22:29.

There are several cases of near-synonymous additions where the translator added a (third) colon to produce a line parallel to the previous one, e.g. Prov 4:10 (1.2.1.5.1); Prov 8:10 (1.2.1.5.3); Prov 6:10 (1.2.1.5.6); Prov 1:27; 8:34 (1.2.1.5.7); Prov 6:25 (1.2.2.4); (Prov 1:14 (1.2.3)).

In the light of the translator's predilection for closely corresponding lines, J. de Waard's view that the translator dislikes the synonymous parallelism of the Masoretic text in regard to Prov 23:24 and in general, following G. Gerleman, may not reflect the translation technique of the translator of LXX Proverbs accurately.

SECONDARY PARALLELISM

In the second part, 1.2.2 "Grammatical relationships," I have looked mostly at near-synonymous Hebrew parallelisms from the viewpoint of their grammatical structure. There are numerous possible grammatical combinations, such as in Prov 1:24 where a second person is paired with an impersonal construction (1.2.2.1); Prov 13:20 where a preposition plus adjective is paired with a noun (1.2.2.2); Prov 9:6 where a personal object is paired with an impersonal object (1.2.2.3); Prov 6:25 where the second person imperfect (and third person object) is paired with a third person imperfect (and second person object) (1.2.2.4); Prov 4:26 where an imperative is paired with an imperfect; (1.2.2.5); Prov 12:4 where a construct form is paired with a participle (1.2.2.6); Prov 20:9 where a direct quotation is paired with a direct quotation (1.2.2.7); Prov 7:4 where a direct quotation is paired with an indirect quotation (1.2.2.8); Prov 30:13 where an exclamation with מָה־ is paired with a statement (1.2.2.9). As regards elliptical constructions (1.2.2.10), there are many possibilities, such as in Prov 17:26 and 18:5 where the complement is omitted in *B* (1.2.2.10.1); Prov 3:9; 5:17; 7:18; 8:20; 9:7; 11:24; 24:30; 8:4,6; 1:3 where the verb (or adverb) is omitted in *B* (1.2.2.10.2.1), also 8:2,3; 13:1 where the verb is omitted in *A* (1.2.2.10.2.2); Prov 18:12 where a verbal clause is paired with a nominal clause (1.2.2.11). All of these the translator translated making clearly more parallel structures.

There are cases with more extensive deviations, Prov 19:28; 1:14; 5:23; 3:3 (1.2.3), which are more difficult to explain on the basis of translation techniques. Therefore, in such instances there is a certain degree of uncertainty regarding their translational character, although possible translational explanations have been given.

After having looked at Hebrew parallelisms from various angles, such as semantics (synonymous and antithetical forms) and grammatical structure, as well as the various relations between the parallel lines (e.g. logical relations, time sequence, comparative and emblematic relations), and having investigated how these Hebrew parallelisms are translated in the LXX, it is quite evident that the translator sought to produce forms that are more parallel both semantically and grammatically.

There are, however, couplets in the LXX of Proverbs that may be regarded as less nearly parallel than the MT. The reasons for such occurrences are given in the following Chapter Two.

2. HEBREW PARALLELISM RENDERED AS A LESS NEARLY PARALLEL FORM

Despite the translator's predilection for producing more closely corresponding colons, there are exceptions where the MT may be regarded as more closely parallel than the LXX. In this chapter I deal with possible reasons and features that could account for this disturbance of the translator's general pattern.

2.1 COHESION AND PARALLEL FORMS

In order to understand the translation technique of the translator of Proverbs it is important to understand how he applied the linguistic feature of cohesion. In the LXX of Proverbs there are many instances of the translator's adding words, phrases and even whole clauses in an effort to make the translation more cohesive. The application of grammatical cohesion, especially on the discourse level (beyond the couplet level), at times influenced the lexical cohesion of the couplet or bicolon[1] (cf. 1.2.1.1) leading to less nearly parallel forms.

Before we turn to the parallel forms, I will demonstrate the coherent character in general of the LXX of Proverbs.

2.1.1 LINGUISTIC SIGNALS OF COHESION IN GENERAL

Features or linguistic signals of cohesion[2] linking information into groups may include the same tense/aspect or person and number, deictic links such as demonstratives or articles, participants introduced with nouns and referred to thereafter with pronouns or zero reference, and certain connectives or particles.

According to R. A. Dooley and S. H. Levinsohn, such

> signals of cohesion indicate how the part of the text with which they occur links up conceptually with some other part. It is common to speak of such signals as **COHESIVE TIES**. . . . Each language will, of course, have its own range of devices which can be used for cohesion, but some general types will be found cross-linguistically.[3]

---

[1] A couplet or bicolon is made up of two lines, halves, or cola that are more or less parallel. The two-colon unit can almost be taken as standard Hebrew poetry. Watson, *Classical*, 12.

[2] These are linguistic means to signal coherence. Robert A. Dooley and Stephen H. Levinsohn, *Analyzing Discourse: Basic Concepts* (SIL and UND, 1998), 15.

[3] *Ibid.*

Such general signals of cohesion will be discussed now as they occur in the LXX of Proverbs.

2.1.1.1 Connectives, Markers or Particles

M. A. K. Halliday and R. Hasan treat items of this group under "Conjunction," distinguishing between "Additive" (e.g. and, nor, or), "Adversative" (e.g. yet, but, however), "Causal" (e.g. so, therefore, because, for this purpose) and "Temporal" (e.g. then, previously, finally) conjunctive relations.[4]

Among linguistic signals or ties of cohesion in LXX Proverbs, the following connectives may be mentioned.

The connector τε is "a marker of a close relationship between coordinate, nonsequential items–'and.'"[5]

1. Prov 1:2,3

MT: 2 לָדַעַת חָכְמָה וּמוּסָר לְהָבִין אִמְרֵי בִינָה
"To know wisdom and instruction, to understand words of insight";
לָקַחַת מוּסַר הַשְׂכֵּל צֶדֶק וּמִשְׁפָּט וּמֵישָׁרִים
3 "To receive the instruction of wisdom (or: in wise behavior), righteousness, and justice, and equity"

LXX: 2 γνῶναι σοφίαν καὶ παιδείαν νοῆσαί τε λόγους φρονήσεως
"to know wisdom, and instruction, *and* to understand words of insight"
3 δέξασθαί τε στροφὰς λόγων νοῆσαί τε δικαιοσύνην ἀληθῆ καὶ κρίμα κατευθύνειν
"*and* to receive hard saying, *and* to understand true justice, and (how) to direct judgment (or: make just decisions)"

The marker τε is added following an infinitive in Prov 1:2,3[6] in order to connect the purpose clauses with their close relationship more naturally in Greek,[7] whereas in the MT the clauses are juxtaposed without any conjunction.

This is not to say, however, that there is no coherence in the Hebrew text since "The coherence of a text is, in essence, a question of whether the hearer can make it 'hang together' conceptually, that is, interpret it within a single

---

[4] Halliday and Hasan, *Cohesion in English*, chap. 5, here 242–243.

[5] J. P. Louw and E. A. Nida, eds., *Greek-English Lexicon of the New Testament Based on Semantic Domains* (2 vols; New York: UBS, 1988).

[6] The particle τε occurs only in the first six verses.

[7] According to J. Cook τε "is an unmistakable sign of the translator's free style and first-hand knowledge of the Greek language." Cook, *Proverbs*, 49.

mental representation."[8] Rather, "coherence is a matter of conceptual unity and cohesion is linguistic form, [thus] it is in principle possible to have coherence without cohesion."[9]

Other signals of cohesion that occur are particles or conjunctions of logical relation, which the translator added to connect verses more closely with each other and explicate their relationship.

The particle τοιγαροῦν indicates result and may be translated "for this very reason, therefore, hence, therefore indeed, so then." In the following instances, the translator added it to connect with what precedes.

2. Prov 1:26

MT: גַּם־אֲנִי בְּאֵידְכֶם אֶשְׂחָק אֶלְעַג בְּבֹא פַחְדְּכֶם
"I also (or: in return) will laugh at your calamity, I will mock when your fear/dread comes (or: when panic strikes you)"

LXX: τοιγαροῦν κἀγὼ τῇ ὑμετέρᾳ ἀπωλείᾳ ἐπιγελάσομαι καταχαροῦμαι δὲ ἡνίκα ἂν ἔρχηται ὑμῖν ὄλεθρος
"*therefore* I also will laugh at your destruction, and I will rejoice when ruin comes upon you"

The translator connected Prov 1:26 with the previous verse by inserting τοιγαροῦν "for that very reason then" at the beginning of the verse. J. Cook, however, suggests that "The Hebrew particle גַּם is rendered by means of τοιγαροῦν, ..."[10] But this is incorrect, because גַּם־אֲנִי is usually translated by κἀγώ, cf. Lev 26:24; Deut 12:30; Isa 66:4; Jer 13:26; Ezek 24:9, etc. There is one other instance of גַּם־אֲנִי in Proverbs, rendered καὶ τὴν ἐμήν, Prov 23:15. As for τοιγαροῦν there is one other occurrence in Prov 1:31 which reflects a free rendering of waw/vav. Further occurrences of τοιγαροῦν are in Job 22:10 where it renders על־כן literally,[11] and in Job 24:22 and Isa 5:26 where it is translational. It is mostly found in books of the Alexandrine canon: 2 Macc 7:23; 4 Macc 1:34; 9:7; 13:16; 17:4; Sir 41:16. Thus Cook's view cannot be sustained, as τοιγαροῦν is clearly a signal of cohesion rather than a translation of גַּם.

In the following cases the translator inserted conjunctions such as ἐάν "if, when," ἵνα "that, in order that," and γάρ "for, then" for the sake of cohesion.

---

[8] Dooley and Levinsohn, *Analyzing Discourse*, p 11.

[9] *Ibid*, 18. For instance, K. M. Heim in his article "Coreferentiality, Structure and Context in Proverbs 10:1–5," *JOTT* 6/3 (1993), shows how these verses build a coherent discourse in Hebrew, contrary to W. McKane who describes them as having an "atomistic character." McKane, *Proverbs*, 413.

[10] Cook, *Proverbs*, 89.

[11] This is the only literal rendering.

3. Prov 2:10

MT: כִּי־תָבוֹא חָכְמָה בְלִבֶּךָ וְדַעַת לְנַפְשְׁךָ יִנְעָם
"For wisdom will come into your heart/mind, and knowledge will be pleasant to your soul"

LXX: ἐὰν γὰρ ἔλθῃ ἡ σοφία εἰς σὴν διάνοιαν ἡ δὲ αἴσθησις τῇ σῇ ψυχῇ καλὴ εἶναι δόξῃ
"For *if/when* wisdom comes into your mind/understanding, and discernment seems pleasing to your soul"

By means of adding ἐὰν "when, if" in Prov 2:10 the translator connected v. 11 more closely to the previous verse.

4. Prov 29:20

MT: חָזִיתָ אִישׁ אָץ בִּדְבָרָיו תִּקְוָה לִכְסִיל מִמֶּנּוּ
"Do you see a man who is hasty in his words? There is more hope for a fool than for him"

LXX: ἐὰν ἴδῃς ἄνδρα ταχὺν ἐν λόγοις γίνωσκε ὅτι ἐλπίδα ἔχει μᾶλλον ἄφρων αὐτοῦ
"*If* you see a man hasty in (his) words, know that the fool has more hope than he"

In Prov 29:20 the logical relationship of the colons of MT is, according to C. H. Toy, one of condition and consequence[12] ("Do you see a man who is hasty in his words? There is more hope for a fool than for him"). In any case, the focus in this verse is on the one who is hasty with his words and speaks before thinking something through.[13] Apparently the translator changed the question into a conditional clause by adding ἐὰν "if" in the first colon and connected it more closely to the second colon by inserting γίνωσκε ὅτι "know that" ("*If* you see a man hasty in (his) words, *know that* the fool has more hope than he").

5. Prov 31:12

MT: גְּמָלַתְהוּ טוֹב וְלֹא־רָע כֹּל יְמֵי חַיֶּיהָ
"She does him good and not evil/harm all the days of her life"

LXX: ἐνεργεῖ γὰρ τῷ ἀνδρὶ ἀγαθὰ πάντα τὸν βίον
"*For* she employs all her living for her husband's good"

---

[12] Toy, *Proverbs*, 514.

[13] Ross, "Proverbs," n.p.

In Prov 31:12 the translator added γάρ "for" to connect to the previous verse, perhaps giving the reason why such a woman's husband would never be in need.

In Prov 6:5, for example see under 3.3.1.1, the translator connected v. 4 more closely with v. 5 by joining them with ἵνα "that (you may deliver yourself . . .)" and thus altering the independent imperative clause of the MT ("deliver yourself . . .") into a dependent final clause.

In summary, these connectives, markers or particles are translational additions intended to join clauses together by using linguistic signals of cohesion.

2.1.1.2 Agreement in Tense/Aspect or Person and Number

According to M. L. Larson, "The fact that a series of clauses or sentences have the same tense, mood, or voice adds a feature of cohesion to the unit in which they occur."[14] And, "Many languages have affixes on the verbs which carry tense, mood, voice and person. These affixes are very important in adding cohesion."[15]

The translator's concern to employ linguistic signals of cohesion can be demonstrated in cases where he altered the number and person as well as tense/aspect of a verb to agree with the preceding verb.

1. Prov 1:22

For example see 3.3.1.5.6.

The translator seems to have changed the rhetorical question in Prov 1:22 ("How long, O simple ones, will you love being simple? And scoffers delight in their scoffing, and fools hate knowledge?") into a statement ("As long as the simple cleave to righteousness/justice, they will not be ashamed, but the foolish being lovers of hubris/haughtiness, having become ungodly they have hated knowledge"), altering the second person of the verb תֶּאֱהֲבוּ "you will love" into the third person ἔχωνται "they cleave" and adding αἰσχυνθήσονται "they will . . . be ashamed" in agreement with the verb that follows ἐμίσησαν "they hated"; MT: יִשְׂנְאוּ "they hate." Thus the translator did not switch from the second to the third person as is the case in the MT but rather kept the third person.

---

[14] Larson, *Meaning-based Translation*, 403. R. Blass mentions "agreement" as one of the characteristic features of cohesion in the following quotation: "the phenomena which create syntactic cohesion includes ellipses, pronouns, agreement, connecting particles, and conjunctions. These devices are governed by language-particular rules." R. Blass, "Cohesion, coherence, and relevance," *NOL* 34 (1986): 41–64.

[15] Larson, *Meaning-based*, 403.

2. Prov 2:19,20

MT: 19 כָּל־בָּאֶיהָ לֹא יְשׁוּבוּן וְלֹא־יַשִּׂיגוּ אָרְחוֹת חַיִּים
"None who go to her return again, nor do they regain/reach the paths of life"
20 לְמַעַן תֵּלֵךְ בְּדֶרֶךְ טוֹבִים וְאָרְחוֹת צַדִּיקִים תִּשְׁמֹר
"So you will walk in the way of good men, and keep the paths of the righteous"

LXX: 19 πάντες οἱ πορευόμενοι ἐν αὐτῇ οὐκ ἀναστρέψουσιν οὐδὲ μὴ καταλάβωσιν τρίβους εὐθείας οὐ γὰρ καταλαμβάνονται ὑπὸ ἐνιαυτῶν ζωῆς
"None who go to her return again, nor do they take hold of right paths, for they are not apprehended by the years of life"
20 εἰ γὰρ ἐπορεύοντο τρίβους ἀγαθάς εὕροσαν ἂν τρίβους δικαιοσύνης λείους
"For had they gone in good paths, they would have found the paths of righteousness easy"

In Prov 2:20 the MT switches to second person תֵּלֵךְ "you may walk" and starts a new paragraph,[16] whereas the translator keeps the third person of the previous verse as well as the following verse. He continues the argumentation of the previous verse by using a conditional clause, an "impossible" condition,[17] in which the verbs ἐπορεύοντο "they had gone" and εὕροσαν "they would have found" agree both in number and person with the three previous verbs in v. 19. For the additional clause in v. 19 (LXX) see 2.2.1.

Similarly in Prov 24:10, see 1.2.1.5.1, the MT switches from third person (v. 9) to second person, whereas the LXX continues referring to the same third person mentioned in v. 9.

One form of verbal agreement in number, person and tense/aspect occurs in verbs that are added to nominal constructions for translational reasons, as in the following case.

---

[16] Ross writes, "**20–22** The passage ends on the more positive note that wisdom will enable people to do what is right and to enjoy God's blessing." Ross, "Proverbs," n.p. Similarly W. McKane takes vv. 20–22 together and starts a new section. McKane, *Proverbs*, 288.

[17] The so called impossible condition or conditional three as used here in the LXX occurs hardly at all in the MT (Gen 43:10; Esth 7:4; Jer 23:22) which speaks in favor of the change in Prov 2:20 being translational. In the NT, however, the conditional three is used more frequently (e.g. Matt 11:23; 12:7; Luke 10:13; John 11:32; 15:22,24; 18:30; 1 Cor 2:8; Heb 11:15; 1 John 2:19).

3. Prov 2:9

MT: אָז תָּבִין צֶדֶק וּמִשְׁפָּט וּמֵישָׁרִים כָּל־מַעְגַּל־טוֹב:
"Then you will understand righteousness and justice and equity, every good path"

LXX: τότε συνήσεις δικαιοσύνην καὶ κρίμα καὶ κατορθώσεις πάντας ἄξονας ἀγαθούς
"Then you will understand righteousness and justice, and you will direct all your course aright"

In Prov 2:9 the verb κατορθώσεις "you will direct aright (or: walk straight),"[18] which is used to render the noun מֵישָׁרִים, agrees with the previous verb συνήσεις—MT: תָּבִין—"you shall understand" (first half) in tense, person and number.[19]

4. Prov 4:4

MT: וַיֹּרֵנִי וַיֹּאמֶר לִי יִתְמָךְ־דְּבָרַי לִבֶּךָ שְׁמֹר מִצְוֹתַי וֶחְיֵה:
"he taught me and said to me, 'Let your heart retain my words, keep my commandments and live'"

LXX: οἳ ἔλεγον καὶ ἐδίδασκόν με ἐρειδέτω ὁ ἡμέτερος λόγος εἰς σὴν καρδίαν[20]
"who spoke and instructed me, (saying), 'Let our speech be fixed in your heart'"

In Prov 4:4 the translator rendered the verbs ἔλεγον καὶ ἐδίδασκόν "they spoke and instructed" (first colon), and the possessive pronoun ἡμέτερος "our" (second colon), in the plural in order to attribute the instructions to both father and mother mentioned in the previous verse 3, whereas in the MT the instructions are given by the father alone וַיֹּרֵנִי וַיֹּאמֶר "he taught me and said."[21] It may have seemed to the translator quite natural to use the plural forms and thus connect the verbs to both father and mother. In addition, he may have sought to avoid relating the subject back as far as the first colon of the previous verse

---

[18] Note that the same verb is used in v. 7 referring to the same group of people spoken of here.

[19] For further examples of this kind see 1.2.2.10.2.

[20] In the Rahlfs edition the second colon φύλασσε ἐντολάς μὴ ἐπιλάθῃ "keep (our) commandments, forget them not" occurs in the following v. 5, whereas in the Cambridge edition it goes with v. 4 following the MT.

[21] In this kind of parallelism one element of a word-pair is in focus, in this case the male parent. Watson, *Classical*, 139.

where the father is mentioned. This would have led to a lesser degree of cohesion and continuity because of not connecting with the immediate.[22]

5. Prov 12:13

MT: בְּפֶשַׁע שְׂפָתַיִם מוֹקֵשׁ רָע וַיֵּצֵא מִצָּרָה צַדִּיק[23]
"(There is) a snare for the wicked in the transgression of (his) lips, but the righteous will escape from trouble"

LXX: δι' ἁμαρτίαν χειλέων ἐμπίπτει εἰς παγίδας ἁμαρτωλός ἐκφεύγει δὲ ἐξ αὐτῶν δίκαιος[24]
"For the sin of (his) lips a sinner falls into snares, but a righteous man escapes from them"

In Prov 12:13 the translator referred to παγίδας "snares" (first colon) by αὐτῶν "them" (second colon) connecting the two halves closely: "a righteous man escapes from them (the snares)." In the MT, however, the second half has the more general word צָרָה "trouble," compared to the more specific מוֹקֵשׁ[25] "snare" (first half). Thus the change in LXX is clearly translational with regard to the agreement mentioned.

In summary, the translator's concern to make the translation more cohesive than a literal rendering is demonstrated in maintaining the third person rather than frequently switching between second and third person,[26] as well as in keeping agreement in tense/aspect.

2.1.1.3 *Participant Reference*

In general terms participant reference is concerned with reference to the people involved in a narrative or other genre of discourse.[27] More specifically, participant reference is concerned with the identification and tracking of participants in a discourse, and answers such questions as: How are participants introduced into a narrative or other form of discourse? Once introduced, how are

---

[22] For a similar case of connecting with the immediate see Prov 3:5–6, 2.2.1.

[23] According to W. McKane מוֹקֵשׁ should not be emended to נוֹקֵשׁ on the basis of the LXX (ἐμπίπτει εἰς παγίδας). McKane, *Proverbs*, 452.

[24] V. 13a is not treated here. E. Tov lists it under inner-translational pluses. Tov, "Recensional Differences," 48.

[25] "מוֹקֵשׁ n.m. prop. a bait or lure in fowler's net; then fig. snare—bait or lure, in a net for birds." BDB.

[26] According to L. Zogbo and E. R. Wendland "in Hebrew poetry there may be abrupt shifts between third and second person, third and first, or first and second." Zogbo and Wendland, *Hebrew Poetry*, 102.

[27] Richard C. Blight, *Translation Problems from A to Z* (Dallas: SIL, 1992), 34.

they identified from then on? How are participants taken out of the narrative or saying, and how are they re-introduced? Which are the main participants? Which are the lesser ones?[28]

According to J. C. and K. Callow languages may differ in the use of devices for participant reference to ensure cohesion.

> In any language, a spontaneous discourse will show cohesion, both of participants and of events. In other words, it will be quite clear to the listener which participant performed which event, and in what order the events occurred. It is not often realized how widely languages can diverge in the devices they use for maintaining this cohesion. In referring to participants, for example, the SD [Source Discourse] uses verb and participle endings, free pronouns, class nouns (for example, woman), role terms (for example, magistrates), and proper names . . . But in most languages, to use a free pronoun or a proper name whenever the SD does would sound very awkward. In many of these languages it would render the passage quite unintelligible, and the listener would be quite at a loss to know which participant performed which event.[29]

Since languages may differ in the way they introduce participants and refer back to them, Hebrew may not correspond to Greek one-to-one as regards participant reference.[30] This mismatch is also reflected in freer translations[31] such as LXX Proverbs.

1. Prov 1:11–13

MT: 11 אִם־יֹאמְרוּ לְכָה אִתָּנוּ נֶאֶרְבָה לְדָם נִצְפְּנָה לְנָקִי חִנָּם
"If they say, 'Come with us, let us lay in wait for blood, let us ambush an innocent without cause"

12 נִבְלָעֵם כִּשְׁאוֹל חַיִּים וּתְמִימִים כְּיוֹרְדֵי בוֹר
"Let us swallow them alive like Sheol, and/even whole, as those that go down to the pit"

13 כָּל־הוֹן יָקָר נִמְצָא נְמַלֵּא בָתֵּינוּ שָׁלָל
"We shall find all precious substance/goods, we shall fill our houses with spoil'"

---

[28] Tauberschmidt, *Sinaugoro*, 92.

[29] John C. and Kathleen, Callow, "Translation Theory," *NOT* 64 (1977): 3–37.

[30] For this topic see also Tauberschmidt, "Principles," 90–94.

[31] Among these are also LXX Joshua and Esther, in which examples of freely rendered participant reference have been found. *Ibid.*

LXX: 10b/11 ἐὰν παρακαλέσωσί σε³² λέγοντες ἐλθὲ μεθ' ἡμῶν
κοινώνησον αἵματος κρύψωμεν δὲ εἰς γῆν *ἄνδρα δίκαιον* ἀδίκως
"If they should exhort you, saying, 'Come with us, take part in blood, and let us unjustly hide *a just/righteous man* in the earth"
12 καταπίωμεν δὲ *αὐτὸν* ὥσπερ ᾅδης ζῶντα καὶ ἄρωμεν *αὐτοῦ* τὴν μνήμην ἐκ γῆς
"and let us swallow *him* alive, like Hades (would), and let us remove the memorial of *him* from the earth"
13 τὴν κτῆσιν *αὐτοῦ* τὴν πολυτελῆ καταλαβώμεθα πλήσωμεν δὲ οἴκους ἡμετέρους σκύλων
"let us seize on *his* valuable property, and let us fill our houses with spoils'"

In Prov 1:11 ἄνδρα δίκαιον "a just man" is referred to by αὐτὸν "him" in v. 12. The MT, however, switches to the plural, using the suffix ם- "them" in v. 12 to refer back to נָקִי "an innocent person" in v. 11.³³ Likewise in v. 12b and v. 13a αὐτοῦ is used to refer to that same person, whereas in the MT the participant is not marked but the point of reference is still "them" (v. 12a). Thus the Greek translation uses more linguistic signs of cohesion than the MT, and in addition, does not switch to the plural but stays with the first person singular.

2. Prov 3:27,28

MT: 27 אַל־תִּמְנַע־טוֹב מִבְּעָלָיו בִּהְיוֹת לְאֵל יָדְךָ לַעֲשׂוֹת
"Do not withhold good from those to whom it is due (lit.: from its owners), when it is in your hand (=power) to do it"
28 אַל־תֹּאמַר לְרֵעֲךָ לֵךְ וָשׁוּב וּמָחָר אֶתֵּן וְיֵשׁ אִתָּךְ
"Do not say to your neighbor, 'Go, and come again, and tomorrow I will give it,' when you have it with you"

LXX: 27 μὴ ἀπόσχῃ εὖ ποιεῖν *ἐνδεῆ* ἡνίκα ἂν ἔχῃ ἡ χείρ σου βοηθεῖν
"Forbear not to do good to the poor, whenever your hand may have (power) to help him"
28 μὴ εἴπῃς ἐπανελθὼν ἐπάνηκε καὶ αὔριον δώσω δυνατοῦ σου ὄντος εὖ ποιεῖν οὐ γὰρ οἶδας τί τέξεται ἡ ἐπιοῦσα
"Say not, 'Come back another time, tomorrow I will give,' while you are able to do (him) good, for you do not know what the next day will bring forth"

---

[32] The beginning of v. 11 is part of v. 10 in Rahlfs' edition, in the Cambridge edition it starts with v. 11.

[33] Apparently the translator rendered נָקִי freely by ἄνδρα δίκαιον which is probably due to contrasting it with ἄνδρες ἀσεβεῖς in the previous verse.

SECONDARY PARALLELISM

In Prov 3:27 the participant ἐνδεῆ "the poor" is probably used as a free rendering in place of מִבְּעָלָיו "those to whom good is due"[34] in the MT. In the following verse 28 the Hebrew text then introduces a new participant, רֵע "neighbor,"[35] whereas the LXX refers to the participant already mentioned in v. 27 with zero reference. A further indication that the translator viewed the two verses as closely related is the fact that in v. 28 the phrase εὖ ποιεῖν "to do good," which also occurs in v. 27 to render טוֹב, is repeated to signal cohesion.

3. Prov 23:11

MT: כִּי־גֹאֲלָם חָזָק הוּא־יָרִיב אֶת־רִיבָם אִתָּךְ
"for their redeemer is strong; he will plead their cause with/against you"

LXX: ὁ γὰρ λυτρούμενος αὐτοὺς *κύριος* κραταιός ἐστιν καὶ κρινεῖ τὴν κρίσιν αὐτῶν μετὰ σοῦ
"for the Lord is their redeemer; he is mighty,[36] and will plead their cause with/against you"

In Prov 23:11 the translator first introduced the new participant, the Lord, ὁ γὰρ λυτρούμενος αὐτοὺς κύριος "for the Lord is their redeemer" (first colon) and thereafter he referred to him as κραταιός ἐστιν "he is mighty" (second colon), whereas the MT starts off with כִּי־גֹאֲלָם חָזָק "for their redeemer is mighty" without introducing the new participant first.

A further case is Prov 22:11 (see 3.3.1.5.4), where the translator may have read אהב as a third person singular *qal* verb "he loves" adding κύριος "the Lord" as subject, and may have formed the second half as a parallel to the first, making αὐτῷ "to him" correspond to "the Lord."

In summary, the translator of Proverbs is concerned to refer to participants introduced by nouns (or noun phrases)—or if they are not introduced to introduce them first (23:11; also 22:11)—by using pronouns, the person affix in the verb, or zero reference. In the MT, however, there are fewer cohesive links

---

[34] "In der Gefolgschaft der Septuaginta hat man darunter einen Bedürftigen unter der Annahme verstanden, daß jemand, der eine Wohltat nötig hat, sie auch verdient. Der hebräische Text faßt den Bedeutungsspielraum weiter und verlangt vom Wohltäter, darüber zu befinden, wer Anspruch hat und wer nicht." Meinhold, *Sprüche*, 1:86. Whybray too is against interpreting this phrase in the light of the LXX rendering, although he states that "LXX's rendering may be based on a different text." Whybray, *Proverbs*, 72. According to R. L. Giese "A Hebrew correspondent for ἐνδεῆ here is highly unlikely." Giese, "Compassion," 111.

[35] Or else a different term for "those to whom good is due" (previous verse) is used.

[36] This translation is according to *The Septuaginta Version: Greek and English* (London: Bagster; New York: Pott, n.d.), 809. An alternative rendering is "for their redeemer, the Lord, is mighty."

(22:11; 1:11–13). Also the MT switches more often from e.g. singular to plural (1:11,12), or does not maintain the same participant (3:28) as the LXX does.

2.1.1.4 Deixis or Deictic Links

Deixis may be described as "reference by means of an expression whose interpretation is relative to the (usually) extralinguistic context of the utterance, such as who is speaking, the time or place of speaking, the gestures of the speaker, or the current location in the discourse."[37] There are different kinds of deixis one of which is discourse deixis. This type may be described as "deictic reference to a portion of a discourse relative to the speaker's current "location" in the discourse."[38]

Deictic reference is a particular type of cohesion which is characterized by the specific nature of the information that is signaled for retrieval. The cohesion lies in the continuity of reference, the same thing entering the discourse a second time.[39]

In the translation of Proverbs, the following cases of deictic links (that have no equivalent in the MT) have been found.

1. Prov 1:5

In Prov 1:5 (A wise person will hear and increase learning) the translator added the deictic τῶνδε "these" ("For by hearing *these* a wise man will become wiser") which points back to παροιμίαι "proverbs" (v. 1) and thus serves as a linguistic signal of cohesion.

2. Prov 9:10,11

MT: 10 תְּחִלַּת חָכְמָה יִרְאַת יְהוָה וְדַעַת קְדֹשִׁים בִּינָה
"The fear of the Lord is the beginning of wisdom, and the knowledge of the Holy One is insight"
11 כִּי־בִי יִרְבּוּ יָמֶיךָ וְיוֹסִיפוּ לְךָ שְׁנוֹת חַיִּים
"For by me your days will be multiplied, and years will be added to your life"

LXX: 10 ἀρχὴ σοφίας φόβος κυρίου καὶ βουλὴ ἁγίων σύνεσις
10a τὸ γὰρ γνῶναι νόμον διανοίας ἐστὶν ἀγαθῆς

---

[37] "Linguistics Bookshelf: Glossary (Linguistics): D" in *Lingua Links*.
[38] *Ibid.*
[39] Halliday and Hasan, *Cohesion*, 31.

"The fear of the Lord is the beginning of wisdom, and the counsel of saints is understanding, 10a for to know the law is the sign of a sound mind[40]"

11 *τούτῳ γὰρ τῷ τρόπῳ πολὺν ζήσεις χρόνον καὶ προστεθήσεταί σοι ἔτη ζωῆς σου*
"For in this way you will live long, and years of your life will be added to you"

In Prov 9:11 the phrase τούτῳ . . . τῷ τρόπῳ, which includes the deictic or demonstrative τούτῳ "this," is substituted by the translator for בִי "by me," in order to connect with the previous verse 10 more smoothly and to avoid the MT's sudden switch in which "wisdom" speaks unexpectedly and directly like a person. The *BHS* apparatus suggests that כִּי־בָהּ "by her (the fear)" should probably be read based on the LXX reading. But this seems inadvisable because not only is the LXX more general[41] but also the translational change is quite obvious and is in line with the kind of adjustments the translator often made, as can be seen throughout this section and beyond.[42]

3. Prov 24:34

In Prov 24:34 ("and poverty will come upon you like one who travels, and want like an armed warrior"[43]) the translator inserted the deictic τοῦτο as part of the conditional clause ἐὰν δὲ τοῦτο ποιῇς "but if you do this (your poverty will come speedily, and your want like a swift courier")," pointing back to the words of the sluggard in the previous verse 33, "I slumber a little, and thus sleep a little . . ." and connecting them more closely with verse 34, "your poverty will come . . ."[44]

4. Prov 25:22

MT: כִּי גֶחָלִים אַתָּה חֹתֶה עַל־רֹאשׁוֹ וַיהוָה יְשַׁלֶּם־לָךְ
"for you will heap coals of fire on their heads, and the Lord will reward you"

---

[40] J. Cook uses this addition as a main support for his thesis that the translator deliberately promoted the value of the law. Cook, "The Law in Septuagint Proverbs," 211–223. On the other hand, G. Gerleman holds "that there is no trace whatever in the LXX Prov of an identification of Wisdom and *Torah*." Gerleman, *Studies*, 42. Apparently the translator paralleled wisdom and counsel with the law by adding v. 10(a) perhaps to provide further explanation, cf. Sir 19:20. A reference to the law cannot be ruled out.

[41] Cf. Plöger, *Sprüche*, 100.

[42] J. Cook too regards the adjustment mentioned as the work of the translator, Cook, *Proverbs*, 266, although his explanation is different.

[43] Cf. Prov 6:11.

[44] M. B. Dick lists this case under "Lines in the LXX emphasizing retribution" and writes that such a passage as this "makes nexus between action and consequence more explicit." Dick, "Ethics," 26–27. However, in this case the addition may simply be for the sake of cohesion.

LXX: τοῦτο γὰρ ποιῶν ἄνθρακας πυρὸς σωρεύσεις ἐπὶ τὴν κεφαλὴν αὐτοῦ ὁ δὲ κύριος ἀνταποδώσει σοι ἀγαθά
"for so doing you will heap coals of fire upon his head, and the Lord will reward you with good"

In Prov 25:22 τοῦτο . . . ποιῶν ". . . so doing" (cf. 9:11) was probably added by the translator as a cohesive link to point back to the previous verse and also to make the logical relationship of the two verses more explicit.

In summary, the translator added deictic links (that may consist of from one word to a whole clause) as signals of cohesion connecting the line or verse more closely to what precedes and making the relationship between the lines or verses more explicit.

2.1.1.5 Conclusion

The translator of Proverbs takes considerable pains to employ linguistic signals of cohesion linking information into groups. He does this by using certain connectives or particles, the same tense/aspect or person and number, participant reference, and deictic links such as demonstratives. This characteristic of linking information can be observed in the translation technique of the LXX translator of Proverbs in general, and at times it influences parallel forms as described below.

2.1.2 LINGUISTIC SIGNALS OF COHESION OR INCREASED COHESIVENESS INFLUENCE PARALLEL FORMS

The translator's concern for cohesiveness and using linguistic signals of cohesion led at times to forms that are less nearly parallel than the MT, as the following cases show.

2.1.2.1 Parallelism and Agreement in Tense/Aspect or Person and Number

Prov 1:28

MT: אָז יִקְרָאֻנְנִי וְלֹא אֶעֱנֶה יְשַׁחֲרֻנְנִי וְלֹא יִמְצָאֻנְנִי
"Then they will call upon me, but I will not answer; they will seek me diligently, but will not find me"

Q: . . . ישחרנני]ו[לא ימצאנני .[45]

---

[45] De Waard, "4QProv," 88.

LXX: ἔσται γὰρ ὅταν ἐπικαλέσησθέ με ἐγὼ δὲ οὐκ
εἰσακούσομαι ὑμῶν ζητήσουσίν με κακοὶ καὶ οὐχ εὑρήσουσιν
"For it shall be that when you call me, I will not listen to you, wicked men will seek me, but they will not find (me)"

The parallel form in Prov 1:28 is affected negatively with respect to agreement in person and number. In Prov 1:27 and the preceding verses the second person is used, but in v. 28 the MT suddenly switches to third person ("Then they will call upon me . . ."). The translator of the LXX, however, maintains the second person of the direct speech in v. 28a ("For it shall be that when you call me . . ."), probably for the sake of making the transition to third person in the following verses smoother. However, this disturbs the Hebrew parallelism of v. 28. In this case the translator seems to be more concerned to ensure a smooth transition than to keep the parallel structure. The fact that the translator added or explicated the participant κακοὶ "wicked men" in v. 28b supports this view, as further explained in the following section.

2.1.2.2 *Parallelism and Participants*

In Prov 1:28b the participant κακοὶ "wicked men" is added by the translator in the second colon of the parallelism. In the first colon the direct speech of vv. 22–27 still continues, coming to an end in v. 28a. It then changes to indirect speech in v. 28b in accordance with the pattern of the context of vv. 29–31. In the MT, however, there is a sudden switch from second to third person. To make a smoother transition to third person the translator kept the direct speech in v. 28a and then added the participant κακοὶ "wicked men" to introduce the participant for the following verses.[46] But by doing so the parallel form was disturbed.

1. Prov 2:7

MT: וְצָפַן לַיְשָׁרִים תּוּשִׁיָּה מָגֵן לְהֹלְכֵי תֹם
"And he stores up sound wisdom for the upright, he is a shield to those who walk blamelessly"

---

[46] Fritsch in "Hexaplaric Signs," 170, lists κακός of Prov 1:28 etc. under frequently added moralizing terms. Similarly Dick, "Ethics," 22–23. But the translator's decision can also (at least partly) be interpreted translationally.

LXX: καὶ θησαυρίζει τοῖς κατορθοῦσι σωτηρίαν⁴⁷ ὑπερασπιεῖ τὴν πορείαν αὐτῶν
"and he treasures up salvation for those that walk uprightly, he will protect their way"

In Prov 2:7 the participant τοῖς κατορθοῦσι "for those that walk uprightly" (לַיְשָׁרִים) (first colon) is referred to by (τὴν πορείαν) αὐτῶν "their (way)" (second colon), whereas the MT has the noun phrase לְהֹלְכֵי תֹם "to those who walk blamelessly" which is more closely parallel to A. The reason for this change is translational; the metaphor expressed by the noun מָגֵן "shield" (second colon) has been dropped and its meaning re-expressed by the verb ὑπερασπιεῖ "he will protect" (מגן) (similarly in Prov 30:5⁴⁸), the participant not being repeated but being referred to by a pronoun (plus a noun which is semantically related to the Hebrew participle). The result is a less nearly parallel rendering in the LXX structurally.

2. Prov 2:16,(17)

MT: 16 לְהַצִּילְךָ מֵאִשָּׁה זָרָה מִנָּכְרִיָּה אֲמָרֶיהָ הֶחֱלִיקָה
"to deliver you from the strange woman, from the adulteress who flatters with her words"

17 הַעֹזֶבֶת אַלּוּף נְעוּרֶיהָ וְאֶת־בְּרִית אֱלֹהֶיהָ שָׁכֵחָה
"who forsakes the partner of her youth and forgets the covenant of her God (or: sacred covenant)"

LXX: 16 τοῦ μακράν σε ποιῆσαι ἀπὸ ὁδοῦ εὐθείας καὶ ἀλλότριον τῆς δικαίας γνώμης
"to remove you far from the straight way, and to estrange you from a righteous purpose"

17 υἱέ μή σε καταλάβῃ κακὴ βουλὴ ἡ ἀπολείπουσα διδασκαλίαν νεότητος καὶ διαθήκην θείαν ἐπιλελησμένη
"(My) son, let not evil counsel overtake you (of her) who has forsaken the instruction of her youth, and forgotten the divine covenant"

Prov 2:16 in the LXX, although it need not necessarily be regarded as a less nearly parallel structure, is different from the MT. This may be for the sake of making a connection with the figure "way(s)/paths" of the previous verses (MT:

---

⁴⁷ This rendering may be due to erroneously reading תּוּשִׁיָּה "sound wisdom" as תְּשׁוּעָה "salvation," or else the translator adapted purposefully to make a closer parallel with B, "salvation" being more closely connected with protection than wisdom.

⁴⁸ This adjustment seems purely translational and does not need to be explained as an exegetical rendering, as J. Cook does in *Proverbs*, 120. J. de Waard supports the translational character of this rendering. De Waard, "Septuagint of Proverbs," 307–308.

vv. 12,13,15) rather than rendering the new participant אִשָּׁה זָרָה "strange woman" explicitly straightaway (first colon). For in the LXX that woman is referred to in the following verse by the participle ἡ ἀπολείπουσα "she who has forsaken" after the transitional insertion υἱέ μή σε καταλάβῃ κακὴ βουλή "(My) son, let not evil counsel overtake you" (v. 17). Thus the changes in the LXX, although quite extensive, look very much like translational adaptations in accordance with the pattern the translator follows.[49]

To sum up, due to his introduction of new participants the translator made quite extensive translational adjustments and it may have been these that led to some less nearly parallel forms.

2.1.2.3 Parallelism and Deictic Links as well as Other Discourse Considerations

1. Prov 20:3

MT: כָּבוֹד לָאִישׁ שֶׁבֶת מֵרִיב וְכָל־אֱוִיל יִתְגַּלָּע
"It is honorable for a man to refrain from strife/dispute, but every fool is quick to quarrel"

LXX: δόξα ἀνδρὶ ἀποστρέφεσθαι λοιδορίας πᾶς δὲ ἄφρων τοιούτοις συμπλέκεται
"(It is) a glory to a man to turn aside from railing, but every fool is entangled with such matters"

In Prov 20:3 ("It is honorable for a man to refrain from strife/dispute, but every fool is quick to quarrel") the translator used τοιούτοις "with such matters" (second colon) to refer back to λοιδορίας "railings, reproach" (first colon) instead of rendering גלע "quarrel" literally which is a near-parallel to ריב "strife/dispute." Thus the use of τοιούτοις functioning as a deictic led to a less synonymous parallelism lexically.

There are further discourse considerations that may be responsible for less nearly parallel renderings as described and demonstrated in the following cases.

---

[49] Toy regards the rendering of the LXX as "a bit of rabbinical or Alexandrian allegorizing" (but he admits that in Prov 7:5 "the Heb. is literally translated"). Toy, *Proverbs*, 46. In addition, M. B. Dick notes that there is a similar deletion in Prov 21:9 "where the Hebrew 'living with a contentious woman' becomes generalized in the Greek to 'living μετὰ ἀδικίας.'" Dick, "Ethics," 25. Nevertheless, our case here may even so be best explained in terms of translational considerations as stated above.

2. Prov 2:1

MT: בְּנִי אִם־תִּקַּח אֲמָרָי וּמִצְוֺתַי תִּצְפֹּן אִתָּךְ
"My son, if you accept my words and treasure up my commandments within you"

Q: [בְּנִי אם תקח אמרי ומ]צותי תצפן אתּךָ⁵⁰

LXX: υἱέ ἐὰν δεξάμενος ῥῆσιν ἐμῆς ἐντολῆς κρύψῃς παρὰ σεαυτῷ
"(My) son, if you accept the word of my commandment (and) hide (or: treasure) it with you"⁵¹

In Prov 2:1 אֲמָרָי . . . וּמִצְוֺתַי "my words . . . and my commandments" are used synonymously in a co-ordinate relationship and occur each in one colon of a parallel form. But in the LXX the translator rendered these two nouns by only one phrase, ῥῆσιν ἐμῆς ἐντολῆς "the word of my commandment" (first colon), taking the Hebrew as a construct chain. The reason for this adjustment may have been the many conditional clauses that follow v. 1 and precede the main clause in v. 5. The translator may have wished to bind these conditional clauses together more closely and thus increase cohesiveness.

3. Prov 3:32

MT: כִּי תוֹעֲבַת יְהוָה נָלוֹז וְאֶת־יְשָׁרִים סוֹדוֹ
"For the perverse are an abomination to the Lord, but the upright are in his confidence"

LXX: ἀκάθαρτος γὰρ ἔναντι κυρίου πᾶς παράνομος ἐν δὲ δικαίοις οὐ συνεδριάζει
"For every transgressor is unclean before the Lord, he does not sit among the righteous"

The antithetically parallel form of Prov 3:32 has apparently been changed by the translator and may be regarded as less nearly parallel. One possible motivation for this change in the LXX may have been to produce a smoother shift from a synonymous parallelism (v. 31) to a number of antithetical parallelisms (vv. 32–35). The translator may have wanted in v. 32 *B* to stay with the same participant, "he," that is the transgressor, to produce a smoother transition from v. 31 which talks about "bad men" to verse 33 *A* where "ungodly men" are spoken of before turning to the antithetical statements in verses 33–35 that follow the same

---

⁵⁰ De Waard, "4QProv," 88. Q agrees with the MT.

⁵¹ Lit.: "My son, if you having accepted the word of my commandment you hide it with you."

pattern of negative-positive statements with a similar content to v. 32 ("33 The Lord's curse is on the house of the wicked, but he blesses the abode of the righteous. 34 Toward the scorners he is scornful, but to the humble he shows favor. 35 The wise will inherit honor, but stubborn fools, disgrace."). Thus the translator may have chosen to change even an antithetic parallelism for the sake of cohesion.

Prov 31:1–9 is a good example that illustrates how discourse considerations can overrule the symmetry of parallel forms. In Prov 31:8 the MT is nearsynonymous, whereas in the LXX rendering *B* is a continuation of *A*.

4. Prov 31:8

MT: פְּתַח־פִּיךָ לְאִלֵּם אֶל־דִּין כָּל־בְּנֵי חֲלוֹף
"Open your mouth (or: speak out) for those who cannot speak, for the rights of all the destitute"

LXX: ἄνοιγε σὸν στόμα λόγῳ θεοῦ καὶ κρῖνε πάντας ὑγιῶς
"Open your mouth (or: speak) with the word of God, and judge all fairly"

The reason for this deviation from the Hebrew text may be purely translational and exegetical, as it was apparently the translator's concern to emphasize the fact that these instructions were given by God. So in addition to mentioning that these sayings are an "oracle" מַשָּׂא,[52] χρηματισμός, he rendered למואל "Lemuel" differently (למו־אל) as εἴρηνται ὑπὸ θεοῦ "spoken by God" (v. 1). In the following verse 2 he again expressed the importance of God's word by adding τί τέκνον τηρήσεις τί ῥήσεις θεοῦ "What will you keep, my son, what? The words of God," emphasizing the aspect of keeping the word of God. Then in v. 8 the phrase λόγῳ θεοῦ "the word of God" was inserted to show the importance of speaking God's word in judging. This, however, led to dropping the nearsynonymous parallelism. But since the following verse 9 is more or less a repetition of verse 8, the translator may have felt freer to alter the text in this way.

To sum up, the replacement of synonymous lexical items with deictics (20:3) as well as other changes due to discourse considerations that increase cohesiveness may have led to less nearly parallel forms in the LXX of Proverbs.

There is a further feature employed by the translator of Proverbs called "cohesive ties and thematic groupings," which is responsible for restructuring the discourse and thus bringing about less nearly parallel forms.

---

[52] משׂא may either be read as "oracle" (MT, LXX), or as a place "Massa." NRSV, NIV, NASB prefer the former, and RSV, REB, McKane, Meinhold and Plöger the latter.

2.1.3 COHESIVE TIES AND THEMATIC GROUPINGS

Thematic groupings can be described as dividing a discourse into smaller units or paragraphs.

> Humans typically process large amounts of information in CHUNKS, somewhat like we eat a meal in bites. This helps us deal with complexity . . . In a longer discourse there will indeed be many items of information; the speaker chunks material into parts which can be dealt with separately.[53]

Such smaller units are often knit closely together. In discourse, it is common to find cohesive ties occurring in patterns, which are based on thematic groupings. Such cohesive ties will be described below as they occur in LXX Proverbs.

The translator of Proverbs tends to group longer stretches of discourse into shorter units especially where it is more difficult to spot the theme of a larger discourse. But even when the idea is less complex he tends to employ cohesive ties and to refer to the immediate.

2.1.3.1 Cohesive Ties and Thematic Groupings in General

Prov 2:12–17

MT: 12 לְהַצִּילְךָ מִדֶּרֶךְ רָע מֵאִישׁ מְדַבֵּר תַּהְפֻּכוֹת׃
13 הַעֹזְבִים אָרְחוֹת יֹשֶׁר לָלֶכֶת בְּדַרְכֵי־חֹשֶׁךְ׃
14 הַשְּׂמֵחִים לַעֲשׂוֹת רָע יָגִילוּ בְּתַהְפֻּכוֹת רָע׃
15 אֲשֶׁר אָרְחֹתֵיהֶם עִקְּשִׁים וּנְלוֹזִים בְּמַעְגְּלוֹתָם׃
16 לְהַצִּילְךָ מֵאִשָּׁה זָרָה מִנָּכְרִיָּה אֲמָרֶיהָ הֶחֱלִיקָה׃
17 הַעֹזֶבֶת אַלּוּף נְעוּרֶיהָ וְאֶת־בְּרִית אֱלֹהֶיהָ שָׁכֵחָה׃

"12 To deliver you from the way of evil,
From the man who speaks perverse things;
13 From those who leave the paths of uprightness,
To walk in the ways of darkness;
14 Who delight in doing evil,
And rejoice in the perversity of evil;
15 Whose paths are crooked,
And who are devious in their ways;
16 To deliver you from the strange woman,
From the adulteress who flatters with her words;
17 That leaves the companion of her youth,
And forgets the covenant of her God"

---

[53] Dooley and Levinsohn, *Analyzing Discourse*, 21.

LXX: 12 ἵνα ῥύσηταί σε ἀπὸ ὁδοῦ κακῆς καὶ ἀπὸ ἀνδρὸς λαλοῦντος μηδὲν πιστόν
13 ὢ οἱ ἐγκαταλείποντες ὁδοὺς εὐθείας τοῦ πορεύεσθαι ἐν ὁδοῖς σκότους
14 οἱ εὐφραινόμενοι ἐπὶ κακοῖς καὶ χαίροντες ἐπὶ διαστροφῇ κακῇ
15 ὧν αἱ τρίβοι σκολιαὶ καὶ καμπύλαι αἱ τροχιαὶ αὐτῶν
16 τοῦ μακράν σε ποιῆσαι ἀπὸ ὁδοῦ εὐθείας καὶ ἀλλότριον τῆς δικαίας γνώμης
17 υἱέ μή σε καταλάβῃ κακὴ βουλὴ ἡ ἀπολείπουσα διδασκαλίαν νεότητος καὶ διαθήκην θείαν ἐπιλελησμένη

"12 to deliver you from the evil way, and from the man who speaks nothing faithfully.
13 Alas/Oh for those who forsake right paths to walk in ways of darkness;
14 who rejoice in evils, and delight in wicked perverseness;
15 whose paths are crooked, and their courses winding;
16 to remove you far from the straight way, and to estrange you from a righteous purpose.
17 (My) son, let not evil counsel overtake you of her who has forsaken the instruction of her youth, and forgotten the covenant of God"

The insertion of ὢ "oh, alas" in Prov 2:13, as well as the vocative υἱε in v. 17, serve the purpose of making the units smaller. The particle as such marks discontinuity, and it seems that the translator disconnected v. 13 from the previous verse in order to give the paragraph more cohesion, as otherwise the argument would have become too long and thus less coherent. This is supported by the fact that v. 16, a substitution by the translator,[54] expresses the evil purpose of the "evil men" who have been characterized and described in vv. 13–15, and is thus joined closely to the previous verses. In the MT, however, v. 16 refers far back to the "wisdom" in v. 10 that will save the man from the adulteress (cf. v. 12).[55]

The insertion of υἱε in v. 17 (and the whole of the first colon of Prov 2:17 has nothing corresponding in the MT) is not surprising considering the translator's endeavor to group big units into smaller paragraphs. For this purpose he not only used ὢ in v. 13 as a discourse marker, but similarly in v. 17 he inserted the vocative υἱε plus imperative (e.g. Prov 1:8; 3:11,21; 4:10,20; 5:1,7;

---

[54] The construction τοῦ μακράν σε ποιῆσαι is quite Greek and can be found in Isa 8:1 and Gen 47:29 where the Hebrew text is not followed literally.

[55] Both verses 12 and 16 start with לְהַצִּילְךָ "to save you" and give the purpose of the "wisdom" (v. 10) entering one's heart.

6:20; 7:1,24; 8:32), a very frequent beginning of a new unit in Proverbs, in order to connect the preceding unit to v. 17b.[56]

In summary, the translator of Proverbs divided the long unit of Prov 2:12–17 into smaller chunks in order to make the pieces "bite-sized," thus making it easier for the reader or hearer to comprehend. He did this without regard for the original meaning of his assumed *Vorlage*.[57] This conclusion is supported by the following cases.

2.1.3.2 Cohesive Ties and Thematic Groupings as Affecting Parallel Forms

The translator's fondness for grouping larger units or even clauses differently from the MT affected parallel forms, resulting in renderings that were less parallel than the MT.

1. Prov 4:15

MT: פְּרָעֵהוּ אַל־תַּעֲבָר־בּוֹ שְׂטֵה מֵעָלָיו וַעֲבוֹר
"Avoid it, do not pass by it, turn away from it, and pass on"

LXX: ἐν ᾧ ἂν τόπῳ στρατοπεδεύσωσιν μὴ ἐπέλθῃς ἐκεῖ ἔκκλινον δὲ ἀπ' αὐτῶν καὶ παράλλαξον
"In whatever place they will pitch their camp, go not thither; but turn from them, and pass by"

Prov 4:15 is a fairly synonymously parallel structure. The LXX rendering, however, due to the translational introductory clause describing the circumstance, may be regarded as less parallel. In the MT the verse is linked to the previous verse, the object "it" referring to "the way of evil men" (v. 14).[58] The translator, however, instead of referring back, started a new unit and even developed the thought further by adding, "In whatever place they will pitch their

---

[56] But the "adulteress" which is mentioned in the MT of v. 16 has not been introduced *expressis verbis* in the LXX, only described in v. 17.

[57] J. Cook sees the translator's religious intentions behind the division(s) into smaller units. Cook, *Proverbs*, 135, 149. Cook states, "This extremely competent translator had the literary tools with which to elaborate on his religious views brilliantly." *Ibid.*, 150. It is, however, difficult to know whether these divisions are religiously motivated, and if they are, as Cook thinks, the translator can hardly be called "an extremely competent translator," *Ibid.*, 317.

[58] 4:14 MT: בְּאֹרַח רְשָׁעִים אַל־תָּבֹא וְאַל־תְּאַשֵּׁר בְּדֶרֶךְ רָעִים "Do not enter the path of the wicked, and do not go/proceed in the way of evil men."

LXX: ὁδοὺς ἀσεβῶν μὴ ἐπέλθῃς μηδὲ ζηλώσῃς ὁδοὺς παρανόμων "Do not go in the ways of the ungodly, neither desire the ways of transgressors."

camp." Or he may just have explicated what he thought was implied already. In either case, he produced smaller units to the detriment of the parallelism.

2. Prov 6:1–3

MT: 1 בְּנִי אִם־עָרַבְתָּ לְרֵעֶךָ תָּקַעְתָּ לַזָּר כַּפֶּיךָ׃
2 נוֹקַשְׁתָּ בְאִמְרֵי־פִיךָ נִלְכַּדְתָּ בְּאִמְרֵי־פִיךָ׃
3 עֲשֵׂה זֹאת אֵפוֹא בְּנִי וְהִנָּצֵל כִּי בָאתָ
בְכַף־רֵעֶךָ לֵךְ הִתְרַפֵּס וּרְהַב רֵעֶיךָ׃

"1 My son, if you have become surety for your neighbor, (if) you have struck your hand with a stranger.
2 You are snared with the words of your mouth, you are caught with the words of your mouth.
3 Do this now, my son, and deliver yourself, when you have come into the hand (power) of your neighbor: go, humble yourself, and importune your neighbor"

LXX: 1 υἱέ ἐὰν ἐγγυήσῃ σὸν φίλον παραδώσεις σὴν χεῖρα ἐχθρῷ
2 παγὶς γὰρ ἰσχυρὰ ἀνδρὶ τὰ ἴδια χείλη καὶ ἁλίσκεται χείλεσιν ἰδίου στόματος
3 ποίει υἱέ ἃ ἐγώ σοι ἐντέλλομαι καὶ σῷζου ἥκεις γὰρ εἰς χεῖρας κακῶν διὰ σὸν φίλον ἴθι μὴ ἐκλυόμενος παρόξυνε δὲ καὶ τὸν φίλον σου ὃν ἐνεγυήσω

"1 (My) son, if you become surety for your friend, you shall deliver your hand to an enemy.
2 For a man's own lips become a strong snare to him, and he is caught with the lips of his own mouth.
3 (My) son, do what I command you and deliver yourself; for on your friend's account you have come into the hands of evil men; do not lose courage, but stir up even your friend for whom you have become surety (or: to whom you have pledged yourself)"

In the LXX Prov 6:1–2 is grouped differently from the MT, and this affects the parallel form in v. 1. In the MT, לְרֵעֶךָ "to your neighbor" and לַזָּר "to a stranger" are probably the same person.[59] In the LXX, however, the second noun phrase ἐχθρῷ "to an enemy" is quite different from φίλον, and may refer to a second participant to whom the pledge or promise is made.[60] Structurally colon one and

---

[59] According to D. Kidner, *friend* is parallel with *stranger*. Kidner *Proverbs*, 72. Similarly Ross, ". . . the debtor is a neighbor who is a misfit . . ." Ross, "Proverbs," n.p. Also Toy, *Proverbs*, 120. *IB*, 4:817. Clifford, *Proverbs*, 75. But A. Meinhold sees in the "stranger" the creditor, probably a Phoenician businessperson. Meinhold, *Sprüche*, 1:109–110.

[60] J. Cook regards both "friend" and "enemy" as the same person, and as the translator's dualistic interpretation. Cook, *Proverbs*, 155–156.

two in the MT are the compound protasis of the conditional clause (vv. 1–2),[61] preceding the apodosis in v. 3. In the LXX, however, colon one is the protasis and colon two the apodosis, and verse 2 (introduced by γάρ) gives further explanation of the "misery" in relation to the "enemy" mentioned in the previous v. 1b.

One reason for grouping vv. 1–2 differently is probably to avoid the compound protasis of the conditional clause and make smaller and more digestible units. Another reason may be the alteration of לָזָר to ἐχθρῷ (v. 1), adding another participant explicitly which was then referred to as κακῶν "evil (men)" in v. 3.[62] In this connection it is interesting to note that the translator rendered כִּי בָאתָ בְכַף־רֵעֶךָ "when you have come into the hand (power) of your neighbor" by ἥκεις γὰρ εἰς χεῖρας κακῶν διὰ σὸν φίλον "for on your friend's account you have come into the hands of evil men," thus making his friend appear in a better light. Perhaps in a similar vein the first alteration was partly influenced by the translator's hesitation to call a "friend" a "stranger" and that is why he reinterpreted the verse. This is quite likely because the translator seems to emphasize the positive aspect of friendship throughout his translation, e.g. 3:29 . . . καὶ πεποιθότα ἐπὶ σοί "and trusting you" is added; also 15:28a . . . καὶ οἱ ἐχθροὶ φίλοι γίνονται ". . . even enemies become friends";[63] in 16:29 which reads אִישׁ חָמָס יְפַתֶּה רֵעֵהוּ "A violent man entices his neighbor/ friend . . . ," the translator avoids reflecting any negative relationship between neighbors/friends and renders more freely ἀνὴρ παράνομος ἀποπειρᾶται φίλων . . . "A transgressor tries to ensnare friends . . ." keeping the friends as friends. Another example is 25:10; the addition of 25:10a χάρις καὶ φιλία ἐλευθεροῖ "Favor and friendship set a man free, . . ." speaks highly of friendship. Thus the translator may not only have been influenced by his desire for grouping, but also by his positive view of friendship. These considerations, whether it be translational, exegetical, or probably both, led to dropping the parallelism in v. 1.

To sum up, the translator's fondness for grouping units differently from the MT sometimes affected parallel forms and led to rendering them less parallel than the MT.

There are other linguistic and translational reasons, and interpretational considerations, which led the translator to depart from his normal practice of producing closely corresponding lines. These will be dealt with in the following section.

---

[61] Cf. Meinhold, *Sprüche*, 1:109.

[62] J. Cook interprets the "evil men" as identical with "the neighbor." Cook, *Proverbs*, 158.

[63] J. Cook mentions an example from Sir 6:9 where a friend becomes an enemy, *ibid.*, 156, but it seems that our translator had the opposite emphasis of an enemy becoming a friend.

2.2 Linguistics, Translation, Interpretation and Parallel Forms

This section deals with further linguistic and translational reasons, as well as interpretational considerations, that may have been responsible for the translator having less regard than usual for the Hebrew parallel form.

2.2.1 Various Linguistic and Translational Considerations Influence Parallel Forms

1. Prov 1:31

MT: וְיֹאכְלוּ מִפְּרִי דַרְכָּם וּמִמֹּעֲצֹתֵיהֶם יִשְׂבָּעוּ
"therefore they shall eat the fruit of their own way, and be filled with their own plans"

Q: ויאכלו מ[פרי דרכם] [ו]ממעצתיהם ישבעו [64]

LXX: τοιγαροῦν ἔδονται τῆς ἑαυτῶν ὁδοῦ τοὺς καρποὺς καὶ τῆς ἑαυτῶν ἀσεβείας πλησθήσονται
"Therefore they shall eat the fruits of their own way, and shall be filled with their own ungodliness"

In Prov 1:31 דֶּרֶךְ "way" (first colon) and מוֹעֵצָה "plan, scheme" (second colon) correspond closely, but while the former is rendered literally, the latter is rendered more freely by ἀσεβείας "ungodliness" which is slightly less parallel to the first colon. There are several possible reasons for this translational adjustment. Perhaps "filled with their own plans" may not have been a possible collocation[65] because πίμπλημι "fill" never occurs in combination with "plan"[66] or may not have made much sense in Greek. Another reason may have been that the translator chose to be more specific and wanted to spell out the negative meaning of מוֹעֵצָה "plan" in this context.[67]

---

[64] De Waard, "4QProv," 88. Q agrees with the MT.

[65] For collocations see Tauberschmidt, "Principles," 43–47.

[66] In Prov 22:20 מוֹעֵצָה is rendered βουλή.

[67] "Except in 22:20, [מוֹעֵצָה] is used in a bad sense in the O.T." IB, 4:792. G. Gerleman thinks that the "LXX makes the religious point of view more clear." Gerleman, *Studies*, 41. According to M. B. Dick "the additional Greek ἀσεβείας further specifies the ethical tenor of MT . . . 'of their plans' . . ." Dick, "Ethics," 24.

2. Prov 2:22

MT: וּרְשָׁעִים מֵאֶרֶץ יִכָּרֵתוּ וּבוֹגְדִים יִסְּחוּ מִמֶּנָּה
"but the wicked will be cut off from the land, and the treacherous will be rooted out of it"[68]

LXX: ὁδοὶ ἀσεβῶν ἐκ γῆς ὀλοῦνται οἱ δὲ παράνομοι ἐξωσθήσονται ἀπ' αὐτῆς
"The paths of the ungodly will perish from the earth, and transgressors will be driven away from it"

The addition of ὁδοὶ "ways" preceding ἀσεβῶν "ungodly" in Prov 2:22 may be due to the frequent occurrence of ways/paths in the preceding verses (2:8,12,13,15,16,19,20) with which the translator sought to connect this verse. In fact, ὁδοὶ ἀσεβῶν is a familiar phrase which occurs also in 4:14 and 15:9—out of a total of five occurrences in the Hebrew Bible (see also Ps 1:6; Jer 12:1). The explanation given by R. J. Clifford that the phrase may have been borrowed from Ps 1:6 is less plausible at this point.[69] Again, the translator's concern to make links of cohesion is demonstrated here. This led, however, to a parallelism, that is slightly less parallel structurally than the MT.

3. Prov 4:16

MT: כִּי לֹא יִשְׁנוּ אִם־לֹא יָרֵעוּ וְנִגְזְלָה שְׁנָתָם אִם־לֹא יַכְשִׁילוּ
"For they cannot sleep unless they have done wrong; and their sleep is taken away unless they cause someone to fall"

LXX: οὐ γὰρ μὴ ὑπνώσωσιν ἐὰν μὴ κακοποιήσωσιν ἀφήρηται ὁ ὕπνος αὐτῶν καὶ οὐ κοιμῶνται
"For they cannot sleep unless they have done evil; their sleep is taken away, and they rest not"

In the MT of Prov 4:16 the first half corresponds fairly well with the second half. In the LXX, however, the last clause in the second colon is dropped and an extra clause added in parallel with the previous clause. There is no simple explanation for this but it is perhaps possible that the translator made this alteration on purpose to explain further the somewhat uncommon phrase וְנִגְזְלָה שְׁנָתָם "their sleep is taken away,"[70] adding καὶ οὐ κοιμῶνται "and they

---

[68] Synonymous parallelism. *IB*, 4:797. Toy, *Proverbs*, 52.

[69] Clifford, "Observations" 54.

[70] This phrase occurs only here in the MT.

rest not" because otherwise it may have been unclear who took away their sleep.[71]

4. Prov 5:3

MT: כִּי נֹפֶת תִּטֹּפְנָה שִׂפְתֵי זָרָה וְחָלָק מִשֶּׁמֶן חִכָּהּ
"For the lips of a loose woman drip honey, and her palate (or: speech) is smoother than oil"

LXX: μὴ πρόσεχε φαύλῃ γυναικί· μέλι γὰρ ἀποστάζει ἀπὸ χειλέων γυναικὸς πόρνης ἣ πρὸς καιρὸν λιπαίνει σὸν φάρυγγα
"Give no heed to a worthless woman; for honey drops from the lips of a harlot, who for a season pleases your palate"

Prov 5:3 in the LXX may be regarded as less parallel than the MT[72] due to translational adjustments. The first clause μὴ πρόσεχε φαύλῃ γυναικί "Give no heed to a worthless woman," which repeats the command of v. 1 although in a negated and more specific way, has been added in order to connect v. 3 (and what follows) more smoothly to the preceding verses. The translator's concern to make a smooth transition from vv. 2–3 is clearly demonstrated; in the MT the description of the loose woman follows on from the exhortation abruptly.[73] The second clause agrees with the MT (first colon), but the third clause differs, the MT reading וְחָלָק מִשֶּׁמֶן חִכָּהּ "and her palate is smoother than oil," whereas the LXX renders ἣ πρὸς καιρὸν λιπαίνει σὸν φάρυγγα "who for a season pleases your palate." It may have been that the translator simply dropped the second comparative construction[74] and rendered more directly; he even went one step further and expressed the effect "a harlot" may have on a man more explicitly by changing "her palate" to "your palate."

---

[71] Similarly PsSol 4:16 ἀφαιρεθείη ὕπνος ἀπὸ κροτάφων αὐτοῦ ἐν νυκτί "may the sleep be taken from his temples in the night." "Although a Greek original for the *Psalms* has been suggested (Hilgenfeld 1868), most scholars have argued that the Greek version is a translation of a Hebrew original." J. L. Trafton, "Psalms of Solomon," n.p., *ABD on CD-ROM*. Version 2.1, 1997.

[72] Watson says that "In Prov 5,3 the metaphorical word-pair "honey // oil" is used, to good effect." Watson, *Classical*, 133.

[73] Cf. Toy, *Proverbs*, 102. According to Whybray "*LXX*, whose text is otherwise inferior to *MT*, nevertheless perhaps preserves here a trace of the missing couplet . . . : 'Give no heed to a worthless woman who for a season pleases thy palate.'" *Proverbs*, 85. But it is quite surprising that Whybray prefers the longer reading of LXX at this point although otherwise he regards LXX inferior to MT.

[74] There are some serious problems with the translation of comparisons and similes in Proverbs, as in Prov 1:12b; 3:12; 7:22; 11:28; 12:4; 18:8b,11b,19; 23:28a,32,34; 26:1 where the whole figure is dropped and/or often translated differently altogether. See also Tauberschmidt, "Principles," 72, 79.

5. Prov 5:5

MT: רַגְלֶיהָ יֹרְדוֹת מָוֶת שְׁאוֹל צְעָדֶיהָ יִתְמֹכוּ
"Her feet go down to death, her steps follow the path to Sheol"

LXX: τῆς γὰρ ἀφροσύνης οἱ πόδες κατάγουσιν τοὺς χρωμένους αὐτῇ μετὰ θανάτου εἰς τὸν ᾅδην τὰ δὲ ἴχνη αὐτῆς οὐκ ἐρείδεται
"For the feet of folly lead those who deal with her down to Hades with death, and her steps are not established"

The MT of Prov 5:5 appears to be a quite closely parallel couplet, but the LXX rendering is less so for translational reasons. The translator rendered the first colon more explicitly, expressing the meaning of the figurative language, that is, that also those who deal with her (the harlot) will go down to death and Hades.[75] The second colon is similar to the MT, except that "Sheol" is not rendered since it has already been covered in the first half.

6. Prov 7:25

MT: 25 אַל־יֵשְׂטְ אֶל־דְּרָכֶיהָ לִבֶּךָ אַל־תֵּתַע בִּנְתִיבוֹתֶיהָ
"Do not let your heart turn aside to her ways, do not stray into her paths"

LXX: 25 μὴ ἐκκλινάτω εἰς τὰς ὁδοὺς αὐτῆς ἡ καρδία σου
"Do not let your heart turn aside to her ways"

In Prov 7:25 there is fairly close synonymous parallelism in the MT, but in the LXX the second colon is missing.[76] This may be due to a scribal error, as suggested by C. H. Toy,[77] or more probably, the translator dropped the second line on purpose, because of the argumentation that continues in v. 26 ("For many she has wounded and cast down . . . = MT/LXX") giving the reason why one should not follow the adulteress. This translational alteration helps to bind the two parts of the argument together more closely and thus increase the cohesiveness.

7. Prov 9:17

MT: מַיִם־גְּנוּבִים יִמְתָּקוּ וְלֶחֶם סְתָרִים יִנְעָם
"Stolen water is sweet, and bread of secrecy (eaten in secret) is pleasant"

---

[75] "The wicked woman's way of life is fatal to her and to those who consort with her." *IB*, 4:813.

[76] In codex A the second half occurs probably due to a later scribal addition.

[77] Toy, *Proverbs*, 157–158.

LXX: ἄρτων κρυφίων ἡδέως ἅψασθε καὶ ὕδατος κλοπῆς γλυκεροῦ
"Take gladly secret bread, and the sweet water of theft"

In Prov 9:17 a foolish woman offers the secret enjoyments of sexual immorality[78] in a statement of two near parallel lines, whereas in the LXX the translator addresses the recipients directly and more forcefully. This directness is clearly shown in the addition of παρακελεύομαι "I exhort" in v. 16b and is in line with the command in the imperative mood in v. 16a. It may have been this adaptation, which is influenced by the context, that led to a less parallel structure, and the switching of the two halves may have been partly responsible for this.[79]

8. Prov 21:18

MT: כֹּפֶר לַצַּדִּיק רָשָׁע וְתַחַת יְשָׁרִים בּוֹגֵד
"The wicked is a ransom for the righteous, and the faithless for the upright"

LXX: περικάθαρμα δὲ δικαίου ἄνομος
"and a transgressor is a ransom of a righteous man"

Prov 21:18 is in synonymous parallelism with a correspondence between "the wicked" and "the faithless" as well as between "the righteous" and "the upright." Perhaps the translator left out the second half on purpose, sacrificing the parallel structure and connecting the colon directly to the previous verse 17 (which is slightly altered presumably by the translator): ἀνὴρ ἐνδεὴς ἀγαπᾷ εὐφροσύνην φιλῶν οἶνον καὶ ἔλαιον εἰς πλοῦτον "A poor man loves mirth, loving wine and oil in abundance." The particle δὲ (v. 18), indicating further development, supports this view.[80]

9. Prov 22:26

MT: אַל־תְּהִי בְתֹקְעֵי־כָף בַּעֹרְבִים מַשָּׁאוֹת
"Do not be one of those who strike hands (=who give pledges), among those who become sureties for debts"

---

[78] *Ibid.*, 838.

[79] As reason for the transposal of the lines may be suggested that secret bread is less figurative than sweet stolen water. Or else the translator followed the pattern of v. 5 where bread also comes first.

[80] E. Tov regards this case as support for a different *Vorlage* because it is shorter. Tov, "Recensional Differences," 56.

LXX: μὴ δίδου σεαυτὸν εἰς ἐγγύην αἰσχυνόμενος πρόσωπον
"Do not give yourself as surety/security from respect of a person (=due to standing in awe of a person)"

In Prov 22:26 the translator dropped בְתֹקְעֵי־כָף "one of those who strike hands" in the first half and translated the meaning of the symbolic action ("give yourself as security"). The second colon is less parallel to the first and quite different from the MT, as the translator seems to have added the reason why one would give pledges: out of respect for a person. These translational considerations led to departing from the near-synonymous parallelism to produce a kind of logical relation. Normally, however, the translator tended to transform Hebrew parallelisms of logical relations into (near-) synonymous/antithetical forms, cf. 1.2.1.5.1.

10. Prov 23:32

MT: אַחֲרִיתוֹ כְּנָחָשׁ יִשָּׁךְ וּכְצִפְעֹנִי יַפְרִשׁ
"At the last it bites like a serpent, and poisons like an adder"

LXX: τὸ δὲ ἔσχατον ὥσπερ ὑπὸ ὄφεως πεπληγὼς ἐκτείνεται καὶ ὥσπερ ὑπὸ κεράστου διαχεῖται αὐτῷ ὁ ἰός
"But at last (such a one) stretches himself out as one smitten by a serpent, and venom is diffused through him as by a horned serpent"

In Prov 23:32 the MT appears to be parallel, as כְּנָחָשׁ יִשָּׁךְ ". . . it bites like a serpent" (first colon) corresponds closely to וּכְצִפְעֹנִי יַפְרִשׁ "and poisons like an adder"[81] (second colon), whereas the translator produced less parallel colons for translational reasons. The subject in the MT is the wine mentioned in the previous verse, which is compared to the biting of a serpent and adder. In the LXX, however, the subject is the person mentioned in the previous verse, and v. 32 speaks about the effect which the bite of a serpent has on him. The second colon then picks up again the last part of the previous line: "smitten by a serpent," but with further detail as it mentions specifically that "venom is diffused through him," the simile being nevertheless maintained in parallel with the first colon. It may be mentioned here that the translator had a rather free approach to rendering metaphors as well as similes.[82]

11. Prov 26:13

MT: אָמַר עָצֵל שַׁחַל בַּדָּרֶךְ אֲרִי בֵּין הָרְחֹבוֹת
"The lazy person says, 'There is a lion in the road, there is a lion in the streets'"

---

[81] Watson regards the two phrases mentioned as Onomatopoeia that "evokes the well-known hissing of snakes." Watson, *Classical*, 27.

[82] Tauberschmidt, "Principles," 70–72.

LXX: λέγει ὀκνηρὸς ἀποστελλόμενος εἰς ὁδὸν λέων ἐν ταῖς ὁδοῖς[83]
"A sluggard when sent on a journey says, 'There is a lion in the ways'"

In Prov 26:13 the translator rendered the verse as a less parallel couplet than the MT, and this is probably due to the application of translation principles. In the orienter to the speech quotation he translated ἀποστελλόμενος εἰς ὁδόν "when sent on a journey" as a clarification, specifying the circumstances of the direct speech act according to how he understood it.[84] This rendering may have been prompted by שׁלח בדרך. According to J. de Waard the translator employed the technique of metathesis (of שׁחל "lion" (MT) and שׁלח "send" (LXX) to avoid monotonous repetition.[85] The reason for not repeating the direct speech quotation may partly be due to having only one word for lion, λέων, available.[86] Instead of repeating the same word the translator may have rather chosen to drop one line, since variation of style is a feature of Greek[87] which he has applied, e.g. Prov 3:13,24; 8:5; 18:15, see under 3.3.

12. Prov 27:8

MT: כְּצִפּוֹר נוֹדֶדֶת מִן־קִנָּהּ כֵּן־אִישׁ נוֹדֵד מִמְּקוֹמוֹ
"Like a bird that strays from her nest, so is a man who strays from his place (home)"

LXX: ὥσπερ ὅταν ὄρνεον καταπετασθῇ ἐκ τῆς ἰδίας νοσσιᾶς οὕτως ἄνθρωπος δουλοῦται ὅταν ἀποξενωθῇ ἐκ τῶν ἰδίων τόπων
"As when a bird flies down from its own nest, so a man is brought into bondage whenever he estranges himself from his own places"

The near-synonymous comparison in Prov 27:8 may be regarded as slightly less parallel grammatically in the LXX, this being due to the translational insertion of δουλοῦται "he is brought into bondage" in the second half to make the point of comparison clear. There are other similar cases of making explicit information that is implied by a logical argument, e.g. in Prov 23:18; 23:35; 24:14; 25:13; 31:2.[88]

---

[83] Cambridge edition adds: ἐν δὲ ταῖς πλατείαις φονευταί "and (there are) murderers in the streets," probably a gloss from Prov 22:13. Rahlfs adopts the shorter text of B* (original hand of Codex Vaticanus).

[84] J. Weingreen regards the LXX rendering as rabbinic-type commentary. Weingreen, "Rabbinic-Type Commentary," 408–409. But this is far from certain.

[85] Cf. also Clifford "Observations," 54.

[86] The translator used this one word throughout Proverbs whereas in the Hebrew different terms are used, cf. Prov 19:12; 20:2; 28:1 פִּיר; Prov 22:13; 28:15; 26:13 אֲרִי; Prov 30:30 לַיִשׁ; Prov 26:13 שָׁחַל.

[87] For stylistic variation see Tauberschmidt, "Principles," 88-90.

[88] See also Tauberschmidt, "Principles," 68–70.

13. Prov 30:3

MT: וְלֹא־לָמַדְתִּי חָכְמָה וְדַעַת קְדֹשִׁים אֵדָע

"I have not learned wisdom, nor do I have knowledge of the holy ones (or: Holy One)"

LXX: θεὸς δεδίδαχέν με σοφίαν καὶ γνῶσιν ἁγίων ἔγνωκα

"God has taught me wisdom, and I know the knowledge of the holy ones"

In Prov 30:3 apparently the figure of sarcasm or irony is used,[89] which the translator changed into a plain statement by inserting θεὸς δεδίδαχέν με "God has taught me." This is not surprising since the translator has the tendency to render irony or sarcasm straightforwardly, see Prov 19:27 under 3.3.1.5.1. By doing so, he contrasts human wisdom in v. 2 with the wisdom God gives (v. 3), thus producing an antithesis; this is in line with his approach. The addition led to a slightly less parallel structure as the subject switches from third person (God) to first person (I). It is possible that the insertion was not purely translational in nature but was motivated by the translator's piety. According to W. McKane the alteration "has the characteristic marks of a reinterpretation of the vocabulary of wisdom dictated by piety."[90]

14. Prov 31:17,18

MT: 17 חָגְרָה בְעוֹז מָתְנֶיהָ וַתְּאַמֵּץ זְרֹעוֹתֶיהָ

"She girds her loins (or: herself) with strength, and strengthens her arms"

18 טָעֲמָה כִּי־טוֹב סַחְרָהּ לֹא־יִכְבֶּה[91] בַלַּיְל נֵרָהּ

"She sees that her merchandise is good (or: that her business goes well), her lamp does not go out by night"

LXX: 17 ἀναζωσαμένη ἰσχυρῶς τὴν ὀσφὺν αὐτῆς ἤρεισεν τοὺς βραχίονας αὐτῆς εἰς ἔργον

"She strongly girds her loins, she strengthens her arms for work"

---

[89] Cf. D. Kidner, *Proverbs*, 178–179. Similarly Graeme Goldsworthy, *The Tree of Life: Reading Proverbs Today* (Sydney: Aio, 1993), 181–182. Toy writes about Prov 30:2–3: "Apparently a sarcastic avowal of intellectual dullness." *Proverbs*, 521.

[90] McKane, *Proverbs*, 646.

[91] Qere reads בַּלַּיְלָה.

18 ἐγεύσατο ὅτι καλόν ἐστιν τὸ ἐργάζεσθαι καὶ οὐκ
ἀποσβέννυται ὅλην τὴν νύκτα ὁ λύχνος αὐτῆς
"She finds by experience that working is good, and her lamp does not go out all night"

Prov 31:17 may be regarded as a near-synonymous parallelism. In the LXX, εἰς ἔργον "for work" (second colon) is presumably an addition by the translator making explicit what is already implied.[92] This addition influenced the parallel line (but not necessarily towards a less parallel rendering). In the following verse 18 the translator then continued with the concept of ἔργον expressing it by ἐργάζεσθαι "to work" in place of סַחְרָהּ "her merchandise/ business." This is in line with his overall concern to increase the cohesion. Thus the alterations in the two verses are clearly of a translational nature.

15. Prov 31:20

MT: כַּפָּהּ פָּרְשָׂה לֶעָנִי וְיָדֶיהָ שִׁלְּחָה לָאֶבְיוֹן
"She stretches out her hand to the poor, and reaches out her hands to the needy"

LXX: χεῖρας δὲ αὐτῆς διήνοιξεν πένητι καρπὸν δὲ ἐξέτεινεν πτωχῷ
"And she opens her hands to the needy, and reaches out fruit to the poor"

Prov 31:20 is semantically and structurally a parallel couplet. According to A. Meinhold the stretching out of the hands has a charitable purpose, although it is not clear if it signifies the giving of food (22:9) or represents an invitation.[93] Apparently the translator made his source text more meaningful by rendering פָּרְשָׂה "she stretches" by διήνοιξεν "she opens," which implies giving something (first colon), and instead of "her hands" (יָדֶיהָ)[94] rendering καρπὸν "fruit," a more explicit rendering that expressed his understanding of the text. These adjustments are clearly of translational nature and led to a slightly less parallel form lexically.

The translator preferred to connect with the immediate rather than refer back to something mentioned earlier. The application of this principle may have affected parallel forms, as shown in the following case.

---

[92] R. E. Murphy notes: "The Greek adds 'for work' (cf. *BHS*), but this seems merely redundant." Murphy, *Proverbs*, 244.

[93] Meinhold, *Sprüche*, 2:526.

[94] In LXX Proverbs "hand" (יד) is often not translated literally, e.g. Prov 1:24 λόγους "words"; Prov 6:5 ἐκ βρόχων "from the toils" . . . ἐκ παγίδος "out of a snare"; Prov 10:4 πενία ἄνδρα ταπεινοῖ "poverty brings a man low."

16. Prov 3:5–6

MT: 5 בְּטַח אֶל־יְהוָה בְּכָל־לִבֶּךָ וְאֶל־בִּינָתְךָ אַל־תִּשָּׁעֵן׃
6 בְּכָל־דְּרָכֶיךָ דָעֵהוּ וְהוּא יְיַשֵּׁר אֹרְחֹתֶיךָ׃

"5 Trust in the Lord with all your heart; and lean not unto your own understanding.
6 In all your ways acknowledge him, and he will direct your paths"

LXX: 5 ἴσθι πεποιθὼς ἐν ὅλῃ καρδίᾳ ἐπὶ θεῷ ἐπὶ δὲ σῇ σοφίᾳ μὴ ἐπαίρου 6 ἐν πάσαις ὁδοῖς σου γνώριζε αὐτήν ἵνα ὀρθοτομῇ τὰς ὁδούς σου ὁ δὲ πούς σου οὐ μὴ προσκόπτῃ

"5 Trust in God with all your heart; and be not exalted in your own wisdom. 6 In all your ways acquaint yourself with her, that she may rightly direct your paths and (that) your foot may not stumble"

In Prov 3:5–6 the translator's tendency to connect to the nearest approximant is shown in v. 6 where he apparently altered the masculine suffix -הוּ into the feminine pronoun αὐτήν to refer to σοφία in the previous colon (not to the Lord in the colon before) thus changing the meaning of the original. As a consequence he left וְהוּא "and he (the Lord)" untranslated in v. 6 B. The second verb of v. 5, ἐπαίρου "be exalted," is different from the MT תִּשָּׁעֵן "lean" and prepares for the alteration in the following verse. Thus, according to the LXX rendering, to be exalted in ones own wisdom is to be avoided, whereas to be acquainted with her is to be preferred, as she makes straight or directs ones paths. In this rendering then the emphasis is on the right use of wisdom rather than on the Lord as in the MT.

Although at times the addition of colons led to more parallel forms, this is not always the case, as the translator did not apply his principle consistently.[95] There are cases where the addition of a colon does not necessarily improve the parallel structure. However, such "additions" were often made for translational reasons and/or for the sake of cohesion, as in the following examples.

17. Prov 2:19

MT: כָּל־בָּאֶיהָ לֹא יְשׁוּבוּן וְלֹא־יַשִּׂיגוּ אָרְחוֹת חַיִּים

"None who go to her return again, nor do they regain/reach the paths of life"

---

[95] In fact none of the LXX translator's applied translation principles consistently.

LXX: πάντες οἱ πορευόμενοι ἐν αὐτῇ οὐκ ἀναστρέψουσιν οὐδὲ μὴ καταλάβωσιν τρίβους εὐθείας οὐ γὰρ καταλαμβάνονται ὑπὸ ἐνιαυτῶν ζωῆς
"None who go to her return again, nor do they take hold of right paths, for they are not apprehended by the years of life"

In Prov 2:19, see also 2.1.1.2, a third colon is added ("for they are not apprehended by the years of life"), probably for several reasons. The most obvious one is that the translator wanted to give further explanation why they will not return from the way to death, although this reason by itself may not be convincing enough. Further reasons are: the translator rendered אָרְחוֹת חַיִּים "paths of life" (second half) by τρίβους εὐθείας "straight paths" probably under the influence of similar phrases in the preceding verses, e.g. v. 13 ὁδοὺς εὐθείας; v. 15 τρίβοι σκολιαί; v. 16 ὁδοῦ εὐθείας (this last case deviates from the MT and is presumably of a translational nature). But since this rendering covers only half of the Hebrew phrase, the translator may have wanted to cover the other half, חַיִּים, also. This he did by rendering ἐνιαυτῶν ζωῆς "years of life," adding one colon. The use of the same verb καταλαμβάνω as in the second colon speaks in favor of the translational character of the addition. Another reason for adding the clause may have been to produce a smoother transition to v. 20, since vv. 19c and 20 agree in person and number, whereas in the MT they are different. Also, the verbal tense/aspect of καταλαμβάνονται "they are (not) apprehended" (v. 19c) emphasizes the present reality of these evil people not sharing in "the years of life." This connects smoothly with v. 20 that says: εἰ γὰρ ἐπορεύοντο τρίβους ἀγαθάς εὕροσαν ἂν τρίβους δικαιοσύνης λείους "For if they had walked in good paths, they would have found the paths of righteousness easy." Thus the addition, which led to a less parallel structure can be explained translationally.[96]

In the present context it may be helpful to consider also the following verse 21, the parallel structure of which has not been distorted as such in the LXX, but the parallel form is somewhat repeated.

18. Prov 2:21

MT: כִּי־יְשָׁרִים יִשְׁכְּנוּ־אָרֶץ וּתְמִימִים יִוָּתְרוּ בָהּ
"For the upright will live in the land, and the blameless/innocent will remain in it"

---

[96] P. A. de Lagarde regards the second and third colon as a double translation and sees the latter as the original. De Lagarde, *Anmerkungen*, 12. Similarly C. T. Fritsch thinks that the third colon is OG and the second Hexaplaric. Fritsch, "Hexaplaric Signs," 172. Against: According to J. Cook "Both the second and third stichs are partly related to the Hebrew. It is therefore possible that the double translation has been constructed by the translator." Cook, *Proverbs*, 143. For the issue of so-called "double translations" see Talshir, "Double Translations," 21–63.

LXX: χρηστοὶ ἔσονται οἰκήτορες γῆς ἄκακοι δὲ ὑπολειφθήσονται ἐν αὐτῇ ὅτι εὐθεῖς κατασκηνώσουσι γῆν καὶ ὅσιοι ὑπολειφθήσονται ἐν αὐτῇ
"The good-natured will become dwellers in the land, and the innocent will be left in it; because the upright will live in the land, and the holy/devout will be left in it"

A possible reason for this seemingly unnecessary repetition may be as follows. Since v. 20 had been altered into a conditional sentence stating that these people did not go in good paths, it would have been difficult to continue the new sentence in v. 21 with כִּי, ὅτι "because (the upright will dwell in the land)" as in the MT and codex B. Apparently, therefore, the translator inserted the first two colons (without ὅτι) in order to first introduce the good people without any mention of the reason (for a smoother transition) and then add the actual representation of the Hebrew text starting with ὅτι. The fact that χρηστοὶ "the good-natured" does not occur anywhere else in Proverbs and that ἄκακοι "the simple, innocent" is used in parallel with it may indicate that it is unlikely that these reflect a different Hebrew *Vorlage*, and thus support the translational character of the addition. On the other hand, the corresponding words in the second couplet, εὐθεῖς "the upright" and ὅσιοι "the holy," reflect the MT reading.[97]

19. Prov 16:28

MT: אִישׁ תַּהְפֻּכוֹת יְשַׁלַּח מָדוֹן וְנִרְגָּן מַפְרִיד אַלּוּף
"A perverse person spreads strife, and a slanderer/ whisperer separates intimate friends"

LXX: ἀνὴρ σκολιὸς διαπέμπεται κακὰ καὶ λαμπτῆρα δόλου πυρσεύει κακοῖς καὶ διαχωρίζει φίλους
"A perverse person spreads evil/harm, and he will kindle a torch of deceit with evil/harm, and he separates friends"

Prov 16:28 may be regarded as a synonymous parallelism that is more generic in the first line and more specific in the second. The parallelism in the LXX, however, is extended to three lines and appears to be less parallel. The reason for the additional line may be that רגן "whisper (maliciously), backbite, slander" (which occurs as a participle) was rendered freely by λαμπτῆρα δόλου πυρσεύει κακοῖς "he will kindle a torch of deceit with mischief" due to the

---

[97] SH takes colon one and two as OG, and three and four that are closer to the Hebrew as Hexaplaric. Fritsch, "Hexaplaric Signs," 172. But perhaps there is no need for such a distinction since the addition can be explained translationally. In any case, colon one and two in the LXX are secondary.

influence of ἐπὶ δὲ τῶν ἑαυτοῦ χειλέων θησαυρίζει πῦρ "and treasures/ stores fire on his own lips" in the previous v. 27 and to give further explanation. Likewise in Prov 16:30 the clause οὗτος κάμινός ἐστιν κακίας "he is a furnace of wickedness" may have been added[98] to the parallelism for similar reasons, carrying the same picture of "fire" in connection with deceit or wickedness as in the previous vv. 28,29. A further indication of the translational character of the second colon of v. 28 that may be mentioned is the noun phrase κακοῖς "with evil/harm," which has been carried over from the previous clause and, in fact, may have derived from the previous verse.[99]

20. Prov 17:17

MT: בְּכָל־עֵת אֹהֵב הָרֵעַ וְאָח לְצָרָה יִוָּלֵד
"A friend loves at all times, and a brother is born for adversity (or: to help in time of trouble)"

LXX: εἰς πάντα καιρὸν φίλος ὑπαρχέτω σοι ἀδελφοὶ δὲ ἐν ἀνάγκαις χρήσιμοι ἔστωσαν τούτου γὰρ χάριν γεννῶνται
"Have a friend in every time, and let brothers be useful in stress; for on this account they are born"

Prov 17:17 is generally taken as a synonymous parallelism[100] and may be understood as a statement of love being present at all times, even in times of adversity or trouble. In the LXX, however, the verse is in the form of a command, which is perhaps due to the translator's positive view of friendship and the importance he gives it, see also 2.1.3.2 under Prov 6:1–2. The addition of the third line, τούτου γὰρ χάριν γεννῶνται "for on this account they are born," is partly in order to relate the fact that "a brother is born to help in time of trouble" (MT) to both colons, and partly to cover the aspect of the purpose a brother is born for.[101] This resulted in a more cohesive but slightly less parallel form, the LXX rendering consisting of three parts. Colons one and two, however, are fairly parallel.

To sum up, despite the translator's fondness for producing lines that are more parallel than in the MT, at times linguistic and translational considerations influenced parallelisms in his translation leading to less parallel forms structurally and/or semantically.

---

[98] G. Gerleman treats this addition under the stylistical device of assonance. Gerleman, *Studies*, 12.

[99] M. B. Dick lists κακός under moralizing tendency. Dick, "Ethics," 22–23. Unfortunately Dick does not consider other possible influences that may have led to the addition.

[100] Some, however, take the two lines as antithetical. For a discussion see McKane, *Proverbs*, 505–506.

[101] Similarly LXX Prov 4:4.

Some colons may have been added specially out of a desire to make the translation more meaningful and cohesive, while linguistic and translational considerations played a role; this led sometimes to less parallel forms.

Further reasons for some less parallel forms may be related to the Hebrew consonantal text, as the following section shows.

2.2.2 PROBLEMS RELATED TO THE HEBREW CONSONANTAL TEXT(S) (UNDERSTANDING OR TAKING THE HEBREW DIFFERENTLY, OR INNER-TEXTUAL CORRUPTION) INFLUENCE PARALLEL FORMS

The Hebrew consonantal text is often ambiguous because it can be vocalized in various ways. In a number of cases which affect the parallelism of lines, the translator's decision on how to vocalize his source text deviated from that of the MT, or he may have misunderstood his *Vorlage*. In some instances he apparently departed from his source text, or else inner-textual corruption on the part of his *Vorlage* or the MT may have been responsible for the divergence.

In this section examples are discussed of LXX deviations from the MT where the consonantal source text[102] may have given rise to departing from the current Hebrew text, the translator's renderings being influenced by his understanding or misunderstanding of his text, as well as linguistic and translational considerations. Thus, he produced some less parallel forms, as the following cases demonstrate.

1. Prov 4:21

MT: אַל־יַלִּיזוּ מֵעֵינֶיךָ שָׁמְרֵם בְּתוֹךְ לְבָבֶךָ
"Do not let them escape from your sight, keep them within your heart/mind"

LXX: ὅπως μὴ ἐκλίπωσίν σε αἱ πηγαί σου φύλασσε αὐτὰς ἐν σῇ καρδίᾳ
"that your fountains may not fail you, keep them in your heart/mind"

---

[102] There is no agreement on the degree to which the translators were aware of the vocalization of individual words. According to E. Tov, "The translator's decisions with regard to the reading of the consonants must have been similar to those of the persons who read the Bible aloud, with one significant difference. The latter had to commit themselves with regard to the reading of all words, which the translators did not have to do. In fact, the degree to which the translators were aware of the vocalization of individual words is debatable. They certainly were not acquainted with all the details of vocalization, but, apart from some significant exceptions . . . they probably recognized its main features." Tov, *Text-Critical Use*, 107. J. Barr, however, doubts the translator's awareness of the process. James Barr, "Vocalization and the Analysis of Hebrew among the Ancient Translators," VTSup 16 (1967): 1.

The two lines in Prov 4:21 correspond, in that the disciple must use the eyes to watch closely the teacher's words, and the heart or mind to determine to do them.[103] In the LXX, however, the first colon is translated differently from the MT, in that the translator took עַיִן to mean πηγή "fountain, spring" instead of "eye/sight" which is, although a possible meaning, not the correct rendering here. Or the translator may have taken מֵעֵינֶיךָ "from your eye/sight" as מַעְיְנֹתֶיךָ "your fountains" (cf. 5:16) by adding ת. This may have been what led to translating ὅπως μὴ ἐκλίπωσίν σε αἱ πηγαί σου "that your fountains may not fail/forsake you," which may have been understood figuratively in the sense of having sex with other women (cf. 5:16). Also, the first colon is connected to the previous verse 20 as a subordinate clause, a closer connection than in the MT. Apparently these changes led to a less parallel form.

2. Prov 9:18

MT: וְלֹא־יָדַע כִּי־רְפָאִים שָׁם בְּעִמְקֵי שְׁאוֹל קְרֻאֶיהָ
"But he does not know that the shades (=dead)[104] are there, that her guests are in the depths of Sheol"

LXX: ὁ δὲ οὐκ οἶδεν ὅτι γηγενεῖς παρ' αὐτῇ ὄλλυνται καὶ ἐπὶ πέτευρον ᾅδου συναντᾷ[105]
"But he does not know that mighty men perish at her (house), and he falls in with a snare of Hades"

Prov 9:18 ("But he does not know that the shades are there, that her guests are in the depths of Sheol") is a fairly parallel couplet, but the translator took רְפָאִים "shades/dead" to mean "mighty men" or "giants," rendering it γηγενεῖς which is a possible meaning, although not in this verse. And in the second half בְּעִמְקֵי "in the depths" may have been understood figuratively as "deep pit"[106] in the

---

[103] Cf. Ross, "Proverbs," n.p.

[104] "These 'dead' are the [רְפָאִים] often translated 'shades.' It refers to the dead who lead a shadowy existence in Sheol." Ross, "Proverbs," n.p.

[105] The addition of vv. 18a–d is not treated here as this would go beyond the scope of this thesis. E. Tov lists it under inner-translational pluses. Tov, "Recensional Differences," 48. Whybray calls it a "purely homiletic addition by *LXX* after v. 18." Whybray, *Proverbs*, 142.

[106] "The word [עֹמֶק] is used figuratively in the expression 'deep pit' to describe the danger of associating with either an adulteress (Prov 22:14) or prostitute (Prov 23:27)." T. D. Alexander, *NIDOTTE*, 3:439.

sense of a πέτευρον "snare,"[107] hence the rendering ἐπὶ πέτευρον ᾅδου for בְּעִמְקֵי שְׁאוֹל. It may have been these considerations that led to a different and also less parallel rendering.

3. Prov 13:18

MT: רֵישׁ וְקָלוֹן פּוֹרֵעַ מוּסָר וְשׁוֹמֵר תּוֹכַחַת יְכֻבָּד
"Poverty and disgrace are for the one who ignores instruction, but he who regards reproof is//will be honored"

LXX: πενίαν καὶ ἀτιμίαν ἀφαιρεῖται παιδεία ὁ δὲ φυλάσσων ἐλέγχους δοξασθήσεται
"Instruction removes poverty and disgrace, but he who attends to reproofs will be honored"

Prov 13:18 is an antithetically parallel couplet. The translator probably took פרע (MT: "the one who ignores") in the sense of "cast off, remove" (as in 2 Chr 28:19; Prov 29:18),[108] and this led to paralleling an impersonal subject "instruction" (first colon) with a personal subject "he" (second colon), thus producing a less parallel structure.

4. Prov 13:20

For example see 1.2.2.2.

In Prov 13:20 ("He who walks with the wise will be wise, but he who consorts with fools will suffer harm"), an antithetical parallelism, the translator probably read ידוע "he will be known" (and rendered γνωσθήσεται) instead of ירוע "he will suffer harm" (MT), ר and ד being easily confused. This led to a slightly less contrastive form semantically.[109] However, grammatically the LXX appears to be slightly more parallel contrastively than the MT, see 1.2.2.2.

---

[107] πέτευρον a perch for fowls to roost at night, Theocr. deriv. uncertain. H. G. Liddell and R. Scott, comps., *A Greek-English Lexicon* (Oxford and New York: Oxford University Press, 1968). Or "tight-rope?" according to J. Lust, E. Eynikel, and K. Hauspie, comps., *A Greek–English Lexicon of the Septuagint: Part II, K-Ω* (Deutsche Bibelgesellschaft, 1996), 374.

[108] R. A. Taylor, *NIDOTTE*, 3:690.

[109] Although in the MT "will be wise" is not exactly antonymous with "will suffer harm," it corresponds more closely with it contrastively than "shall be wise" corresponds with "shall be known" in the LXX.

5. Prov 13:22

MT: טוֹב יַנְחִיל בְּנֵי־בָנִים וְצָפוּן לַצַּדִּיק חֵיל חוֹטֵא
"A good person leaves his wealth (or: an inheritance) to his children's children, but the wealth of the sinner is laid up for the righteous"[110]

LXX: ἀγαθὸς ἀνὴρ κληρονομήσει υἱοὺς υἱῶν θησαυρίζεται δὲ δικαίοις πλοῦτος ἀσεβῶν
"A good man will inherit children's children, but the wealth of ungodly men is laid up for the righteous"

In Prov 13:22 the translator may have taken נחל (first colon) as a *qal* verb in the sense of "(he) will inherit" and regarded "children's children" as the direct object ("A good man will inherit children's children"). The only problem with this assumption is that the shape of the *hip'il* verb יַנְחִיל "he provides for an hereditary possession" in the MT is slightly different from that of the *qal* verb יִנְחַל "receive possession." But this may not have been a hindrance for the translator considering other adjustments he made, or else he may have misread his text. This could have been what led to a slightly less corresponding parallelism.

6. Prov 14:2

MT: הוֹלֵךְ בְּיָשְׁרוֹ יְרֵא יְהוָה וּנְלוֹז דְּרָכָיו בּוֹזֵהוּ
"He who walks uprightly (lit.: in his uprightness) fears the Lord, but he who is devious/crooked in his ways (=conduct) despises him"

LXX: ὁ πορευόμενος ὀρθῶς φοβεῖται τὸν κύριον ὁ δὲ σκολιάζων ταῖς ὁδοῖς αὐτοῦ ἀτιμασθήσεται
"He who walks uprightly fears the Lord, but he who is crooked in his ways will be dishonored"

Prov 14:2 is antithetical with a close correspondence of the lines. The verb בּוֹזֵהוּ "(he who) despises him" (second colon) stands in contrast with יְרֵא יְהוָה "(he who) fears the Lord" (first colon). The translator, however, apparently rendered בּוֹזֵהוּ as ἀτιμασθήσεται "he shall be dishonored/despised" perhaps by taking the *qal* verb as a *nip'al* verb (נִבְזֶה). This may have been what led to a less parallel construction in the LXX.

---

[110] According to W. McKane "a sinner's wealth is held in store (not for his own posterity but) for a righteous man." McKane, *Proverbs*, 462.

7. Prov 15:6

MT: בֵּית צַדִּיק חֹסֶן רָב וּבִתְבוּאַת רָשָׁע נֶעְכָּרֶת
"In the house of the righteous there is much treasure, but trouble befalls the income of the wicked"

LXX: ἐν πλεοναζούσῃ δικαιοσύνῃ ἰσχὺς πολλή οἱ δὲ ἀσεβεῖς ὁλόρριζοι ἐκ γῆς ὁλοῦνται;[111] οἴκοις δικαίων ἰσχὺς πολλή καρποὶ δὲ ἀσεβῶν ἀπολοῦνται
"In abounding righteousness is much strength, but the ungodly shall completely perish from the earth; in the houses of the righteous there is much strength, but the fruits of the ungodly will perish"[112]

Prov 15:6 may be regarded as an antithetical parallelism.[113] The problem with the LXX is that there is some uncertainty as to whether the first or the second couplet is OG. According to SH the first couplet is to be regarded as OG, and the second, which is closer to the Hebrew, as Hexaplaric.[114] W. McKane, however, assumes that the translator rendered the second couplet and translated נֶעְכָּרֶת as ἀπολοῦνται;[115] also the Cambridge edition favors the second couplet since it puts the first part with v. 5. If this is correct, the translator translated (the second couplet) less antithetically since he rendered חסן by ἰσχὺς "strength, might" (חֹסֶן). This is a possible meaning but in this context "treasures, stores" (חֹסֶן) is more appropriate and fits better with the second colon.[116]

8. Prov 19:6

MT: רַבִּים יְחַלּוּ פְנֵי־נָדִיב וְכָל־הָרֵעַ לְאִישׁ מַתָּן
"Many will seek the favor of the noble, and everyone is a friend to the man that gives gifts"

---

[111] The first part of v. 6 occurs in the Cambridge edition with v. 5. It is not found in the MT.

[112] "The LXX for this verse, however, has no reference to wealth but talks about amassing righteousness." Ross, "Proverbs," n.p.

[113] According to Watson the parallelism may be regarded as "Gender-matched parallelism" (also in Prov 14:13) that is used to reinforce antithesis or contrast. Watson, *Classical*, 125.

[114] Fritsch, "Hexaplaric Signs," 175. Similarly Toy, *Proverbs*, 305.

[115] McKane, *Proverbs*, 484–485.

[116] See also Delitzsch, *Proverbs*, 1:318–319; and V. P. Hamilton, *NIDOTTE*, 2:221.

LXX: πολλοὶ θεραπεύουσιν πρόσωπα βασιλέων πᾶς δὲ ὁ κακὸς γίνεται ὄνειδος ἀνδρί
"Many wait on the favor of kings,[117] but every bad man becomes a reproach to (another) man"

In Prov 19:6 the translator seems to have misread הרע (MT: "friend") and interpreted it as ὁ κακὸς "bad man" rather than as "friend," thus changing the near-synonymous parallelism into an antithetical structure. To explain how ὄνειδος "reproach, insult" could have come about may be more difficult, but there is the possibility that the translator read מדון "contention?" for מתן "gift."[118] This may have been what led to the antithetical and slightly less parallel structure.

9. Prov 23:20

MT: אַל־תְּהִי בְסֹבְאֵי־יָיִן בְּזֹלֲלֵי בָשָׂר לָמוֹ
"Do not be among winebibbers, among riotous eaters of flesh"

LXX: μὴ ἴσθι οἰνοπότης μηδὲ ἐκτείνου συμβολαῖς κρεῶν τε ἀγορασμοῖς
"Do not be a winebibber, neither continue long at feasts, and purchases of flesh"

In Prov 23:20 the two lines are near-synonymous, but the translator produced a slightly less parallel structure. Perhaps this was due to translating זללי "riotous (eaters)" in the sense of the Aramaic זבני,[119] thus rendering (κρεῶν τε) ἀγορασμοῖς "purchases (of flesh)." Or else he was uncertain about the exact meaning of this word, it being rendered πορνοκόπος "fornicator, whoremonger" in 23:21, and ἀσωτίαν "debauchery, wastefulness" in 28:7. He also added ἐκτείνου συμβολαῖς "continue long at feasts," although this was not contrary to the sense. This addition may have been made to give further explanation concerning the circumstances of such drinking and eating.

10. Prov 23:34

MT: וְהָיִיתָ כְּשֹׁכֵב בְּלֶב־יָם וּכְשֹׁכֵב בְּרֹאשׁ חִבֵּל[120]
"You will be like one who lies down in the midst of the sea, like one who lies on the top of a mast"

---

[117] Lust/Eynikel/Hauspie, *Lexicon, Part I*, 204.

[118] Lust/Eynikel/Hauspie, *Lexicon, Part II*, 333.

[119] Delitzsch, *Proverbs*, 2:116.

[120] This word, which only occurs here, is of uncertain meaning. Meinhold, *Sprüche*, 2:398.

LXX: καὶ κατακείσῃ ὥσπερ ἐν καρδίᾳ θαλάσσης καὶ ὥσπερ κυβερνήτης ἐν πολλῷ κλύδωνι
"And you shall lie as in the midst of the sea, and as a pilot in a great storm"

Prov 23:34 may be a near-synonymous couplet. The LXX, however, may be regarded as slightly less parallel, the translator perhaps having taken חבל as חֹבֵל[121] "sailor" (LXX: κυβερνήτης "pilot") instead of חִבֵּל[122] "mast." The probable addition of ἐν πολλῷ κλύδωνι "in a great storm" may have been a result of the previous change, expressing more specifically the feeling of one who is tossed about in the middle of the sea, as the present context speaks of a person who is drunk and uncontrolled.

11. Prov 24:15

MT: אַל־תֶּאֱרֹב רָשָׁע לִנְוֵה צַדִּיק אַל־תְּשַׁדֵּד רִבְצוֹ
"Do not lie in wait like a wicked man (or: O wicked man) against the home of the righteous; do not destroy his resting place"

LXX: μὴ προσαγάγῃς ἀσεβῆ νομῇ δικαίων μηδὲ ἀπατηθῇς χορτασίᾳ κοιλίας
"Do not bring an ungodly man into the dwelling of the righteous, neither be deceived by the feeding of the belly"

In Prov 24:15 the MT appears to be synonymously a more nearly parallel couplet than the LXX, since אַל־תֶּאֱרֹב "do not lie in wait" (first half) corresponds to אַל־תְּשַׁדֵּד "do not destroy" (second half) and נָוֶה "residence, home" (first line) corresponds to רִבְצוֹ "resting place" (second line). The alteration in the LXX may be partly due to the comparison רָשָׁע "like a wicked man" (or else form of address: "O wicked man") which was taken as the object of the verb and thus rendered ἀσεβῆ "an ungodly (man)." The deviation in the second colon is difficult to explain; it does not correspond to the MT at all. This may be due to differences in the source text, or else the translator may have formed the second colon in connection with his first colon in the sense that fellowship with an ungodly man may result in mere "feeding of the belly," although this is uncertain.

---

[121] "8:24 חֹבֵל n.m. sailor (denom. fr. חֶבֶל; i.e. rope-puller); coll." BDB.

[122] "8:23 חִבֵּל n.[m.] prob. mast (as *corded* or *roped* in place; denom. fr. חֶבֶל) only in sim. of drunken man." BDB.

12. Prov 25:15

MT: בְּאֹרֶךְ אַפַּיִם יְפֻתֶּה קָצִין וְלָשׁוֹן רַכָּה תִּשְׁבָּר־גָּרֶם[123]
"With patience a ruler may be persuaded, and a soft tongue breaks the bone"

LXX: ἐν μακροθυμίᾳ εὐοδία βασιλεῦσιν γλῶσσα δὲ μαλακὴ συντρίβει ὀστᾶ
"In long-suffering is success to kings, and a soft tongue breaks the bones"

In Prov 25:15, a near-synonymous parallelism, there is the possibility that the translator may have taken יפתה "he may/will be persuaded" in the sense of "he will be spacious, wide, open"[124] and translated more freely by εὐοδία "good journey" or "success" which will be bestowed on a patient leader, thus producing a less parallel structure.

13. Prov 28:22

MT: נִבְהָל לַהוֹן אִישׁ רַע עָיִן וְלֹא־יֵדַע כִּי־חֶסֶר יְבֹאֶנּוּ
"A man with an evil eye (=miser) hastens after wealth, and does not know that want will come upon him"

LXX: σπεύδει πλουτεῖν ἀνὴρ βάσκανος καὶ οὐκ οἶδεν ὅτι ἐλεήμων κρατήσει αὐτοῦ
"An envious man makes haste to be rich, and does not know that the merciful man will have the mastery over him"

In Prov 28:22 there is some contrast between "hastens after wealth" (first colon) and "want/poverty will come" (second half). The LXX in this respect may be regarded as slightly less parallel, as the translator took חסר (MT: חֶסֶר "lack, poverty") as חֶסֶד = ἐλεήμων "the merciful" and read ד instead of ר.

14. Prov 28:28

MT: בְּקוּם רְשָׁעִים יִסָּתֵר אָדָם וּבְאָבְדָם יִרְבּוּ צַדִּיקִים
"In the rising of the wicked (=When the wicked rise), men hide themselves, but in their destruction (=when they perish), the righteous increase"

---

[123] Usually פתה is used in a negative sense but here it is used in a positive sense: "be persuaded." C.-W. Pan, *NIDOTTE*, 3:715.

[124] "17:351 [פָּתָה] vb. be spacious, wide, open." BDB. Also according to C.-W. Pan the basic meaning of פתה is "be open." *NIDOTTE*, 3:715. In all the other occurrences (1:10; 16:29; 24:28) פתה occurs in *pi'el* with the meaning of "to entice," here it is in *pu'al*.

LXX: ἐν τόποις ἀσεβῶν στένουσι δίκαιοι ἐν δὲ τῇ ἐκείνων
ἀπωλείᾳ πληθυνθήσονται δίκαιοι
"In the places of the ungodly the righteous mourn, but in their destruction the righteous shall be multiplied"

In Prov 28:28 בְּקוּם "in the rising" (first colon) corresponds contrastively to בְּאָבְדָם "in their destruction" (second colon), whereas the LXX may be regarded as less parallel at this point; but see 1.2.1.4. This may be because the translator took בקום as במקום = ἐν τόποις "in the places" due to overlooking the מ, or else a scribal error was responsible.

15. Prov 29:2

MT: בִּרְבוֹת צַדִּיקִים יִשְׂמַח הָעָם וּבִמְשֹׁל רָשָׁע יֵאָנַח עָם
"When the righteous increase (=are in authority), the people rejoice; but when the wicked rule, the people groan"

LXX: ἐγκωμιαζομένων δικαίων εὐφρανθήσονται λαοί ἀρχόντων δὲ ἀσεβῶν στένουσιν ἄνδρες
"When the righteous are praised, the people rejoice; but when the ungodly rule, men mourn"

In Prov 29:2 the MT may be regarded as more nearly parallel than the LXX, considering that behind בִּרְבוֹת צַדִּיקִים "when the righteous increase" (first colon) is the idea of authority belonging to the larger group;[125] this corresponds antithetically to וּבִמְשֹׁל רָשָׁע "but when the wicked rule" (second colon). The translator, however, produced a less parallel structure which may be due to taking ברבות as בְּבִרְכוֹת = ἐγκωμιαζομένων "(when) . . . are praised."

To sum up, inner-textual corruption, understanding or misunderstanding or even taking the Hebrew consonantal text differently for exegetical or translational reasons at times influenced renderings of Hebrew parallelisms in the direction of less parallel forms than the MT.

In addition, the translator's theology or interpretation may have led to less parallel renderings, as discussed in the following section.

---

[125] Delitzsch, *Proverbs*, 2:241–242. Similarly A. Meinhold, "Vom Vielwerden der Gerechten ist auch in 28,28b die Rede. Hier steht es parallel zu dem Herrschen des Frevlers, wodurch das Gewinnen der Macht als Bedeutung offensichtlich ist." Meinhold, *Sprüche*, 2:482.

2.2.3 INTERPRETATION AND THEOLOGY INFLUENCES PARALLEL FORMS

As a further factor the interpretative and theological viewpoint of the translator was sometimes responsible for producing less parallel forms. The following are examples of this.

1. Prov 1:32

MT: כִּי מְשׁוּבַת פְּתָיִם תַּהַרְגֵם וְשַׁלְוַת כְּסִילִים תְּאַבְּדֵם
"For the turning away (=waywardness) of the simple kills them, and the complacency of fools destroys them"

Q: •יכ מושבת פ[תים תהרגם] [וש]לות כסילים תאבדם[126]

LXX: ἀνθ' ὧν γὰρ ἠδίκουν νηπίους φονευθήσονται καὶ ἐξετασμὸς[127] ἀσεβεῖς ὀλεῖ
"For because they wronged the simple/innocent they will be slain, and an inquiry will ruin the ungodly"

While Prov 1:32 appears to be synonymously parallel, the LXX may be regarded as less parallel due to the translator's interpretation. In the MT "turning away" and "complacency" will be the ruin of the simple and fools.[128] In the LXX, however, the phrase מְשׁוּבַת פְּתָיִם "the turning away of the simple" may, by a slight change from ו to י, have been taken as מְשִׁיבַת פְּתָיִם[129] "making the simple turn away" that is, that bad people make the simple turn away, leading to the translation ἠδίκουν νηπίους "they wronged the simple."[130] One reason for this interpretation may have been a different and more positive understanding of "the simple" (νηπίους) than in the usual interpretation of the Hebrew where פְּתָיִם "the simple" generally denotes people without moral direction and who are inclined to evil.[131]

The LXX translation of Prov 1:22 supports this view, as there also the פְּתָיִם "simple" do not appear in such a bad light as in the usual interpretation of the MT. In that verse the translator even used the more positive ἄκακοι "innocent,

---

[126] De Waard, "4QProv," 88–89. The reading משובת of the MT is confirmed by SP, (Vulg. and Tg.).

[127] For a discussion of this rendering see Cook, *Proverbs*, 95–96.

[128] Ross, "Proverbs," n.p.

[129] Feminine *hipʿil* participle.

[130] J. de Waard thinks: "The variant ἠδίκουν of G may be the result of an exegesis which considered משובת פתים to be a genitivus objectivus construction, together with a more generic translation of משובת." De Waard, "4QProv," 90.

[131] See also D. Kidner, *Proverbs*, 39.

unsuspecting."[132] For further translational adjustments to Prov 1:22 see under 3.3.1.5.6.

Similarly in the following case the "fool", אֱוִיל / ἀνοήτῳ, appears in a more positive light in the LXX.

2. Prov 17:27,28

MT: 27 חוֹשֵׂךְ אֲמָרָיו יוֹדֵעַ דָּעַת וְקַר־רוּחַ אִישׁ תְּבוּנָה
"He who restrains his words has knowledge, and a man of understanding has a cool spirit (or: stays calm)"
28 גַּם אֱוִיל מַחֲרִישׁ חָכָם יֵחָשֵׁב אֹטֵם שְׂפָתָיו נָבוֹן
"Even a fool, when he keeps silent, is considered wise, when he closes his lips (he is counted) prudent/intelligent"

LXX: 27 ὃς φείδεται ῥῆμα προέσθαι σκληρὸν ἐπιγνώμων μακρόθυμος δὲ ἀνὴρ φρόνιμος
"He who forbears to utter a hard word is discreet, and a patient man is sensible"
28 ἀνοήτῳ ἐπερωτήσαντι σοφίαν σοφία λογισθήσεται ἐνεὸν δέ τις ἑαυτὸν ποιήσας δόξει φρόνιμος εἶναι
"Wisdom will be imputed to a fool who asks after wisdom, and he who keeps silent will seem to be sensible"

Prov 17:28 expresses that silence is one evidence of wisdom. Even a fool appears wise and intelligent when he keeps his mouth shut and thus conceals his folly. In the LXX the second colon corresponds fairly well with the MT. The first colon, however, is slightly different and corresponds less well, as the translator added the idea that the ἀνοήτῳ "fool, ignorant" who asks for wisdom shall receive it. Here a certain hope is expressed that the fool may become wise, whereas in the MT no such hope is held for the אֱוִיל "fool"; he simply appears as wise when he keeps silent. Just as in the previous examples where the translator makes the פְּתָיִם "simple" appear in a better light as ἄκακοι "innocent, unsuspecting" (Prov 1:22) and νηπίους "simple, innocent" (Prov 1:32), here too the ἀνοήτῳ "fool, ignorant" is viewed more positively.

In addition, in altering the first colon of v. 28 the translator may have also considered the context and wished to bring it more in line with the previous verse 27 which speaks of a man who is sparing with his words due to his knowledge and understanding. According to the translator, then, even to a foolish person such wisdom and knowledge can be given if he asks (v. 28, first colon).

---

[132] For a similar view see Cook, *Proverbs*, 86.

3. Prov 4:14

MT: בְּאֹרַח רְשָׁעִים אַל־תָּבֹא וְאַל־תְּאַשֵּׁר בְּדֶרֶךְ רָעִים
"Do not enter the path of the wicked, and do not go/proceed in the way of evil men"

LXX: ὁδοὺς ἀσεβῶν μὴ ἐπέλθῃς μηδὲ ζηλώσῃς ὁδοὺς παρανόμων
"Do not go in the ways of the ungodly, neither desire the ways of transgressors"

In Prov 4:14, a near-synonymous parallelism, the translator translated in a slightly less parallel way. In place of וְאַל־תְּאַשֵּׁר "and do not go" he rendered freely μηδὲ ζηλώσῃς "neither desire," perhaps to make the command stronger.[133] The phrase may have been shaped according to Prov 3:31 where almost exactly the same phrase μηδὲ ζηλώσῃς τὰς ὁδοὺς αὐτῶν is used, a translation that also deviates from the Hebrew slightly.[134] There is a third case, 6:6, where ζηλόω (also in connection with ὁδός) has been introduced for the sake of emphasis, καὶ ζήλωσον ἰδὼν τὰς ὁδοὺς αὐτοῦ "and desire his ways." There the MT is less emphatic and reads רְאֵה דְרָכֶיהָ "see/consider her ways." Thus the translator's interpretation or emphasis led to a slightly less parallel translation.

4. Prov 10:15

MT: הוֹן עָשִׁיר קִרְיַת עֻזּוֹ מְחִתַּת דַּלִּים רֵישָׁם
"The wealth of the rich is his strong city, (but) the destruction of the poor is their poverty"

LXX: κτῆσις πλουσίων πόλις ὀχυρά συντριβὴ δὲ ἀσεβῶν πενία
"The wealth of the rich is a strong city, but the ruin of the ungodly is poverty"

In Prov 10:15 there is a contrast between the rich and the poor. The rich have security against life's uncertainties which the poor are denied.[135] In the LXX, however, the translator contrasted πλουσίων "the rich" with ἀσεβῶν "the ungodly" instead of "the poor" (דַּלִּים), and thus produced a less contrastive pair.

---

[133] McGlinchey takes this verse as proof of an Egyptian coloring, conjecturing that the LXX read תאבה instead of תאשר. J. M. McGlinchey, *The Teaching of Amen-em-Ope and the Book of Proverbs* (Washington, 1939). Against this view, G. Gerleman writes: "Here a false understanding of the Greek text has caused McGlinchey to assume Egyptian influence. The Greek ζηλώσῃς, no doubt, is a translation (not a very good one, to be sure) of Hebr. תאשר, and means 'esteem happy,' 'praise.' When understood in this way the LXX Prov. in this passage shows no greater similarity to the text quoted from Amen-em-Ope [IV 9] than does the MT." Gerleman, *Studies*, 8.

[134] An emendation from תבחר to תתחר based on the LXX is improbable. See also Whybray, *Proverbs*, 73; and Plöger, *Sprüche*, 41.

[135] Goldsworthy, *Life*, 92.

Apparently he made this alteration on purpose to avoid misunderstanding the proverb as to blame the poor for their poverty.[136]

5. Prov 13:17

MT: מַלְאָךְ רָשָׁע יִפֹּל בְּרָע וְצִיר אֱמוּנִים מַרְפֵּא
"A wicked messenger falls into mischief (or: causes trouble), but a faithful ambassador (brings) healing"

LXX: βασιλεὺς θρασὺς ἐμπεσεῖται εἰς κακά ἄγγελος δὲ πιστὸς ῥύσεται αὐτόν
"A rash king will fall into mischief, but a faithful messenger will deliver him"

Prov 13:17 is antithetically parallel, but less so the LXX, in which the "messenger" appears in a more positive light. Besides this example where the translator apparently avoided translating "wicked" messenger, there is another case in Prov 10:26 where the translator avoided translating a similar phrase, "lazy" messenger.[137] Instead, of "wicked messenger" he substituted βασιλεὺς θρασὺς "a rash king" who will receive help from the faithful messenger. The noun מַרְפֵּא "healing" was read as *pi'el* participle and rendered more freely by ῥύσεται αὐτόν "he shall deliver him." Thus the second half was related to the first by referring to the king with a pronoun, which is quite typical for the translator's style. This led to a slightly less contrastively parallel form, but not to a less cohesive structure.

6. Prov 20:12,13

MT: 12 אֹזֶן שֹׁמַעַת וְעַיִן רֹאָה יְהוָה עָשָׂה גַם־שְׁנֵיהֶם
"The hearing ear, and the seeing eye, the Lord has made even both of them"
13 אַל־תֶּאֱהַב שֵׁנָה פֶּן־תִּוָּרֵשׁ פְּקַח עֵינֶיךָ שְׂבַע־לָחֶם
"Do not love sleep, lest you come to poverty; open your eyes, and you will be satisfied with bread"

LXX: 12 οὖς ἀκούει καὶ ὀφθαλμὸς ὁρᾷ κυρίου ἔργα καὶ ἀμφότερα
"The ear hears, and the eye sees; even both of them are the Lord's work"

---

[136] According to R. L. Giese, the translator objected to the factual observation on the way the world is which is given without comment on the way it should be "perhaps fearful of the fact that it could be misinterpreted as an apathetic determinism." Giese, "Compassion," 110.

[137] Note that in Prov 25:13 where the messenger occurs in a positive light "a trustworthy messenger," the LXX does not avoid the reading of the MT.

13 μὴ ἀγάπα καταλαλεῖν ἵνα μὴ ἐξαρθῇς διάνοιξον τοὺς ὀφθαλμούς σου καὶ ἐμπλήσθητι ἄρτων
"Love not to speak ill, lest you be cut off; open your eyes, and be filled with bread"

Prov 20:13 is synonymously parallel with a contrast between loving sleep and staying awake, as well as their results of growing poor and being satisfied.[138] In the LXX, however, while the second colon reflects the text of the MT quite well, the first colon appears to be less nearly parallel since καταλαλεῖν "to speak ill" (first colon) does not correspond closely with διάνοιξον τοὺς ὀφθαλμούς σου "open your eyes" (second colon), whereas פְּקַח עֵינֶיךָ "open your eyes" (second colon) corresponds quite closely with שֵׁנָה "sleep" (first colon). The divergence in the LXX appears to be at least partly of a translational nature, considering the translator's keenness for cohesion. At this point it is less likely that the *Vorlage* differed than that the translator changed the original proverb on purpose to make a smoother connection and bring it in line with the previous verse 12. There it is stated that God made the eye in order to see (and understand) and the ear to hear (and obey). And according to v. 13a of the LXX a person should not use his speech to καταλαλεῖν "speak ill" but he should rather open his eyes and be observant and sensitive. The command διάνοιξον τοὺς ὀφθαλμούς σου "open your eyes" (v. 13b), therefore may have been reinterpreted in this way and may not have been understood as a warning not to be lazy as in the MT. It is possible that apart from the translational considerations the translator wanted to stress the point that one should not love ill speech rather than that of not being lazy.[139]

7. Prov 21:8

MT: הֲפַכְפַּךְ דֶּרֶךְ אִישׁ וָזָר וְזַךְ יָשָׁר פָּעֳלוֹ
"The way of the guilty[140] is crooked, but as for the pure, his work is right (or: but the conduct of the pure is right)"

---

[138] Ross, "Proverbs," n.p. Cf. Mouser, *Proverbs*, 29.

[139] G. Gerleman sees behind the adaptation in v. 13a the Stoic view of life. Gerleman, *Studies*, 54. This view, however, may be reading more into the text than the translator intended. For a discussion on major deviations between LXX and MT of Prov 20:10–22 see Andreas Scherer, *Das weise Wort und seine Wirkung: Eine Untersuchung zur Komposition und Redaktion von Proverbia 10,1–22,16* (Neukirchener Verlag, 1999), 265–266. According to Scherer these major deviations do not result from differences in the *Vorlage* but the reasons for these deviations are to be sought in the editprial work of the translator(s).

[140] It seems best to derive וָזָר (hapax legomenon) from a cognate Arabic root meaning "guilty" (cf. NIV, NASB, NKJV, RSV, NRSV). E. Carpenter/M. A. Grisanti, *NIDOTTE*, 1:1064–1065.

LXX: πρὸς τοὺς σκολιοὺς σκολιὰς ὁδοὺς ἀποστέλλει ὁ θεός ἁγνὰ γὰρ καὶ ὀρθὰ τὰ ἔργα αὐτοῦ
"To the crooked God sends crooked ways, for his works are pure and right"

In Prov 21:8, an antithetic parallelism, the translator may have added the idea that God is the one who sends crooked ways. There are other instances in LXX Proverbs where θεός is added for various reasons, as in Prov 30:3; 31:1; 31:2; 31:8 (also 4:27(a); 22:8(a)). In the second half the translator gives the reason for God's acting, connecting it logically to the first half and keeping God as the actor. In so doing he changes the meaning of the original proverb, and also sacrifices the antithetical form for the sake of a logical parallelism. This goes against his normal pattern of transforming logical parallelisms into synonymously or antithetically parallel forms, cf. 1.2.1.5.1.

8. Prov 28:4

MT: עֹזְבֵי תוֹרָה יְהַלְלוּ רָשָׁע וְשֹׁמְרֵי תוֹרָה יִתְגָּרוּ בָם
"Those who forsake the law praise the wicked, but those who keep the law strive against them"

LXX: οὕτως[141] οἱ ἐγκαταλείποντες τὸν νόμον ἐγκωμιάζουσιν ἀσέβειαν οἱ δὲ ἀγαπῶντες τὸν νόμον περιβάλλουσιν ἑαυτοῖς τεῖχος
"so they that forsake the law praise ungodliness, but they that love the law fortify themselves with a wall"

Prov 28:4 is antithetic with a contrast between "those who forsake the law" and "those who keep the law" as well as "praise the wicked" and "strive against them." The LXX, however, is slightly less parallel. Apparently the translator substituted περιβάλλουσιν ἑαυτοῖς τεῖχος "fortify themselves with a wall" for יִתְגָּרוּ בָם "strive against them"[142] (second colon). The Targum adds, "so as to induce them to repent," giving the line a positive meaning. Similarly the translator may have wished to avoid the provocative "strive against them," choosing instead the more positive figure of the wall as a protection (from evil). In Prov 25:28 of the MT[143] there is a similar figure of a wall, except that there it is the figure of a broken city wall which is compared to a man that lacks self-control. In the LXX of that verse, however, the translator seems to have changed

---

[141] οὕτως "so, in this way/manner" connects to the previous verse and compares the ungodly men with those who forsake the law.

[142] גרה in *hitpaʿel* means "to engage in strife" in the sense of "to provoke a group of people to war." J. M. Bracke, *NIDOTTE* 1:891.

[143] עִיר פְּרוּצָה אֵין חוֹמָה אִישׁ אֲשֶׁר אֵין מַעְצָר לְרוּחוֹ "Like a city breached, without walls, is a man who lacks self-control."

"who lacks self-control" to "who does anything without advice/counsel."[144] Both cases show that the translator favored the figure of a wall (for protection), in one case in connection with νόμος "law" (28:4) and in the other with βουλή "advice" (25:28). Thus the departure from the Hebrew text which led to a less parallel rendering may be due to the translator's own theology.

To sum up, the translator's interpretation and theological viewpoint may have been responsible for the overruling of his normal pattern of producing renderings that are more nearly parallel.

2.3 Conclusion

Despite the translator's predilection for closely corresponding lines, there are parallelisms in LXX Proverbs that are less parallel semantically and/or grammatically than those in the MT. Quite a number of these instances, however, are the product of the translator's concern to maintain cohesiveness beyond the parallel lines of the couplet (2.1). This concern can be observed in LXX Proverbs in general (2.1.1), as connectives and markers or particles are added by the translator to link information and tie it together more closely and thus make the translation more cohesive, Prov 1:2,3,26; 2:10; 29:20; 31:12 (2.1.1.1). There is considerable agreement in tense/aspect or person and number especially in cases where the Hebrew tends to go back and forth between person, number and tense/aspect, Prov 1:22; 2:19,20; 2:9; 4:4; 12:13 (2.1.1.2). Participants that are introduced with nouns (or noun phrases)—or if they are not introduced the translator introduces them first—are referred to by pronouns, the person affix in the verb, or zero reference, whereas in the MT there are fewer cohesive links, Prov 1:11–13; 3:27,28; 23:11; 22:11 (2.1.1.3). And deictics are added to provide a tighter connection to what precedes and make the relationship of the lines or verses more explicit, Prov 1:5; 9:10,11; 24:34; 25:22 (2.1.1.4). All these linguistic signals of grammatical cohesion reflect the translator's concern to produce a cohesive translation. At times, these linguistic signals of grammatical cohesion, especially at the level of the paragraph, influenced the smaller units of the couplets. This led to less parallel forms. Thus, Prov 1:28; 2:7,16; 20:3; 2:1; 3:32; and 31:8 appear to be less parallel in the LXX than the MT parallelisms (2.1.2). The feature of "Cohesive ties and thematic groupings" (2.1.3) in particular gives evidence that the translator tended to group paragraphs differently and chop up larger units into smaller paragraphs to make them more digestible, again increasing cohesiveness, e.g. Prov 2:12–17 (2.1.3.1). This process sometimes resulted in less parallel forms, Prov 4:15 and 6:1(–3) (2.1.3.2). Thus, although the translator placed a priority on producing closely corresponding lines especially in couplets (which are highly cohesive

---

[144] ὥσπερ πόλις τὰ τείχη καταβεβλημένη καὶ ἀτείχιστος οὕτως ἀνὴρ ὃς οὐ μετὰ βουλῆς τι πράσσει "As a city whose walls are broken down, and which is unfortified, so is a man who does anything without counsel."

especially lexically), he also had the bigger picture in mind and was concerned to get across the overall meaning of larger units using features like linguistic signals and thematic grouping to achieve his goal.

Aside from the features of linguistic signals and cohesive groupings, there are further reasons (2.2) for the appearance of less parallel renderings. Among all these reasons there are first those that are translational and linguistic, Prov 1:31; 2:22; 4:16; 5:3,5; 7:25; 9:17; 21:18; 22:26; 23:32; 26:13; 27:8; 30:3; 31:17,20; 3:5–6; 2:19,21: 16:28; 17:17, (2.2.1). Then there are problems concerning the Hebrew consonantal text(s) (understanding or taking the Hebrew differently, or inner-textual corruption), Prov 4:21; 9:18; 13:18,20,22; 14:2; 15:6; 19:6; 23:20,34; 24:15; 25:15; 28:22,28; 29:2 (2.2.2); and lastly interpretational reasons and theological biases, Prov 1:32; 17:28; 4:14; 10:15; 13:17; 20:13; 21:8; 28:4 (2.2.3).

In some cases (but not all) the addition of colons contributed to producing less parallel renderings, see under 2.2.1, Prov 2:19,21: 16:28; 17:17. These colons may have been added to make the translation more meaningful and cohesive by applying linguistic and translational considerations. Another reason for adding colons is that the translator sought to cover words and phrases which he was not able to render within his normal framework due to translational and contextual considerations, see Prov 2:19 and 17:17 under 2.2.1; (Prov 5:23 under 1.2.3); (see also Prov 22:11 under 3.3.1.5.4, and Prov 11:16 under 3.3.1.3).[145] On the other hand, there are many examples of additions which have led to more parallel forms than the MT reading, Prov 1:14, (1.2.1.2); Prov 18:22 (1.2.1.3); Prov 11:21, (1.2.1.4); Prov 4:10, (1.2.1.5.1); Prov 8:10, (1.2.1.5.3); 6:10,35, (1.2.1.5.6); Prov 1:27; 8:34, (1.2.1.5.7); and Prov 1:22 (2.1.1.2). Generally speaking, additions are a difficult issue because it is not always apparent whether they are due to differences in the source text or to the application of translation principles. However, in this study only those cases have been treated for which convincing translational, exegetical etc. reasons can be given.

Since these less parallel forms can be explained on the basis of the translator's translation practice (linguistically, translationally, interpretationally, textually), they do not invalidate his general predilection for producing more nearly parallel forms.

After evidence has been given for the translator's predilection for producing forms that are more parallel (Chapter One) and after those cases that seem to contradict the thesis have been explained (Chapter Two), the findings will be used to distinguish cases where LXX Proverbs differs from the MT for

---

[145] Similar cases are Prov 28:22 (2.2.2) and 1:23 (1.2.1.1), although in these cases there are no additional colons added. These cases speak in favor of the translator's attempt for a certain degree of accuracy despite the free character of his translation. Cook, however, thinks that "not the details but the (religious) intention was of primary importance" for the translator. Cook, "Aspects," 153. But this assumption seems to be too general and undifferentiated.

translational, linguistic, interpretational, etc. reasons from those where the difference is due to a different text, while working on the basis of the hypothesis that the *Vorlage* of LXX Proverbs was similar to the MT. To this we will now turn.

3. PARALLELISM AND TEXTUAL CRITICISM

3.1 The Value of the LXX

Before using the LXX for textual criticism an important question to ask is the value of the LXX. Does the LXX consist of many independent translations, or one Greek original or proto-LXX? It was de Lagarde who first discussed the principles involved in reconstructing the original form of the LXX. He thought that all manuscripts of the LXX derive from one Greek prototype. He held a similar theory for the MT. The view that all existing LXX manuscripts are based on one prototype has been accepted by the majority of scholars, except that not all agree that the underlying text of the LXX should be called its "Urtext."[1] P. Kahle (1875–1964) was the first scholar who questioned the existence of such an "Urtext."[2] He believed that there never existed an original or proto-LXX and thus he questioned the value of the LXX in reconstructing an early form of the Hebrew text.[3] Kahle saw the LXX as similar to the Aramaic Targums, which were partial or multiple translations made (over a long period of time) to meet practical needs. It follows that the value of the LXX for textual criticism of the Hebrew Bible is fairly minimal.[4] Kahle's hypothesis, however, has remained unsupported by other scholars, except by his pupil Sperber.[5] Recent years have seen the decline of Kahle's theory. For instance, the discovery and publications of a Greek translation of the Minor Prophets from Nahal Hever in the Judean desert is far from showing the great variety of Greek translations in pre-Christian times that Kahle at first proposed. This scroll is now seen as a revision of the LXX from about the turn of the era. It strongly supports the idea that there was once a single original translation of the Bible, a proto-LXX.[6] Also, J. W. Wevers has shown concerning the Greek "Dodekapropheton" scroll of Hab 2:6 (which is based on the LXX) that its text is a revision on the basis of the MT. In

---

[1] P. de Lagarde says, "Es ist Jahre hindurch meine Absicht gewesen, die drei durch Hieronymus uns bezeugten amtlichen Recensionen der Septuaginta herzustellen, sie in Parallel-Columnen drucken zu heißen, und aus der Vergleichung dieser drei Texte Weiteres zu erschließen." Paul de Lagarde, *Septuaginta-Studien* (Göttingen, 1891), 3. By means of comparing the three texts mentioned as well as quotations of church fathers etc. it was Lagarde's aim to arrive at a LXX "Urtext," "wobei der dem masoretischen Text fernste Text als der ursprüngliche zu gelten habe." Cf. Würthwein, *Text*, 71–72.

[2] Tov, "The Septuagint," 165–166.

[3] P. Kahle, *The Cairo Geniza* (Oxford: Basil Blackwell, 1959).

[4] Ralph W. Klein, *Textual Criticism of the Old Testament: The Septuagint after Qumran* (Philadelphia: Fortress, 1974), 3.

[5] Tov, "The Septuagint," 167.

[6] Klein, *Textual Criticism*, 4.

his conclusions he says: "Unser Text sollte nun ein für allemal Kahles Theorie von den 'vielen Übersetzungen' begraben. Hier ist ein Text, der offensichtlich jüdisch ist und der ebenso offensichtlich zeigt, dass er eine Revision des sogenannten 'christlichen' LXX-Textes ist."[7]

Should the LXX then be regarded as a textual witness? In the traditional approach (until 1947) of grading the textual witnesses of the OT, the MT, the LXX, and (for the Pentateuch) the SP were regarded as the three pillars of the biblical text.

The perception of this "tripartite division" is, according to E. Tov, "based partly on the limitations of the textual knowledge until 1947 and partly on analogy with the textual transmission of the LXX and New Testament."[8] After the discovery of Hebrew scrolls in the Judean Desert, however, the traditional description of the main witnesses of the OT text is problematic. Tov thinks that these main witnesses do not reflect different textual types, but should rather be regarded as reflecting three texts. He writes: "These texts relate to each other as all *early* texts of the OT relate to each other: in an intricate web of agreements, differences and exclusive readings. . . . The LXX merely represents a single text and not a family as is the case with the MT, nor a recension as is the case with the SP."[9]

Many scholars, however, maintain the traditional approach, and it has indeed become even more dominant since 1947. "Scholars have attempted to determine the place of each individual scroll within the framework of the tripartite division of the textual witnesses."[10] According to E. B. Brotzman the great majority of Qumran scrolls support the Masoretic Text,[11] "but there are also manuscripts that support the readings of the Septuagint and Samaritan Pentateuch, as well as others that are not aligned with any previously known text type."

M. Müller says that after the discoveries of the Qumran scrolls "Very soon three text families were sorted out. Besides the "proto-Masoretic," some texts

---

[7] J. W. Wevers, *Septuaginta-Forschungen seit 1954*, TRu 33 (1968): 76-77. Cf. Würthwein, *Text*, 75.

[8] Emanuel Tov, *The Hebrew and Greek Texts of Samuel* (Jerusalem: Academon, 1980), 63–64.

[9] Emanuel Tov, "The Contribution of the Qumran Scrolls to the Understanding of the LXX," in *Septuagint, Scrolls and Cognate Writings* (ed. G. J. Brooke and B. Lindars; Atlanta: Scholars Press, 1992), 41.

[10] Tov, *Texts of Samuel*, 63–64.

[11] Brotzman, *Textual Criticism*, 96. About forty percent of the Hebrew biblical texts from Qumran contain the consonantal text of the MT, and only five percent reflect a Hebrew text-type close to the LXX. Jobes and Silva, *Invitation*, 176. See also the evidence from the 4QProv fragments in this thesis. According to J. de Waard, in four out of five instances 4Q103 supports the MT against G. De Waard, "4QProv," 87–96. See also Scherer, *Das weise Wort*, 166–167.

were found to represent the Alexandrian tradition, that is, the Septuagint-tradition and others, the Samaritan Pentateuch."[12]

In the opinion of E. Würthwein, the Hebrew text of the OT which had become the standard text around 100 A.D. must be understood as a product of historical development after the fall of Jerusalem. The view that this text was not a completely new creation but was created by the Rabbis following ancient traditions is supported by those finds of Qumran which are closely related to the MT. For instance, the Isaiah scroll 1Q Is^b is not much different from the MT. This means that we can probably assume that there was a proto-Masoretic text in use. Besides the proto-Masoretic text there were two other text-forms (Textgestalten) in use. There is, however, no indication that the proto-Masoretic text was more authoritative than the other two.[13] It was only later, in connection with the Jewish restoration, that one text, already in use, became authoritative and superseded the other texts which had been in use before 70 A.D. As the texts of Murabba'at (which are almost identical with MT) indicate, this text prevailed in 132–135 A.D. We would not know of the plurality of texts in use if we did not have the SP, the Nash Papyrus, the LXX, and especially the texts of Qumran. Even among these texts, three main groups can be seen, of which one group of texts is closely related to SP, a second group to LXX, and the third group to the MT.[14]

It is, however, not clear how this plurality of textual groups is to be interpreted historically. F. M. Cross follows W. F. Albright's hypothesis that these different types of text must be understood as local types, of which one is Palestinian, another Egyptian, and the third Babylonian. Sh. Talmon holds against this view that it does not explain satisfactorily the plurality of text-types at the end of the pre-Christian era. He thinks that these texts were in use among different social and religious groups, and thus the differences between the texts can be explained by supposing a certain controlled freedom of the authors and scribes. Talmon thinks that there were other texts and families which are not known today.

According to Tov there were no text types, but only independent texts (see above).[15] He thinks that the LXX was not translated from an Egyptian local text

---

[12] Müller, *First Bible,* 34.

[13] M. Müller says in *First Bible,* 66–67, that there is no indication in the writings of Aristeas, Aristobulus, Philo or Josephus "that the Greek version is understood as incomplete or secondary. Only in later rabbinical sources do we meet the assertion that the Seventy-two had altered details in their translation out of regard to king Ptolemy." Against: In D. W. Gooding's view (personal correspondence), "both Aristeas and Philo base the authority of the Greek version on the claim that it is an absolutely exact translation of the original Hebrew. The claim is quite clearly not true (whatever Hebrew *Vorlage* it was based on). But their claim shows quite clearly where they considered the authority lay: not in the translation but in the Hebrew original."

[14] Würthwein, *Text,* 17–18.

[15] *Ibid.,* 18.

type with Egyptian characteristics, but rather from a Palestinian text, as claimed by the Epistle of Aristeas.[16] However, E. Tov partly supports the theory of local text families in the following way:

> When the early editions of these books [of the OT] were completed, they were accepted by the people as final and were accordingly put into circulation, but at a later period, 'revised editions' of the books, intended to replace the earlier ones, were written and circulated. The process of substitution, however, was only partial, so that the early editions did not completely go out of existence. In Palestine, the new edition that was later to become MT—almost identical with the edition contained in Tg, Syr, Vg—replaced the earlier texts but could not replace them completely. Thus, the early editions remained in use in places that were not central from a geographical and sociological point of view, such as the Qumran repository of texts and the various manuscripts from which the Greek translation was prepared in Egypt. These early editions were thus preserved for posterity, by mere chance, in the Septuagint translation and through the discoveries in Qumran.[17]

To sum up, opinions on the value of the LXX differ. Kahle's hypothesis of the LXX being similar to the Aramaic Targums, which were partial or multiple translations to meet practical needs, has remained unsupported by most scholars. The question is whether the LXX *Vorlage* represents merely a single text or a textual family. In Tov's opinion the MT represents a family, the SP a recension, and the LXX *Vorlage* merely a single text that relates to other texts in an intricate web of agreements, differences and exclusive readings. In Müller's view, however, the LXX *Vorlage* represents a textual family. In his opinion the LXX has great value as a more or less reliable text witness of an "original" Bible, or as a witness to the process of transmitting tradition.

My own view is in line with HOTTP and HUBP; both groups agree that period one, the period of the so-called Ur-text, falls outside the province of textual criticism *in sensu stricto*.[18] In any case, even if the LXX should be given great importance as a textual witness, we need to consider its translational character, and particularly that of LXX Proverbs.

---

[16] Tov, *Textual Criticism*, 186.

[17] *Ibid.*, 316.

[18] Cf. INTRODUCTION.

3.2 Evaluation of Textual Witnesses

According to E. Würthwein, as a general rule the MT must be given priority where no fault can be found in it either linguistically or regarding its content, except if there are good reasons for employing other readings in particular cases.[19] As the most important textual witnesses besides the MT he regards SP, Q, and LXX, followed by Aq., Symm., Th., Syr., Tg., Vulg., VL, Sa., Copt., Eth., Ar. in order of importance.[20]

E. Tov, however, does not accept that there is an unequal status of textual sources. Rather, in his view all readings or witnesses have an equal status, including ancient versions, provided the variant has been obtained by reliable methods of reconstruction. Yet he regards the MT readings as, on the whole, preferable to those found in other texts.[21]

According to E. R. Brotzman

> the absolute superiority of the Masoretic Text in every verse of the Old Testament cannot be maintained. But neither should the Masoretic Text be relegated to being just one more witness to the wording of the text. As a whole, the Masoretic Text is certainly to be valued more highly than the witness derived from the versions. But in any one particular text, the various readings of all witnesses must be considered and a valid decision reached based on internal evidence.[22]

Since textual criticism does not proceed according to democratic rules, Tov does not see reliance on a broad attestation of textual evidence as profitable, since it could have been created by coincidence. Rather a reading should be judged on its intrinsic and inherent value.[23]

---

[19] Würthwein, *Text*, 127.

[20] *Ibid.*, 125.

[21] Tov, *Textual Criticism*, 298–299.

[22] Brotzman, *Textual Criticism*, 127. The following is a quotation of the current standard text which is specifically recommended for use by interconfessional groups of translators. The *Biblia Hebraica Stuttgartensia*, published by the German Bible Society, is recommended for use by joint translation committees. "In general the Masoretic text is to be retained as the basis for translation. Where, however, there are special difficulties in the traditional form of the text, scholars should make use of the evidence provided by recent textual discoveries and by ancient versions for other forms of the Hebrew text. New insights provided by related Semitic languages should be given due consideration though they may conflict with traditional renderings. In dealing with textual problems, the volumes of the Hebrew Old Testament Text Project, prepared under the auspices of the United Bible Societies [and Barthélemy], should be considered." J. C. Willebrands et al., *Guidelines for Interconfessional Cooperation in Translating the Bible* (Rome: Vatican Polyglot, 1987), 6–7.

[23] Tov, *Textual Criticism*, 300.

Tov also thinks that the older textual witnesses are not necessarily the better ones since certain copyists may have preserved their source better than others. For instance the MT manuscript written in the tenth century A.D. is closer to the "Urtext" than 1QIs[a] dating from the first century B.C.E. But in general Tov does not regard the external criteria for the evaluation of readings as valid in the case of the Hebrew Bible, whereas internal criteria are to be recognized in textual criticism. (For the evaluation of some witnesses, such as LXX, external rules can be helpful).[24]

K. H. Jobes and M. Silva criticize Tov for minimizing the value of the canons on the basis that they are subjective. Furthermore, they state that "Scholars who minimize the value of the traditional text-critical canons typically argue that we are dependent on the context, which is to say, preference should be given to intrinsic probability."[25]

In my opinion, the internal evidence is of great importance, but the external evidence of the quality of the manuscripts should not be ignored (cf. Brotzman's view above).

The basic principle in choosing between alternative readings can be expressed in the following question: Which would have changed into the other? Or in other words: Which is more likely to have given rise to the other?[26] This appears to be a very general and basic rule, but to give more specific guidelines the following rules may be helpful. These rules, however, cannot always be applied automatically (or "mechanically"), since at times they point in opposite directions.

1. The more difficult reading is to be preferred.

This rule may work if there are no scribal errors involved in the MT, as e.g. in Gen 2:2 "on the seventh day" in the MT, as opposed to "on the sixth day" in the LXX. The former reading is more difficult than the latter. In the case of Jer 23:33, however, a scribal error is involved. The MT reads: אֶת־מַה־מַשָּׂא "What burden?" Most scholars regard the LXX as reflecting the original reading: ὑμεῖς ἐστε τὸ λῆμμα "You are the burden!" which reads אתם המשא when reconstructed into Hebrew.[27]

2. The shorter reading is to be preferred.

Copyists tended to add information to the text, e.g. to make implicit information explicit, add comments to explain difficult words or concepts, and include alternative readings if manuscripts which they were copying varied. One such

---

[24] *Ibid.*, 300ff.

[25] Jobes and Silva, *Invitation*, 131.

[26] McCarter, *Textual Criticism*, 72.

[27] Tov, *Textual Criticism*, 302–303.

SECONDARY PARALLELISM   171

example is 1 Sam 2:22, MT: "And Eli was very old." 4QSam^a: "And Eli was very old, *ninety years*."[28]

3. The reading that is more appropriate to its context is to be preferred.

For example a reading that conforms more to the style of the author is to be preferred to one that does not. This applies also to viewpoint of the passage, characteristics of language and thought, and so on.[29]

4. Assimilation to parallel passages (Harmonization) needs to be considered.

Probably in order to attain greater consistency, copyists assimilated the text of one passage to that of a similar passage. Among the more common types of assimilation are, for instance, assimilation to more explicit details given in a nearby passage, as in Isa 2:10. The LXX adds: ὅταν ἀναστῇ θραῦσαι τὴν γῆν, which is assimilated from Isa 2:19: בְּקוּמוֹ לַעֲרֹץ הָאָרֶץ "when he rises to terrify the earth."[30]

5. Emendation may be used with discretion.

Emendation may be described as "the process of substituting what appears to be a better form of the text for one which is judged to be incorrect."[31] S. Jellicoe writes about this topic:

> Conjectural emendation, so common half a century or more ago, and carried to extremes, for example, by Duhm, and to the point of eccentricity in the later work of Cheyne, is today in some circles virtually rejected, a reaction which is altogether too radical. The main objection, which certainly has validity, is on grounds of subjectivism. Used with discretion, however, it will always have a place.[32]

With regard to making textual decisions E. Tov believes more in common sense than in abstract rules. He says, "It is our understanding that common sense should be the main guide of the textual critic when attempting to locate the most

---

[28] *Ibid.*, 305–306.

[29] McCarter, *Textual Criticism*, 74.

[30] Barthélemy et al., *Preliminary*, XI (factor 5). Also Tov, *Textual Criticism*, 307.

[31] Bratcher and Reyburn, *Psalms*, Glossary.

[32] Jellicoe, *Septuagint*, 320.

contextual appropriate reading. At the same time, abstract rules are often also helpful."[33]

3.3 TRANSLATIONAL CASES OF PARALLEL FORMS

After an investigation of the characteristics of parallelism in LXX Proverbs (see Chapter One), it is now evident that the translator of Proverbs did not produce a literal translation but made many translational changes, particularly by producing forms that are more parallel grammatically and/or semantically. Therefore, it can be problematic to use the LXX of Proverbs as a tool for reconstructing the Hebrew text in order to produce "better" parallelism without taking into consideration the translator's technique of producing "better" parallelisms. Insights into his translation practice provide important guidance for determining whether an apparent divergence between the LXX and the MT is due to a different *Vorlage* or rather to the translation technique of the translator. Differences between LXX and MT may also be due to differences in language[34] as well as inner-textual corruption.[35]

In this chapter, parallel constructions from Proverbs many of which have been regarded as significant for textual criticism will be discussed in the light of the translator's fondness towards producing closer corresponding parallel forms. The thesis is, of course, based on the hypothesis that the Hebrew source text of LXX Proverbs did not differ extensively from the MT. This assumption can, however, not be made for every part of the book, as there are more extensive deviations that cannot be explained on the basis of translation techniques that were applied. Only cases have been chosen where it is reasonable to suppose that the translator of LXX Proverbs was using as his source a text similar to the MT.

---

[33] Tov, *Textual Criticism*, 296. For more information on this topic see Barthélemy et al., *Preliminary*, XI (factor 5). In the book mentioned there are altogether 15 factors included that are involved in textual decisions (IV–XVII).

[34] Stylistic differences may also fall into this category, see under INTRODUCTION.

[35] "A difference in the Greek text may also be due to a different understanding of the vowel tradition of the Hebrew text." Brotzman, *Textual Criticism*, 79. J. W. Wevers, "Use of Versions," 15–24. In my opinion translation techniques include also exegetically motivated changes. According to J. R. Adair, Jr., "Particularly important are studies that address translation technique and retroversion. It is interesting to note, however, that despite the number of OT studies devoted to the use of the versions, it is NT scholars who have produced more complete studies treating the versions as a whole (Metzger 1977; Ehrman and Holmes 1995; cf. Fernández Marcos 1985)!" James R. Adair, Jr., "Old and New in Textual Criticism: Similarities, Differences, and Prospects for Cooperation," *TC* 1 (1996): 12.

3.3.1 SEMANTIC (AND GRAMMATICAL) RELATIONSHIPS

In this category, primarily semantic relationships are treated although grammatical relationships are also discussed whenever they are relevant for our discussion and co-occur with semantic relationships.

3.3.1.1 *Lexical Aspect*

It has been demonstrated under 1.2.1.1 "Lexical aspect" that the translator tended to produce lexical items or phrases of close correspondence in near-synonymous parallelisms. In this section similar cases that have sometimes been regarded as text-critical are being identified as translational.

1. Prov 2:6

MT: כִּי־יְהוָה יִתֵּן חָכְמָה מִפִּיו דַּעַת וּתְבוּנָה
"For the Lord gives wisdom, from his mouth[36] come knowledge and understanding"

LXX: ὅτι κύριος δίδωσιν σοφίαν καὶ ἀπὸ προσώπου αὐτοῦ γνῶσις καὶ σύνεσις
"For the Lord gives wisdom, and from his presence come knowledge and understanding"

Prov 2:6 can be regarded as a near-synonymous parallelism ("For the Lord gives wisdom, from his mouth come knowledge and understanding"). The question is whether ἀπὸ προσώπου αὐτοῦ "from his presence" should be regarded as a translational alteration or a scribal mistake (either on the part of the MT or the LXX[37]) since מפיו "from his mouth" and מפניו "from his presence" look almost alike.[38] The commentaries generally opt for the MT at this point. In the *BHS*

---

[36] A. Meinhold asks the question: "Wenn sie [die Weisheit] aus seinem Munde hervorgeht ... und das den Vorgang seines Gebens ausmacht, verwischt sich dann nicht doch der Unterschied zwischen prophetischer und weisheitlicher Inspiration?" He then answers, "Ein wirklicher Wortempfang des Weisen wird aber kaum gemeint sein. ... Dem Weisen wird die Eingebung zuteil, deren Inhalt er in Worte zu fassen versucht." Meinhold, *Sprüche*, 1:65.

[37] For this latter option see Delitzsch, *Proverbs*, 1:77.

[38] Avoidance of anthropomorphism is not likely since this is not common in LXX Proverbs. See also Cook, *Proverbs*, 119.

apparatus,[39] however, the LXX reading is mentioned as perhaps being the original reading. On the basis of our findings in this thesis it is very likely that the translator altered his source text to make the rendering (προσώπου) in the second colon correspond more closely with κύριος / יְהוָה in the first colon.

2. Prov 3:8

MT: רִפְאוּת תְּהִי לְשָׁרֶּךָ וְשִׁקּוּי לְעַצְמוֹתֶיךָ
"It will be healing/health for/to your navel, and refreshment to your bones"

LXX: τότε ἴασις ἔσται τῷ σώματί σου καὶ ἐπιμέλεια τοῖς ὀστέοις σου
"Then will there be health for your body, and good care of your bones"

In Prov 3:8, a near-synonymous parallelism ("It will be healing/health for/to your navel, and refreshment to your bones"), the exact meaning of שׁר is not without problems. According to C. L. Rogers, Jr. "the exact meaning of the word [שׁר] is not clear, but it could mean body (LXX), navel (KD, *Proverbs*, 1:87–88), or strength (McKane, *Proverbs*, 1970, 293)."[40] According to A. Meinhold, "Der Nabel wird als Teil für den ganzen Körper herangezogen. Er mag so ungefähr die Mitte des menschlichen Körpers darstellen und erinnert an die lebensnotwendige Verbindung zwischen dem Menschen als Embryo und seiner Mutter."[41] A. P. Ross regards "navel" as synecdoche.[42] If this is the case, it is possible that the translator rendered the synecdoche "navel" by "body" to make the two halves of the parallelism fit better, since "bones" corresponds more closely to "body" than to the figurative use of "navel." *BHS* suggests τῷ σώματί σου = לִשְׁאֵרְךָ or לִבְשָׂרְךָ "for your flesh"[43] in place of לְשָׁרֶּךָ "for your

---

[39] The editors of the *BHS* were more cautious than those of in the *BHK*, as the former refrains from merely quoting the retroverted Hebrew text without the versional evidence itself. Thus in the new system the reader has more information available to make his own judgment as to whether a particular reading should be preferred to the MT. The problem, however, according to E. Tov is that "The new system heralds a new and cautious approach, but in actual fact *BHS* blurs the data, because the uninitiated reader is actually unable to distinguish between (retroverted) variants and emendations." Tov, *Text-Critical Use*, 235.

[40] C. L. Rogers Jr., *NIDOTTE*, 4:249.

[41] Meinhold, *Sprüche*, 1:76. O. Plöger also translates *Nabel*. Plöger, *Sprüche*, 32. Similarly Werner Dietrich, *Das Buch der Sprüche* (Wuppertal: Brockhaus, 1985), 54.

[42] Ross, "Proverbs," n.p. For "synecdoche" see Tauberschmidt, "Principles," 72–77. For another example in Prov see 1:14, 1.2.1.2.

[43] According to E. Tov the first option is to be preferred to the second. Tov, *Text-Critical Use*, 75. R. B. Y. Scott, however, chose the latter. Robert Balgarnie Young Scott, *Proverbs, Ecclesiastes: Introduction, Translation, and Notes* (New York: Doubleday, 1965), 44.

navel." This is one possible option to solve the problem, but we cannot be certain that the reading לְאָרֶךְ or לִבְשָׂרֶךָ was in front of the translator because of his translation technique. However, as for לִשְׁאֵרֶךָ a scribal error cannot be ruled out completely.

3. Prov 3:10

MT: וְיִמָּלְאוּ אֲסָמֶיךָ שָׂבָע וְתִירוֹשׁ יְקָבֶיךָ יִפְרֹצוּ
"then your barns[44]/storehouses[45] will be filled with plenty, and your presses will be bursting with wine"

LXX: ἵνα πίμπληται τὰ ταμιεῖά σου πλησμονῆς σίτου οἴνῳ δὲ αἱ ληνοί σου ἐκβλύζωσιν
"that your storehouses may be completely filled with corn, and that your presses may burst with wine"

Prov 3:10 is a near-synonymous parallelism ("then your barns/storehouses will be filled with plenty, and your presses will be bursting with wine"), in which according to R. Alter "the general term [*abundance*] occurs in the first verset and a more specific instance of the general category [*new wine*] in the second verset."[46] There is, however, some disagreement as to how שָׂבָע should be translated. In BDB there are two possible meanings listed: 1. plenty and 2. satiety. The former meaning is favored by e.g. W. McKane,[47] D. Kidner,[48] F. Delitzsch,[49] and the latter is chosen by e.g. A. Meinhold,[50] B. Gemser.[51] Now, there is a third possibility: Since Phoenician has a cognate which has the meaning "satiety, produce/grain," it has been suggested that it may be related to the Heb. noun שָׂבָע.[52] R. J. Clifford favors this third interpretation and writes that "plenty" acquires the concrete meaning "grain" when paired with "wine" as in a

---

[44] Most translations render "barns."

[45] Cf. V. P. Hamilton, *NIDOTTE*, 1:468; also BDB: "storehouse."

[46] Alter, "Dynamics," 92. Alter's interpretation is on the basis of stylistic features used in Hebrew poetry. However, L. Zogbo and E. R. Wendland come to a different solution by judging the couplet based on stylistic features of Hebrew poetry. According to their view if we adopt "to overflowing" or "with plenty," the chiastic structure is incomplete. In their opinion, "the original meaning was 'grain' rather than 'over-flowing.'" (See discussion below). Zogbo and Wendland, *Hebrew Poetry*, 167–169.

[47] McKane, *Proverbs*, 214.

[48] Kidner, *Proverbs*, 64.

[49] Delitzsch, *Proverbs*, 1:89.

[50] "Sättigung," Meinhold, *Sprüche*, 1:71.

[51] "Sättigung," Gemser, *Sprüche Salomos*, 26.

[52] R. H. O'Connell, *NIDOTTE*, 3:1210. Note that O'Connell lists this possibility with a question mark.

Phoenician inscription from the eighth century B.C.E.[53] It is, however, far from certain that the Heb. term has actually taken on the specific meaning "grain," even here in this context. C. H. Toy emends the text to add "corn" as suggested by the LXX,[54] and similarly the *BHS* suggests according to the LXX rendering πλησμονῆς σίτου "completely filled with corn" the addition of שֶׁבֶר after שָׂבָע "plenty." Considering the translator's habitual approach, however, it is more probable that he adjusted the first colon to make a parallel with the second. To render the more general term שָׂבָע "plenty" he added the specific σίτου "corn" to πλησμονῆς. This adjustment is in accordance with the second colon where also a specific term, "wine," is used. For a similar adjustment of substituting a specific term for a generic term see Prov 15:27, 1.2.1.1.

4. Prov 3:26

MT: כִּי־יְהוָה יִהְיֶה בְכִסְלֶךָ וְשָׁמַר רַגְלְךָ מִלָּכֶד
"For the Lord will be your confidence, and will keep your foot from being caught"

LXX: ὁ γὰρ κύριος ἔσται ἐπὶ πασῶν ὁδῶν σου καὶ ἐρείσει σὸν πόδα ἵνα μὴ σαλευθῇς
"For the Lord will be over/on all your ways, and will establish your foot that you be not moved"

In Prov 3:26 ("For the Lord will be your confidence, and will keep your foot from being caught") the word כֶּסֶל is often translated "confidence,"[55] but some understand it as "side."[56] Apparently the translator rendered the noun phrase rather freely by ἐπὶ πασῶν ὁδῶν σου "on all your ways" (first colon) to make it correspond better semantically with ἐρείσει σὸν πόδα "will establish your foot" (second colon).[57] This is in line with his translation technique. The suggestion of

---

[53] Clifford, *Proverbs*, 50.

[54] Toy, *Proverbs*, 62.

[55] So e.g. McKane, *Proverbs*, 215. Also e.g. (N)RSV, NIV, NASB. And Gemser, *Sprüche Salomos*, 28: "Zuversicht." Plöger, *Sprüche*, 39: "Zuversicht."

[56] E.g. Clifford, *Proverbs*, 56: "at your side." Also REB. The senses of the word according to BDB are 1. loins, 2. stupidity, 3. confidence. A. Meinhold thinks that the meaning in focus here is not "confidence," but "side" as an extension of the meaning "loins." He writes, "Wegen der Präposition 'an' dürfte hier 'Seite' als erweiterte Bedeutung von 'Lende' zum Tragen kommen und nicht—wie oft vertreten wird—'(leichtfertiges oder ernsthaftes) Vertrauen.'" Meinhold, *Sprüche*, 1:85.

[57] Note: The prepositional noun phrase מִלָּכֶד "from being caught" is expressed more idiomatically by using an extra clause ἵνα μὴ σαλευθῇς "that you be not moved."

the *BHS*[58] that the LXX reading, ἐπὶ πασῶν ὁδῶν σου = בְּמִסְלֹתֶיךָ, may perhaps be the original is thus not necessary.[59]

5. Prov 5:9

MT: פֶּן־תִּתֵּן לַאֲחֵרִים הוֹדֶךָ וּשְׁנֹתֶיךָ לְאַכְזָרִי
"lest you give your honor (or: vigor) to others, and your years to a cruel one"

LXX: ἵνα μὴ πρόῃ ἄλλοις ζωήν σου καὶ σὸν βίον ἀνελεήμοσιν
"lest you give away your life to others, and your life/livelihood to the merciless"

In Prov 5:9 ("lest you give your honor (or: vigor) to others, and your years to a cruel one") הוֹד according to C. J. Collins refers to "a man's natural strength,"[60] and A. P. Ross writes, "The 'strength' ([הוֹד] v. 9) may refer to health and vigor that might be relinquished to a cruel enemy."[61] The LXX rendering, however, is less specific and clearly more parallel as there is a close correspondence between ζωήν "life" (first colon) and βίον "life/livelihood" (second colon). It seems that these words have been paralleled on purpose in place of the less parallel "honor/vigor" (first colon) and "years" (second colon) in the MT. For similar translational combinations of these two Greek words see Prov 3:2a and 3:16, 1.2.1.5.8.

6. Prov 5:18

MT: יְהִי־מְקוֹרְךָ בָרוּךְ וּשְׂמַח מֵאֵשֶׁת נְעוּרֶךָ
"Let your fountain be blessed, and rejoice in the wife of your youth"

LXX: ἡ πηγή σου τοῦ ὕδατος ἔστω σοι ἰδία καὶ συνευφραίνου μετὰ γυναικὸς τῆς ἐκ νεότητός σου
"Let your fountain of water be truly your own, and rejoice in the wife of your youth"

In Prov 5:18 according to W. McKane "'Let your fountain be blessed' (v. 18a) has in mind the blessing of the wife who bears many children,[62] and is superior to LXX, 'Let your fountain be for yourself alone.'"[63] A. Meinhold, however, while following the reading of the MT, interprets "fountain" as referring to the

---

[58] Gesenius-Buhl 17 ed. attributes this proposal to Lagarde.

[59] According to W. McKane the first colon in the LXX "is probably a paraphrase which attempts to make sense of a difficult Hebrew text." McKane, *Proverbs*, 298.

[60] C. J. Collins, *NIDOTTE*, 1:1016.

[61] Ross, "Proverbs," n.p.

[62] Similarly G. Goldsworthy, "*fountain*. Probably a metaphor for the wife as the bearer of children." Goldsworthy, *Life*, 66.

[63] McKane, *Proverbs*, 319.

wife of one's youth who is to be enjoyed as "Quell der Lebensfreude," adducing support from an Ugaritic text.[64] Although there are these different views on "fountain," the MT is generally maintained. The differences in LXX, however, appear to be of a translational nature. This conclusion is reached on the basis of the translation techniques that were applied in regard to synonymous parallelism and (especially in this case) contextual considerations. First of all the translator supplied τοῦ ὕδατος "of water" naturally (as he did in Prov 5:16). Then in place of בָּרוּךְ "(be) blessed" he translated freely ἰδία "(your) own" (first colon) which is somewhat parallel to "the wife of your youth" (second colon), the parallel thought being that she alone is his to rejoice in, no other one. This idea is emphasized by the translator in the immediate context using expressions that are related to ἰδία, e.g. in v. 17 ἔστω σοι μόνῳ "Let (her) be your own";[65] v. 19 ἡ δὲ ἰδία ἡγείσθω σου "and let her be considered your own";[66] v. 20 τῆς μὴ ἰδίας "(a woman) not your own."[67] Thus it is most likely that ἰδία v. 18 has been added by the translator not only to make the colons more parallel, but also because of contextual reasons.[68]

7. Prov 6:5

MT: הִנָּצֵל כִּצְבִי מִיָּד וּכְצִפּוֹר מִיַּד יָקוּשׁ
"save yourself like a gazelle from the hand, like a bird from the hand of the fowler"

LXX: ἵνα σῴζῃ ὥσπερ δορκὰς ἐκ βρόχων καὶ ὥσπερ ὄρνεον ἐκ παγίδος
"that you may deliver yourself like a doe out of a snare, and like a bird out of a trap"

In Prov 6:5 ("save yourself like a gazelle from the hand, like a bird from the hand of the fowler"), see also 2.1.1.1, מִיָּד "from the hand" has been variously explained. RSV emends to צַיָּד "hunter." Similarly W. McKane, who thinks that

---

[64] Meinhold, *Sprüche*, 1:105. Also Ross who writes that "The first line, calling for the 'fountain' to be blessed, indicates that sexual delight is God-given." Ross, "Proverbs," n.p. Similarly D. Kidner, *Proverbs*, 70–71.

[65] Note: In the MT יִהְיוּ־לְךָ לְבַדֶּךָ "let them be your own" refers to the waters in the previous verse.

[66] Note: This text is not represented in the MT.

[67] Note: Similarly this text is not represented in the MT and has been added for translational reasons.

[68] Against: R. J. Clifford lists the LXX of Prov 5:18 under superior readings. Clifford, "Observations," 56. See also Clifford, *Proverbs*, 67–68.

"hunter" (צָיָד) is a smaller alteration than "net" (מָצוֹד).[69] C. H. Toy, however, holds that it is simpler to read *snare* or *trap*, with G, Tg., Syr. (*mn nšbʾ*) than supplying "of the hunter" (so KJV) by conjecture.[70] As for the Targum it was apparently based on the Peshitta.[71] And as for the latter, according to M. P. Weitzman the LXX was used by the Jewish translators of the Syriac version of the Old Testament, especially in the books of Proverbs, Ezekiel, The Twelve, Song of Songs and Qohelet. For other books the LXX was less used (Genesis, Joshua, Isaiah, Jeremiah, Psalms and Esther) and for some not at all (Samuel, Kings, Job, Lamentations and Chronicles).[72] But A. Meinhold favors the MT and thinks that an emendation is not necessary at this point.[73] These different options seem to indicate that it is difficult to be sure of the original reading, but at least in regard to the LXX the deviation may be explained in terms of a translational change, as it is quite likely that the translator altered מִיַּד יָקוּשׁ "from the hand of the fowler" to ἐκ παγίδος "out of a trap" (second colon), rendering in the first colon ἐκ βρόχων in order to achieve a synonymous parallelism. According to W. McKane "ἐκ βρόχων, 'from meshes (of the net),' is an attempt to deal with this difficulty [of the MT] rather than an indication of an original [מָצוֹד], 'net.'"[74] R. J. Clifford, however, lists this case under superior

---

[69] McKane, *Proverbs*, 323. R. J. Clifford also emends to "hunter." Clifford, *Proverbs*, 73–74.

[70] Toy, *Proverbs*, 121.

[71] Cook, *Proverbs*, 28, who refers to P. E. Steyn, "External Influence in the Peshitta Version of Proverbs" (unpublished doctoral dissertation, University of Stellenbosch 1992), 33. Similarly B. Gemser: "Das Targum beruht weithin auf der syrischen Übersetzung (cf gegen Kaminka bes. Gerleman, S. 46 bis 51), folgt aber in einigen Fällen dem hebräischen Text." Gemser, *Sprüche Salomos*, 10.

[72] M. P. Weitzman, *The Syriac Version of the Old Testament: An Introduction* (Cambridge University Press, 1999), chapter 3. E. Tov thinks that "The close relationship between the LXX and the Peshitta often resulted from common exegetical traditions." Tov, *Text-Critical Use*, 188. A. Kaminka's view, put forward in "LXX und Targum zu Proverbia," *HUCA* 8/9 (1931/2): 169–191, of a Targumic influence upon the LXX Proverbs is refuted by Gerleman, *Studies*, 46–51. Gerleman holds that Kaminka's opinion that the Targum is older than the LXX Proverbs is a mere presupposition, and according to his view, "The sources themselves are most likely to suggest that the priority belongs to the LXX Prov." *Ibid.*, 51. This is supported by B. Gemser who writes that the Syriac version "hat . . . offenbar schon in ihrer Urgestalt die [G] benutzt." Gemser, *Sprüche Salomos*, 10. Similarly R. J. Clifford: "Frequently S finds the Hebrew text difficult, in which case it turns to G for help." Clifford, *Proverbs*, 29.

[73] "Die Erwähnung der 'Hand,' des 'Griffes,' verweist zurück auf V.1, besonders aber auf V.3b. In 1.Kön. 20,42 wird die Wendung 'aus der Hand/aus dem Griff' auch ohne Näherbestimmung verwendet, so daß hier keine Textänderung erforderlich ist." Meinhold, *Sprüche*, 1:111.

[74] McKane, *Proverbs*, 40.

readings of LXX Proverbs in his article "Observations on the Texts and Versions of Proverbs,"[75] while in his commentary he emends to "hunter."[76]

8. Prov 19:29

MT: נָכוֹנוּ לַלֵּצִים שְׁפָטִים וּמַהֲלֻמוֹת לְגֵו כְּסִילִים

"Judgments (or: punishment; or: penalties) are prepared for scoffers, and blows for the back of fools"

LXX: ἑτοιμάζονται ἀκολάστοις μάστιγες καὶ τιμωρίαι ὤμοις ἀφρόνων

"Scourges are prepared for the intemperate/undisciplined, and punishments likewise for fools"

In Prov 19:29 F. Delitzsch understands שְׁפָטִים "judgments" as God's judgments on people for despising him and the מַהֲלֻמוֹת "stripes/blows" as punishment inflicted on them by men for their betterment.[77] But, according to R. Schultz, although שפט is always used for God's judgments, Prov 19:29 is an exception: "a wordplay pairs this verse with the preceding (v. 28): The worthless who makes a mockery of justice [מִשְׁפָּט] is destined for judgment [שְׁפָטִים]."[78] Yet another explanation is offered by A. P. Ross who holds that שְׁפָטִים "judgments" "is a metonymy and may be rendered 'penalties.'"[79] In any case, it is likely that the translator rendered μάστιγες "scourges" (first colon) to make a parallel with τιμωρίαι "punishments" (second colon) rather than translating שְׁפָטִים "judgments" literally. Thus the emendation of שְׁפָטִים to שְׁבָטִים "rods" on the basis of the LXX rendering as suggested by e.g. C. H. Toy, B. Gemser, and BHS does not seem to be needed,[80] although in translation one may depart from the literal "judgments."

9. Prov 23:25

MT: יִשְׂמַח־אָבִיךָ וְאִמֶּךָ וְתָגֵל יוֹלַדְתֶּךָ.

"Let your father and your mother be glad, and let her who bore you rejoice"

---

[75] Clifford, "Observations," 56.

[76] Clifford, *Proverbs*, 73–74.

[77] Delitzsch, *Proverbs*, 2:38.

[78] R. Schultz, *NIDOTTE*, 4:219. R. E. Murphy too holds that "'judgment' is used here in the sense of punishment." Murphy, *Proverbs*, 141.

[79] Ross, "Proverbs," n.p.

[80] Cf. also A. Meinhold who holds that this emendation is not necessary. Meinhold, *Sprüche*, 2:324, fn. 82.

LXX: εὐφραινέσθω ὁ πατὴρ καὶ ἡ μήτηρ ἐπὶ σοί καὶ χαιρέτω ἡ τεκοῦσά σε

"Let your father and your mother rejoice over you, and let her who bore you be glad"

Prov 23:25 is fairly parallel semantically, except that both father and mother are mentioned in the first half, but just the mother is referred to in the second half[81] ("Let your father and your mother be glad, and let her who bore you rejoice"). C. H. Toy leaves out וְאִמֶּךָ "and your mother" to achieve a better parallelism.[82] O. Plöger emends וְאִמֶּךָ to מִמֶּךָ "for your sake" because the mother is mentioned in v. 25b,[83] and also *BHS* mentions this reading to be perhaps more original on the basis of the LXX. However, the translator seems to have added the prepositional phrase (ἐπὶ) σοί "(over) you" in the first colon to make a parallel with the object σε "you" in the second colon; MT: ךְ- "you." But the correspondence is not total, as in the first colon the governing verb is "be glad, rejoice" and in the second colon it is "bore."

Stylistic variation or variation for the sake of style is a common feature of Greek as of other languages. This feature can also be observed more or less in LXX renderings,[84] and it occurs in some instances in parallel forms of the LXX of Proverbs. The use of synonyms or closely related concepts to avoid a stereotyped translation[85] does not necessarily make the forms more parallel or less parallel semantically (although most of the following examples are more parallel structurally), but they are indicators of the translational nature of such texts.

10. Prov 3:13

MT: אַשְׁרֵי אָדָם מָצָא חָכְמָה וְאָדָם יָפִיק תְּבוּנָה

"Happy/Blessed is the man who finds//has found wisdom, and the man who gets understanding"

LXX: μακάριος ἄνθρωπος ὃς εὗρεν σοφίαν καὶ θνητὸς ὃς εἶδεν φρόνησιν

"Happy/Blessed is the man who finds//has found wisdom, and the mortal who

---

[81] W. McKane accepts the MT as it stands. McKane, *Proverbs*, 247, 388–389.

[82] Toy, *Proverbs*, 436.

[83] Plöger, *Sprüche*, 263.

[84] For further information on "Variation and style," see Tauberschmidt, "Principles," 88–90. See also J. A. L. Lee, "Translations of the Old Testament. I. Greek," in *Handbook of Classical Rhetoric*, 776–778.

[85] Watson writes, "Since not every word in Hebrew (or the other related languages) has its apposite synonym it was often inevitable that the same word (or verbal root) had to be used in both lines of a parallel couplet." Watson, *Classical*, 279.

receives//has received (lit.: has seen) prudence"

In Prov 3:13 ("Happy/Blessed is the man who finds//has found wisdom, and the man who gets understanding") the verbs in colon one, εὗρεν "finds//has found" and colon two, εἶδεν "receives//has received (lit.: has seen)" are both third person singular, aorist, active, indicative, whereas in the MT the first verb is in the perfective מָצָא "finds//has found" and the second in the imperfective aspect יָפִיק "will get/gets." Thus the LXX rendering appears to be more parallel in this respect. For אָדָם "man" the Hebrew text has only the one word in both instances, but the LXX uses two different words, because as the translator apparently chose the device of stylistic variation and put θνητός "mortal" in the second colon rather than repeating ἄνθρωπος "man." The same combination is used in Prov 20:24 in a parallel manner in translating the pair אָדָם–גֶּבֶר[86]. Therefore it is not to be supposed that θνητός reflects a different Hebrew text on the basis of the LXX translation.

11. Prov 3:24

MT: אִם־תִּשְׁכַּב לֹא־תִפְחָד וְשָׁכַבְתָּ וְעָרְבָה שְׁנָתֶךָ
"When you lie down, you will not be afraid; when you lie down, your sleep will be sweet"[87]

LXX: ἐὰν γὰρ κάθῃ ἄφοβος ἔσῃ ἐὰν δὲ καθεύδῃς ἡδέως ὑπνώσεις
"For if you sit down, you will be undismayed, and if you sleep, you will slumber sweetly"

In Prov 3:24 the LXX rendering appears to be a more parallel couplet structurally, as ἐὰν is repeated in the second colon; the verbs of colon one, κάθῃ "you sit down" and colon two, καθεύδῃς "you sleep" agree in tense/aspect, mood, and person; and the negative particle לֹא־ (in "you will *not* be afraid") is avoided by the rendering ἄφοβος "undismayed" in the first colon to fit the structure of the second colon. In all the structural aspects mentioned, the MT shows less correspondence. As regards the translation of תִּשְׁכַּב "you lie down"[88] by κάθῃ "you sit down" (first colon), this may be explained on the basis of the translator's preference for employing stylistic variation. Thus he may have sought to avoid rendering the same word twice. So we do not need to

---

[86] גֶּבֶר is normally translated "young or strong man." Ross translates מִצְעֲדֵי־גָבֶר "steps of a mighty man." Ross, "Proverbs," n.p. But it is not certain that the notion of strength plays a role in this parallelism.

[87] A. Meinhold renders, "Wenn du dich niederlegst, brauchst du nicht zu erschrecken, und wenn du liegst, wird dein Schlaf süß sein." Meinhold, *Sprüche*, 1:83.

[88] According to Toy, "The repetition of the verb is somewhat strange, though it is defensible on rhetorical grounds." Toy, *Proverbs*, 75.

assume that the translator had תֵּשֵׁב "you sit down" in his *Vorlage*, as suggested by R. J. Clifford,[89] and with some degree of uncertainty *BHS* (frt l).

12. Prov 8:5

MT: הָבִינוּ פְתָאיִם עָרְמָה וּכְסִילִים הָבִינוּ לֵב
"O simple ones, learn prudence; and, O fools, learn intelligence/understanding"

LXX: νοήσατε ἄκακοι πανουργίαν οἱ δὲ ἀπαίδευτοι ἔνθεσθε καρδίαν
"O simple, understand prudence; and you untaught, imbibe intelligence/understanding"

In Prov 8:5 the LXX translator apparently did not slavishly render הָבִינוּ "learn" in both colons by one and the same verb but varied his style using two verbs νοήσατε (first colon) and ἔνθεσθε (second colon) to convey the same idea. A scribal error cannot be ruled out completely because הָבִינוּ and הָכִינוּ = ἔνθεσθε (see the suggestion in the *BHS* apparatus) may well have been confused, but if we consider the translation technique applied in this book with regard to stylistic variation, it is not surprising that the translator did not use the same word twice to render הָבִינוּ. Therefore the LXX reading need not reflect a variant text.[90]

13. Prov 18:15

MT: לֵב נָבוֹן יִקְנֶה־דָּעַת וְאֹזֶן חֲכָמִים תְּבַקֶּשׁ־דָּעַת
"The mind of the prudent receives knowledge, and the ear of the wise seeks knowledge"

LXX: καρδία φρονίμου κτᾶται αἴσθησιν ὦτα δὲ σοφῶν ζητεῖ ἔννοιαν
"The mind of the sensible gets knowledge, and the ears of the wise seek insight"

In Prov 18:15 the translator rendered presumably דָּעַת (colon one and two) by two different Greek words, αἴσθησις "knowledge" (first colon) and ἔννοια "insight" (second colon), for the sake of stylistic variation. Therefore it need not be assumed that the *Vorlage* of the LXX differed from the MT, and the

---

[89] Clifford, "Observations," 56, fn. 20. In his commentary, however, Clifford follows the MT. Clifford, *Proverbs*, 56. The LXX reading has been adopted by some translations such as RSV, NRSV, REB, for textual and/or translational reasons.

[90] According to W. McKane "The reading of LXX in v. 5b . . . has no clear superiority over MT, apart from the aesthetic objection which may be levelled against the repetition . . . in v. 5b." McKane, *Proverbs*, 345.

suggestion by B. Gemser that the LXX reading should perhaps be preferred[91] may not be needed.

To sum up, since the translator tended to render lexical items or phrases in near-synonymous parallelisms in a more exactly parallel fashion, it is important to identify translational cases and not treat them as text-critical.

3.3.1.2 Emphatic Phrases or Various Figures of Speech

It has been demonstrated under 1.2.1.2 how the translator tended to alter parallelisms of emphatic phrases or various figures of speech into more nearly parallel lines. This tendency should be considered before using the following cases as variant readings.

1. Prov 3:22

MT: וְיִהְיוּ חַיִּים לְנַפְשֶׁךָ וְחֵן לְגַרְגְּרֹתֶיךָ
"that they be life[92] for your soul/life/being[93] (or: that they increase your vitality[94]), and adornment to your neck"[95]

LXX: ἵνα ζήσῃ ἡ ψυχή σου καὶ χάρις ᾖ περὶ σῷ τραχήλῳ
22a ἔσται δὲ ἴασις ταῖς σαρξί σου καὶ ἐπιμέλεια τοῖς σοῖς ὀστέοις
"that you may live, your soul/life/being, and that there may be adornment round your neck, 22a and it shall be health to your flesh, and safety to your bones"

Prov 3:22 may be regarded as near-synonymous with a figure of speech in the second half ("that they be life for your soul/life/being, and adornment to your neck"). He who hangs on to insight (v. 21) will find strength or vitality, and beauty in wisdom, the metaphor "adornment to your neck" standing for "honor and respect."[96] The translator, however, rendered the clause וְיִהְיוּ חַיִּים "that they be life" by ἵνα ζήσῃ "that you may live" (first colon) and as a parallel to it he added the verb ᾖ "it shall be" ("adornment round your neck") in the second colon where the MT has a verbless clause (וְחֵן לְגַרְגְּרֹתֶיךָ "and adornment to your neck"), thus producing a more nearly parallel structure. But more strikingly, in addition to "soul/life" and the figurative "neck" in colon one and two he added

---

[91] Gemser, *Sprüche Salomos*, 74–75.

[92] "The *life* is physical, as in 3:2, 16." Toy, *Proverbs*, 74.

[93] "*Being* is here better than *soul* . . ." Ibid.

[94] McKane, *Proverbs*, 215.

[95] Watson lists Prov 3:22 under "Gender-matched Parallelism" where the gender of the nouns involved match with each other: m. + f. // m. + f. Watson, *Classical*, 123–124.

[96] Cf. NLT, HfA. See also Clifford, *Proverbs*, 58.

"flesh" and "bones" (v. 22a) in a parallel manner apparently to further explicate what is already conveyed by נֶפֶשׁ.[97] The particle δὲ, which marks further development, supports the translational nature of the addition. A similar parallelism can be found a few verses earlier in v. 8, τότε ἴασις ἔσται τῷ σώματί σου καὶ ἐπιμέλεια τοῖς ὀστέοις σου "Then shall there be health to your body,[98] and good keeping to your bones," which may have influenced the translator here. In emphasizing the physical aspect he may also have had in mind the following verse, since the addition helps towards a smoother transition to v. 23 in which the physical aspect is in focus with its reference to walking safely without stumbling. E. Tov is of the opinion that the added colon 3:22a is due to differences in the *Vorlage*.[99] But it is more likely at this point that the translator added the parallel form for the reasons that have been stated.

2. Prov 11:28

MT: בּוֹטֵחַ בְּעָשְׁרוֹ הוּא יִפֹּל וְכֶעָלֶה צַדִּיקִים יִפְרָחוּ
"He who trusts in his riches will fall, but the righteous will bloom/flourish like leaves (or: a branch)"

LXX: ὁ πεποιθὼς ἐπὶ πλούτῳ οὗτος πεσεῖται ὁ δὲ ἀντιλαμβανόμενος δικαίων οὗτος ἀνατελεῖ
"He who trusts in wealth will fall, but he who helps righteous men will rise"

Since in Prov 11:28 ("He who trusts in his riches will fall, but the righteous will bloom/flourish like leaves") the MT contrasts "fall" with "bloom" the emendation of יִפֹּל "fall" to יִבֹּל "wither" has been suggested to improve the parallelism.[100] There is, however, no good reason why the MT reading should be corrupt at this point, as "The image of the 'green leaf' is a figure of prosperity and fertility throughout the ancient Near East."[101] Moreover, parallelisms in Hebrew tend in any case to be more dynamic. The LXX, however, provides two lexical items that clearly correspond more closely. This shows again the tendency of the translator to make the second half correspond to the first half, as πεσεῖται = יִפֹּל "he shall fall" (first colon) and ἀνατελεῖ "he shall rise"

---

[97] "14:375 נֶפֶשׁ n.f. soul, living being, life, self, person, desire, appetite, emotion, and passion." BDB.

[98] The MT has navel, but apparently the translator dropped the figure and rendered parallel to the second colon, see under 3.3.1.1.

[99] Tov, "Recensional Differences," 50.

[100] *IB*, 4:850, and *BHS*. Also RSV and NRSV renderings. Against: McKane, *Proverbs*, 436.

[101] Ross, "Proverbs," n.p. Similarly McKane, *Proverbs*, 436. NLT: "like leaves in spring." NIV: "like a green leaf." R. J. Clifford too supports the MT. Clifford, *Proverbs*, 126.

correspond in a contrastive manner, whereas the MT has יִפְרָ֑חוּ ... כֶּעָלֶ֥ה "... they shall bloom like leaves."

In addition, the two colons in Prov 11:28 agree also grammatically: A participle (singular) is paired with an adjective (plural).

The translator rendered the participle (singular) and corresponding adjective (plural) of the MT by using two participles that agree in number (singular). Also, he repeated οὗτος, which corresponds with הוּא "he,"[102] in the second colon, each preceding the verb; and the two verbs agree in number, person, tense/aspect, and mood. Thus the LXX rendering is clearly influenced by the translator's technique of producing a more closely parallel form grammatically as well as semantically.

3. Prov 14:11

MT: בֵּ֣ית רְ֭שָׁעִים יִשָּׁמֵ֑ד וְאֹ֖הֶל יְשָׁרִ֣ים יַפְרִֽיחַ
"The house of the wicked will be destroyed, but the tent of the upright will flourish"

LXX: οἰκίαι ἀσεβῶν ἀφανισθήσονται σκηναὶ δὲ κατορθούντων στήσονται
"The houses of the ungodly will be destroyed, but the tents of the upright will stand"

In Prov 14:11 according to the MT the house of the upright will not only be preserved, but it will even flourish or increase in prosperity ("The house of the wicked will be destroyed, but the tent of the upright will flourish"). The translator, however, seems to have altered the metaphor יַפְרִֽיחַ "it will flourish," by rendering it στήσονται "it will stand" (second colon) as a contrastive parallel to ἀφανισθήσονται "it will be destroyed" (first colon). In addition, the Hebrew parallelism is clearly more dynamic than that of the translation, a feature that is very common in Proverbs.

4. Prov 14:15

MT: פֶּ֭תִי יַאֲמִ֣ין לְכָל־דָּבָ֑ר וְ֝עָר֗וּם יָבִ֥ין לַאֲשֻׁרֽוֹ
"The simple believes every word, but the prudent considers his steps"

---

[102] For further cases where הוּא is rendered οὗτος see Prov 5:23; 13:13; 28:24.

LXX: ἄκακος πιστεύει παντὶ λόγῳ πανοῦργος δὲ ἔρχεται εἰς μετάνοιαν
"The simple believes every word, but the prudent betakes himself to afterthought (or: proceeds with deliberation)"

In Prov 14:15 ("The simple believes every word, but the prudent considers his steps") the translator may have dropped the figurative לַאֲשֻׁרוֹ "his steps"[103] and instead translated εἰς μετάνοιαν "to after-thought" (second colon) in antithetic parallelism to "believes every word" (first colon). Thus the LXX may be regarded as secondary, since in Hebrew parallelism figures of speech are quite common especially in the second half of the parallelism, and they are frequently dropped by the translator (see examples under 1.2.1.2).

The last three cases fit also into the category of "Near-antithetical parallelisms rendered with a clearer contrast" (3.3.1.4).

To sum up, the translator's technique of rendering emphatic phrases or various figures of speech more exactly parallel needs to be considered before such cases can be used as variant readings in LXX Proverbs.

3.3.1.3 Near-Synonymous Parallelisms Transformed into Antithetical Forms

The translator's predilection for antithesis is demonstrated in cases where he transformed near-synonymous parallelisms into antithetical forms, see 1.2.1.3. This translation technique should be kept in mind before using the following cases to correct the MT.

1. Prov 10:18

MT: מְכַסֶּה שִׂנְאָה שִׂפְתֵי־שָׁקֶר וּמוֹצִא דִבָּה הוּא כְסִיל
"Lying lips conceal hatred, and whoever utters slander is a fool"

LXX: καλύπτουσιν ἔχθραν χείλη δίκαια οἱ δὲ ἐκφέροντες λοιδορίας ἀφρονέστατοί εἰσιν
"Righteous lips cover enmity, but they that utter railings are most foolish"

There are different interpretations of Prov 10:18[104] ("Lying lips conceal hatred, and whoever utters slander is a fool"). According to W. McKane, "If MT is

---

[103] According to W. McKane "v.15b appears to resume the metaphor of the road in the manner of v.8a . . ." McKane, *Proverbs*, 467. The nominal form אֶשֶׁר occurs primarily in poetry and wisdom texts with figurative meaning. E. H. Merrill, *NIDOTTE*, 1:567–568.

[104] The second half may be regarded as climactic in the sense that hypocrisy is bad enough, slander is worse. For this view see Ross, "Proverbs," n.p. Similarly Meinhold, *Sprüche*, 2:176–177. Less likely is B. Gemser's view that takes the verse as single sentence. Gemser, *Sprüche Salomos*, 50.

retained, this is one of the few verses in the chapter which does not have an antithetic structure."[105] R. J. Clifford, while translating the MT literally, prefers the interpretation (which he finds in McKane) that takes "who conceals hatred" as the subject, rather than the interpretation of NRSV and RSV that takes "lying lips" as the subject. As the reason why Clifford prefers the former interpretation he writes: "for it makes possible an antithetic parallelism." The antithesis that Clifford sees is between "who conceals hatred" and "who reveals a slander."[106] In fact, however, McKane does not regard the parallelism as antithetic. In his view, "The syntax ('he who conceals hatred (is) lying lips') presents some difficulty, but the construction should be tolerated and is equivalent to 'He who speaks lies conceals hatred'"; and it is the latter option that McKane chose for his translation. In other words, McKane takes "Lying lips" as metonymy for the person "who speaks lies"; he takes this as the subject of the clause, not as Clifford represents his view. Similarly, the translator of Proverbs took "lips" (the person who speaks) as the subject, but he modified the first colon changing שִׂפְתֵי־שָׁקֶר "lying lips" to χείλη δίκαια "righteous lips," thus producing an antithetic form. This is not surprising considering his love of antithesis. In addition, the environment of antithetical parallelisms may have influenced his decision, as the immediate context often had an impact on the translator's choices.[107] Thus the LXX rendering may not be representing a variant text, as adopted in the NEB.

2. Prov 11:25

MT: נֶפֶשׁ־בְּרָכָה תְדֻשָּׁן וּמַרְוֶה גַּם־הוּא יוֹרֶא
"A generous person[108] will be enriched,[109] and he who makes (others) saturated will himself be saturated"[110]

LXX: ψυχὴ εὐλογουμένη πᾶσα ἁπλῆ ἀνὴρ δὲ θυμώδης οὐκ εὐσχήμων
"Every sincere/generous person[111] is blessed, but a passionate man is not graceful"

---

[105] McKane, *Proverbs*, 419.

[106] Clifford, *Proverbs*, 115.

[107] M. B. Dick lists δίκαια under moralizing tendency. Dick, "Ethics," 22–23. Dick does not consider other possible influences that may have led to the addition.

[108] Lit.: "the soul of blessing."

[109] "The verb 'made rich' [תְדֻשָּׁן] is literally 'to be made fat,' drawing on the standard comparison between fatness and abundance or prosperity (Deut.32:15)." Ross, "Proverbs," n.p.

[110] For the second half of the translation cf. R. H. O'Connell, *NIDOTTE*, 2:537.

[111] Lit.: "soul."

In Prov 11:25 the two lines are in near-synonymous parallelism,[112] ("A generous person will be enriched, and he who makes others saturated will himself be saturated"). While the first colon of the LXX is somewhat similar to the MT ("Every generous person is blessed"), the second colon deviates from it ("but a passionate man is not graceful"). But it is possible that the translator took וּמַרְוֶה to mean "but he who makes (himself) saturated," which would explain the rendering θυμώδης "passionate." Such a person according to the LXX is οὐκ εὐσχήμων "not graceful" in contrast to the "generous" person. These adjustments may be due to the translator's fondness for producing contrastive parallelisms as well as the context of antithetical forms that precede and follow.

In addition to the translator's general fondness for producing antithetical parallelism, he may have been influenced by the immediate context of antithetical forms. The following are examples of such altered parallelisms.

3. Prov 11:16

MT: אֵשֶׁת־חֵן תִּתְמֹךְ כָּבוֹד וְעָרִיצִים יִתְמְכוּ־עֹשֶׁר
"A gracious woman obtains honor, and ruthless/violent men obtain riches"

LXX: γυνὴ εὐχάριστος ἐγείρει ἀνδρὶ δόξαν θρόνος δὲ ἀτιμίας γυνὴ μισοῦσα δίκαια. πλούτου ὀκνηροὶ ἐνδεεῖς γίνονται οἱ δὲ ἀνδρεῖοι ἐρείδονται πλούτῳ
"A gracious wife brings glory to her husband, but a wife hating righteousness is a theme (lit.: throne/seat) of dishonor. The lazy (or: timid) come to be in need of wealth, but the manly/courageous support themselves with wealth"

Prov 11:16 contrasts the ability of the graciousness of a woman and the force of men to acquire honor and riches.[113] The translator seems to have made several adjustments, seeking to make a clearer antithesis. Apparently he added ἀνδρὶ "(her) husband" and thus related the proverb to a γυνὴ εὐχάριστος "a gracious wife" rather than the more general "gracious woman" (MT).[114] In the second half he produced a stronger contrast by inserting δὲ . . . γυνὴ μισοῦσα δίκαια "but a wife hating righteousness." Also he made a contrast with δόξαν "honor" (first colon) by employing ἀτιμίας "dishonor" (second colon). The additional

---

[112] Similarly Toy, *Proverbs*, 235. Ross, "Proverbs," n.p. R. J. Clifford states that the parallelism is synthetic without giving any indication that would explain how it might be synthetic. Clifford, *Proverbs*, 125–126.

[113] According to W. McKane, "A man must strive for wealth, but a gracious woman gets honour through the natural effect of her presence and personality. Or the emphasis may rather be on [עֹשֶׁר] and [כָּבוֹד]. The woman who is gracious gets *honour*, but men have to be energetic to get *wealth*." McKane, *Proverbs*, 431.

[114] It is true that the Hebrew and the Greek word cover both "woman" and "wife," but the context, that is, the addition of "(her) husband," suggests that the translation is more specific than the MT.

antithetical parallelism is probably derived from the second half of the Hebrew text the second colon of the LXX reflecting the MT,[115] while the first half was probably added to form an antithesis. If this is so, which is quite likely, the LXX rendering may not be due to a different text (against Gemser, Ringgren, cf. *BHS*) but may be due to the translator's fondness for producing sharper antitheses, especially in environments of antithetical parallelisms such as this.[116] In regard to whole colons that are not found in the MT, it is of course more difficult to know whether these go back to a *Vorlage* or not, but as has been discussed earlier the translator was quite capable of adding parallel forms, especially in cases where a part of the Hebrew text was not covered in the translation due to some extensive changes in the preceding colon(s).[117]

4. Prov 11:30

MT: פְּרִי־צַדִּיק עֵץ חַיִּים וְלֹקֵחַ נְפָשׁוֹת חָכָם
"The fruit of the righteous is a tree of life, and he who is wise wins souls"

LXX: ἐκ καρποῦ δικαιοσύνης φύεται δένδρον ζωῆς ἀφαιροῦνται δὲ ἄωροι ψυχαὶ παρανόμων
"Out of the fruit of righteousness grows a tree of life, but the souls of transgressors are cut off before their time"

Prov 11:30 has been interpreted in various ways. Especially the second half is difficult. Some interpreters say that the verb לקח "take" is to be taken as "destroy" in a negative sense since it occurs mostly as such;[118] and along with that חָכָם "wise" is sometimes emended to חָמָס "violence" to achieve an antithesis.[119] Thus v. 30b may read something like "but violence takes lives away" (cf. NRSV, similarly TEV).[120] But there are those who defend the MT,

---

[115] עָרִיצִים was probably taken as ἀνδρεῖοι.

[116] E. Tov too regards the LXX reading as by the translator. Tov, "Recensional Differences," 46–47. GN2 and most translations follow the MT, whereas the JB, NEB, NRSV, TEV follow the LXX reading.

[117] According to R. E. Murphy "there is no sufficient reason to depart from the Hebrew text" at this point. Murphy, *Proverbs*, 82. Whybray lends support to those commentators who regard the additional lines as an attempt to make sense out of a difficult Hebrew text. *Proverbs*, 182. Similar cases are Prov 2:19; 17:17; 5:23; 22:11.

[118] R. J. Clifford writes, "Colon B is problematic. It is, literally, 'the wise person takes lives/souls.'" Clifford, *Proverbs*, 126.

[119] Cf. McKane, *Proverbs*, 432–433.

[120] McKane translates the second half: "but (the fruit) of him who takes life is *violence*." *Proverbs*, 228. Clifford, however, is of the opinion that: "The one who takes souls is not the violent but the wise person. The meaning of this strange statement is that the wise have power over life. The surprising reversal of the idiom is dictated by colon A. In short, a wise person promotes life." Clifford, *Proverbs*, 127.

arguing that לקח can also be taken in a positive sense (cf. 2:1)[121] and so there is no need to emend חָכָם. In any case, it is difficult to rely on the LXX for support at this point, because the translator may well have altered the more or less parallel lines of the Hebrew to an antithesis in accordance with his general tendency, and also because of the context, since most of the parallelisms in chapter 11 are antithetical. Thus ψυχαὶ παρανόμων "souls of the transgressors" was apparently produced to make a contrast with the first half of the verse,[122] and similarly ἀφαιροῦνται . . . ἄωροι "are cut off before their time." In other words, whereas those who produce the fruits of righteousness remain and live, the transgressors are cut off from life. The *BHS* suggestion (cf. B. Gemser[123]) that חָכָם "wise" should perhaps be replaced by παρανόμων, חָמָס "transgressors, violent" may thus not be necessary.

5. Prov 12:28

MT: בְּאֹרַח־צְדָקָה חַיִּים וְדֶרֶךְ נְתִיבָה אַל־מָוֶת
"In the way of righteousness is life, and in its pathway there is no death (lit.: and the way of a path not death)"

LXX: ἐν ὁδοῖς δικαιοσύνης ζωή ὁδοὶ δὲ μνησικάκων εἰς θάνατον
"In the ways of righteousness is life, but the ways of those that remember injuries lead to death"

In Prov 12:28 the second colon is often regarded as problematic, and consequently the text has either been emended to e.g. "but the way of error leads to death" (RSV)[124] or אל has been read differently and the colon translated "there is a path that leads to death."[125] But more recently there has been some tendency to go back to the Masoretic Text as it stands, e.g. "in walking its path there is no death" (NRSV).[126] Some regard "no death" as referring to

---

[121] For further support of the argument see Meinhold, *Sprüche*, 1:201. Also Plöger, *Sprüche*, 143.

[122] The deviation of καρποῦ δικαιοσύνης "fruit of righteousness" from the MT may be due to the translator's free approach in rendering metaphors as well as similes, see Tauberschmidt, "Principles," 70–72, and also to rendering a nominal clause by adding a verb as he frequently did.

[123] Gemser, *Sprüche Salomos*, 56.

[124] Similarly TEV.

[125] Old versions, mlt Mss read אֶל, instead of אַל, also McKane, *Proverbs*, 450–452, and Murphy, *Proverbs*, 88. Against: Delitzsch, *Proverbs*, 1:268–270.

[126] Also NIV, NASB, NLT, CEV translate according to the MT. Similarly Meinhold, *Sprüche*, 1:214–215. R. J. Clifford, however, follows the LXX fairly closely by rendering, "but the way of malice leads to death." Clifford, *Proverbs*, 128–129.

"immortality,"[127] others see it as avoidance of untimely death.[128] In any case, the translator was probably influenced by the surrounding antithetical parallel forms in addition to his general predilection for antithetical parallelisms; this led him to contrast חַיִּים = ζωή "life" (first colon) with מָוֶת = θάνατον "death" (second colon), which meant interpreting אל as אֶל "to" rather than אַל "not." In addition he seems to have altered the subject, inserting μνησικάκων "(the ways of) those that remember injuries" (second colon) to make an antithetically near-parallel to δικαιοσύνης "(the way of) righteousness" (first colon). Thus the two suggested LXX readings in the *BHS* apparatus (cf. B. Gemser[129]) may not in fact be supported by the LXX due to their translational origin.

6. Prov 14:17

MT: קְצַר־אַפַּיִם יַעֲשֶׂה אִוֶּלֶת וְאִישׁ מְזִמּוֹת יִשָּׂנֵא
"He who is quick to anger acts foolishly, and a man of evil plans/devices is hated"

LXX: ὀξύθυμος πράσσει μετὰ ἀβουλίας ἀνὴρ δὲ φρόνιμος πολλὰ ὑποφέρει
"A man who is quick to anger acts recklessly, but a sensible man bears up under many things"

In Prov 14:17 the question is whether אִישׁ מְזִמּוֹת (second colon) is to be taken in a good or a bad sense. W. McKane takes the phrase in a positive sense of a person who can remain calm even under provocation,[130] whereas J. E. Hartley takes the opposite view and regards מְזִמּוֹת in v. 17 as denoting evil plans or

---

[127] E. H. Merrill takes the second colon as semantically parallel to the first "only in this pathway . . . is there 'no death' (Dahood, 340)." *NIDOTTE*, 3:203. M. Dahood finds immortality promised here. "Immortality in Proverbs 12:28," *Bib* 41 (1960): 176–181. W. McKane comments that the meaning here may be "no death," "immortality," but the balance of probability is still, in his view, against Dahood's solution. McKane, *Proverbs*, 451.

[128] According to G. Goldsworthy, "In this context ['not death'] may mean that the wise man avoids untimely death." Goldsworthy, *Life*, 106–107. Similarly GN2: "Gott gehorchen ist ein Weg zum Leben, eine gut gebaute Straße ohne tödliche Gefahren." A. Meinhold who translates, "und der Weg 'ihres' Steiges (kann) kein (Straf-) Tod sein (?)," holds that "Wahrscheinlich haben der Weise, der den Spruch geschaffen hat, so wenig wie derjenige, der ihn als krönenden Abschluß an seine jetzige Stelle gesetzt hat, dabei an Unsterblichkeit und ein Fortleben im Jenseits nach dem Sterben gedacht. Ein solches Denken ist in den kanonischen Schriften des Alten Testaments nicht wirklich zu greifen . . ." Meinhold, *Sprüche*, 1:216.

[129] Gemser, *Sprüche Salomos*, 60.

[130] McKane, *Proverbs*, 468. McKane, however, understands the occurrence of the same phrase in Prov 12:2b in the negative sense. *Ibid.*

schemes.[131] Some recent translations or revised translations favor the latter view, e.g. NRSV, CEV, NLT, NASB, GN2.[132] As for the LXX, the translator may have been influenced by the antithetical parallelisms of the immediate context besides his general predilection. This may have led to changing וְאִישׁ מְזִמּוֹת "and a man of evil plans," rendering it ἀνὴρ δὲ φρόνιμος "but a sensible/ discreet man" (second colon) to make an antithetical parallel with ὀξύθυμος "a man who is quick to anger" (first colon). Likewise the change to πολλὰ ὑποφέρει "he bears up under many things" (second colon) may have been motivated by the translator's desire to produce a clear antithesis to יַעֲשֶׂה אִוֶּלֶת "he acts foolishly," πράσσει μετὰ ἀβουλίας "he acts recklessly" (first colon). If this is the case, the LXX reading ὑποφέρει, which is taken to support a (possible) variant reading (ישׂא instead of ישׂנא) by e.g. Gemser, BHS may be of translational origin.

The translator's fondness for antithetic forms can also be observed in the cases which he rendered with a clearer contrast, as demonstrated in the following section.

3.3.1.4 Near-Antithetical Parallelisms Rendered with a Clearer Contrast

The translator rendered many near-antithetical parallelisms with a clearer contrast, see 1.2.1.4. Therefore, the translator's fondness for producing sharp antitheses must be considered in textual criticism, as the following cases indicate.

1. Prov 10:6

MT: בְּרָכוֹת לְרֹאשׁ צַדִּיק וּפִי רְשָׁעִים יְכַסֶּה חָמָס
"Blessings are on the head of the righteous, but the mouth of the wicked conceals violence"

LXX: εὐλογία κυρίου ἐπὶ κεφαλὴν δικαίου στόμα δὲ ἀσεβῶν καλύψει πένθος ἄωρον
"The blessing of the Lord is upon the head of the righteous, but the mouth of the ungodly will cover untimely grief"

---

[131] And similarly in Prov 12:2. NIDOTTE, 1:1112–1113. This view is supported by A. Meinhold, who regards the word under discussion which he renders "Anschläge" as negative. Meinhold, Sprüche, 1:237.

[132] RSV, LB, TEV support the former view.

In Prov 10:6 the second half seems unrelated to the first half[133] ("Blessings are on the head of the righteous, but the mouth of the wicked conceals violence"). According to W. McKane "The antithesis of blessing would be curse or punishment, but what follows is an assertion that behind the speech of wicked men there is a deep-seated aggressiveness and hostility [חָמָס]."[134] Similarly A. P. Ross who states, "The focus of this contrast is on rewards. We would expect a curse to be the antithesis of 'blessings.' But the point is rather that behind the speech of the wicked is aggressive 'violence' [חָמָס]; so he cannot be trusted (McKane, p. 422)."[135] The translator, however, seems to have altered חָמָס "violence" to πένθος ἄωρον "untimely grief" in order to produce a stronger antithesis with εὐλογία κυρίου "the blessing of the Lord."[136] Thus the LXX reading πένθος ἄωρον may be regarded as secondary.

2. Prov 10:10

MT: קֹרֵץ עַיִן יִתֵּן עַצָּבֶת וֶאֱוִיל שְׂפָתַיִם יִלָּבֵט
"He that winks with the eye causes pain/trouble, but (or: and[137]) foolish lips (=a chattering fool) comes to ruin"

LXX: ὁ ἐννεύων ὀφθαλμοῖς μετὰ δόλου συνάγει ἀνδράσι λύπας ὁ δὲ ἐλέγχων μετὰ παρρησίας εἰρηνοποιεῖ
"He that winks with his eyes deceitfully procures griefs for men, but he that reproves boldly is a peacemaker"

In Prov 10:10 the second half does not seem to fit the first half as a parallel or contrast[138] ("He that winks with the eye causes pain/trouble, but (or: and) foolish lips comes to ruin"). Therefore many commentators follow the LXX (e.g. Toy, McKane, Scott, Gemser, Clifford).[139] Some of the more recent commentaries,

---

[133] According to R. E. Murphy "there is probably some confusion in the text (v 6b = v 11b), which has never been solved." Murphy, *Proverbs*, 73. A. Scherer, however, writes: "Zwei Dubletten liegen innerhalb des engeren Kontexts des Großabschnitts Prov 10 vor. Die exakte Identität von 10,6b und 11b einerseits und 10,8b und 10b andererseits, an die hierbei gedacht ist, hat sich als kompositorisch sinnvoll erwiesen. Schon deswegen ist hier kaum an textkritische Operationen zur Beseitigung der Wiederholungen zu denken." Scherer, *Das weise Wort*, 66–67.

[134] McKane, *Proverbs*, 422.

[135] Ross, "Proverbs," n.p.

[136] The same phrase occurs in 10:22. It is possible that the addition "of the Lord" may have been made to agree with v. 22.

[137] Scherer, *Das weise Wort*, 48.

[138] Cf. Goldsworthy, *Life*, 91.

[139] Also e.g. (N)RSV, REB, TEV and NLT.

however, retain the reading of the MT (e.g. Meinhold, Plöger,[140] Ross, Scherer,[141] Dietrich).[142] A. P. Ross, for instance, writes, "Verse 10 departs from the normal antithetical pattern to form a comparison: shifty signs, although grievous, are not as ruinous as foolish talk."[143] The translator has probably made some adjustments especially to the second colon to make it correspond to the first colon, since ὁ . . . ἐλέγχων "he that reproves" appears to be parallel to ὁ . . . ἐννεύων "he that winks" in a contrasting manner and likewise συνάγει ἀνδράσι λύπας "he procures griefs for men" (first half) with εἰρηνοποιεῖ "he is a peacemaker" (second half). Thus it seems that the translator produced a striking contrast by applying his translation technique.[144] In view of this, the suggestion in the *BHS* apparatus to perhaps follow the LXX reading ὁ δὲ ἐλέγχων μετὰ παρρησίας εἰρηνοποιεῖ may not be needed, nor may R. J. Clifford's assertion that "G preserves a superior reading, for it has antithetic parallelism and gives a syllable count closer to colon A . . ."[145] be appropriate.

3. Prov 12:21

MT: לֹא־יְאֻנֶּה לַצַּדִּיק כָּל־אָוֶן וּרְשָׁעִים מָלְאוּ רָע

"No harm/ill[146] happens to the righteous, but the wicked are filled with trouble"

LXX: οὐκ ἀρέσει τῷ δικαίῳ οὐδὲν ἄδικον οἱ δὲ ἀσεβεῖς πλησθήσονται κακῶν

---

[140] O. Plöger writes, "*G*, sonst nicht sonderlich an Antithesen interessiert, hat hier eine Antithese gebracht: . . . , die von den meisten Exegeten übernommen wird, da sie sinnvoller ist als *M*. Ob sie ursprünglicher ist, muß dahingestellt bleiben . . ." Plöger, *Sprüche*, 125. I do not, however, agree with Plöger's comment that *G* was not very interested in antitheses.

[141] According to A. Scherer the reading of the LXX, ὁ δὲ ἐλέγχων μετὰ παρρησίας εἰρηνοποιεῖ, "ist offensichtlich sekundär. Sie will, lediglich einem ästhetischen Bedürfnis folgend, eine Wiederholung, wie sie in **M** durch die Identität von 8b und 10b vorliegt, vermeiden . . . Die Tendenz, die hier sichtbar wird, ist für **G** auch über den vorliegenden Fall hinaus typisch . . . Als weiteres Beispiel sei nur auf Prov 21:9b und 21:19b verwiesen. Dort liegt in **M** der Sinn beider Halbverse eng beieinander. **G** hat diese Gemeinsamkeit aufgelöst, indem sie 9b einen völlig neuen Sinn gegeben hat." Scherer, *Das weise Wort*, 48.

[142] Also e.g. GN2, HfA, CEV, NCV.

[143] Ross, "Proverbs," n.p.

[144] This is supported by G. Gerleman who regards the LXX rendering as (trans)formed according to Greek style. Gerleman, "Septuagint Proverbs," 16.

[145] Clifford, *Proverbs*, 111. Clifford lists this case (10:10b) under "obviously corrupt verses" with regard to the MT. Clifford, "Observations," 51.

[146] "No immoral act or condition is meant here, but some outward misfortune." *IB*, 4:854.

"No injustice is pleasing to the righteous, but the ungodly are (or: will be) full of evil"[147]

In Prov 12:21 אָוֶן "harm" and רָע "trouble" are synonymous, but the צַדִּיק "righteous" and רְשָׁעִים "wicked" stand in contrast with each other ("No harm/ill happens to the righteous, but the wicked are filled with trouble"). The verse speaks of "a relative truth about the contrast between the righteous and the wicked with respect to calamity."[148] Apparently the translator understood or took the verse not as referring to outward misfortune or trouble, but to an inward condition perhaps because he connected v. 21 with the previous v. 20[149] where it speaks of inner conditions and intentions of good and bad people. Accordingly he altered the first half and substituted יְאֻנֶּה "happens" with ἀρέσει "pleasing" ("No injustice is pleasing to the righteous, but the ungodly are full of evil"). This translational adjustment is certainly in line with the translator's technique concerning his effort for cohesion as well as making the halves correspond with each other. Thus the suggested LXX reading ἀρέσει in place of יְאֻנֶּה by e.g. Toy[150] (cf. *BHS* apparatus) may not reflect a Hebrew *Vorlage*.

4. Prov 13:9

MT: אוֹר־צַדִּיקִים יִשְׂמָח וְנֵר רְשָׁעִים יִדְעָךְ
"The light of the righteous rejoices (=shines brightly), but the lamp of the wicked goes out"

Q: [אור צדיקים ישמח ונר רש]עים י[דעך] [151]

LXX: φῶς δικαίοις διὰ παντός φῶς δὲ ἀσεβῶν σβέννυται[152]
"The righteous always have light, but the light of the ungodly is quenched"

Prov 13:9 is antithetically parallel with a contrast of the righteous and the wicked. The light of the former shines brightly, but that of the latter goes out, "light" being a symbol that represents life, joy, and prosperity; and "dark" signifying adversity and death.[153] It is most likely that the translator dropped the

---

[147] For the translation cf. Toy, *Proverbs*, 255.

[148] Ross, "Proverbs," n.p.

[149] Cf. O. Plöger who writes, "*G:* ἀρέσει ('der Gerechte hat keinen Gefallen . . .') bemüht sich um eine Anknüpfung an V.20." Plöger, *Sprüche*, 147.

[150] Toy thinks that the LXX ". . . (representing a somewhat different Heb. text from ours) is appropriate, and may be the original form of the couplet." Toy, *Proverbs*, 255. But unfortunately Toy did not take the translator's technique into consideration.

[151] De Waard, "4QProv," 89. Prov 13:9 is very fragmentary.

[152] The addition in v. 9(a) is not discussed here, as it cannot be explained translationally.

[153] Cf. Ross, "Proverbs," n.p. Meinhold, *Sprüche*, 1:220–221.

Hebrew figure of "the light . . . rejoices"[154] and rendered more straightforwardly φῶς . . . διὰ παντός ". . . always have light" as an antithetical parallel to the second colon φῶς . . . σβέννυται "the light . . . is quenched."[155] Thus διὰ παντός need not be regarded as reflecting a variant reading (against *BHS*) due to its translational nature.

5. Prov 13:15

MT: שֵׂכֶל־טוֹב יִתֶּן־חֵן וְדֶרֶךְ בֹּגְדִים אֵיתָן
"Good understanding gives favor, but the way of the faithless is hard"

LXX: σύνεσις ἀγαθὴ δίδωσιν χάριν τὸ δὲ γνῶναι νόμον διανοίας ἐστὶν ἀγαθῆς ὁδοὶ δὲ καταφρονούντων ἐν ἀπωλείᾳ
"Good understanding gives favor, and to know the law belongs to a sound understanding, but the ways of scorners tend to destruction"

The two lines in Prov 13:15 do not correspond very well antithetically ("Good understanding gives favor, but the way of the faithless is hard"). Also the reading אֵיתָן is problematic[156] and I do not intend to give a solution here. It is, however, possible that the translator modified his text translationally in line with his predilection for a more contrastively parallel rendering. Accordingly he may have sought to contrast ἀπωλεία "destruction" with χάριν "favor" ("Good understanding gives favor, and to know the law belongs to a sound understanding, but the ways of scorners tend to destruction"). In fact, ἀπώλεια seems to be one of his favorite words as he used it quite frequently even without any correspondence in the MT, and interestingly he used it in the second part of antithetical parallelisms also in Prov 11:6; 13:1,15; 16:26,26(a) to emphasize the

---

[154] According to W. McKane the meaning is "bright" rather than "joyful" and an emendation is not required. McKane, *Proverbs*, 461. Driver illustrates the semantic relationship between "brightness" and "joy" by Ugaritic examples. G. R. Driver, "Problems in the Hebrew Text of Proverbs," *Bib* 32 (1951): 180.

[155] G. Gerleman lists this case under the stylistic device of anaphora because of the repetition of the same word in the beginning of the two colons. Gerleman, *Studies*, 14. See also Lee, "Translations of the Old Testament," 779.

[156] G. R. Driver suggests that the rare negative particle 'e was dropped before 'ethan by haplography and so the reading should be "is not lasting." Driver, "Problems in the Hebrew Text," 181. Some emend on the basis of the LXX and read "their destruction" (*BHS*, Gemser, Plöger, etc.). R. J. Clifford also regards the LXX reading as superior. Clifford, "Observations," 56. And there are those who try to maintain the MT, e.g. Meinhold "aber der Weg der Treulosen ist andauernd fest(-gelegt) (?)." A. Scherer adopts the LXX reading at this point and regards Meinhold's solution as "nicht überzeugend." Scherer, *Das weise Wort*, 121. W. Dietrich favors the MT and thinks that there is no need to read with LXX. He translates אֵיתָן with "steinig" and writes: "Der **Weg der Treulosen** ist . . . wie ein ausgetrocknetes, **steiniges** Flußbett. Hier ist das Vorwärtskommen schwierig." Dietrich, *Sprüche*, 128. HOTTP, 489, opts for the MT.

fate of the transgressors etc. The reason for adding τὸ δὲ γνῶναι νόμον διανοίας ἐστὶν ἀγαθῆς "and to know the law belongs to a sound understanding" after the first line is perhaps to further explicate and even specify the object of good understanding according to the translator's perception, and to connect it with the previous verse 14 where νόμος "law" has already been mentioned. An additional reason for the addition may be that the translator wished to emphasize the law in LXX Proverbs.[157]

6. Prov 13:23

MT: רָב־אֹכֶל נִיר רָאשִׁים וְיֵשׁ נִסְפֶּה בְּלֹא מִשְׁפָּט
"Abundant food is in the unbroken soil of the poor (or: notables/grandees[158]), but it (or: substance) is swept away through want of justice (or: lack of judgment; or: through injustice)"

LXX: δίκαιοι ποιήσουσιν ἐν πλούτῳ ἔτη πολλά ἄδικοι δὲ ἀπολοῦνται συντόμως
"The righteous will spend many years in wealth, but the unrighteous will perish suddenly"

The MT of Prov 13:23 is difficult to understand and thus numerous emendations have been suggested[159] ("Abundant food is in the unbroken soil of the poor, but it is swept away through want of justice"). The versions too give evidence that the verse is hard to understand.[160] According to C. H. Toy the Hebrew text appears to be corrupt beyond emendation.[161] The LXX rendering is quite different from the MT, but this may be due to the difficulty of the Hebrew text, and thus the translator may have simplified the text and eliminated the difficult word נִיר.[162] In any case, the two lines in the LXX have a high degree of correspondence, certainly more than the MT ("The righteous will spend many years in wealth, but the unrighteous will perish suddenly"). It is possible that the translator rendered רָאשִׁים "the poor" freely by δίκαιοι "the righteous" in parallel with ἄδικοι "the unrighteous"—and בְּלֹא מִשְׁפָּט "want of justice" or "injustice" is usually done by ἄδικοι (second colon). There is the possibility that theological considerations may have played a role in the translator's

---

[157] Cook, "The Law of Moses," 455–457.

[158] Although most translations render "poor," "notables/grandees" is another possible understanding of the MT and is followed by McKane, *Proverbs*, 463.

[159] For a discussion see McKane, *Proverbs*, 462–463.

[160] Cf. Ross, "Proverbs," n.p. *IB*, 4:860.

[161] Toy, *Proverbs*, 278.

[162] Cf. Plöger, *Sprüche*, 157.

decision to change to a more parallel rendering.[163] Thus δίκαιοι = יְשָׁרִים "the righteous" need not be regarded as a variant reading.

7. Prov 14:9

MT: אֱוִלִים יָלִיץ אָשָׁם וּבֵין יְשָׁרִים רָצוֹן
"Fools scoff at a guilt-offering/guilt (or: sin; or: Fools do not care if they sin), but among upright men there is approval (or: good understanding)"

LXX: οἰκίαι παρανόμων ὀφειλήσουσιν καθαρισμόν οἰκίαι δὲ δικαίων δεκταί
"The houses of transgressors will need purification, but the houses of the just are acceptable"

In Prov 14:9 the meaning of the MT is not very clear and thus many emendations have been suggested.[164] W. McKane with a minor change of the MT renders, "Fools scoff at guilt, but upright men discern (וּבָנוּ) what is acceptable."[165] The deviation in the LXX especially in the first colon may be partly due to the difficulty of the Hebrew. In the second colon it agrees closely with the MT except that it takes בֵּין "among" with a minor change as בֵּית "house" (οἰκίαι). It may have been this that led to employing the contrasting phrase οἰκίαι παρανόμων "the houses of transgressors" (first colon) in place of אוילים "fools."[166] Also ὀφειλήσουσιν καθαρισμόν "will need purification" (first colon) may have its origin in the translator's desire for a contrast to "are acceptable" (second colon). Certainly, the LXX ("The houses of transgressors will need purification, but the houses of the just are acceptable") can be regarded as more parallel antithetically than MT, and this is most probably due to the translator's translation technique. Thus the suggested variants in the *BHS* that are derived from the LXX as perhaps reflecting the original readings may be of a translational nature.

8. Prov 14:16

MT: חָכָם יָרֵא וְסָר מֵרָע וּכְסִיל מִתְעַבֵּר וּבוֹטֵחַ
"A wise person fears and departs from evil, but the fool rages and is confident"

LXX: σοφὸς φοβηθεὶς ἐξέκλινεν ἀπὸ κακοῦ ὁ δὲ ἄφρων ἑαυτῷ

---

[163] According to W. McKane the "LXX transforms the sentence into a clear-cut expression of the doctrine of theodicy: 'The righteous will pass many years in wealth, but the unrighteous will be speedily destroyed.'" McKane, *Proverbs*, 462.

[164] For a discussion see McKane, *Proverbs*, 475–476.

[165] *Ibid.*, 476.

[166] G. Gerleman lists this case under anaphora because of the repetition of οἰκίαι. Gerleman, *Studies*, 14.

πεποιθὼς μείγνυται ἀνόμῳ
"A wise person fears and departs from evil, but the fool trusts in himself and joins himself with the transgressor"

In Prov 14:16 ("A wise person fears and departs from evil, but the fool rages and is confident") it is very likely that the translator adjusted the second half to correspond to the first half, since μείγνυται ἀνόμῳ "he joins himself with the transgressor" (second half) appears to be antithetically parallel to "(he) departs from evil" (first half). Similarly the translator paralleled ἑαυτῷ πεποιθὼς[167] "(he) trusts in himself" (second colon) with "(he) fears."[168] It is possible that a scribal error was involved, מִתְעַבֵּר "he rages" and מִתְעָרֵב = μείγνυται "he joins himself" being liable to confusion, but it is more probable that the translator altered his source text by applying his translation technique.[169] The LXX reading as mentioned in the *BHS* apparatus does not make much sense on its own without ἀνόμῳ "with the transgressor." Most of the translations and commentators follow the MT.[170]

9. Prov 14:21

MT: בָּז־לְרֵעֵהוּ חוֹטֵא וּמְחוֹנֵן עֲנָיִים אַשְׁרָיו
"He that despises his neighbor sins (or: commits sin), but he that has mercy on the poor is blessed/happy"

LXX: ὁ ἀτιμάζων πένητας ἁμαρτάνει ἐλεῶν δὲ πτωχοὺς μακαριστός
"He that dishonors the needy sins, but he that has pity on the poor is most blessed"

In Prov 14:21 the sin of despising a neighbor (who is poor or in need) is contrasted with showing kindness and mercy to the needy.[171] Most of the

---

[167] The translator understood בוֹטֵחַ as "self-assured," see also McKane, *Proverbs*, 465.

[168] According to W. McKane "'fearful' does not mean that he is excessively timid and irresolute, but that he does not overestimate his own capabilities and does not underrate the difficulties and dangers involved in a given course of action." McKane, *Proverbs*, 464.

[169] J. de Waard also thinks that the reading in the LXX is of translational nature but he explains the difference in the LXX (*mit'areb* compared to *mit'aber* in the MT) in terms of the translator's application of metathesis as a translation technique. Jan de Waard, "Metathesis as a Translation Technique?" In *Traducere Navem* (ed. J. Holz-Mänttäri and C. Nord; Tampere: Universitätsbibliothek, 1993), 250–251.

[170] E.g. RSV, NRSV, GN1, GN2, HOTTP, Meinhold, McKane, Toy.

[171] Cf. Ross, "Proverbs," n.p.

commentators follow the MT reading "his neighbor."[172] The LXX translator seems to have altered this, rendering πένητας "the needy" (first colon) as a semantic parallel to πτωχούς "the poor"—MT: עֲנִיִּים—(second colon), rather than translating לְרֵעֵהוּ "to his neighbor" literally. Thus the LXX reading given in the *BHS* apparatus (πένητας = לְרָעֵב) as perhaps representing the original text (also Gemser and Scott) may be attributed to the translator's translation technique rather than to a different *Vorlage*. A scribal mistake may not be ruled out completely because the shapes of לְרֵעֵהוּ and לְרָעֵב are fairly similar,[173] but the translational explanation is more convincing, as it is in line with the translator's common practice.

10. Prov 14:32

MT: בְּרָעָתוֹ יִדָּחֶה רָשָׁע וְחֹסֶה בְמוֹתוֹ צַדִּיק
"The wicked is overthrown by his wickedness, but the righteous has hope in his death (or: has a refuge when he dies)"

Q: [ברעתו י]דחה רש[ע וחס]ה במות[ו צדיק] [174]

LXX: ἐν κακίᾳ αὐτοῦ ἀπωσθήσεται ἀσεβής ὁ δὲ πεποιθὼς τῇ ἑαυτοῦ ὁσιότητι δίκαιος
"The ungodly will be removed in/by his wickedness, but he who is secure in/by (or: who relies on) his own holiness/piety is righteous"

In Prov 14:32 the commentators are divided between those who favor the MT and those who follow the LXX reading. B. K. Waltke (although he prefers the reading of the MT[175]) assumes that the LXX rendering goes straight back to a Hebrew *Vorlage*. He says that "The consonants of the MT are *bmtw*, and those of the (assumed) Vorlage (i.e., the retroverted text lying before a translator) behind the LXX were *btmw*. The slight difference due to metathesis of *m* and *t*, however, profoundly affects the exegesis of that text and the theology of the book."[176]

---

[172] Toy, *Proverbs*, 293–294. McKane, *Proverbs*, 473. Plöger, *Sprüche*, 166. Meinhold, *Sprüche*, 1:238.

[173] R. J. Clifford regards the reading of the MT as a copyist's error from the preceding v. 20 and follows the LXX. Clifford, *Proverbs*, 142.

[174] De Waard, "4QProv," 89.

[175] B. K. Waltke, "Proverbs: Theology of," *NIDOTTE*, 4:1091–1092.

[176] B. K. Waltke, *NIDOTTE*, 1:51. Against: A. Meinhold does not agree with the suggested metathesis, for this would mean "daß sich der Mensch bei sich selbst zu bergen versuchte, und das wäre trügerisch." Meinhold, *Sprüche*, 1:245.

W. McKane writes that the reading of the MT "would have to be taken as evidence of a belief in an after-life. I do not believe that the sentence originally asserted this, and LXX (v. 32b) supplies a more apt antithesis to v. 32a."[177]

The arguments in favor of the LXX are based on avoidance of the teaching of immortality or an after-life. McKane's argument that LXX supplies a more apt antithesis does, however, speak for the thesis presented here.

Those who think that the reading of the MT is original argue as follows.

D. Kidner, for instance, holds that "The Heb. text . . . must not be discarded merely as implying too advanced a doctrine of death: Job and the Psalms show occasional glimpses, such as this, of what lies normally beyond their view."[178]

F. Delitzsch points out that

> Yet though there was no such revelation [as faith in immortality and in the resurrection] then, still the pious in death put their confidence in Jahve, the God of life and of salvation—for in Jahve there was for ancient Israel the beginning, middle, and end of the work of salvation—and believing that they were going home to Him, committing their spirit into His hand (Ps. xxxi.6), they fell asleep, though without any explicit knowledge, yet not without the hope of eternal life.[179]

G. Goldsworthy holds that "This does not necessarily indicate an understanding of life after death, but it does express confidence that the righteous are vindicated."[180]

A. P. Ross writes, "A problem often raised is that nowhere in the Book of Proverbs is hope for immortality found. Rather death is seen as a misfortune. Nevertheless, this verse may be a shadowy forerunner of that truth."[181]

The uncertainty of the text is also reflected in the decision of the HOTTP, as one half of the committee favored the MT and the other half followed the LXX, both with a C rating.[182] As for the LXX it appears that it is antithetically a more parallel couplet, as "the ungodly will be removed in/by his wickedness," but the righteous "is secure in/by his own holiness" and is thus not driven away. So it may be that the translator purposely rendered בְּמוֹתוֹ "in/by his death" by τῇ ἑαυτοῦ ὁσιότητι "in/by his own holiness" (= בְּתֻמּוֹ) in parallel with "in/by his

---

[177] McKane, *Proverbs*, 475. According to A. Scherer, however, the MT does not imply a belief in an after-life. "Dem Spruch geht es um ein die Todesfurcht überwindendes JHWH-Vertrauen, nicht um ein zukünftiges, jenseitiges Leben." Scherer, *Das weise Wort*, 143.

[178] Kidner, *Proverbs*, 111.

[179] Delitzsch, *Proverbs*, 312.

[180] Goldsworthy, *Life*, 113.

[181] Ross, "Proverbs," n.p.

[182] Barthélemy et al., *Preliminary*, 3:496–497.

wickedness" following his frequent translation practice.[183] If this is so, the LXX reading followed by B. Gemser,[184] O. Plöger,[185] and the *BHS* apparatus is of a translational nature.[186] To conclude, although both sides may have presented valid arguments, on the basis of the translator's technique the LXX rendering may be regarded as translational. As for the Qumran evidence, it supports the reading of the MT.[187]

11. Prov 14:33

MT: בְּלֵב נָבוֹן תָּנוּחַ חָכְמָה וּבְקֶרֶב כְּסִילִים תִּוָּדֵעַ
"Wisdom rests in the heart of a person of understanding, and/but in the inward part (=heart) of fools it is made known"

Q: [בלב נבון] תנוח חכמה ו[ב]קרב כסילי[ם תודע] [188]

LXX: ἐν καρδίᾳ ἀγαθῇ ἀνδρὸς σοφία ἐν δὲ καρδίᾳ ἀφρόνων οὐ διαγινώσκεται
"There is wisdom in the good heart of a man, but in the heart of fools it is not known"

In Prov 14:33 the second colon is difficult, and consequently different possible solutions have been offered. A. P. Ross translates it "even among fools she lets herself be known" and suggests it is to be understood ironically or sarcastically: "the fool, anxious to appear wise, blurts out what he thinks is wisdom but in the process turns it to folly."[189] A. Meinhold tries to solve the problem by taking the second half as a rhetorical question.[190] D. W. Thomas connects תִּוָּדֵעַ to the

---

[183] Whybray in support of the LXX reading writes that "in his holiness" makes a good parallelism with "through his evildoing." *Proverbs*, 223. However, a "good parallelism" is no indication for the priority of the LXX reading, but rather for its translational nature according to this thesis.

[184] Gemser, *Sprüche Salomos*, 66–67.

[185] Plöger, *Sprüche*, 166,168.

[186] The RSV and NRSV follow the LXX reading, whereas the NLT and NIV follow the MT.

[187] R. J. Clifford, who favors the reading of the MT notes that "The Qumran scroll 4QProv^b supports MT." Clifford, *Proverbs*, 143. Similarly De Waard, "4QProv," 92–93. Furthermore de Waard regards LXX reading as translational and explains the difference in the LXX in terms of the translator's application of metathesis as a translation technique. De Waard, "Metathesis," 251–252.

[188] De Waard, "4QProv," 89. As far as the evidence is concerned Q agrees with the MT.

[189] Ross, "Proverbs," n.p.

[190] Meinhold, *Sprüche*, 1:242. Similarly Murphy, *Proverbs*, 101–102.

Arabic root *wd*ʿ and translates it "in fools it is suppressed."¹⁹¹ C. H. Toy suggests emending תִּוָּדֵעַ to אִוֶּלֶת "folly."¹⁹² The LXX appears to have solved the textual problem by inserting the negative particle.¹⁹³ By this means the translator made the second colon correspond to the first colon in a contrastive manner: there is wisdom in the heart of a good man, that is, the one who understands, whereas in the heart of the fool there is no wisdom. *BHS* uses the LXX as support for לֹא תִוָּדֵעַ (οὐ διαγινώσκεται) "will not be known" in place of תִּוָּדֵעַ "will be known." The LXX reading,¹⁹⁴ although it may be a possible solution to the problem, may not be regarded as evidence for a variant text due to its translational nature.

12. Prov 14:34

MT: צְדָקָה תְרוֹמֵם־גּוֹי וְחֶסֶד לְאֻמִּים חַטָּאת
"Righteousness exalts a nation, but sin is a reproach/disgrace to any people/ nation"¹⁹⁵

Q: [צדקה] תרומם גוי ו[ח]סד לאמים [חטאת] ↓¹⁹⁶

LXX: δικαιοσύνη ὑψοῖ ἔθνος ἐλασσονοῦσι δὲ φυλὰς ἁμαρτίαι
"Righteousness exalts a nation, but sins diminish (or: lower) tribes"

In Prov 14:34 the MT makes good sense, and according to W. McKane "There is no difficulty in translating [חֶסֶד] 'disgrace,' and the sense is weaker if [חֹסֶר], 'want,' is read, as it apparently was by the Greek translator."¹⁹⁷ There is also the possibility that the translator understood ἐλασσονόω not only in the sense of

---

¹⁹¹ D. W. Thomas, "The Root *yd*ʿ in Hebrew," *JTS* 35 (1934): 302–303. Cf. also McKane, *Proverbs*, 466. Against: W. Johnstone who states: "If there is a Hebrew root *yd*ʿ II, there is no philological basis in Arabic for rendering it 'be humbled, humiliated.'" "*YD*ʿ II, 'Be Humbled, Humiliated'?," *VT* XLI, 1 (1991): 49–62, here 57–58. See also Plöger, *Sprüche*, 168.

¹⁹² Toy, *Proverbs*, 300–301. Against: W. McKane argues that this solution "does not at all grapple with MT." McKane, *Proverbs*, 466.

¹⁹³ According to Whybray it is generally assumed that the negative particle "not" has fallen out of the Hebrew text accidentally and the LXX reflects the original text. *Proverbs*, 223. The most recent commentaries (e.g. Murphy, Clifford, Ross, Meinhold), however, favor the MT as its stands in this case.

¹⁹⁴ The RSV, NRSV and NLT follow the LXX reading.

¹⁹⁵ "Righteousness elevates the status of a nation, gives it a standing in the world and makes it a power for good; sin depresses its influence and brings it into disrepute." McKane, *Proverbs*, 475.

¹⁹⁶ De Waard, "4QProv," 89. Q agrees with the MT.

¹⁹⁷ McKane, *Proverbs*, 475. O. Plöger also regards the LXX reading as translational. Plöger, *Sprüche*, 175.

"diminish," but also in the sense of "lower,"[198] thus: sins make a people small and unimportant, in contrast to the first half which states that righteousness exalts a nation. If we consider the translator's technique of producing forms that are more parallel than the Hebrew, it is quite likely that he purposely rendered by ἐλασσονοῦσι "they diminish/lower," since "exalt" and "diminish/lower" are more parallel antithetically than "exalt" and "reproach." Therefore the LXX reading need not be regarded as a possible variant as suggested in the *BHS* apparatus. As for the Qumran evidence, it supports the MT.

13. Prov 15:19

MT: דֶּרֶךְ עָצֵל כִּמְשֻׂכַת חָדֶק וְאֹרַח יְשָׁרִים סְלֻלָה
"The way of the sluggard is as a hedge of thorns, but the way of the righteous is made plain (or: is a level highway)"

Q: ‏וארח ישרים [...] סוללה[199]

LXX: ὁδοὶ ἀεργῶν ἐστρωμέναι ἀκάνθαις αἱ δὲ τῶν ἀνδρείων τετριμμέναι
"The ways of sluggards are strewn with thorns, but those of the diligent are made smooth"

In Prov 15:19 there is a dead metaphor that is coupled with a live one[200] ("The way of the sluggard is as a hedge of thorns, but the way of the righteous is made plain"). The Hebrew יְשָׁרִים "the righteous" in contrast with עָצֵל "the sluggard" may be a little unexpected but is quite possible,[201] especially in the light of dynamic Hebrew parallelism. The translator's fondness for producing colons that are more parallel can be seen clearly in the word pair ἀεργῶν "sluggards"

---

[198] Cf. LXX Ps 8:6.

[199] De Waard, "4QProv," 90. Q of Prov 15:19 is very fragmentary.

[200] Mouser, *Proverbs*, 94.

[201] D. Kidner suggests that the contrast of the sluggard with the upright is "a reminder (a) that there is an element of dishonesty in laziness . . . ; (b) that the straight course is ultimately the easiest." Kidner, *Proverbs*, 115. O. Plöger also supports the MT when he writes that wisdom "sieht die Weisen, Gerechten, Klugen usw. in einer zusammengehörigen Gruppierung gegenüber ihren Gegenspielern, so daß die einzelnen Bezeichnungen austauschbar sein können." Plöger, *Sprüche*, 183. For further support of the MT see Meinhold, *Sprüche*, 255–256. And Clifford, *Proverbs*, 149, 153.

(first colon) and ἀνδρείων "(the) diligent" (second colon).²⁰² Thus the LXX reading (which is favored by e.g. W. McKane,²⁰³ C. H. Toy²⁰⁴ and *BHS*) may be regarded as translational. Furthermore, it may be that ἐστρωμέναι "strewn with (thorns)" originated as a rather free rendering by the translator of the simile כִּמְשֻׂכַת "as a hedge (of thorns)."²⁰⁵ Thus ἐστρωμέναι = מְשֻׂכָּת (cf. *BHS* apparatus) may as well be of a translational nature.

14. Prov 15:32

MT: פּוֹרֵעַ מוּסָר מוֹאֵס נַפְשׁוֹ וְשׁוֹמֵעַ תּוֹכַחַת קוֹנֶה לֵּב
"He who refuses correction/discipline rejects his own soul/life, but he who listens to reproof gets understanding"

LXX: ὃς ἀπωθεῖται παιδείαν μισεῖ ἑαυτόν ὁ δὲ τηρῶν ἐλέγχους ἀγαπᾷ ψυχὴν αὐτοῦ
"He who rejects instruction hates himself, but he who minds/considers reproofs loves his soul"

Considering the translator's translation technique it is not surprising that in Prov 15:32 he introduced ἀγαπᾷ "loves" (second colon) corresponding antithetically to μισεῖ "hates"—MT: מוֹאֵס "rejects"—(first colon) for the sake of a sharper contrast.²⁰⁶ Thus the LXX reading ἀγαπᾷ ψυχὴν αὐτοῦ = אֹהֵב נַפְשׁוֹ "loves his soul" in place of קוֹנֶה לֵב "gets understanding" does not seem to be superior over the MT reading.²⁰⁷

---

[202] R. E. Murphy in his translation follows the MT and renders "upright," and in his notes he writes: "The parallelism is rather loose, and many adopt 'diligent,' supposedly on the basis of the Greek, but ἀνδρείων means 'strong.'" Murphy, *Proverbs*, 110–111. However, in the present context ἀνδρείων may be taken in the sense of "diligent" (cf. Lust/Eynikel/Hauspie, *Lexicon*, *Part I*, 34) which is still within the semantic range of the word.

[203] McKane, *Proverbs*, 482.

[204] Toy, *Proverbs*, 310–311.

[205] For adjustments of similes see under "Metaphor and simile" by Tauberschmidt, "Principles," 70–72.

[206] "The Greek translator abandons the text in order to get the sharp contrast: *hates himself . . . loves his own soul*." Toy, *Proverbs*, 318.

[207] Note that the two verbs מאס and שמע also occur in combination in Hos 9:17: יִמְאָסֵם אֱלֹהַי כִּי לֹא שָׁמְעוּ לוֹ "My God will reject them, because they have not listened to him; . . ."

15. Prov 18:2

MT: לֹא־יַחְפֹּץ כְּסִיל בִּתְבוּנָה כִּי אִם־בְּהִתְגַּלּוֹת לִבּוֹ
"A fool takes no pleasure in understanding, but only in revealing his own mind (=expressing his opinion[208])"

LXX: οὐ χρείαν ἔχει σοφίας ἐνδεὴς φρενῶν μᾶλλον γὰρ ἄγεται ἀφροσύνῃ
"A senseless man feels no need of wisdom, for[209] he is rather led by folly"

In Prov 18:2 the translator seems to have made translational adjustments, rendering the second colon freely by introducing ἀφροσύνη "folly" (second colon) to make a contrast with σοφίας "wisdom"; MT: בִּתְבוּנָה "understanding" (first colon). This is in line with his tendency to make the second half correspond to the first. The *BHS* mentions the LXX reading ἀφροσύνη = בְּהוֹלֵלוֹת? "by folly" for בְּהִתְגַּלּוֹת "in expressing/exposing/ revealing" in the apparatus. A scribal mistake may not be totally excluded since the beginnings and endings of the two words look alike. None of the commentators (or translations) consulted, however, suggests following the LXX reading at this point. In any case, the LXX translation looks very much like a translational adjustment as mentioned above. Thus we should not regard this case as text-critical.

16. Prov 21:20

MT: אוֹצָר נֶחְמָד וָשֶׁמֶן בִּנְוֵה חָכָם וּכְסִיל אָדָם יְבַלְּעֶנּוּ
"There is desirable treasure and oil in the dwelling of the wise, but a foolish man devours it (or: destroys[210] it; or: uses it up)"[211]

LXX: θησαυρὸς ἐπιθυμητὸς ἀναπαύσεται ἐπὶ στόματος σοφοῦ ἄφρονες δὲ ἄνδρες καταπίονται αὐτόν
"A desirable treasure rests//will rest on the mouth of the wise, but foolish men swallow//will swallow it up"

The mention of וָשֶׁמֶן "and oil" in Prov 21:20 is regarded by some interpreters as not suitable.[212] But A. Meinhold argues in favor of "oil" on the grounds that it

---

[208] Cf. McKane, *Proverbs*, 515–516. Kidner, *Proverbs*, 127. Ross, "Proverbs," n.p.

[209] γάρ "for" (explanation).

[210] For this meaning see P. J. J. S. Els, *NIDOTTE*, 1:666.

[211] "The verse basically means that the wise gain wealth but the foolish squander it." Ross, "Proverbs," n.p.

[212] Cf. McKane, *Proverbs*, 553. McKane follows Eitan's proposal, although he regards it as speculative, to suspect in שֶׁמֶן (according to the Arabic tḥmn) a further adjective "precious."

makes a connection with v. 17, and oil was an important treasure that was used in many ways in a household or "the dwelling."²¹³ It is likely that the translator left out the noun phrase וָשֶׁמֶן "and oil" on purpose because it disturbed the parallelism. Perhaps he regarded "oil" as symbolic²¹⁴ and therefore would not have taken it literally, in which case it would not have added much to the meaning. In addition he changed בִּנְוֵה "in the dwelling" to ἀναπαύσεται ἐπὶ στόματος "will rest on the mouth"²¹⁵ (first colon), which is antithetically parallel to καταπίονται αὐτόν "(they) will swallow it up." In doing so, he even paralleled one figure of speech with another one. Thus the suggestion of the LXX reading ἀναπαύσεται ἐπὶ στόματος, *frt* יָשׁוּן בְּפִי, in the *BHS* apparatus as possible alternative reading may not be needed.

17. Prov 21:26

MT: כָּל־הַיּוֹם הִתְאַוָּה תַאֲוָה וְצַדִּיק יִתֵּן וְלֹא יַחְשֹׂךְ
"All day long he desires eagerly, but the righteous gives and does not hold back"

LXX: ἀσεβὴς ἐπιθυμεῖ ὅλην τὴν ἡμέραν ἐπιθυμίας κακάς ὁ δὲ δίκαιος ἐλεᾷ καὶ οἰκτίρει ἀφειδῶς
"An ungodly man entertains evil desires all day, but the righteous is unsparingly merciful and compassionate"

In Prov 21:26 the subject of the first half is not explicit. Some interpreters assume a continuation from v. 25 to v. 26 and take "the sluggard" as the subject of v. 26.²¹⁶ Others hold to the contrary that the subject in v. 26a does not necessarily have to be "the sluggard" of v. 25 and regard the subject as indefinite, "one who craves,"²¹⁷ or as "the ungodly/impious" in contrast to "the righteous" in v. 26b.²¹⁸ In any case, it is most likely that the translator added

---

²¹³ For further details see, Meinhold, *Sprüche*, 2:356. Also R. J. Clifford supports the MT reading "wine and oil." Clifford, *Proverbs*, 192.

²¹⁴ Cf. NLT which renders it "luxury."

²¹⁵ B. Gemser is the only commentator who regards the LXX as superior here and suggests to read בְּפִי for "in der Wohnung." Gemser, *Sprüche Salomos*, 81.

²¹⁶ G. R. Driver, "Hebrew Notes on Prophets and Proverbs," *JTS* 41 (1940): 174. Kidner, *Proverbs*, 145. Similarly McKane, *Proverbs*, 557.

²¹⁷ "This verse has been placed with the preceding because of the literary connection with 'desire'• 'he craves for more' [הִתְאַוָּה תַאֲוָה], but it provides an independent thought. The verse contrasts the one who craves with the righteous who give generously." Ross, "Proverbs," n.p. Similarly Clifford, *Proverbs*, 193.

²¹⁸ Cf. Meinhold, *Sprüche*, 2:359–360: "Sinngemäß richtig hat die Septuaginta das Wort für 'Frevler' ergänzt und entsprechend übersetzt. Notwendig ist eine solche Textänderung allerdings nicht, wenn das unpersönliche Subjekt 'man' in der Verbform zur Geltung kommt."

ἀσεβής "an ungodly (man)" (first colon) to make a parallel with צַדִּיק, ὁ ...
δίκαιος "the righteous (man)" (second colon), whereas in the MT there is no explicit subject in the first half. In addition to the translator's predilection for closely corresponding items, it may be mentioned at this point that he also tended to explicate• that is, introduce new• participants, cf. 2.1.1.3. The *BHS* suggests the LXX reading ἀσεβής, עַוָּל, or אֱוִיל, or רָשָׁע in the apparatus, but it should not be regarded as a variant reading at all,[219] although in translation a subject may be added according to the interpretation chosen.

18. Prov 28:2

MT: בְּפֶשַׁע אֶרֶץ רַבִּים שָׂרֶיהָ וּבְאָדָם מֵבִין יֹדֵעַ כֵּן יַאֲרִיךְ
"Through the transgression/wickedness of a land the rulers become many, but through a man of understanding and knowledge the state (or: authority) continues"[220]

LXX: δι' ἁμαρτίας ἀσεβῶν κρίσεις ἐγείρονται ἀνὴρ δὲ πανοῦργος κατασβέσει αὐτάς
"Because of the sin of ungodly men quarrels arise, but a wise man will extinguish them"

For Prov 28:2 many emendations have been suggested to achieve a better contrast between the two halves.[221] A. Meinhold holds that the MT makes sense as it stands and therefore no emendations are needed.[222] Apparently the better antithetical correspondence of the two halves in the LXX is due to the translator smoothening out the "apparent difficulties" of the MT. Thus ἀσεβῶν "ungodly (men)" (first colon) is contrasted with ἀνὴρ ... πανοῦργος "a wise man" (second colon), and κρίσεις ἐγείρονται "quarrels arise" with κατασβέσει αὐτάς "will quell them." It is also important to note that the pronoun αὐτάς agrees with κρίσεις which is typical for the style of the translator and his striving for coherence. This means that the deviations of the LXX may simply

---

[219] W. McKane thinks that "ἀσεβής (v. 26a) may have no significance for textual criticism, since it is the type of moralizing expansion which would be encouraged by [צַדִּיק] (v. 26b)." McKane, *Proverbs*, 557.

[220] "In just over two centuries, northern Israel, for its sins, had nine dynasties, each, after the first, inaugurated by an assassination ... In three and a half centuries, Judah, for David's sake, had only one." Kidner, *Proverbs*, 168–169. Similarly McKane, *Proverbs*, 630–631.

[221] See discussion in McKane, *Proverbs*, 630–631.

[222] Meinhold, *Sprüche*, 2:467.

be due to the translator's technique rather than to a different *Vorlage* as has been proposed by some (cf. *BHS*, Gemser et al.).²²³

19. Prov 29:18

MT: בְּאֵין חָזוֹן יִפָּרַע עָם וְשֹׁמֵר תּוֹרָה אַשְׁרֵהוּ
"Where there is no prophecy/vision, the people run wild, but happy is he who keeps the law"

LXX: οὐ μὴ ὑπάρξῃ ἐξηγητὴς ἔθνει παρανόμῳ ὁ δὲ φυλάσσων τὸν νόμον μακαριστός
"There will be no interpreter to a lawless nation, but he who observes the law is blessed"

Prov 29:18 may be regarded as a near-parallel couplet contrastively²²⁴ ("Where there is no prophecy/vision, the people run wild, but happy is he who keeps the law"), but the LXX is a slightly more closely parallel form ("There will be no interpreter to a lawless nation, but he who observes the law is blessed"). This is probably due to the translator's translation technique, as he seems to have rendered παρανόμῳ "lawless" (where the MT has פרע "run wild"; first colon) as a contrastive semantic parallel to וְשֹׁמֵר תּוֹרָה = ὁ δὲ φυλάσσων τὸν νόμον "but he who keeps the law" (second colon). The rendering ἐξηγητὴς "guide, interpreter" for חָזוֹן²²⁵ may be due to the translational adjustment made to fit the parallelism. In addition, it may also be possible that the translator wished to emphasize the importance of the law. C. H. Toy, however, thinks that "We should probably substitute for *vision* some such word as *guidance*" following the LXX, because in his opinion "the most calamitous period of Israel's history, politically and morally, was that during which prophecy was at its height . . . , and the people were obedient at a time when God hid his face and there was no prophet"; and in addition, "Pr. nowhere else mentions prophetic teaching, its guide being wisdom, the instruction of the sages."²²⁶ In response A. P. Ross writes, "It should be stated, however, that the prophetic ministry was usually in

---

²²³ The NEB follows the LXX, and K. Aitken also suggests this reading, Kenneth T. Aitken, *Proverbs* (Louisville: Westminster John Knox, 1986), 260, whereas most versions are largely in agreement with the meaning proposed by Kidner, McKane, and others, following the MT closely. R. E. Murphy also follows the MT closely, and he seems to reject the LXX reading on the ground that it reflects a different *Vorlage*, which is quite surprising. Murphy, *Proverbs*, 212–213.

²²⁴ In *IB*, 4:944, it is listed under antithetic.

²²⁵ According to W. McKane the word חָזוֹן refers to prophetic vision. McKane, *Proverbs*, 640–641. Also D. Kidner, *Proverbs*, 175. Similarly Ross who writes, "The word [חָזוֹן] refers to divine communication to prophets (as in 1 Sam.3:1) and not to individual goals that are formed." Ross, "Proverbs," n.p.

²²⁶ Toy, *Proverbs*, 512.

response to the calamitous periods, calling the people back to God."[227] Apart from the fact that the Hebrew word חָזוֹן may fit quite well, the LXX should not be adopted at this point due to its translational nature.

To sum up, the translator's fondness for producing antitheses and clearer contrasts is important to note in order to avoid using translational cases as variant readings.

3.3.1.5 Additional Aspects

The following cases of additional aspects, see also 1.2.1.5, demonstrate the importance of considering the translator's predilection for closely corresponding lines before using these parallel forms as variant readings.

3.3.1.5.1 Parallelisms of logical relations

1. Prov 17:14

MT: פּוֹטֵר מַיִם רֵאשִׁית מָדוֹן וְלִפְנֵי הִתְגַּלַּע הָרִיב נְטוֹשׁ

"The beginning of strife is a seepage of water (or: is as when one lets out water), therefore leave off contention, before it breaks out (or: stop before the quarrel breaks out)"

LXX: ἐξουσίαν δίδωσιν λόγοις ἀρχὴ δικαιοσύνης προηγεῖται δὲ τῆς ἐνδείας στάσις καὶ μάχη

"Just rule gives authority to words, but sedition/discord and strife precede poverty"

Prov 17:14 states the cause (or reason) first where "the beginning of strife" is compared to "a seepage of water" and then the effect (or result) follows[228] ("The beginning of strife is a seepage of water, therefore leave off contention, before it breaks out"). In the LXX, however, ἀρχὴ δικαιοσύνης "just rule" (first colon) is contrasted with στάσις καὶ μάχη "sedition and strife" (second colon) and appears to be more parallel antithetically ("Just rule gives authority to words, but sedition/discord and strife precede poverty"). It is not apparent how the translator arrived at this translation. O. Plöger suggests that he misread his source text, and that led to a totally different sense.[229] However, this seems relatively unlikely. Rather, the translator may have dropped the metaphor on purpose[230] and recast the whole verse, although it is not totally unrelated to the

---

[227] Ross, "Proverbs," n.p.

[228] See also Ross, "Proverbs," n.p.

[229] Plöger, *Sprüche*, 199.

[230] Note that the translator often dropped figures of speech as in Prov 1:12b; 3:12; 7:22; 11:28; 12:4; 18:8b,11b,19; 23:28a,32,34; 26:1 and often translated differently altogether.

MT reading since ἀρχὴ δικαιοσύνης "just rule" avoids מָדוֹן "strife." C. H. Toy prefers the Greek and writes: "The Grk. gives what is perhaps a better text by reading *words* instead of *water*."[231] But the LXX rendering does not seem to be superior at this point due to its translational nature.

2. Prov 19:27

MT: חֲדַל־בְּנִי לִשְׁמֹעַ מוּסָר לִשְׁגוֹת מֵאִמְרֵי־דָעַת
"Cease, my son, to hear the instruction, to stray from the words of knowledge"

LXX: υἱὸς ἀπολειπόμενος φυλάξαι παιδείαν πατρὸς μελετήσει ῥήσεις κακάς
"A son who ceases to attend to the instruction of a father will cherish evil designs"

The imperative in Prov 19:27 uses irony in the first part, in other words, one should not cease to listen to instruction, while the second part may be understood as a final clause[232] or else as result.[233] The translator, however, altered the imperative into a coherent statement[234] with a positive ("attend to instruction") – negative ("will cherish evil designs") contrast typical of the translator's approach, the latter term of the contrast being substituted for מֵאִמְרֵי־דָעַת "words of knowledge." The translator's preference for rendering irony or sarcasm straightforwardly is also demonstrated in Prov 30:3, 2.2.1. Therefore the suggestion to perhaps follow the LXX for textual reasons (cf. *BHS*) is not needed at this point. This case shows particularly that in addition to the tendency of the translator to render Hebrew parallelism in a more parallel fashion, linguistic and contextual considerations played a role in influencing parallel forms.

---

[231] Toy, *Proverbs*, 345.

[232] W. McKane writes, "The construction is that of imperative and final clause—characteristic of the Instruction—but the intention, contrary to the meaning which lies on the surface, is to enter a dissuasive against the neglect of [מוּסָר]." McKane, *Proverbs*, 525. Similarly Meinhold, *Sprüche*, 2:324, 326–327.

[233] Ross regards the second part as result: "The result of ceasing to listen is that the son will stray from the words of knowledge." Ross, "Proverbs," n.p. Similarly Plöger, *Sprüche*, 218.

[234] For this kind of translational adjustment see Tauberschmidt, "Principles," 77–80.

3.3.1.5.2 *Parallelism of addition relations*

Prov 22:13

MT: אָמַר עָצֵל אֲרִי בַחוּץ בְּתוֹךְ רְחֹבוֹת אֵרָצֵחַ
"The sluggard says, 'There is a lion outside! I shall be slain/killed in the streets!'"

LXX: προφασίζεται καὶ λέγει ὀκνηρός λέων ἐν ταῖς ὁδοῖς ἐν δὲ ταῖς πλατείαις φονευταί
"The sluggard makes excuses, and says, 'There is a lion in the ways, and murderers in the streets'"

In Prov 22:13 "with humor and irony, the proverb mocks the lazy person's excuse-making to avoid going to work,"[235] the second half being a continuation of the first half ("The sluggard says, 'There is a lion outside! I shall be slain/killed in the streets!'"). The translator, however, made certain adjustments towards a more parallel rendering ("The sluggard makes excuses, and says, 'There is a lion in the ways, and murderers in the streets'"). He substituted ὁδοῖς "ways" for חוּץ "outside" to make a parallel with "streets" (second half), and he altered אֵרָצֵחַ "I shall be killed" slightly so as to read רֹצֵחַ instead and rendered φονευταί "murderers" in parallel with (the murderer) "lion" (first half).[236] Thus the proposed reading mentioned in the *BHS* apparatus, φονευταί = רֹצֵחַ, may be regarded as translational.[237]

3.3.1.5.3 *Parallelisms of comparisons*

Among the parallelisms of comparisons, different combinations of parts of speech may be paired; and A. Berlin lists Prov 16:16 under "Miscellaneous Contrast."[238] The MT (emphasis) of 16:16 has been retained in various

---

[235] Goldsworthy, *Life*, 146. Similarly McKane, *Proverbs*, 569. The translator of LXX Proverbs by adding προφασίζεται "he makes excuses" explicated what is already implied in the MT. Thus J. Weingreen's explanation that this addition is a Rabbinic-type commentary may not be needed at this point. Weingreen, "Rabbinic-Type Commentary," 408.

[236] W. McKane thinks that the LXX translation "may be due to the circumstance that [רצח] is elsewhere used only of death by human hands." McKane, *Proverbs*, 569. Similarly Ross, but he gives the additional reason that the variation in the LXX is intended to form a better parallelism: "The LXX changes it to 'murderers in the street' to form a better parallelism, possibly because [רצח] is used only of humans in the Bible." Ross, "Proverbs," n.p.

[237] G. Gerleman lists this example among cases the lines of which are more conformable, balanced and made congruent one with another. Gerleman, *Studies*, 25.

[238] Berlin, *Dynamics*, 52.

translations,[239] although it has often been regarded as a scribal error due to its less common construction.[240]

1. Prov 16:16

MT: קָנֹה־חָכְמָה מַה־טּוֹב מֵחָרוּץ וּקְנוֹת בִּינָה נִבְחָר מִכָּסֶף
"Acquiring wisdom—how much better than gold, and to acquire understanding is to be chosen rather than silver"

LXX: νοσσιαὶ σοφίας αἱρετώτεραι χρυσίου νοσσιαὶ δὲ φρονήσεως αἱρετώτεραι ὑπὲρ ἀργύριον
"The brood of wisdom is more to be chosen than gold, and the brood of prudence more to be chosen than silver"

In Prov 16:16 there are two comparisons that are equivalent at the level of their deep structure although they differ in surface structure ("Acquiring wisdom—how much better than gold, and to acquire understanding is to be chosen rather than silver"). Apparently the translator rendered the comparison in a more natural way in Greek, omitting מה "how" and instead inserting αἱρετώτεραι "more to be chosen" in parallel with the second colon and expressing the comparative by a genitive in parallel with the ὑπέρ construction[241] in the second line ("The brood of wisdom is more to be chosen than gold, and the brood of prudence more to be chosen than silver"). The particle מה is sometimes regarded as dittography,[242] and R. J. Clifford mentions in this connection that it is not attested in the versions.[243] For R. E. Murphy, however, "There is no compelling reason to eliminate מה, "what? how?" as dittography from the preceding חכמה, 'wisdom.'"[244] In any case, the LXX (and those versions that depend on it) cannot be taken as support at this point, even if a scribal error was involved.

2. Prov 17:7

MT: לֹא־נָאוָה לְנָבָל שְׂפַת־יֶתֶר אַף כִּי־לְנָדִיב שְׂפַת־שָׁקֶר
"Lips of excess (excellent speech[245]) is not becoming to a fool, much less are lying lips to a ruler"

---

[239] E.g. NRSV (note that RSV follows LXX etc.), NIV, REB, NASB, similarly TEV.

[240] See discussion below.

[241] Cf. note on Prov 8:10.

[242] Gemser, *Sprüche Salomos*, 71.

[243] Clifford, *Proverbs*, 157.

[244] Murphy, *Proverbs*, 118.

[245] The meaning of "superiority," "excellence" is derived from "lip of excess." *IB*, 4:880. "The word [יֶתֶר] ('arrogant') could also be rendered 'excellent' . . ." Ross, "Proverbs," n.p.

LXX: οὐχ ἁρμόσει ἄφρονι χείλη πιστὰ οὐδὲ δικαίῳ χείλη ψευδῆ
"Faithful lips will not suit a fool, nor lying lips a just man"

Prov 17:7 is a comparison that shows which of two things is worse,[246] the first half being illustrative and the main point of the verse being found in the second half[247] ("Lips of excess is not becoming to a fool, much less are lying lips to a ruler"). It is most likely that in 17:7 the translator did not render שְׂפַת־יֶתֶר "lip of excess (excellent speech)" literally but instead translated it as χείλη πιστὰ "faithful lips" (first colon), which is lexically antonymous to שְׂפַת־שָׁקֶר "lying lip" = χείλη ψευδῆ (second colon), thus producing a closer correspondence of the two lines ("Faithful lips will not suit a fool, nor lying lips a just man"). This makes the LXX reading clearly translational. This is supported by O. Plöger who states (against *BHS*), ". . . es geht hier nicht, wie *G* meint, um eine genaue Antithese, sondern um eine Überbietung, . . ."[248] R. E. Murphy regards the LXX reading as "far from certain," but he still adopts it in his translation and renders "honest lips."[249]

3. Prov 18:19

MT: אָח נִפְשָׁע מִקִּרְיַת־עֹז וּמִדְיָנִים כִּבְרִיחַ אַרְמוֹן
"A brother offended is harder (to be won) than a strong city, and quarrels are like the bars of a castle"[250]

LXX: ἀδελφὸς ὑπὸ ἀδελφοῦ βοηθούμενος ὡς πόλις ὀχυρὰ καὶ ὑψηλή ἰσχύει δὲ ὥσπερ τεθεμελιωμένον βασίλειον
"A brother helped by a brother is as a strong and high city, and is as strong as a well founded palace"

In Prov 18:19 the Hebrew text is difficult. A possible interpretation is as NLT translates: "It's harder to make amends with an offended friend than to capture a

---

[246] Ross, "Proverbs," n.p.

[247] McKane, *Proverbs*, 507. Similarly A. Meinhold who writes, "Die zweite Vershälfte bildet gegenüber der ersten eine Steigerung . . . , auf ihr liegt der Ton." Meinhold, *Sprüche*, 2:286.

[248] Plöger, *Sprüche*, 202.

[249] Murphy, *Proverbs*, 126–127.

[250] Similarly W. McKane who translates, "An aggrieved brother is more inaccessible than a fortified city, and quarrels are like the bars of a palace." McKane, *Proverbs*, 239.

fortified city. Arguments separate friends like a gate locked with iron bars."[251] The LXX rendering improves the text[252] and has a clearer antithesis,[253] which is probably due to the translator's technique ("A brother helped by a brother is as a strong and high city, and is as strong as a well founded palace"). The metaphor or comparison in the first colon was probably changed into a simile[254] by inserting ὡς in correspondence with the second colon, since the translator loves to make the lines correspond to each other. Thus the LXX reading ὡς πόλις (cf. BHS, frt l כְּקִרְיָה "like a city") instead of מִקִּרְיָה "than a city," may not represent the original Hebrew text.[255]

4. Prov 27:9

MT: שֶׁמֶן וּקְטֹרֶת יְשַׂמַּח־לֵב וּמֶתֶק רֵעֵהוּ מֵעֲצַת־נָפֶשׁ
"Oil and incense make the heart glad, so does the sweetness of a man's friend (or: friendship) because of the counsel of the soul (or: the sweetness of friendship strengthens the spirit[256])"

LXX: μύροις καὶ οἴνοις καὶ θυμιάμασιν τέρπεται καρδία
καταρρήγνυται δὲ ὑπὸ συμπτωμάτων ψυχή
"The heart delights in ointments and wines and perfumes, but the soul is broken by calamities"

In Prov 27:9 the second colon of the MT is difficult, but it may be understood in terms of the advice or counsel of a friend sweetening or strengthening the soul or spirit.[257] The whole verse is expressed fittingly by the NLT: "The heartfelt

---

[251] In short, "Serious disputes create insurmountable barriers among friends." Ross, "Proverbs," n.p. A. Meinhold writes, "Beide Hälften von V.19 werden durch die Erwähnung von Befestigungs- und Sicherungsgrößen miteinander verbunden. Was mit diesem Spruch letztlich gesagt sein soll, ist offen. Soll es heißen, daß aus Freundschaft oder Verwandtschaft im Enttäuschungsfall umso härtere Feindschaft und kaum überwindliche Barrieren werden? Oder ist gemeint, daß Streit unter Brüdern/Freunden am schwersten zu schlichten ist? Oder wird gewarnt, mit einem solchen Streit überhaupt erst zu beginnen (vgl. 17,14)? Wie es im einzelnen auch sei, der Spruch deutet einen Fall an, der das Gegenteil von 17,17 darstellt." Meinhold, Sprüche, 2:306.

[252] Cf. IB, 4:888.

[253] Cf. Ross, "Proverbs," n.p.

[254] For further information on translating "Metaphor and simile" see Tauberschmidt, "Principles," 70–72.

[255] R. E. Murphy seems to favor the LXX when he writes, "The comparative min before 'strong city' is obscure; perhaps it should be changed to 'like' with the LXX ὡς." Murphy, Proverbs, 134. In his translation, however, Murphy follows the MT. Ibid., 133.

[256] Cf. McKane, Proverbs, 253.

[257] Ross, "Proverbs," n.p. Similarly McKane, Proverbs, 612–613.

counsel of a friend is as sweet as perfume and incense."²⁵⁸ The translator, however, seems to have altered the parallel form of the comparison into an antithetic parallelism according to his habitual pattern (cf. 1.2.1.5.3) employing καταρρήγνυται "(it is) broken" (second colon) as a contrast to יִשְׂמַח = τέρπεται "(it) delights" (first colon). Both verbs even agree in number (singular), tense (present), voice (middle), mood (indicative) and person (third). Also ὑπὸ συμπτωμάτων "by calamities" was apparently used to make a contrast with μύροις καὶ οἴνοις²⁵⁹ καὶ θυμιάμασιν "ointments and wines and perfumes"; MT: שֶׁמֶן וּקְטֹרֶת "ointments and perfumes." Consequently there is no need to suppose, as proposed by Gemser and the *BHS* apparatus, and adopted by several translations such as RSV, NRSV, REB, TEV, that the LXX reading καταρρήγνυται δὲ ὑπὸ συμπτωμάτων represents the original text.²⁶⁰

3.3.1.5.4 Less closely parallel or single-sentence constructions

Prov 22:11

MT: אֹהֵב טְהָר־לֵב חֵן שְׂפָתָיו רֵעֵהוּ מֶלֶךְ
"He that loves pureness of heart, (and) graciousness of his lips (speech), the king (shall be) his friend"

LXX: ἀγαπᾷ κύριος ὁσίας καρδίας δεκτοὶ δὲ αὐτῷ πάντες ἄμωμοι χείλεσιν ποιμαίνει βασιλεύς
"The Lord loves holy hearts, and all blameless persons are acceptable to him, the king rules with his lips"

Prov 22:11 is difficult²⁶¹ and several emendations have been suggested²⁶² ("He that loves pureness of heart, (and) graciousness of his lips/speech, the king shall be his friend"). To reconstruct the verse based on the LXX ("The Lord loves holy hearts, and all blameless persons are acceptable to him, the king rules with his lips"), however, is highly questionable, as there are several fairly obvious translational adaptations that can be detected on the basis of the translator's

---

²⁵⁸ On the basis of the MT G. R. Driver suggests a comparative ("more than") rather than a correspondence ("is as") relation. "Hebrew Notes," *ZAW* 52 (1934): 54. Similarly GN2, "Duftendes Öl und Weihrauch geben eine festliche Stimmung; aber noch beglückender als süße Düfte ist die Zuneigung eines Menschen." Also NCV, "The sweet smell of incense can make you feel good, but true friendship is better still."

²⁵⁹ "And wines" does not occur in the MT.

²⁶⁰ The MT is supported by NASB, NIV, NLT, also Meinhold and Plöger.

²⁶¹ According to Ross "The simplest interpretation is that someone who is honest and gracious will be welcomed in the courts of the palace. The same theme is found in 16:13." Ross, "Proverbs," n.p.

²⁶² For a discussion see McKane, *Proverbs*, 567–568.

commonly applied principles. First, he may have read אהב as third person singular *qal* verb "he loves" adding κύριος "the Lord" as subject, and may have formed the second line as a parallel to it, making αὐτῷ "to him" correspond to "the Lord." This kind of explication of participants as well as the agreement is quite common in LXX Proverbs, see 2.1.1.3. The translator's interest in religious or spiritual interpretation may have played a role in the decision to insert "Lord," cf. Prov 3:9 under 1.2.1.1. Furthermore, πάντες ἄμωμοι "all blameless persons" (second colon) corresponds with ὁσίας καρδίας "holy hearts" (first colon) and δεκτοὶ "(are) acceptable" (second colon) with ἀγαπᾷ "he loves" (first colon). In the MT, however, there is less correspondence. The third line in the LXX may have come about as an attempt to cover the final three words in the MT. Thus the LXX rendering may not be helpful (against Gemser, *BHS*) for reconstructing the Hebrew text in this case.

3.3.1.5.5 Near-synonymous parallelisms with three parts

Prov 8:2

MT: בְּרֹאשׁ־מְרוֹמִים עֲלֵי־דָרֶךְ בֵּית נְתִיבוֹת נִצָּבָה
"On the heights, beside the way, at the crossroads she takes her stand"

LXX: ἐπὶ γὰρ τῶν ὑψηλῶν ἄκρων ἐστίν ἀνὰ μέσον δὲ τῶν τρίβων ἕστηκεν
"For she is on the highest points, and stands in the midst of the ways"

In Prov 8:2 the MT consists of three parts, whereas the LXX has only two parts. The latter has been reduced to two colons leaving עֲלֵי־דָרֶךְ "beside the way" untranslated probably in order to parallel τῶν ὑψηλῶν ἄκρων "the highest points" (first colon) with τῶν τρίβων "the ways" (second colon). This alteration may be regarded as translational, since the translator's tendency to make the two halves correspond to each other can be clearly seen here and is also evident in the addition of the verb ἐστίν, see 1.2.2.10.2.2. For further examples of parallelisms with three parts which have been reduced to two lines, see 1.2.1.5.6.

3.3.1.5.6 Triplets

1. Prov 1:22

MT: עַד־מָתַי פְּתָיִם תְּאֵהֲבוּ פֶתִי וְלֵצִים לָצוֹן חָמְדוּ לָהֶם וּכְסִילִים יִשְׂנְאוּ־דָעַת
"How long, O simple ones, will you love being simple? And scoffers delight in their scoffing, and fools hate knowledge?"

LXX: ὅσον ἂν χρόνον ἄκακοι ἔχωνται τῆς δικαιοσύνης οὐκ
αἰσχυνθήσονται οἱ δὲ ἄφρονες τῆς ὕβρεως ὄντες ἐπιθυμηταί
ἀσεβεῖς γενόμενοι ἐμίσησαν αἴσθησιν
"As long as the simple cleave to righteousness/justice, they will not be ashamed,
but the foolish being lovers of hubris/haughtiness, having become ungodly they
have hated knowledge"

In Prov 1:22, see 2.1.1.2, the translator of LXX Proverbs altered a triplet ("How
long, O simple ones, will you love being simple? And scoffers delight in their
scoffing, and fools hate knowledge?") into an antithetical form ("As long as the
simple cleave to righteousness/justice, they will not be ashamed, but the foolish
being lovers of hubris/haughtiness, having become ungodly they have hated
knowledge"). R. J. Clifford, disputes the originality of v. 22b,c, regarding it as
"an early and intrusive addition to the Hebrew text" partly for contextual
reasons, but mainly on the basis that "no version except V certainly interpreted
the verse like MT. Accordingly, we omit vv. 22bc as secondary, . . ."[263] The
deviation of the LXX rendering, however, cannot be taken as support for
Clifford's argument due to the translator's technique of adapting triplets into
more nearly parallel forms, and of course his general fondness for producing
antithetical colons, cf. 1.2.1.3.

2. Prov 5:22

MT: עֲווֹנוֹתָיו יִלְכְּדֻנוֹ אֶת־הָרָשָׁע וּבְחַבְלֵי חַטָּאתוֹ יִתָּמֵךְ
"His own iniquities will capture him, the wicked, and he will be held with the
cords of his sins"

LXX: παρανομίαι ἄνδρα ἀγρεύουσιν σειραῖς δὲ τῶν ἑαυτοῦ
ἁμαρτιῶν ἕκαστος σφίγγεται
"Iniquities ensnare a man, and each one is bound in the chains of his own sins"

W. G. E. Watson regards Prov 5:22 as chiastic tricolon of the pattern ABA,[264]
the function of which is to relieve the monotony and in this case to close the
stanza.[265] However, אֶת־הָרָשָׁע "the wicked" although fitting, is often regarded as
a scribal gloss,[266] a view that is mainly based on its omission in the LXX, where
the object is translated by the more neutral ἄνδρα "man"[267] (first colon). In the
second colon the LXX has in parallel with it ἕκαστος "each one," whereas in
the MT the subject (third person singular) is expressed in the verb referring back

---

[263] Clifford, *Proverbs*, 40–42.

[264] Watson, *Classical*, 182.

[265] *Ibid.*, 205.

[266] Meinhold, *Sprüche*, 1:106.

[267] Further senses are "husband" and "person."

to "the wicked." Aside from the translator's tendency to make the two halves correspond to each other, the wider context was probably drawn into consideration when employing ἄνδρα, as it agrees with ἀνδρός in the previous verse. Thus the suggestion in the *BHS* apparatus that אֶת־הָרָשָׁע should perhaps be deleted on the basis of the LXX rendering may not be necessary. Nevertheless, the apposition may be rearranged in a translation as it is frequently done.[268]

3.3.1.5.7 Conclusion

The translator's fondness for closely corresponding lines as reflected in rendering parallelisms of additional aspects, such as parallelisms of logical relations, comparisons, single-sentence constructions, near-synonymous parallelisms with three parts, and triplets, should be drawn into consideration when differentiating translational from text-critical cases.

3.3.2 GRAMMATICAL RELATIONSHIPS

The translator's predilection for close correspondence is also reflected in grammatical relationships, see 1.2.2, which should be considered in textual criticism.

3.3.2.1 Noun Phrase Subject, Paralleled with Prepositional Noun Phrase

Prov 2:15

MT: אֲשֶׁר אָרְחֹתֵיהֶם עִקְּשִׁים וּנְלוֹזִים בְּמַעְגְּלוֹתָם
"whose paths are crooked, and who are devious in their ways"

LXX: ὧν αἱ τρίβοι σκολιαὶ καὶ καμπύλαι αἱ τροχιαὶ αὐτῶν
"whose paths are crooked, and winding are their wheel tracks"

In Prov 2:15 the perversion of evil men is again described by taking up the path/way terminology of previous verses,[269] using synonymous parallelism in the deep structure. The surface structure of the two halves, however, differs slightly ("whose paths are crooked, and who are devious in their ways"). The translator seems to have altered the prepositional phrase בְּמַעְגְּלוֹתָם "in their ways" to a subject noun phrase αἱ τροχιαί "(their) wheel tracks," matching it with the first half αἱ τρίβοι "(their) paths"—MT: אָרְחֹתֵיהֶם "their paths"—and

---

[268] "The iniquities of the wicked ensnare them, . . ." (NRSV), or "The evil deeds of a wicked man ensnare him, . . ." (NIV).

[269] Cf. Meinhold, *Sprüche*, 1:68.

thus producing a more symmetrical parallelism ("whose paths are crooked, and winding are their wheel tracks"). Thus the suggestion to perhaps delete בְּ on the basis of the LXX rendering (cf. *BHS*) may not be supported.

3.3.2.2 *Elliptical Constructions*

3.3.2.2.1 *Verb (adverb), omitted in B*

1. Prov 7:16

MT: מַרְבַדִּים רָבַדְתִּי עַרְשִׂי חֲטֻבוֹת אֵטוּן מִצְרָיִם
"I have decked my bed with coverings, with colored linens from Egypt"

LXX: κειρίαις τέτακα τὴν κλίνην μου ἀμφιτάποις δὲ ἔστρωκα τοῖς ἀπ' Αἰγύπτου
"I have spread my bed with sheets, and I have covered it with tapestry from Egypt"

Prov 7:16 is a nearly parallel couplet, the first half being more general and the second more specific ("I have decked my bed with coverings, with colored linens from Egypt"). The MT omits the verb in *B*, whereas in the LXX rendering the verb ἔστρωκα "spread, cover" is added as a structural (and also semantic) parallel to τέτακα "spread, stretch" (first colon). Thus the LXX is clearly more closely parallel. The LXX rendering ἔστρωκα has been proposed (cf. *BHS*) in place of חֲטֻבוֹת[270] but it is less likely that the LXX translation reflects a superior reading at this point.

2. Prov 8:16

MT: בִּי שָׂרִים יָשֹׂרוּ וּנְדִיבִים כָּל־שֹׁפְטֵי צֶדֶק
"By me princes rule, and nobles (and) all the righteous rulers"

LXX: δι' ἐμοῦ μεγιστᾶνες μεγαλύνονται καὶ τύραννοι δι' ἐμοῦ κρατοῦσι γῆς
"By me nobles become great, and monarchs by me rule over the earth"

Prov 8:16 is a fairly synonymous couplet semantically but less so structurally ("By me princes rule, and nobles (and) all the righteous rulers"). The LXX rendering, however, shows a considerable degree of parallel structure compared to the MT ("By me nobles become great, and monarchs by me rule over the earth"). The two verbs μεγαλύνονται ". . . become great" (first colon) and κρατοῦσι ". . . rule" (second colon) are quite parallel, whereas the MT has

---

[270] For the meaning of "colored" see R. L. Alden, *NIDOTTE*, 2:104.

only one verb, יִשְׂרוּ "... rule" which covers the whole verse. It is most likely that the translator adapted the second colon to achieve a structure that corresponds more closely to the first colon. A further indication that he added κρατοῦσι for the sake of parallelism rather than giving a rendering for שׁפט is that the latter is always translated κρίνω in Proverbs, 29:9,14; 31:9, and is used in contexts of just justice or righteous judging. Furthermore, the prepositional phrase δι' ἐμοῦ "by me" (MT: בִּי) is repeated in the second colon; and μεγιστᾶνες "nobles" (first colon) and τύραννοι "monarchs" (second colon) are in parallel, and apparently the third phrase כָּל־שֹׁפְטֵי צֶדֶק "all the righteous rulers"[271] is dropped to produce a more parallel structure. The noun γῆς "earth" may have been added because the verb κρατέω "to exercise power or force over someone or something"[272] (e.g. Prov 16:32; 17:2; 18:21; 30:4; 28:22) is likely to have some dependent word or phrase follow it.[273] Thus the LXX rendering may not be used to support a possible superior variant text, as suggested in *BHS* and adopted by RSV and REB.

3.3.2.3 Structural Differences

Prov 4:4–5

MT: 4 וַיֹּרֵנִי וַיֹּאמֶר לִי יִתְמָךְ־דְּבָרַי לִבֶּךָ שְׁמֹר מִצְוֹתַי וֶחְיֵה
5 קְנֵה חָכְמָה קְנֵה בִינָה אַל־תִּשְׁכַּח וְאַל־תֵּט מֵאִמְרֵי־פִי

"4 He taught me, and said to me, 'Let your heart retain my words, keep my commandments, and live.
5 Get wisdom, get understanding, forget (them) not; neither decline from the words of my mouth'"

---

[271] Similarly NRSV "govern rightly," NCV "judge fairly," NLT "righteous judgments," but RSV and REB have "... earth." W. McKane does not regard the textual point of great moment here as it does not affect the interpretation much. McKane, *Proverbs*, 348. Meinhold, *Sprüche*, 1:141, and also Plöger, *Sprüche*, 90, follow the MT (in *BHS* edition). D. J. Estes too is in favor of the MT as he states in the fn, but in his translation he follows the NIV. J. Daniel, Estes, *Hear, my Son: Teaching and Learning in Proverbs 1–9* (Grand Rapids: Eerdmans, 1997), 52. Similarly R. E. Clements, who writes, "The Hebrew 'all of them are righteous rulers,' which may be correct, but the emended text presupposed here has received wide acceptance." Roland E. Clements, *Wisdom in Theology* (Carlisle: Paternoster & Grand Rapids: Eerdmans, 1992), 115.

[272] Louw and Nida, *Lexicon*.

[273] Similarly Prov 14:18 κρατήσουσιν αἰσθήσεως "they will hold fast on knowledge." The only case in Proverbs that is somewhat different is Prov 12:24 χεὶρ ἐκλεκτῶν κρατήσει εὐχερῶς "the hand of the chosen will rule easily" but even there an adverb follows κρατέω.

LXX: 4 οἳ ἔλεγον καὶ ἐδίδασκόν με ἐρειδέτω ὁ ἡμέτερος λόγος εἰς σὴν καρδίαν
5 φύλασσε ἐντολάς μὴ ἐπιλάθῃ μηδὲ παρίδῃς ῥῆσιν ἐμοῦ στόματος
"4 who spoke and instructed me (saying), 'Let our speech be fixed in your heart, 5 keep (our) commandments, forget (them) not, neither neglect the speech of my mouth'"

In Prov 4:4–5[274] the translator seems to have made some adjustments towards a more parallel as well as more coherent rendering. In the LXX the translator left out the last clause וֶחְיֵה "and live" in v. 4 as this would have disturbed the parallel structure. In the MT of v. 5 there are two clauses, קְנֵה חָכְמָה קְנֵה בִינָה "Get wisdom, get understanding," which are not represented in the LXX and have probably been dropped on purpose in order to obtain a more parallel structure.[275] Also the translator seems to have been concerned to ensure that the flow of the main idea, the command to keep the father's (parent's) commandments/speech, would not be interrupted by the two clauses about wisdom and understanding. In addition, the following command μηδὲ ἐγκαταλίπῃς αὐτήν "Forsake it not" in verse 6 refers to ῥῆσιν "speech," whereas in the MT it refers to "wisdom" and "understanding." These two terms are mentioned again in v. 7 in the MT. The LXX, however, drops the whole of that verse, perhaps because the translator chose already in v. 5 not to include "wisdom" and "understanding" as explained above.[276] And in verses 8 and 9, other than in the MT, the reference is still to the "speech" of v. 5. Since discourse considerations as well as the desire to keep the structure fairly parallel may have led the translator to make these adjustments, the LXX reading should, contrary to the *BHS* apparatus, not be taken as perhaps reflecting a different Hebrew text in vv. 4–5.

To sum up, the translator's fondness for producing closely corresponding lines concerning semantic as well as grammatical relationships should be considered to avoid using translational cases as text critical cases.

3.4 Conclusion

There are different opinions regarding the value of the Septuagint as a textual witness. For instance, Tov thinks that the Hebrew *Vorlage* of the LXX represents merely a single text, but Müller holds that it represents a textual

---

[274] For Prov 4:4 see 2.1.1.2.

[275] There is a similar case in Prov 11:10–11, 1.2.1.4, where the translator dropped clauses with the same intention.

[276] B. Gemser (in common with most commentators) retains v. 7 (MT) despite its omission in the LXX. Gemser, *Sprüche Salomos*, 32. R. J. Clifford, however, regards it as a later addition, because "It is not in G and ill suits the context . . ." But "In v. 5, MT is superior to G . . ." according to his view. Clifford, *Proverbs*, 60.

family. In Müller's view the LXX has great value and he even thinks that the Septuagint ought to be the text translated in an authorized Christian version of the Old Testament,[277] and that it should be a witness to the process of transmitting tradition. But such a hypothesis falls outside the area of textual criticism *in sensu stricto*. Würthwein, on the other hand, gives priority to the MT where no fault can be found in it. Tov, however, does not go as far as Würthwein because he does not accept an unequal status of textual sources. Yet overall he regards the MT readings preferable to those found in other texts.

In my opinion, the MT cannot be given priority automatically. However, at any point in the text, before the reading of LXX Proverbs can serve as a variant text, the translator's technique needs to be considered seriously, especially in regard to the freedom with which he adjusted dynamic Hebrew parallelisms towards forms that are more parallel and symmetrical. At the same time it is important to consider the influence that the immediate context may have had on the translator's choices, and to recognize stylistic variation as well as theological biases and inner-textual corruption.

In section 3.3 translational cases of parallel forms have been discussed using the same categories as in 1.2. While Chapter One has provided the basis for the translator's style and adaptations, in this chapter his particular technique was considered in identifying translational cases that have often be regarded as text-critical. There are the following cases that have been identified as translational: Prov 2:6; 3:8,10,26; 5:9,18; 6:5; 12:21; 19:29; 22:13; 23:25; 3:3,24; 8:5; 18:15 (3.3.1.1 "Lexical aspect"); Prov 3:22; 11:28; 14:11,15 (3.3.1.2 "Emphatic phrases or various figures of speech"); Prov 10:18; 11:25; 16:30; 12:28; 14:17 (3.3.1.3 "Near-synonymous parallelisms transformed into antithetical forms"); Prov 10:6,10; 12:21; 13:9,15,23; 14:9,16,21,32,33,34; 15:19,32; 18:2; 21:20,26; 28:2; 29:18 (3.3.1.4 "Near-antithetical parallelisms rendered with a clearer contrast"); Prov 17:14; 19:27 (3.3.1.5.1 "Parallelisms of logical relations"); Prov 22:13 (3.3.1.5.2 "Parallelism of addition relations"); Prov 16:16; 17:7; 18:19; 27:9 (3.3.1.5.3 "Parallelisms of comparisons"); Prov 22:11 (3.3.1.5.4 "Less closely parallel or single-sentence constructions"); Prov 8:2 (3.3.1.5.5 "Near-synonymous parallelism with tree parts"); Prov 1:22; 5:22 (3.3.1.5.6 "Tiplet"); Prov 2:15 (3.3.2.1 "Noun phrase subject, paralleled with prepositional noun phrase"); Prov 7:16; 8:16 (3.3.2.2.1 "Verb (adverb), omitted in *B*"); Prov 4:4–5 (3.3.2.3 "Structural differences").

---

[277] Müller, *First Bible*, 113. Against: K. Jeppesen while agreeing with Müller's thesis that the Greek text should play an important role in biblical theology (as important as the Hebrew text), Jeppesen does not agree with Müller's hypothesis mentioned above. K. Jeppesen, "Biblia Hebraica–Et Septuaginta: A Response to Mogens Müller," *SJOT* 10, 2 (1996): 271–281.

Therefore, care should be taken when using LXX Proverbs for "better" parallelisms in cases where they can be explained translationally.[278]

---

[278] Cf. J. Cook writes, "the Septuagint version of Proverbs should be treated with the utmost caution when utilised for text-critical purposes. By far the greatest number of differences compared to the MT are the result of the translator's creative approach." Cook, *Proverbs*, 334. Cook, however, may at times give different reasons for the deviations in LXX Proverbs than are given in this thesis.

GENERAL CONCLUSIONS

The translator of LXX Proverbs tended to render Hebrew parallelisms so that the lines in couplets have closer correspondence semantically and/or grammatically in the translation than in his Hebrew source text. This thesis is based on the hypothesis that the Hebrew *Vorlage* was similar to the MT in the book of Proverbs, at least in (most of) the cases treated in the present work. I do, however, not deny that there are deviations that are more extensive, but for such cases no translational explanation can be given. The more extensive deviations should be explained on the basis of differences in the *Vorlage*. But this issue has not been dealt with in the present study, as this would go beyond its scope.

As for deviations where colons are added in LXX Proverbs we cannot be certain whether these are due to differences in the source text, the application of translation principles, or recensional activity.[1] But some additions (e.g. Prov 1:14,22,27; 4:10; 6:10,25; 8:10,22,34; 11:21; 17:5,21; 18:22) may have resulted from the translator's technique and fondness for closely corresponding lines. And some of the additions may have come about because the translator sought to cover words and phrases which he was not able to render within his normal framework due to translational and contextual considerations, see Prov 2:19; 5:23; 11:16; 17:17; 22:11.

On the basis of texts where it is reasonable to suppose that the translator of LXX Proverbs was using as his source a text similar to the MT I have demonstrated that when the translator produced forms that are more closely parallel this was due to the application of his translation technique. The study thus provides a tool which can assist in evaluating LXX Proverbs as a source of variant readings, thus avoiding the misuse of LXX Proverbs for the sake of "better" parallelisms.

In Hebrew parallelism, which is the heart of Hebrew poetry, there exist many different parallel forms and innumerable possible ways of combining the lines. This statement is supported by recent studies (e.g. Alter, Berlin, Kugel, Watson) that have shown that Hebrew parallelism is much more dynamic than has been assumed in the past. That is why the three categories that R. Lowth established to classify the whole spectrum of Hebrew parallelism are insufficient and too narrow, although they may serve as general and very broad guidelines. Therefore, the forcing of parallelisms into a straitjacket of synonymity where it does not exist and the practice of emending the text in order to create "better" parallelisms can have disastrous results in textual criticism. Certainly, a broad view of parallelism needs to be adopted, taking into account a wide range of grammatical and semantic possibilities for parallel forms.

---

[1] N. Fernández Marcos points out that it is difficult to isolate recensional activity from original translation technique. N. Fernández Marcos, *Scribes and Translators: Septuagint and Old Latin in the Books of Kings* (VTSup 54; Leiden: Brill, 1994), chap. 2. Cf. Jobes and Silva, *Invitation*, 281.

Parallelism occurs in other languages too, and it is found in the literature of the Hellenistic period, where parallel forms often appear to be more structured and symmetrical than in Hebrew parallelism. Although the translator of LXX Proverbs may have been influenced by the style of his time,[2] the investigation of his individualistic style and how he applied translation techniques/principles is crucial in isolating the translational elements and particularly detecting the "better" parallelisms in LXX Proverbs.

Aside from LXX Proverbs there are some other books (especially the less literally translated ones) which also adapted Hebrew parallelisms to a certain degree. Examples from Genesis and Isaiah show that some of the LXX translators felt free to produce rather non-literal renderings of Hebrew parallelisms using forms that were more natural to them, some of which renderings were even quoted by NT authors.

The translator of Proverbs, however, produced the freest renderings, both in general and particularly in regard to translating parallel forms; he had a strong tendency to alter Hebrew parallelisms to more parallel and symmetrical forms both as regards semantics as well as grammatical structure.

The translator's adaptations are, of course, not always purely linguistically, translationally and stylistically motivated, since no translation is free from certain biases. For instance, in Prov 3:9 the translator reinterpreted the only cultic demand in the book of Proverbs ethically. Also, he has a more positive understanding of "the simple" in Prov 1:22,32. Furthermore, he seems to emphasize the positive aspect of friendship throughout his translation, e.g. Prov 6:1; 3:29; 15:28a; 16:29; 17:17; 25:10a. And, apparently the translator used "destruction" (ἀπωλεία) as one of his favorite words without any correspondence to the MT, e.g. Prov 11:6; 13:15; 16:26+26a, to emphasize the fate of the transgressors. In Prov 30:3 it is possible that the insertion "God has taught me" was partly motivated by the translator's piety. In Prov 31:1–9 the translator adapted his Hebrew source text in order to emphasize the fact that these instructions were given by God. Furthermore, it is likely that the translator of LXX Proverbs wished to emphasize the law in his translation, cf. J. Cook,[3] e.g. Prov 9:10; 13:15; and Prov 6:23. Similarly, he may have had the tendency to moralize, cf. M. B. Dick, e.g., Prov 10:18; 11:7; 15:23.[4] Thus, there are adaptations that are exegetically motivated.[5]

But in order to understand the translator's approach fully, it seems best to start the investigation of the translator's practice by looking at linguistically,

---

[2] See also Gerleman, "Septuagint Proverbs," 15–27.

[3] Cook, "The Law of Moses," 448–461.

[4] Dick, "Ethics," 20–50.

[5] According to Jobes and Silva "it is impossible to know if the theological elements introduced by a translator were common to the thought of Judaism at that time, peculiar to the particular theological tradition of the translator, or idiosyncrasies of the translator alone." Jobes and Silva, *Invitation*, 94.

translationally and stylistically motivated changes, and as a second step consider exegetically or theologically motivated biases. It is true that translation principles and theological biases are not always separable (e.g. Prov 29:18), but translational etc. adaptations are often more concrete and clear-cut. Starting the investigation with translation principles has the advantage that it gives a broader picture for what the translator is doing overall, not just with regard to rendering certain lexical items. For instance, Dick mentions that "Frequently the LXX converts Hebrew synonymous parallelism to antithetic parallelism, and so displays sensitivity to Greek style,"[6] and he adds Prov 1:22, and some other stylistically motivated cases in a footnote (Prov 10:10; 11:25; 17:4; 11:30; 17:21; 21:14), although at the same time he writes that "These changes, however, may not be solely due to a Greek poetic dislike for synonymous parallelism"[7] but to a moralizing tendency in LXX Proverbs.[8] Dick does, however, not attempt to explain stylistically motivated cases and so just those instances with an apparent theological bias are treated in his approach. In a model that includes linguistics and translation principles, however, it can be shown in a vast number of instances that the translator in general tended to transform near-synonymous parallelisms, not only in those cases that are exegetically motivated. Thus, such an approach provides a more objective picture, as it views translated words, phrases and clauses in context rather than in isolation.

It is of great importance to investigate the individual character of a translation. It is not enough to compare a translation to contemporary Greek style with apparent dislike for synonymous parallelism (e.g., Gerleman), nor to investigate lexical items in isolation and look for certain biases (e.g., Dick). An outstanding characteristic of the translator's style is the application of cohesion, in particular grammatical and lexical cohesion. The translator applied grammatical cohesion in that he added, e.g., conjunctions and pronouns to make paragraphs more cohesive, as well as lexical cohesion by using synonyms and antonyms, or phrases that are closely parallel. Since the effect of grammatical cohesion is more dominant than that of lexical cohesion, it is not surprising that grammatical cohesion at times overruled the translator's tendency to produce more closely parallel lines. But there is much evidence that the translator adapted his source text in order to produce lines that are more closely parallel, not only in the case of near-antithetical parallelisms, but also in the case of near-synonymous forms; this is because the translator applied the principle of cohesion to both types of parallelism. Therefore we cannot maintain the view of the translator's dislike for synonymous parallelism.

The application of grammatical cohesion to higher units of discourse beyond the couplet level, however, at times led to less parallel renderings. But

---

[6] Dick, "Ethics," 22.

[7] Here Dick simply assumes that Gerleman's thesis about the translator's "dislike for synonymous parallelism" is correct.

[8] *Ibid.*, 22.

there are also other reasons that may have been responsible for less parallel couplets, such as interpretational reasons, linguistic and translational reasons, and reasons related to the Hebrew consonantal text.

If we consider the translation techniques of the translator, especially with regard to rendering Hebrew parallelisms in a more parallel way, it is difficult to attempt to reconstruct cases of "better" parallelisms and obtain reliable results. Many such instances have been treated as variant readings in the *BHS* apparatus (and by other scholars) but they often appear to be treated in an isolated fashion and without any serious consideration of the translator's technique. The present work has demonstrated that a considerable number of these suggested LXX readings can be explained on the basis of our findings concerning the translator's practice and should thus be regarded as translational and secondary rather than as variant readings of the Hebrew text (cf. 3.3).

Although we cannot automatically assume that the MT does always provide the correct reading due to problems that are particularly related to the transmission of the text, the LXX should only be used as a source of preferred readings after careful study of the translator's techniques.

R. J. Clifford does not seem to take into account the translator's technique when he decides on superior readings in G, especially Prov 3:24; 5:18; 6:5; 10:10; 13:15; 14:21, etc.[9] These cases are very questionable as "superior readings." Thus it would only be appropriate to use more caution in claiming renderings in LXX Proverbs to be superior readings. Clifford's criticism that HOTTP "seldom recommends emendations on the basis of LXX"[10] is unjustified, since he resorts to the LXX Proverbs without serious consideration of the translator's practice.

Although this study is based on the hypothesis that the *Vorlage* of LXX Proverbs is similar to the MT, there are recognizable translational elements in a free translation such as LXX Proverbs. Particularly the recurring patterns in couplets and the translator's application of cohesion are characteristic for the translator's individual style.

Therefore, before using LXX Proverbs for superior readings, the translation technique of the Greek translation should be studied carefully. The thesis will thus provide a tool to assist in evaluating LXX Proverbs as a source of variant readings in textual criticism, and so avoid misusing LXX Proverbs for the sake of "better" parallelisms.

---

[9] Clifford, "Observations," 56.

[10] *Ibid.*

APPENDIX

In order to get a more complete picture of the preferences of different commentaries and Bible versions with regard to textual decisions in Proverbs, the following chart may help to give an overview of the approach taken by six translations and five commentaries.

Explanation for charts: * = the translation does not correspond one-to-one, but is similar to the source mentioned; ? = uncertainty, or no textual decision was made; diff. = the translation differs from both MT and LXX; sl. em. = slight emendation, which means that the MT is slightly emended but not on the basis of the LXX; tr. = translational case.

	RSV	NRSV	GN1	GN2	NEB	REB
Prov 1:21	LXX	MT	MT	MT	MT	MT
Prov 2:9 tr.	MT	MT	MT	MT	LXX	LXX
Prov 2:17	MT	MT	MT	MT	LXX	MT
Prov 3:3 tr.	MT	MT	LXX	LXX	LXX	MT
Prov 3:8 tr.	LXX	LXX	MT	MT	MT	MT
Prov 3:12 tr.	MT	MT	MT	MT	LXX	LXX
Prov 3:24 tr.	LXX	LXX	MT	MT	LXX	LXX
Prov 4:5	MT	MT	MT	MT	LXX	MT
Prov 4:7	MT	MT	MT	MT	LXX	LXX
Prov 5:7	MT	LXX	MT	MT	LXX	LXX
Prov 5:18 tr.	MT	MT	MT	MT	MT	MT
Prov 6:5 tr.	slight em.	slight em.	MT*	MT*	LXX	LXX
Prov 6:24	MT	LXX	MT	MT	LXX	LXX
Prov 8:32	MT	MT	MT	MT	MT	MT
Prov 10:10 tr.	LXX	LXX	MT	MT	LXX	LXX
Prov 10:18 tr.	MT	MT	MT	MT	LXX	MT
Prov 11:16 tr.	MT	LXX	MT	MT	LXX	MT
Prov 11:28 tr.	LXX	LXX	LXX*	MT	MT	MT
Prov 11:30 tr.	LXX	LXX	MT	MT	LXX	LXX
Prov 12:28 tr.	LXX	MT	MT	MT	LXX	LXX
Prov 13:11	LXX	LXX	LXX	LXX	LXX	LXX
Prov 13:15 tr.	LXX	LXX	LXX*	MT*	LXX	LXX
Prov 14:21 tr.	MT	MT	MT	MT	LXX	LXX
Prov 14:32 tr.	LXX	LXX	LXX	LXX	LXX	LXX

APPENDIX

	RSV	NRSV	GN1	GN2	NEB	REB
Prov 15:19 tr.	MT	MT	MT	LXX	LXX	LXX
Prov 16:16	LXX	MT	MT*	MT*	MT	LXX
Prov 18:19 tr.	LXX	Diff.	MT	MT	MT	MT
Prov 20:28 tr.	LXX	LXX	MT	MT	LXX	LXX
Prov 26:21	MT	MT	MT	MT	LXX	MT
Prov 27:10	MT	MT	MT	MT	LXX	MT
Prov 29:18 tr.	MT	MT	MT	MT	LXX*	LXX*
Prov 30:17	MT	MT	MT	MT	LXX	LXX
Prov 31:21	MT	MT	LXX*	LXX*	LXX	LXX
MT:	58%	58%	82%	85%	21%	39%
LXX:	39%	36%	18%	15%	79%	61%
Different or no decision	3%	6%	0%	0%	0%	0%

	HOTTP	Clifford[1]	Meinhold[2]	McKane[3]	Toy[4]
Prov 1:21	MT	MT	MT	LXX	diff.
Prov 2:9 tr.	MT	MT	MT	MT	LXX
Prov 2:17	MT	MT	MT	LXX*	MT
Prov 3:3 tr.	LXX	LXX	MT	MT	LXX
Prov 3:8 tr.	MT	LXX	MT	MT	LXX
Prov 3:12 tr.	MT/LXX divided[5]	MT	MT	MT	LXX
Prov 3:24 tr.	MT	LXX, later MT[6]	MT	MT	LXX
Prov 4:5	MT	MT	MT	MT	Diff.
Prov 4:7	MT	LXX	MT	MT	LXX
Prov 5:7	MT	LXX	MT	MT	LXX
Prov 5:18 tr.	Not	LXX	MT	MT	LXX

---

[1] Clifford, *Proverbs*. And Clifford, "Observations," 47–61. Note: The commentary is a later publication (1999) than the article (1997).

[2] Meinhold, *Sprüche*.

[3] McKane, *Proverbs*.

[4] Toy, *Proverbs*.

[5] The committee was equally divided in favor of the LXX and the MT.

[6] The preference for the LXX is expressed in Clifford, "Observations," 56, and the preference for the MT in his commentary on *Proverbs*.

	HOTTP	Clifford	Meinhold	McKane	Toy
Prov 6:5 tr.	MT	LXX*, later sl. em.	MT	slight em.	LXX
Prov 6:24	MT	LXX	MT	MT	LXX*
Prov 8:32	not	LXX	MT	MT	MT
Prov 10:10 tr.	MT	LXX	MT	LXX	LXX
Prov 10:18 tr.	MT	MT	MT	MT	MT
Prov 11:16 tr.	MT	MT	MT	MT	MT
Prov 11:28 tr.	MT	MT	MT	MT	MT
Prov 11:30 tr.	MT	MT	MT	LXX	LXX
Prov 12:28 tr.	MT	LXX	MT	LXX	LXX
Prov 13:11	MT	LXX	MT	MT*	LXX
Prov 13:15 tr.	MT	LXX	MT	LXX	diff.
Prov 14:21 tr.	MT	LXX	MT	MT	MT
Prov 14:32 tr.	MT/LXX divided	MT	MT	LXX	LXX
Prov 15:19 tr.	MT	MT	MT	LXX	LXX
Prov 16:16	MT	LXX	MT	MT	LXX
Prov 18:19 tr.	MT	MT	MT	MT	LXX?
Prov 20:28 tr.	MT	LXX, later MT	MT	MT	LXX
Prov 26:21	MT	MT	MT	MT	MT
Prov 27:10	MT	MT	MT	MT	not?
Prov 29:18 tr.	MT	MT	MT	MT	LXX
Prov 30:17	MT	MT	MT	LXX	LXX
Prov 31:21	LXX	LXX	MT	MT	diff.
MT:	85%	55%	100%	70%	21%
LXX:	9%	45%	0%	27%	64%
Different or no decision	6%	0%	0%	3%	15%

Thirty-three references have been taken[7] in order to illustrate the approach of four English (RSV, NRSV, NEB, REB) and two German (GN1, GN2) Bible versions as well as five commentaries (HOTTP, Clifford, Meinhold, McKane, Toy) with regard to the textual decisions they made. Meinhold did not draw upon the LXX and used the MT exclusively (100%), second comes the HOTTP

---

[7] The selection of passages was made from texts that are corrupted or unintelligible, otherwise no specific criteria were used in choosing these texts.

with 9% LXX use (MT: 85%),[8] followed by the GN2 with 15% (MT: 85%), and the GN1 with 18% (MT: 82%). McKane drew upon the LXX in 27% (MT: 70%) of the cases discussed. The NRSV used the LXX in 36% of cases and the RSV in 39% (MT: 58% in both versions), followed by Clifford with 45% LXX use (MT: 55%). Next comes REB with 61% readings from the LXX (MT: 39%), followed by Toy with 64% (MT: 21%), and finally comes NEB with 79% dependency on the LXX (MT: 21%). It may be noted that the revised translations (NRSV, GN2, REB) drew less heavily from the LXX. One needs to keep in mind that these figures are just indications and can therefore not be taken as representative for the whole book of Proverbs.

---

[8] Note that for the remaining 6% (9% + 85% = 94%) no decision was made. Similarly in some of the following cases either no decision or comment was made, or a reading different from MT and LXX was chosen.

BIBLIOGRAPHY

Adair, James R., Jr. "Old and New in Textual Criticism: Similarities, Differences, and Prospects for Cooperation." *Textual Criticism* 1 (1996): 1–19.
Aejmelaeus, Anneli. *Parataxis in the Septuagint: A Study of the Renderings of the Hebrew Coordinate Clauses in the Greek Pentateuch.* Helsinki: Suomalainen Tiedeakatemia, 1982.
———. *On the Trail of the Septuagint Translators*, (Collected Essays). Kampen: Kok Pharos, 1993.
Aitken, Kenneth T. *Proverbs.* Louisville: Westminster John Knox, 1986.
Albrektson, Bertil. "Textual Criticism and the Textual Basis of a Translation of the Old Testament." *The Bible Translator* 26/3 (1975): 314–324.
Alter, Robert. "The Dynamics of Parallelism." *Hebrew University Studies in Literature and the Arts* 11/1 (1983): 71–101.
———. *The Art of Biblical Poetry.* New York: Basic Books, 1985.
Anbar, M. "Proverbs 11:21; 16:15: *yd lyd* 'sur le champ,'" *Biblica* 53/4 (1972): 537–538.
Armerding, Carl E. *The Old Testament and Criticism.* Grand Rapids: Eerdmans, 1983.
Auld, A. Graeme. *Joshua, Moses and the Land: Tetrateuch-Pentateuch-Hexateuch in a Generation of Study since 1938.* Edinburgh: T & T Clark, 1980.
Barnwell, Katharine. *Introduction to Semantics and Translation.* Second edition. England: Summer Institute of Linguistics, 1980.
Barr, James. *The Semantics of Biblical Language.* Oxford University Press, 1961.
———. "Vocalization and the Analysis of Hebrew among the Ancient Translators." *Vetus Testamentum Supplements* 16 (1967).
———. *The Typology of Literalism in Ancient Biblical Translations.* Mitteilungen des Septuaginta-Unternehmens (MSU) 15. Göttingen: Vandenhoeck & Ruprecht, 1979.
Barthélemy, Dominique et al., *Preliminary and Interim Report on the Hebrew Old Testament Text Project.* Vol. 3 Poetical Books. New York: United Bible Societies, 1973–1980.
Barthélemy, Dominique, David W. Gooding, Johan Lust, and Emanuel Tov. *The Story of David and Goliath.* Textual and Literary Criticism. Papers of a Joint Research Venture. Göttingen: Vandenhoeck & Ruprecht, 1986.
Bauer, Walter. *Griechisch-deutsches Wörterbuch zu den Schriften des Neuen Testaments und der frühchristlichen Literatur.* 6., völlig neu bearbeitete Auflage. Herausgegeben von Kurt Aland und Barbara Aland. Berlin & New York: Walter de Gruyter, 1988.
Baumgartner, A. J. *Étude critique sur l'état du texte du Livre des Proverbes d'après les principales traductions anciennes.* Leipzig, 1890.
Beckwith, R. T. *The Old Testament Canon of the New Testament Church.* London: SPCK, 1985.
Beekman, John, and John Callow. *Translating the Word of God.* Grand Rapids: Zondervan, 1974.
Beentjes, P. C. *The Book of Ben Sira in Hebrew: A Text Edition of all Extant Hebrew Manuscripts and A Synopsis of all Parallel Hebrew Ben Sira Texts.* Supplements to Vetus Testamentum Vol. LXVIII. Leiden, New York, Köln: Brill, 1997.

Berlin, Adele. *The Dynamics of Biblical Parallelism.* Bloomington: Indiana University Press, 1985.
——. "Parallelism." In *The Anchor Bible Dictionary on CD-ROM.* Logos Library System Version 2.1, 1997. Print ed.: David Noel Freedman, ed. *Anchor Bible Dictionary.* 6 vols. New York: Doubleday, 1992.
Berry, D. K. *An Introduction to Wisdom and Poetry of the Old Testament.* Nashville: Broadman & Holman, 1994.
Bertram, Georg. "Die religiöse Umdeutung altorientalischer Lebensweisheit in der griechischen Übersetzung des AT." *Zeitschrift für die alttestamentliche Wissenschaft* NF 13 (1936): 153–167.
Bible Windows 4.5 CD-ROM. Tanglewood Cedar Hill Tex.: Silver Mountain Software, 1996.
Biblia Hebraica Stuttgartensia. Edited by K. Elliger and W. Rudolph. Deutsche Bibelstiftung Stuttgart. Stuttgart: Biblia-Druck, 1976/77.
Bickerman, E. "The LXX as a Translation." *Proceedings of the American Academy of Jewish Research* 28 (1959): 1–39.
Blass, Friedrich, Albert Debrunner, and Friedrich Rehkopf, eds. *Grammatik des neutestamentlichen Griechisch.* 15. durchgesehene Auflage. Göttingen: Vandenhoeck & Ruprecht, 1979.
Blass, R. "Cohesion, coherence, and relevance." *Notes on Linguistics* 34 (1986): 41–64.
Blight, Richard C. *Translation Problems from A to Z.* Dallas: Summer Institute of Linguistics, 1992.
Bratcher, Robert G. and William D. Reyburn. *A Translator's Handbook on the Book of Psalms.* New York: United Bible Societies, 1991.
Brock, Sebastian P. "The Phenomenon of the Septuagint." *Old Testament Studies* 17 (1972): 11–36.
——. "Aspects of Translation Techniques in Antiquity." *Greek, Roman, and Byzantine Studies* 20 (1979): 67–87.
Brock, S. P., C. T. Fritsch, and S. Jellicoe, eds. *A Classified Bibliography of the Septuagint.* Leiden: Brill, 1973.
Brockington, L. H. *The Hebrew Text of the Old Testament.* Oxford University Press, Cambridge University Press, 1973.
Bromiley, G. W., ed. *International Standard Bible Encyclopedia.* 4 vols. Grand Rapids: Eerdmans, 1988.
Brooke, George J. and Barnabas Lindars, S.S.F., eds. *Septuagint, Scrolls and Cognate Writings.* Septuagint and Cognate Studies 33. Society of Biblical Literature. Atlanta: Scholars Press, 1992.
Brotzman, Ellis R. *Old Testament Textual Criticism: A Practical Introduction.* Grand Rapids: Baker Books, 1994.
Brown, F., S. R. Driver, and C. A. Briggs, eds. *A Hebrew and English Lexicon of the Old Testament with an Appendix containing the Biblical Aramaic.* Corrected edition, Oxford & New York: Oxford University Press, 1952.
Burkhardt, Helmut et al., eds. *Das grosse Bibellexikon.* Band 1–6. 1. Taschenbuchausgabe. Wuppertal: Brockhaus & Giessen: Brunnen, 1996.
Buttrick, George Arthur et al., eds. *The Interpreter's Bible.* Vol. IV. Nashville: Abingdon, 1955.
Caird, G. B. *The Language and Imagery of the Bible.* First published by Gerald Duckworth & Co.Ltd., 1980.

Callow, John C. and Kathleen. "Translation Theory." *Notes on Translation* 64 (1977): 3–37.

Carson, D. A. *Exegetical Fallacies*. Second edition. Grand Rapids: Baker & Carlisle: Paternoster, 1996.

Claassen, W., ed. *Text and Context: Old Testament and Semitic Studies for F. C. Fensham*. Sheffield Academic Press, 1988.

Clements, Ronald E. *Wisdom in Theology*. Carlisle: Paternoster & Grand Rapids: Eerdmans, 1992.

Clifford, Richard J. "Observations on the Text and Versions of Proverbs." Pages 47–61 in *Wisdom You Are My Sister: Studies in Honor of Roland E. Murphy, O. Carm. on the Occasion of His Eightieth Birthday*. Edited by M. L. Barre. Catholic Biblical Quarterly Monograph Series 29. Washington, DC: Catholic Biblical Association, 1997.

———. *Proverbs: A Commentary*. The Old Testament Library. Louisville: Westminster John Knox, 1999.

Coenen, Lothar, Erich Beyreuther, and Hans Bietenhard, eds. *Theologisches Begriffslexikon zum Neuen Testament*. Band 1 & 2. Studien-Ausgabe 1979. Theologischer Verlag Brockhaus, 1971.

Conybeare, F. C. and St. George Stock. *Grammar of Septuagint Greek*. Hendrickson, 1905/95.

Cook, Johann. "Hellenistic Influence in the Book of Proverbs (Septuagint)?" *Bulletin of the International Organization for Septuagint and Cognate Studies* 20 (1987): 30–42.

———. "The Hexaplaric Text, Double Translations and Other Textual Phenomena in the Septuagint (Proverbs)." *Journal of Northwest Semitic Languages* 22/2 (1996): 129–140.

———. "Aspects of the Translation Technique Followed by the Translator of LXX Proverbs." *Journal of Northwest Semitic Languages* 22/1 (1996): 143–153.

———. *The Septuagint of Proverbs–Jewish and/or Hellenistic Proverbs? Concerning the Hellenistic Colouring of LXX Proverbs*. Brill, 1997.

———. "The Law in Septuagint Proverbs." *Journal of Northwest Semitic Languages* 23/1 (1997): 211–223.

———. "Contrasting as a Translation Technique in the LXX Proverbs." In *The Quest for Context and Meaning: Studies in Biblical Intertextuality in Honor of J. A. Sanders*. Edited by C. A. Evans and S. Talmon. Brill, 1997.

———. "The Law of Moses in Septuagint Proverbs." *Vetus Testamentum* 49:4 (1999): 448–461.

———. "The Translator(s) of the Septuagint of Proverbs." *Textual Criticism* 7 (2002): 1–27.

Corbett, Edward P. J. *Classical Rhetoric for the Modern Student*. New York: Oxford University, 1971.

Cox, C. "Review of Cook, The Septuagint of Proverbs" (review of J. Cook, *The Septuagint of Proverbs–Jewish and/or Hellenistic Proverbs? Concerning the Hellenistic Colouring of LXX Proverbs*). TC: A Journal of Biblical Textual Criticism 3 (1998).

Crenshaw, J. L. "Proverbs, Book of." In *The Anchor Bible Dictionary on CD-ROM*. Logos Library System Version 2.1, 1997. Print ed.: David Noel Freedman, ed. *Anchor Bible Dictionary*. 6 vols. New York: Doubleday, 1992.

Crystal, David. *A Dictionary of Linguistics and Phonetics*. Third edition updated and enlarged. Blackwell, 1991.
Dahood, M. "Immortality in Proverbs 12:28." *Biblica* 41 (1960): 176–181.
Deissmann, Adolf. *The Philology of the Greek Bible: Its Present and Future*. London, 1908.
———. *Licht vom Osten: Das Neue Testament und die neuentdeckten Texte der hellenistisch-römischen Welt*. Tübingen: Mohr (Siebeck), 1909.
De Lagarde, Paul A. *Anmerkungen zur griechischen Übersetzung der Proverbien*. Leipzig, 1863.
———. *Septuaginta-Studien*. Göttingen, 1891.
Delitzsch, Franz. *Biblical Commentary on the Proverbs of Solomon*. Translated by M. G. Easton. 2 vols. Grand Rapids: Eerdmans, 1971. (German original, 1872).
De Waard, Jan and Eugene A. Nida. *From One Language to Another: Functional Equivalence in Bible Translating*. Nashville: Nelson, 1986.
De Waard, Jan. "Metathesis as a Translation Technique." Pages 249–260 in *Traducere Navem*. (Festschrift für Katharina Reiß zum 70. Geburtstag). Edited by Justa Holz-Mänttäri and Christiane Nord, Tampere: Universitätsbibliothek, 1993.
———. "4QProv and Textual Criticism." *Textus* 19 (1998): 87–96.
———. "The Septuagint of Proverbs as a Translational Model." *The Bible Translator* 50/3 (1999): 304–314.
Dick, Michael Brennan. "The Ethics of the Old Greek Book of Proverbs." Pages 20–50 in *The Studia Philonica Annual: Studies in Hellenistic Judaism*. Edited by D. T. Runia. Vol. II. Atlanta: Scholars Press, 1990.
Dietrich, Werner. *Das Buch der Sprüche*. Wuppertaler Studienbibel. Reprint 1992. Wuppertal: Brockhaus, 1985.
Dooley, Robert A. and Stephen H. Levinsohn. *Analyzing Discourse: Basic Concepts*. Summer Institute of Linguistics and University of North Dakota, 1998.
Driver, G. R. "Problems in Proverbs." *Zeitschrift für die alttestamentliche Wissenschaft* 50 (1932): 141–148.
———. "Hebrew Notes." *Zeitschrift für die alttestamentliche Wissenschaft* 52 (1934): 51–56.
———. "Hebrew Notes on Prophets and Proverbs." *Journal of Theological Studies* 41 (1940): 162–175.
———. "Problems in the Hebrew Text of Proverbs." *Biblica* 32 (1951): 173–197.
Dutton, Tom, ed. *Culture Change, Language Change: Case studies from Melanesia*. Pacific Linguistics Series C-120. The Australian National University, 1992.
Elliger, Winfried, Gerhard Fink, Günter Heil, and Thomas Meyer. *ΚΑΝΘΑΡΟΣ Griechisches Unterrichtswerk. Lese- und Arbeitsbuch*. Stuttgart, Düsseldorf, Berlin, Leipzig: Klett, 1996.
Erman, A. *Die aegyptische Literatur in Die orientalischen Literaturen*. ET: *The Literature of the Ancient Egyptians*. Translated by A. M. Blackman. London, 1927.
Estes, J. Daniel. *Hear, My Son: Teaching and Learning in Proverbs 1–9*. New Studies in Biblical Theology. Grand Rapids: Eerdmans. Cambridge, U.K., 1997.
Fanning, B. M. *Verbal Aspect in New Testament Greek*. Oxford Theological Monographs. Oxford: Clarendon, 1990.
Fox, Michael V. *Proverbs 1–9: A New Translation with Introduction and Commentary*. The Anchor Bible. New York: Doubleday, 2000.

Frankel, Z. *Über den Einfluß der palästinischen Exegese auf die alexandrinische Hermeneutik.* Leipzig, 1851.
Fraser, P. M. *Ptolemaic Alexandria.* Jewish-Alexandrian Literature. Oxford: Clarendon, 1972.
Fritsch, Charles T. "The Treatment of the Hexaplaric Signs in the Syro-Hexapla of Proverbs." *Journal of Biblical Literature* 72 (1953): 169–181.
Gammie, John G. "The Septuagint of Job: Its Poetic Style and Relationship to the Septuagint of Proverbs." *Catholic Biblical Quarterly* 49/1 (1987): 14–31.
Geller, Stephen A. *Parallelism in Early Biblical Poetry.* Harvard Semitic Monographs, 20. Scholars Press, 1979.
Gemser, Berend. *Sprüche Salomos.* Handbuch zum Alten Testament, 16. 2. Auflage. Tübingen, 1963.
Gerleman, G. "The Septuagint Proverbs as a Hellenistic Document." *Oudtestamentische Studiën* 8 (1950): 15–27.
———. 1956 *Studies in the Septuagint. III. Proverbs.* Lunds Universitets Årsskrift. N.F. Avd. 1. Bd 52 Nr 3, Lund, 1956.
Gesenius, Wilhelm. *Hebräisches und Aramäisches Handwörterbuch über das Alte Testament.* Bearbeitet von Dr. Frants Buhl. 17. Auflage. Berlin, Göttingen, Heidelberg: Springer, 1962.
Giese Jr., Ronald L. "Qualifying Wealth in the Septuagint of Proverbs." *Journal of Biblical Literature* 111/3 (1992): 409–425.
———. "Dualism in the LXX of Prov 2:17: A Case Study in the LXX as Revisionary Translation." *Journal of the Evangelical Theological Society* 36/3 (1993): 289–295.
———. "Compassion for the Lowly in Septuagint Proverbs." *Journal for the Study of the Pseudepigrapha* 11 (1993): 109–117.
Goerling, Fritz. "Criteria for the Translation of Key Terms in Jula Bible Translations." Ph.D. diss., Fuller Theological Seminary. School of World Mission, 1995.
Goldsworthy, Graeme. *The Tree of Life: Reading Proverbs Today.* Sydney: Aio, 1993.
Gooding, D. W. *Current Problems and Methods in the Textual Criticism of the Old Testament.* The Queen's University of Belfast. New Lecture Series No. 118, 1979.
Goodwin, William Watson. *Syntax of the Moods and Tenses of the Greek Verb.* London: Macmillan & Co., 1889.
Greenspoon, L. and O. Munnich, eds. *VIII Congress of the International Organization for Septuagint and Cognate Studies: Paris 1992.* Society of Biblical Literature Septuagint and Cognate Studies, 41. Atlanta: Scholars Press, 1995.
Greenstein, E. L. "How Does Parallelism Mean? A Sense of Text." *Jewish Quarterly Review Supplement* (1982): 41–70.
———. "Humor and Wit." In *The Anchor Bible Dictionary on CD-ROM.* Logos Library System Version 2.1, 1997. Print ed.: David Noel Freedman, ed. *Anchor Bible Dictionary.* 6 vols. New York: Doubleday, 1992.
Gutt, Ernst-August. *Translation and Relevance: Cognition and Context.* Oxford: Basil Blackwell, 1991.
Halliday, M. A. K. and Ruqaiya Hasan. *Cohesion in English.* English Language Series. Title No. 9. Longman, 1976.
Hazlitt, William. *The Table-Talk of Martin Luther.* Philadelphia: The Lutheran Publication Society, 1997.

Healey, A. "The Role of Function Words in the Paragraph Structure of Koine Greek." *Notes on Translation* 69 (1978): 2–16.
Heater, Homer, Jr. *A Septuagint Translation Technique in the Book of Job*. Catholic Biblical Quarterly Monograph Series 11. Washington, DC, 1982.
Heilmann, Willibald, Kurt Roeske, and Rolf Walther. τύποι *Griechische Kurzgrammatik*. Frankfurt am Main: Moritz Diesterweg, 1994.
Heim, K. M. "Coreferentiality, Structure and Context in Proverbs 10:1–5." *Journal of Translation and Textlinguistics* 6/3 (1993): 1–23.
Helbing, Robert. *Die Kasussyntax der Verba bei den Septuaginta: Ein Beitrag zur Hebraismenfrage und zur Syntax der Koine*. Göttingen: Vandenhoeck & Ruprecht, 1928.
Hengel, Martin. *Judentum und Hellenismus*. Tübingen, 1973.
Hess, R. S. "Reflections on Translating Joshua." In *Handbook of Classical Rhetoric in the Hellenistic Period 330 B.C.–A.D. 400*. Edited by S. E. Porter. Leiden, New York, Köln: Brill, 1997.
Jacob, I. & W. "Saffron." Under "Flora." In *The Anchor Bible Dictionary on CD-ROM*. Logos Library System Version 2.1, 1997. Print ed.: David Noel Freedman, ed. *Anchor Bible Dictionary*. 6 vols. New York: Doubleday, 1992.
Jakobson, Roman. "Grammatical Parallelism and Its Russian Facet." *Language* 42 (1966): 399–429.
———. "Poetry of Grammar and Grammar of Poetry." Pages 37–46 in *Verbal Art, Verbal Sign, Verbal Time*. Edited by Krystyna Pomorska and Stephen Rudy. University of Minnesota Press, 1985.
Jellicoe, Sidney. *The Septuagint and Modern Study*. Oxford: Clarendon, 1968.
Jenni, Ernst. *Lehrbuch der hebräischen Sprache des Alten Testaments*. Basel und Stuttgart: Helbing & Lichtenhahn, 1978.
Jenni E. and C. Westermann. *Theologisches Handwörterbuch zum Alten Testament*. Band I & II. München: Kaiser. Theologischer Verlag Zürich, 1978.
Jeppesen, K. "Biblia – Et Septuaginta: A Response to Mogens Müller." *Scandinavian Journal of the Old Testament* 10, 2 (1996): 271–281.
Jobes, Karen H. and Moisés Silva. *Invitation to the Septuagint*. Grand Rapids: Baker. United Kingdom: Paternoster, 2000.
Johnstone, William. "YDʿ II, 'Be Humbled, Humiliated'?" *Vetus Testamentum* XLI, 1 (1991): 49–62.
Kahle, Paul. *The Cairo Geniza*. (1st ed. London 1947). 2nd ed. Oxford: Basil Blackwell, 1959.
Kaminka, A. "LXX und Targum zu Proverbia." *Hebrew Union College Annual* 8/9 (1931/2): 169–191.
Kelly, Page H. *Biblical Hebrew: An Introductory Grammar*. Grand Rapids: Eerdmans, 1992.
Kidner, D. *The Proverbs: An Introduction and Commentary*. London: Tyndale, 1964.
Kittel, G., fnd., Gerhard Friedrich, ed. *Theologisches Wörterbuch zum Neuen Testament*. Band I–X. Studienausgabe 1990, unveränderter Nachdruck. Stuttgart, Berlin, Köln: Kohlhammer, 1933–79.
———. *Theological Dictionary of the New Testament*. ET. Volume I–X. Grand Rapids: Eerdmans, 1974.
Klein, Ralph W. *Textual Criticism of the Old Testament: The Septuagint after Qumran*. Philadelphia: Fortress, 1974.

Kraft, Robert A., ed. *Septuagintal Lexicography.* Septuagint and Cognate Studies 1. Society of Biblical Literature. University of Montana, 1992.
Kugel, James L. *The Idea of Biblical Poetry: Parallelism and Its History.* Yale University Press, New Haven and London, 1981.
Larson, Mildred L. *Meaning-based Translation: A Guide to Cross-Language Equivalence.* University Press of America, Lanham, New York, London, 1984.
LaSor, William Sanford, D. A. Hubbard, and F. W. Bush. *Old Testament Survey: The Message, Form and Background of the Old Testament.* Grand Rapids: Eerdmans, 1982.
Lee, J. A. L. "Translations of the Old Testament. I. Greek." Pages 777–778 in *Handbook of Classical Rhetoric in the Hellenistic Period 330 B.C.–A.D. 400.* Edited by S. E. Porter. Leiden, New York, Köln: Brill, 1997.
———. *A Lexical Study of the Septuagint Version of the Pentateuch.* Society of Biblical Literature Septuagint and Cognate Studies, 14. Chico, California: Scholars Press, 1983.
Lemeire, A. "Education." In *The Anchor Bible Dictionary on CD-ROM.* Logos Library System Version 2.1, 1997. Print ed.: David Noel Freedman, ed. *Anchor Bible Dictionary.* 6 vols. New York: Doubleday, 1992.
Leech, G. N. *A Linguistic Guide to English Poetry.* London: Longmans, 1969.
Liddell, H. G. and R. Scott, comps. *A Greek-English Lexicon.* 9th rev. and augmented edition, H. S. Jones, et al. 1940. With a Supplement. Oxford and New York: Oxford University Press, 1968.
Liddell & Scott. Edited by P. G. W. Glare with A. A. Thompson. *Revised Supplement.* Greek-English Lexicon. Oxford: Clarendon, 1996.
Lingua Links CD-ROM. Version 4.0 LT. SIL International, 1999.
Longacre, Robert. *Joseph: A Story of Divine Providence: A Text Theoretical and Text Linguistic Analysis of Genesis 37 and 39–48.* Winona Lake: Eisenbrauns, 1989.
Louw, J. P. and E. A. Nida, eds. *Greek-English Lexicon of the New Testament Based on Semantic Domains.* 2 vols. New York: UBS, 1988.
Lowth, Robert. *Lectures on the Sacred Poetry of the Hebrews.* ET 1835, London, 1753.
———. *Isaiah: A New Translation with a Preliminary Dissertation and Notes.* Repr. 1848, London, 1778.
Lust, J., E. Eynikel, and K. Hauspie, comps.; with the collaboration of G. Chamberlain, *A Greek-English Lexicon of the Septuagint: Part I, A-I.* Deutsche Bibelgesellschaft, 1992.
Lust, J., E. Eynikel, and K. Hauspie, comps. *A Greek-English Lexicon of the Septuagint: Part II, K-Ω.*. Deutsche Bibelgesellschaft, 1996.
Marcos, N. Fernández. *Scribes and Translators: Septuagint and Old Latin in the Books of Kings.* Vetus Testamentum Supplements 54. Leiden: Brill, 1994.
———, Review of J. Cook, *The Septuagint of Proverbs–Jewish and/or Hellenistic Proverbs? Concerning the Hellenistic Colouring of LXX Proverbs. Journal of the Study of Judaism in the Persian, Hellenistic, and Roman Periods,* XXX, 1 (1997): 95–98.
Margolis, M. L. *The Book of Joshua in Greek.* Paris: Geuthner, 1931/38.
Mayser, Edwin. *Grammatik der griechischen Papyri aus der Ptolemäerzeit. Band I. Laut und Wortlehre.* Leipzig: Teubner, 1906.
———. *Grammatik der griechischen Papyri aus der Ptolemäerzeit. Band II. Satzlehre.* Berlin und Leipzig: Walter de Gruyter & Co., 1926.
McCarter, P. Kyle, Jr. *Textual Criticism: Recovering the Text of the Hebrew Bible.* Philadelphia: Fortress, 1986.

McGlinchey, J. M. *The Teaching of Amen-em-Ope and the Book of Proverbs.* Washington, 1939.
McKane, William. *Proverbs: A New Approach.* London: SCM, 1970.
Meinhold, Arndt. *Die Sprüche. Teil 1: Sprüche Kapitel 1–15.* Zürcher Bibelkommentare 16.1. Theologischer Verlag Zürich, 1991.
———. *Die Sprüche. Teil 2: Sprüche Kapitel 16–31.* Zürcher Bibelkommentare 16.2. Theologischer Verlag Zürich, 1991.
Mezzacasa, G. *Il libro dei proverbi di Salomone: Studio critico sulle aggiunte greco-alessandrine.* Roma: Instituto Biblico Pontificio, 1913.
Motyer, Alex. *The Prophecy of Isaiah.* Leicester: InterVarsity, 1993.
Mouser, William E. *Getting the Most Out of Proverbs.* Grand Rapids: Zondervan, 1991.
Moulton, J. H. *A Grammar of NT Greek. Vol. I: Prolegomena.* Third edition. Edinburgh: T & T Clark, 1908.
Murphy, Roland E. "Wisdom in the OT." In *The Anchor Bible Dictionary on CD-ROM.* Logos Library System Version 2.1, 1997. Print ed.: David Noel Freedman, ed. *Anchor Bible Dictionary.* 6 vols. New York: Doubleday, 1992
———. *Proverbs.* World Biblical Commentary. Volume 22. Nashville: Nelson, 1998.
Müller, Mogens. *The First Bible of the Church: A Plea for the Septuagint.* Journal for the Study of the Old Testament, Supplement Series 206. Copenhagen International Seminar 1. Sheffield Academic Press, 1996.
Nestle, Eberhard and Kurt Aland, eds. *Novum Testamentum Graece.* 26. neu bearbeitete Auflage. Stuttgart: Biblia-Druck 1979.
Newman, Louis I. *Studies in Biblical Parallelism. Part I: Parallelism in Amos.* Semicentennial Publications of the University of California, 1868–1918.
Newmark, Peter. *Approaches to Translation.* Oxford, New York, Toronto, Sydney, Paris, Frankfurt: Pergamon, 1981.
Niccacci, Alviero. "Analysing Biblical Hebrew Poetry." *Journal for the Study of the Old Testament* 74 (1997): 77–93.
Nida, Eugene A. *Toward a Science of Translation.* Leiden: Brill, 1964.
Nida, Eugene A. and C. R. Taber. *The Theory and Practice of Translation.* Leiden: Brill, 1969.
Oikonomos, E. "Die Bedeutung der deuterokanonischen Schriften in der orthodoxen Kirche." In *Die Apokryphenfrage im ökumenischen Horizont: Die Stellung der Spätschriften des Alten Testaments im biblischen Schrifttum und die Bedeutung in den kirchlichen Traditionen des Ostens und Westens.* Edited by Siegfried Meurer. Bibel im Gespräch 3. Stuttgart: Deutsche Bibelgesellschaft, 1989.
Olofsson, Staffan. *The LXX Version: A Guide to the Translation Technique of the Septuagint.* Coniectanea Biblica, Old Testament Series 30. Stockhlom: Almqvist & Wiksell, 1990.
———. *God Is My Rock: A Study of Translation Technique and Theological Exegesis in the Septuagint.* Coniectanea Biblica, Old Testament Series 31. Stockholm: Almqvist & Wiksell, 1990.
Orlinsky, H. M. "The Septuagint as Holy Writ and the Philosophy of the Translators." *Hebrew Union College Annual* 46 (1975): 89–114.
Orlinsky, Harry M. and Robert G. Bratcher. *A History of Bible Translation and the North American Contribution.* Society of Biblical Literature. Atlanta: Scholars Press, 1991.
Packard Humanities Institute CD-ROM #7. Contents: (1) Inscriptions (Cornell, Ohio State, et al.). (2) Papyri (Duke, U. of Michigan), 1996.

Parker, D. C. *The Living Text of the Gospels.* Cambridge University Press, 1996.
———. "The Hexapla of Origen." In *The Anchor Bible Dictionary on CD-ROM.* Logos Library System Version 2.1, 1997. Print ed.: David Noel Freedman, ed. *Anchor Bible Dictionary.* 6 vols. New York: Doubleday, 1992.
Pearson, Brook W. R. "Remainderless Translations? Implications of the Tradition Concerning the Translation of the LXX for Modern Translation Theory." Pages 63–84 in *Translating the Bible.* Edited by S. E. Porter and R. S. Hess. Sheffield Academic Press, 1999.
Peters, M. K. H. "Septuagint." In *Anchor Bible Dictionary on CD-ROM.* Logos Library System Version 2.1, 1997. Print ed.: D. N. Freedman, ed. *Anchor Bible Dictionary.* 6 vols. New York: Doubleday, 1992.
Petersen, David L. and Kent Harold Richards. *Interpreting Hebrew Poetry.* Minneapolis: Fortress, 1992.
Perowne, T. T. *The Proverbs.* Cambridge Bible for Schools and Colleges. Cambridge University Press, 1899.
Perseus Project. Gregory Crane, Editor-in-Chief, Tufts University. Online: http://www.perseus.tufts.edu.
Plöger, Otto. *Sprüche Salomos (Proverbia).* Biblischer Kommentar Altes Testament. Band XVII. Neukirchener Verlag, 1984.
Porter, Stanley E. *Idioms of the Greek New Testament.* Second edition with corrections. Reprint 1995. Biblical Languages: Greek Series. Sheffield Academic Press, 1992.
Porter, Stanley E. and D. A. Carson. *Biblical Greek Language and Linguistics: Open Questions in Current Research.* Journal for the Study of the New Testament: Supplement Series 80. Sheffield Academic Press, 1993.
Porter, Stanley E., ed. *Handbook of Classical Rhetoric in the Hellenistic Period 330 B.C.– A.D. 400.* Leiden, New York, Köln: Brill, 1997.
Porter, Stanley E. and Richard S. Hess, eds. *Translating the Bible: Problems and Prospects.* Journal for the Study of the New Testament. Supplement Series 173. Sheffield Academic Press, 1999.
Pritchard, James B., ed. *Ancient Near Eastern Texts: Relating to the Old Testament.* Third edition with Supplement. Princeton, New Jersey: Princeton University Press, 1969.
Rabin, Chaim. "The Translation Process and the Character of the Septuagint." *Textus* 6 (1968): 1–26.
Rahlfs, Alfred. *Septuaginta.* Stuttgart: Deutsche Bibelgesellschaft, 1935/79.
Rehkopf, Friedrich. *Septuaginta-Vokabular.* Göttingen: Vandenhoeck & Ruprecht, 1989.
Renkema, Jan. *Discourse Studies: An Introductory Textbook.* Amsterdam/Philadelphia: John Benjamins, 1993.
Robinson, T. H. *The Poetry of the Old Testament,* 1947.
Ross, A. P. "Proverbs." In *The Expositor's Bible Commentary on CD-ROM.* Edited by Frank E. Gaebelein. Grand Rapids: Zondervan, 1991.
Sanders, J. A. "Hermeneutics of Text Criticism." *Textus* XVIII (1995).
Schäfer, Rolf. *Die Poesie der Weisen: Dichotomie als Grundstruktur der Lehr- und Weisheitsgedichte in Proverbien 1–9.* Wissenschaftliche Monographien zum Alten und Neuen Testament. 77. Band. Neukirchener Verlag, 1999.
Scherer, Andreas. *Das weise Wort und seine Wirkung: Eine Untersuchung zur Komposition und Redaktion von Proverbia 10,1–22,16.* Wissenschaftliche Monographien zum Alten und Neuen Testament. 83. Band. Neukirchener Verlag, 1999.

Schmidt, J. "Studien zur Stilistik der alttestamentlichen Spruchliteratur." *Alttestamentliche Abhandlungen* 13/1 (1936), Münster.
Schmidt, Werner H., Winfried Thiel, and Robert Hanhart. *Altes Testament*. Grundkurs Theologie Band 1. Stuttgart, Berlin, Köln, Mainz: Kohlhammer, 1989.
Schneider, T. R. *The Sharpening of Wisdom: Old Testament Proverbs in Translation*. New Series. Old Testament Essays. Supplement Nu. 1. Pretoria: OTSSA, 1992.
Scott, Robert Balgarnie Young. *Proverbs, Ecclesiastes: Introduction, Translation, and Notes*. The Anchor Bible. Vol. 18. Garden City, New York: Doubleday, 1965.
Seligmann, I. L. *The Septuagint Version of Isaiah: A Discussion of Its Problems*. Leiden, 1948.
Septuaginta. *The Septuaginta Version: Greek and English*. London: Bagster. New York: Pott, n.d.
Segert, S. "Hebrew Poetic Parallelism as Reflected in the Septuagint." International Organization for Septuagint and Cognate Studies 18 (1985): 133–148.
Soderlund, S. K. "Septuagint." Pages 400–409 in *The International Standard Bible Encyclopedia*. Vol. 4. Edited by G. W. Bromiley. Grand Rapids: Eerdmans, 1988.
Soisalon-Soininen, Ilmari. *Studien zur Septuaginta-Syntax*. Herausgegeben von Anneli Aejmelaeus und Raija Sollamo. Helsinki: Suomalainen Tiedeakatemia, 1987.
Steyer, Gottfried. *Satzlehre des neutestamentlichen Griechisch: Handbuch für das Studium des neutestamentlichen Griechisch. Band II. Satzlehre*. Gütersloher Verlagshaus: Mohn, 1979.
Steyn, P. E. "External Influence in the Peshitta Version of Proverbs." Unpublished doctoral dissertation, University of Stellenbosch, 1992.
Stine, Philip C., ed. *Issues in Bible Translation*. UBS Monograph Series, No. 3. London, New York, Stuttgart: United Bible Societies, 1988.
———. *Bible Translation and the Spread of the Church: The Last 200 Years*. Leiden, New York, Kobenhavn, Köln: Brill, 1990.
Swete, Henry Barclay. *The Old Testament in Greek according to the Septuagint*. Cambridge, 1901.
———. *An Introduction to the Old Testament in Greek*. Revised by R. R. Ottley. Cambridge University Press, 1914.
Talmon, Shemaryahu. "Double Readings in the Masoretic Text." *Textus* 1 (1984): 144–184.
Talshir, Zipora. "Double Translations in the Septuagint." Pages 21–63 in *LXX VI Congress of the International Organization for Septuagint and Cognate Studies, Jerusalem 1986*. Edited by C. E. Cox. Septuagint and Cognate Studies 23, Atlanta 1987.
Tauberschmidt, Gerhard. "Principles of Bible Translation and the Septuagint." M.Phil. diss., University of Aberdeen, 1997.
———. *A Grammar of Sinaugoro: An Austronesian Language of the Central Province of Papua New Guinea*. Pacific Linguistics C-143. Canberra: The Australian National University, 1999.
Taylor, Archer. "The Style of Proverbs." *De Proverbio* 5/1 (1999): 1–18.
Thackeray, Henry St. John. *A Grammar of the Old Testament in Greek according to the Septuagint, I*. Cambridge University Press, 1909.
———. "The Poetry of the Greek Book of Proverbs." *Journal of Theological Studies* 13 (1911): 46–66.

Thesaurus Linguae Graecae CD-ROM#D. Contents: 1. TLG Data Bank Texts. 2. Index to TLG Data Bank Texts. 3. TLG Canon. University of California, Irvine.
Thomas, D. W. "The Root yd‛ in Hebrew." *Journal of Theological Studies* 35 (1934): 298–306.
Tov, Emanuel, ed. *The Hebrew and Greek Texts of Samuel*. 1980 Proceedings IOSCS–Vienna. Jerusalem: Academon, 1980.
———, ed. *A Computerized Data Base for Septuagint Studies*: *The parallel aligned text of the Greek and Hebrew Bible*. Computer assisted tools for Septuagint Studies (CATSS) Volume 2. Journal of Northwest Semitic Languages. Supplementary Series 1, Stellenbosch, 1986.
———. "The Septuagint." Pages 161–188 in *Mikra: Text, Translation, Reading and Interpretation of the Hebrew Bible in Ancient Judaism and Early Christianity*. Edited by M. J. Mulder and Harry Sysling. Assen/Maastricht: Van Gorcum. Philadelphia: Fortress, 1988.
———. "Recensional Differences between the Masoretic Text and the Septuagint of Proverbs." Pages 43–56 in *Of Scribes and Scrolls, Studies on the Hebrew Bible, Intertestamental Judaism, and Christian Origins Presented to John Strugnell*. Edited by H. W. Attridge et al. Lanham, Maryland, 1990.
———. *Textual Criticism of the Hebrew Bible*. Minneapolis: Fortress. Assen/Maastricht: Van Gorcum, 1992.
———. "The Contribution of the Qumran Scrolls to the Understanding of the LXX." In *Septuagint, Scrolls and Cognate Writings*. Edited by G. J. Brooke and B. Lindars, S.S.F. Atlanta: Scholars Press, 1992.
———. *The Dead Sea Scrolls on Microfiche*. Leiden: Brill, 1993.
———. *The Text-Critical Use of the Septuagint in Biblical Research*. Revised and Enlarged Second edition. Jerusalem: Simor, 1997.
Toy, Crawford H. *The Book of Proverbs: A Critical and Exegetical Commentary*. Edinburgh: T & T Clark, 1899.
Trafton, J. L. "Psalms of Solomon." In *The Anchor Bible Dictionary on CD-ROM*. Logos Library System Version 2.1, 1997. Print ed.: David Noel Freedman, ed. *Anchor Bible Dictionary*. 6 vols. New York: Doubleday, 1992.
Translator's Workplace CD-ROM. Version 3.0. A joint project of the Summer Institute of Linguistics and the United Bible Societies, 1999.
Turner, Nigel. *A Grammar of New Testament Greek Vol. III: Syntax*. T & T Clark, Edinburgh, 1963.
———. *A Grammar of New Testament Greek. Vol. IV: Style*. T & T Clark, Edinburgh, 1976.
Tur-Sinai, Naftali Herz. *Die Heilige Schrift*. 2. Auflage 1995. Neuhausen-Stuttgart: Hänsler, 1993.
VanGemeren, Willem A. *New International Dictionary of Old Testament Theology and Exegesis*. 5 vols. Grand Rapids: Zondervan, 1997.
Walters, Peter (formerly Katz), D. W. Gooding, ed. *The Text of the Septuagint: Its Corruptions and their Emendation*. Cambridge University Press, 1973.
Waltke, Bruce. "Proverbs: Theology of." Pages 1091–1092 in *New International Dictionary of Old Testament Theology and Exegesis*. Vol. 4. Edited by W. A. VanGemeren. Grand Rapids: Zondervan, 1997.
Watson, Francis. *Text and Truth: Redefining Biblical Theology*. Grand Rapids: Eerdmans, 1997.

Watson, Wilfred G. E. *Classical Hebrew Poetry: A Guide to Its Techniques*. Journal for the Study of the Old Testament: Supplement Series 26. Reprinted with corrections by Sheffield Academic Press, 1995.

Weingreen, J. "Rabbinic-Type Commentary in the LXX Version of Proverbs." Pages 407–415 *Proceedings of the Sixth World Congress of Jewish Studies*. Edited by A. Shinan. Jerusalem: World Union of Jewish Studies, 1973.

Weitzman, M. P. *The Syriac Version of the Old Testament: An Introduction.* Chapter 3. University of Cambridge Oriental Publications, 56. Cambridge University Press, 1999.

Wendland, Ernst R. *Analyzing the Psalms*. Summer Institute of Linguistics, 1998.

Wevers, J. W. "Septuaginta Forschungen seit 1954." *Theologische Rundschau* 33 (1968): 18–76.

———. "The Göttingen Septuagint." *Bulletin of the International Organization for Septuagint and Cognate Studies* 8 (1975).

———. "An Apologia for LXX Studies." *Bulletin of the International Organization for Septuagint and Cognate Studies* 18 (1985): 16–38.

———. "The Use of Versions for Text Criticism: The Septuagint." *La Septuaginta en la Investigacion Contemporanea.* (V Congreso de la IOSCS). Edited by N. Fernández Marcos. Consejo Superior de Investigaciones Cientificas. Madrid, 1985.

Whorf, Benjamin Lee. *Language, Thought, and Reality: Selected Writings of Benjamin Lee Whorf*. Edited by J. B. Carroll. Cambridge: M.I.T. Press, 1956.

Whybray, R. N. *Proverbs*: *New Century Bible Commentary*. Grand Rapids: Eerdmans, 1994.

———. *The Book of Proverbs: A Survey of Modern Study*. Leiden, New York, Köln: Brill, 1995.

Willebrands, J. C. et al. *Guidelines for Interconfessional Cooperation in Translating the Bible*. The New Revised Edition. Rome: Vatican Polyglot, 1987.

Wright, C. J. H. *New International Dictionary of Old Testament Theology and Exegesis*. 5 vols. Grand Rapids: Zondervan, 1997.

Würthwein, Ernst. *Der Text des Alten Testaments: Eine Einführung in die Biblia Hebraica*. Fünfte, neubearbeitete Auflage. Stuttgart: Deutsche Bibelgesellschaft, 1988.

Zogbo, Lynell and Ernst R. Wendland. *Hebrew Poetry in the Bible: A Guide for Understanding and for Translating*. United Bible Societies, 2000.

INDEX

Prov 1:2,3, 110
Prov 1:3, 97
Prov 1:5, 120
Prov 1:11–13, 117
Prov 1:12, 93
Prov 1:14, 102
Prov 1:22, 113, 218
Prov 1:23b,c, 33
Prov 1:24, 39
Prov 1:26, 111
Prov 1:27, 79
Prov 1:28, 122
Prov 1:28b, 123
Prov 1:31, 133
Prov 1:32, 155
Prov 2:1, 126
Prov 2:10, 112
Prov 2:12–17, 128
Prov 2:15, 220
Prov 2:16,(17), 124
Prov 2:19, 142
Prov 2:19,20, 114
Prov 2:21, 143
Prov 2:22, 134
Prov 3:2a, 80
Prov 3:3, 104
Prov 3:5–6, 142
Prov 3:8, 174
Prov 3:9, 34, 93
Prov 3:10, 175
Prov 3:12, 11
Prov 3:13, 181
Prov 3:18, 75
Prov 3:22, 184
Prov 3:24, 182
Prov 3:25, 35
Prov 3:26, 176
Prov 3:27,28, 118
Prov 3:32, 126
Prov 4:4, 115

Prov 4:4–5, 222
Prov 4:10, 62
Prov 4:14, 157
Prov 4:15, 130
Prov 4:16, 134
Prov 4:21, 146
Prov 4:26, 88
Prov 5:3, 135
Prov 5:5, 136
Prov 5:9, 177
Prov 5:17, 93
Prov 5:18, 177
Prov 5:22, 219
Prov 5:23, 103
Prov 6:1–3, 131
Prov 6:5, 178
Prov 6:10, 76
Prov 6:11, 47
Prov 6:23, 76
Prov 6:25, 87
Prov 6:35, 78
Prov 7:4, 90
Prov 7:16, 221
Prov 7:17, 74
Prov 7:18, 94
Prov 7:25, 136
Prov 8:2, 98, 218
Prov 8:3, 98
Prov 8:4, 96
Prov 8:5, 183
Prov 8:6, 97
Prov 8:10, 70
Prov 8:16, 221
Prov 8:20, 94
Prov 8:34, 80
Prov 9:6, 86
Prov 9:7, 95
Prov 9:10,11, 120
Prov 9:17, 136
Prov 9:18, 147

Prov 10:6, 193
Prov 10:10, 194
Prov 11:10–11, 60
Prov 10:15, 157
Prov 10:18, 187
Prov 11:7, 44
Prov 11:16, 189
Prov 11:21, 50
Prov 11:22, 72
Prov 11:24, 51, 95
Prov 11:25, 188
Prov 11:28, 185
Prov 11:30, 190
Prov 12:4, 89
Prov 12:10, 52
Prov 12:13, 116
Prov 12:14, 35
Prov 12:21, 195
Prov 12:25, 52
Prov 12:28, 191
Prov 13:1, 99
Prov 13:9, 196
Prov 13:14, 64
Prov 13:15, 197
Prov 13:17, 158
Prov 13:18, 148
Prov 13:19, 53
Prov 13:20, 86, 148
Prov 13:22, 149
Prov 13:23, 198
Prov 13:25, 54
Prov 14:2, 149
Prov 14:9, 199
Prov 14:11, 186
Prov 14:15, 186
Prov 14:16, 199
Prov 14:17, 192
Prov 14:21, 200
Prov 14:32, 201
Prov 14:33, 203

Prov 14:34, 204
Prov 15:6, 150
Prov 15:10, 45
Prov 15:15, 54
Prov 15:19, 205
Prov 15:21, 55
Prov 15:(22b),23, 43
Prov 15:27, 56
Prov 15:32, 206
Prov 16:16, 214
Prov 16:28, 144
Prov 17:4, 44
Prov 17:5, 67
Prov 17:7, 214
Prov 17:9, 57
Prov 17:10, 69
Prov 17:12, 70
Prov 17:14, 211
Prov 17:17, 145
Prov 17:21, 48
Prov 17:23, 63
Prov 17:26, 40
Prov 17:27,28, 156
Prov 18:2, 207
Prov 18:12, 100
Prov 18:15, 183
Prov 18:19, 215
Prov 18:22, 49
Prov 19:6, 150
Prov 19:27, 212
Prov 19:28, 101

Prov 19:29, 180
Prov 20:3, 125
Prov 20:9, 90
Prov 20:12,13, 158
Prov 20:23, 36
Prov 20:30, 37
Prov 21:8, 159
Prov 21:14, 46
Prov 21:18, 137
Prov 21:20, 207
Prov 21:24, 74
Prov 21:26, 208
Prov 22:3, 57
Prov 22:8, 41
Prov 22:11, 217
Prov 22:13, 213
Prov 22:15, 68
Prov 22:26, 137
Prov 22:29a, 81
Prov 23:11, 119
Prov 23:20, 151
Prov 23:21, 42
Prov 23:25, 180
Prov 23:31, 65
Prov 23:32, 138
Prov 23:34, 151
Prov 24:10, 63
Prov 24:11, 37
Prov 24:15, 152
Prov 24:30, 96
Prov 24:34, 121

Prov 25:15, 153
Prov 25:22, 121
Prov 26:13, 138
Prov 26:20, 72
Prov 27:8, 139
Prov 27:9, 216
Prov 27:11, 64
Prov 27:15, 73
Prov 28:2, 209
Prov 28:4, 160
Prov 28:22, 153
Prov 28:25, 58
Prov 28:27, 59
Prov 28:28, 59, 153
Prov 29:2, 154
Prov 29:4, 60
Prov 29:9, 66
Prov 29:18, 210
Prov 29:20, 112
Prov 30:3, 140
Prov 30:13, 91
Prov 31:6, 38
Prov 31:8, 127
Prov 31:12, 112
Prov 31:17,18, 140
Prov 31:20, 141

www.ingramcontent.com/pod-product-compliance
Lightning Source LLC
Chambersburg PA
CBHW020645300426
44112CB00007B/245